AFTER PRINT

After Print

Eighteenth-Century Manuscript Cultures

Edited by

Rachael Scarborough King

UNIVERSITY OF VIRGINIA PRESS
CHARLOTTESVILLE AND LONDON

University of Virginia Press
© 2020 by the Rector and Visitors of the University of Virginia
All rights reserved

First published 2020

1 3 5 7 9 8 6 4 2

Library of Congress Cataloging-in-Publication Data
Names: King, Rachael Scarborough, editor.
Title: After print : eighteenth-century manuscript cultures / edited by Rachael Scarborough King.
Description: Charlottesville : University of Virginia Press, 2020. | "This volume originated as a double panel at the 2014 Canadian Society for Eighteenth-Century Studies annual meeting in Montreal and as the conference 'After Print: Manuscripts in the Eighteenth Century' held at the University of California, Santa Barbara, on April 24, 2015"—Acknowledgements. | Includes bibliographical references and index.
Identifiers: LCCN 2019030032 (print) | LCCN 2019030033 (ebook) | ISBN 9780813943473 (hardcover ; acid-free paper) | ISBN 9780813943480 (paperback ; acid-free paper) | ISBN 9780813943497 (epub)
Subjects: LCSH: Manuscripts, English—History—18th century. | Manuscripts, English—History—17th century. | Manuscripts, English—History—19th century. | Printing—History. | Authorship—History. | Books and reading—History. | Codicology—Data processing. | Paratext—History. | Intermediality—History.
Classification: LCC Z105 .A29 2020 (print) | LCC Z105 (ebook) | DDC 091.09/033—dc23
LC record available at https://lccn.loc.gov/2019030032
LC ebook record available at https://lccn.loc.gov/2019030033

Cover art: Spider from John Abbot, *Aranea*, ca. 1799 (courtesy of Hargrett Rare Book and Manuscript Library/University of Georgia Libraries); illustrated title page from Wordsworth's *Recollections of a Tour in Scotland* by George Hutchinson (Wordsworth Trust, Dove Cottage, Cumbria); background by Tramont_ana/Shutterstock

CONTENTS

Acknowledgments   vii

Introduction: The Multimedia Eighteenth Century   1

Part I. Coteries, Communities, Collaborations: Manuscript Publication

"Pray for the Unworthy Scribbler": The Textual Cultures of Early Methodist Women   27
    ANDREW O. WINCKLES

Collecting John Abbot's Natural History Notes and Drawings   52
    BETH FOWKES TOBIN

A "Female Accomplishment"? Femininity, Privacy, and Eighteenth-Century Letter-Writing Norms   74
    RACHAEL SCARBOROUGH KING

Bookmaking and Archiving in Dorothy Wordsworth's Notebooks   95
    MICHELLE LEVY

Part II. The Manuscript-Print Interface

Paratextual Readers: Manuscript Verse in Printed Books of the Long Eighteenth Century   123
    PHILIP S. PALMER

Mediating the "Sudden & Surprising Revolution": Official Manuscript Newsletters and the Revolution of 1688   148
    LEITH DAVIS

Manuscript, Print, and the Affective Turn: The Case of Frances Brooke's *The Old Maid*   175
    KATHRYN R. KING

Becoming Dr. Franklin: Benjamin Franklin's Science,
Manuscript Circulation, and "Anti-Authorship" in Print   195
    COLIN T. RAMSEY

Part III. New Methods for Manuscript Studies

Amateur Manuscript Fiction in the Archives: An Introduction   217
    EMILY C. FRIEDMAN

The Language of Notation and the Space of Manuscript
Notebooks   237
    COLLIN JENNINGS

The Circulation of John Keats's Letters on Land, on Sea, Online   263
    BRIAN REJACK

Cooking Hannah Woolley's Printed Recipes from a
Manuscript Recipe Book: UPenn Ms. Codex 785   285
    MARISSA NICOSIA

Epilogue   310
    MARGARET J. M. EZELL

Contributors   321

Index   325

ACKNOWLEDGMENTS

THIS VOLUME originated as a double panel at the 2014 Canadian Society for Eighteenth-Century Studies (CSECS) annual meeting in Montreal and as the conference "After Print: Manuscripts in the Eighteenth Century," held at the University of California, Santa Barbara (UCSB), on April 24, 2015. I am grateful to Andrew Bricker for suggesting and co-organizing the CSECS panels and to the Andrew W. Mellon Fellowship of Scholars in Critical Bibliography at Rare Book School and the UCSB Early Modern Center for supporting the conference, for which the UCSB College of Letters and Science also provided funding. Many thanks to the presenters and participants at the "After Print" conference, whose enthusiasm and expertise demonstrated a call for this collection. The RBS Mellon Fellowship provided the impetus and context for the conference and for this book, and I am grateful to Michael F. Suarez, Donna Sy, and Barbara Heritage for their advice and encouragement. The UCSB Academic Senate generously supported this work with a subvention toward the cost of publication. Finally, I thank Angie Hogan for her excellent editorial guidance and the two anonymous readers at the University of Virginia Press for their thoughtful, incisive readings.

AFTER PRINT

INTRODUCTION

The Multimedia Eighteenth Century

~

EIGHTEENTH-CENTURY readers were frequently enjoined to put down their printed books and personally inspect manuscript documents to authenticate the works they were reading. In prefatory and self-reflexive comments, authors asserted the existence of handwritten "originals" whose material existence proved their claims. In his *Review* of May 30, 1704, Daniel Defoe noted of the sources of his printed news, "The Originals of these and other Letters of this Nature, are left with the Printer of this Paper, for any Person to peruse that doubts the Truth of them."[1] Similarly, the table of contents for the *Bee* no. 22 listed "Copies of two Letters, the *Originals* of which, are left at the Publishers of the BEE, to be perused by the Curious," while in the dedicatory epistle to a volume of Alexander Pope's correspondence, Edmund Curll noted, "Beside, what is here presented to You, I have Several other very valuable Originals in my Custody."[2] In the 1770s, James Macpherson and Samuel Johnson battled over the existence of "originals" of the poems of Ossian, with Macpherson advertising "that there is a design on foot to print the Originals, as soon as the translator shall have time to transcribe them for the press," while Johnson countered, "Macpherson never in his life offered me the sight of any original or of any evidence of any kind."[3] The "originals" trope was so common that Henry Fielding used it to contribute to the satire in *Shamela*, with Parson Oliver writing to Parson Tickletext of Shamela's letters, "The Originals themselves are in my Hands, and shall be communicated to you, if you think proper to make them publick."[4] Such ongoing references to handwritten texts existing alongside printed works encouraged readers to always be reading through the printed page, seeing it not as self-verifying but as drawing its authority from a manuscript source. Although it is impossible to ascertain the extent to which such "originals" actually existed or readers actually consulted them, the appeal to manuscript presumed the interdependence among media of publication.[5]

This interdependence is increasingly coming to the fore of scholarly considerations of eighteenth-century literature. Recent books have emphasized "the interplay of media . . . and the porous boundaries between them," "the co-existence of script and print," and the period's attention to varieties of mediation: "The eighteenth century saw the emergence of a sustained, self-conscious discourse questioning the effects of, and relationship between, different media forms."[6] But while such works foreground the interaction of print with other media, they locate manuscript and orality under the rubric of "print culture"; as the Multigraph Collective's *Interacting with Print* notes, "Do not imagine, because we seek to look beyond print to other media, that we have given up on the idea of a print culture. Rather, we seek to formulate new ways of understanding the centrality of print in our period."[7] The present volume concentrates instead on the medium of manuscript, understanding it as always in contact with other material forms but highlighting its unique affordances in the eighteenth-century literary landscape.[8] As the new attention to the period's multimodality is showing, eighteenth-century authors worked with a heightened awareness of conditions of mediation, and they self-consciously analyzed the relationships between form and content. Manuscript carried a range of meanings that writers and readers could activate: not only the site, as scholarship has often assumed, of privacy, femininity, and amateurism, it also offered accessibility, flexibility, interactivity, exclusivity, authority, timeliness, personalization, entry into print, and forms of publicity (in different contexts and not all at once). By taking into account the varied nature of manuscript writing, this volume therefore calls for media specificity and reveals the complex networks of the multimedia eighteenth century.

For despite the widespread adoption of D. F. McKenzie's argument that "forms effect meaning"—and acknowledgment of what he later called the "frankly diverse nature" and "persistive interaction" of speech, writing, and print[9]—postmedieval literary scholars and book historians continue primarily to focus on printed materials and print culture. This default position is perhaps most evident in studies of the eighteenth century, which often stands as the endpoint for forms of manuscript literary circulation. By the age of Addison and Pope, it is assumed, print had become the dominant medium for public, professional authorship. George Justice pithily summarizes this position when he notes that the eighteenth century is "a period in which the printing press and an attendant public sphere have conventionally been seen as overwhelming the quaint, semi-private circulation of literature in manuscript."[10] Alvin Kernan provides this standard view when he argues that in the mid-eighteenth century "an older system of polite or courtly letters ... was swept away ... and gradually replaced by a new print-based, market-centered, democratic literary system," adding that "print destroyed the old oral and manuscript culture."[11] Studies of manuscript practices and cultures have tended to highlight medieval production and to end in the seventeenth century: Brill's Library of the Written Word series for "The Manuscript World" covers antiquity to the Renaissance, the journals *Manuscript Studies* and *English Manuscript Studies 1100–1700* end in the early modern period, and the annual Saint Louis Conference on Manuscript Studies restricts papers to medieval and Renaissance topics.[12] This periodization in effect denies the possibility of eighteenth-century manuscript studies. It presumes that, by the eighteenth century, manuscript publication was an effect of inability rather than choice—restricted to women and bad authors—or an aristocratic holdover related to the "stigma of print" for the upper classes.[13]

But as our ongoing lived experience of the technological multiplicities of the digital age enables us to look with fresh eyes at past eras of media shift, scholars are turning to the nonprint forms of composition, circulation, and publication that remained central to social, professional, and literary life in the eighteenth century. The essays in this volume show how essential handwritten texts were to eighteenth-century literature, politics, religion, business, and everyday life—so central that they are at times, paradoxically, almost invisible because they were taken for granted by contemporaries. It takes a concerted, collaborative effort to draw out the range of ways manuscript production remained effective, both on its own and in relation to other media. Together, the authors in *After Print* establish how writers and readers continued to rely on responsive handwritten and hybrid communications during the expansion of print, and they challenge the understanding of the eighteenth century as a print culture. In genres from journals and commonplace books to letters, scientific notes, poems, and novels, manuscript offered attractive alternatives to print publication. At the most basic level, printing rested on a manuscript foundation, since copies were delivered to printers in handwritten form; as printing expanded in the eighteenth century, so did printed texts that required the addition of script such as "blanks," errata sheets, and penmanship manuals. For everyday readers and writers, it may not have been apparent that print was becoming the dominant medium of textual production; to the contrary, critiques continued to emphasize print's suspect anonymity and impersonal nature. Eighteenth-century manuscript practices were notable for their variety and vitality, and for their self-awareness about the processes of mediation. This volume thus argues for both the centrality and the diversity of manuscript practices from the Restoration through at least the Romantic period—attempting throughout not to assign an expiry date to manuscript culture—and for a critical stance that questions the solidity of the print-manuscript hierarchy. The constant interactions between media and continuance of an autonomous sphere of handwritten production demonstrate how manuscript did not die out but, rather, may have been revitalized by the advent of printing, as writing elicited more and more writing. This reorientation both offers a clearer picture of the conditions for eighteenth-century literature and has insights for our own moment of protracted media shift, as it highlights aggregate, iterative steps rather than a single revolution.

As the first book to survey eighteenth-century manuscript cultures, *After Print* challenges the predominance of print by drawing together recent trends in book history, media studies, bibliography, the digital humanities, and eighteenth-century literature. The material turn has been particularly pronounced in eighteenth-century studies, where scholars have revisited the "rise" narratives central to the period's understanding of itself—the rise of the novel, of the middle class, of the individual, of print—in light of the new textual formats that proliferated in the period. Scholarly attention to noncanonical and ephemeral genres, particularly in the growing prominence of periodical studies, emphasizes the many channels beyond the codex by which information and entertainment reached readers. Such attention necessarily means noticing the lack of clear borders not only between books and non-books, but also among methods of book production, as we encounter codices filled with marginalia, written and printed materials bound up together, printed forms that required completion by hand, and manuscript documents that provided the basis for printed works. Concurrently, the importance of digital databases, especially Early English Books Online (EEBO) and Eighteenth-Century Collections Online (ECCO), has both offered scholars easy (if institutionally restricted) access to a wider range of print materials and highlighted the frequent need to view such works in physical rather than digital form, where features such as size, paper quality, marginalia, and coloring are difficult or impossible to ascertain and where words and images are often missing or illegible due to poor digitization. This expanded range of topics and objects has sent many scholars back to archives, where they encounter manuscript and mixed-media materials that challenge the print-centric orientation of eighteenth-century studies. Taken together, such efforts are offering a new picture of the eighteenth-century mediascape, revealing persistent fluidity and negotiation rather than a steady rise of print.

A turn to eighteenth-century manuscripts thus builds on the insights of influential scholars of early modern writing. Harold Love and Margaret J. M. Ezell, the latter a contributor to this volume, each has offered persuasive and comprehensive arguments for the continued significance of manuscript circulation to professional literary and scientific writing through the seventeenth century.[14] Love and Ezell use the term "publication," now typically associated with printing, to refer to forms of manuscript authorship, and they note that a range of writers and readers—not only the aristocratic or female—preferred scribal publication for the ability to create communities of readers and to offer texts that were amendable and adaptable.[15] As Ezell writes, "For the majority of writers and readers in the period at the turn of the [eighteenth] century, literary authorship was still understood as an interactive, dynamic, and ongoing exchange."[16] George Justice and Nathan Tinker's edited collection *Women's Writing and the Circulation of Ideas: Manuscript Publication in England, 1550–1800*, draws from Ezell's work to show how, as Justice writes, the "decision to use manuscript rather than print publication resulted from a set of choices, made in positive terms for the most part.... Writers used manuscripts (or print technology, for that matter) because it [sic] suited their needs."[17] Their volume's focus on female writers, however, implies a special connection between manuscript and femininity. Betty Schellenberg's in-depth study of a variety of literary coteries resists such gendering and shows how central scribal exchanges were to professional print production in the second half of the eighteenth century; as she writes, the trajectory over the period is "one not of decline but of constantly shifting local equilibria between the coterie and the commercial print trade."[18] Meanwhile, major studies of that print trade, such as Adrian Johns's *The Nature of the Book* and James Raven's *The Business of Books*, have shown how, in Raven's words, the effects of print constituted "no overnight revolution and change was relatively fitful."[19] But while he notes that "manuscript production and transmission, and the influence of scribal design continued for several centuries," his interest, like that of many book historians, lies in the development of the printed book market.[20] An approach that instead foregrounds the multiplicity of eighteenth-century manuscripts demonstrates, to return to Justice, "not only that we need to 'recover' a practice that has been 'lost,'" but also that "it is perhaps even more important to change the lenses through which we understand literature in history."[21] This means seeing manuscript cultures as in close correspondence with other media but, at the same time, not solely within the worldview of a dominant print culture. This volume takes as its subject manuscripts that came into existence after the rise of print while also looking beyond print to understand manuscript in its own context.

The kinds of scribal works that emerge from this viewpoint occupy coherent but overlapping media spheres. To begin with, there are the handwritten documents that were the stuff of everyday communication in the period. The eighteenth century has long been recognized as, in the words of Jürgen Habermas, "the century of the letter," as the spread of literacy and standardization of the postal system made letter writing a more accessible activity.[22] But as Amanda Gilroy and W. M. Verhoeven point out, "Until quite recently, critical discourse has on the whole accepted female epistolary skill as a truth universally acknowledged, and has subscribed to the fiction of the feminine, private letter."[23] The letter, as a nonliterary genre that did not require extensive formal training, became associated with women and domesticity, a fact that has colored its representation in scholarship. But recent historicist studies of eighteenth-century letters have used extensive archival research to expand beyond a focus on women's correspondence. Konstantin Dierks sees the letter as part of a "culture of documents" for eighteenth-century Britons and Americans, and he tracks commercial, political, bureaucratic, and personal letters— as well as commodities such as inkstands, paper, and desks—to show how letter writing offered a form of personal agency to a wide range of people. As he writes, "Everywhere in the century was an infinity of letters; in an extraordinary growth of transatlantic commerce, just as in the waging of revolution and war. . . . By century's end, that expansion of letter writing was proclaimed in public culture to be universal, routine, and fundamental to what then constituted 'modern' life."[24] Merchants sent bills and received payments by letter; the central task of the diplomat was to report news by letter to his supervisors in London; much of that news was incorporated into written newsletters and printed newspapers; the

Royal Society sent scientific questionnaires through the post, read correspondence aloud at its meetings, and printed letters in its *Philosophical Transactions*. Eve Tavor Bannet argues that eighteenth-century commentary on letters highlighted all of these media states and in doing so "taught users to conceive of 'the letter' as a genre that could easily, even indifferently, present itself in a variety of oral, written or printed modes."[25] In this volume, Andrew O. Winckles, Brian Rejack, and I track disparate collections of letters used for crisscrossing personal, political, literary, and intimate purposes, while Emily C. Friedman collects never-printed manuscript novels—some of them epistolary—that displayed differing approaches to "publication." The ubiquity of letters across public and private realms meant that, on the level of everyday practice, readers and writers were surrounded by handwritten documents, which drew connections to several media of communication.

A similar interest in dismantling the boundaries between public and private spheres—and the association of each with print and manuscript, respectively—extends to scholarly consideration of other handwritten texts. Donald H. Reiman has identified three categories of "modern manuscripts"—the private, the confidential, and the public—that correspond mainly to the author's conception of his or her audience.[26] But many, if not most (if not all), manuscripts crossed such boundaries, and readers both in the past and today have habitually ignored writers' intentions as to audience. The kinds of practices that Love has identified as "scribal publication," the act of making available "texts in handwritten copies within a culture which had developed sophisticated means of generating and transmitting such copies" such as coterie circulation, recopying, and epistolary transmission, remained widespread in the eighteenth century.[27] Both men and women were encouraged to keep commonplace books as scholarly and personal aids, and these were often collaborative works to be shared among and added to by family and friends.[28] Journals and diaries could also be semipublic documents. Frances Burney, for example, wrote long "journal letters" that circulated in manuscript among her sisters, friends, and father, and many of her most famous journal entries, such as those describing her mastectomy and her near-drowning in Devon, were written for commemorative purposes months or years after the events. James Boswell, likewise, shared journal entries with friends, an activity that his father censured but his idol Samuel Johnson sanctioned; at Johnson's implicit request, Boswell's *Journal of a Tour to the Hebrides*, documenting their joint trip to Scotland in 1773, remained in manuscript until after Johnson's death in 1784.²⁹ In the realm of scientific and antiquarian journals, manuscript was the primary medium for the voluminous notes and fragments that scholars compiled, and one of the tasks of the scholar was to arrange his papers for posthumous collection in a library or museum, an act that constituted its own form of publication. The essays by Michelle Levy, Beth Fowkes Tobin, Collin Jennings, and Marissa Nicosia here explore the notebooks, scientific notes, and recipe books that abounded in the eighteenth century. In these and many other arenas, manuscript operated in a variety of public-facing ways.

In addition to such full manuscript works, the period saw a flourishing of documents and books that required or encouraged the mixing of script and print. The eighteenth century experienced a quantitative takeoff in the volume of print production, and this necessarily had an impact on the manuscript medium. The total number of imprints posted double-digit percentage increases in most decades between 1700 and 1800, with the sharpest jumps coming in the final third of the century.³⁰ At the beginning of the period, the post-1695 shift to newspaper and periodical publishing reconfigured the print marketplace. Dror Wahrman has named this the era of "Print 2.0," arguing that the boom in periodical and ephemeral texts following the lapse of the Licensing Act constituted a new epoch in the print medium.³¹ But rather than subsuming manuscript texts, such changes likely led to a concomitant rise in written production. Periodicals, for example, began by requesting readers' feedback in the form of letters to the editor; one of the first major successes of the genre was John Dunton's *Athenian Mercury*, which presented lists of reader-supplied questions and the answers of the "Athenian Society." In September 1691, a few months after beginning the project, Dunton called on his readers "to hold their *Hands* and *Pens*, and let us take *Breath a while*, and get rid of those CART-LOADS of *Questions* which are yet upon the File, and are likely to press us to death under their weight."³² Richard Steele, meanwhile, appealed in *Tatler* no. 7 for readers to send him letters "by the Penny Post" with material for publication, "since, without such assistance, I frankly confess, and am sensible, that I have not a month's wit more."³³ Collections of original letters sent to Steele as editor of the *Tatler* and *Spectator* remain at the British Library, showing that readers responded to the call. In this volume, essays by Leith Davis and Kathryn R. King explore the circular relationship between manuscript letters and printed essays in the seventeenth- and eighteenth-century periodical.

But it was not only that printed texts relied on manuscript bases; they also encouraged handwritten additions and responses. Peter Stallybrass has highlighted the importance of job printing to printers' financial survival, arguing that legal forms, bank bills, and accounting ledgers were as central to the print revolution as Bibles and novels. These documents generally required the addition of handwriting to be complete, proving that "printing has become the great means ... of eliciting writing by hand."[34] William Sherman and Ann Blair have focused on textual marginalia as evidence of how actual consumers reacted to print.[35] Blair notes that such print-centric innovations as the errata list asked for readers to perfect the printed text, but many people went beyond the listed faults to revise grammar, usage, and matters of fact: "By making corrections, readers completed the process of producing a text; despite the guidance of errata lists, readers had the last say, beyond the real control of either printer or author."[36] In addition, as the Multigraph Collective notes, manuscript works in this period began modeling themselves on print, creating new possibilities through intermediation; with manuscripts that circulated to the hundreds of copies and rare printed works that acquired an aura, the "seemingly commonsensical difference between print and manuscript as technologies of writing proves far more slippery than our conventional analyses would have it."[37] The essays in this volume by Philip S. Palmer and Colin T. Ramsey show how readers altered their printed books and how authors in print positioned themselves vis-à-vis manuscript. From the manuscript copy delivered to the printer to the printed volume annotated by hand and the handwritten "title page" complete with colophon, the eighteenth-century takeoff in printing elicited a parallel spurt of manuscript production.

After Print thus pursues a methodology that considers both print and manuscript as continually contingent, in flux, and in conversation with each other. Adrian Johns's influential argument that an association of print with fixity and authority was the result of hard work on the part of printers over centuries—that "the very identity of print itself has had to be *made*"—has had an ongoing impact on print studies, where scholars such as Paula McDowell, Andrew Piper, and Trish Loughran have paid careful attention to the particular, local circumstances of the eighteenth- and nineteenth-century print industry.[38] But the similarly evolving nature of manuscript cultures and interaction between printing and writing remain comparatively underexplored. Manuscript was not a static entity against which the modern form of print defined itself; rather, the two media were coproductive throughout the long and fitful quantitative rise in textual production that characterized the eighteenth-century print marketplace. To fully appreciate the nature of print in the eighteenth century, we must also have a solid understanding of the other media with which it was in conversation.

Scholars who take a media studies-informed approach to the period have offered models for considering diverse forms in conjunction. David McKitterick writes that a conceptual separation of print and manuscript followed a 350-year-long "period of accommodation" in which authors, printers, readers, and booksellers viewed both as forms of textual production that had similarities and differences.[39] McKitterick uses close bibliographical analysis to draw a large-scale framework: "The new can only be understood by reference to the old, and different cultures and media must inevitably exist side by side.... In practice, each new technology does not replace the previous one. Rather, it augments it, and offers alternatives."[40] In a study of colonial New England, Matt Cohen turns his focus from printed publications to the "publication event," defining "'publication' in its broad, seventeenth-century meaning (which included publicly posted or proclaimed information) and insisting on its performative elements." As he notes, "Communication happens on a spectrum of media modes."[41] Both Cohen and McKitterick build on the work of D. F. McKenzie, who argued that, for consumers, media tend to work in complementary, not competitive, ways: "We did not stop speaking when we learned to write, nor writing when we learned to print, nor reading, writing, or printing when we entered the 'electronic age.'"[42] Engaging methodologically with this seemingly obvious, but necessary, observation, the essays in *After Print* operate from an assumption of the complementarity, codependence, and integration of manuscript and print in the long eighteenth century. They follow texts across national borders, noting how both printed and written works traveled together via global postal and commercial routes. And they do not offer these studies as a prehistory of the "rise of print." Instead, they assume that manuscript culture had no determined endpoint. As Paul Duguid has argued, a model of media history that "resist[s] simple ideas of supercession ... encourages richer investigation of those very genealogies supersession makes untraceable."[43] Through specific, in-depth attention to material texts and archival research, this volume establishes the imperative to view particular works and authors as part of an integrated and nonhierarchical multimedia environment.

Such an attitude toward eighteenth-century literature both draws from and has insights for our contemporary sense of media shift as it focuses on the intuitive, everyday accommodations that users make to new and old technologies. As we live through another supposedly revolutionary moment, the negotiations in progress among printed, digital, audio, video, and oral forms—when the "death" of print is repeatedly deferred, digital filters re-create the distortions of film, and social media platforms become archival repositories—provide us with an innate sense of the actual processes by which producers and consumers compare and contrast media. We thus approach the eighteenth century from another perspective "after" print, when the status of print culture is again in upheaval. This volume's authors share an understanding of the eighteenth century as a period of prolonged, obsessive interest in writing, publication, and what we now call communications media, elaborating on John Guillory's observation that "the concept of a medium of communication was absent but *wanted* for the several centuries prior to its appearance."[44] Scholars of present-day media have argued against a teleological model of development and in favor of an "archeological" approach that treats as more illuminating moments "where things and situations were still in a state of flux, where the options for development in various directions were still wide open, where the future was conceivable as holding multifarious possibilities of technical and cultural solutions for constructing media worlds."[45] By viewing the eighteenth century through such a lens, *After Print* provides a clearer picture of the past and present moments, thus offering a new model for combining archival research with a media-history framework and textual interpretation.

Essay Outlines

The authors in this volume establish the imperative to view the print medium in the context of a holistic media environment at the same time that they explore specific moments of manuscript circulation from the late seventeenth century through the early nineteenth century. The book's three sections follow the broad areas of interest within the study of manuscript cultures outlined earlier: manuscript publication, the print-manuscript interface, and new methodologies that explore a digital-manuscript interface. Rather than proceeding chronologically through the period, then, the volume's organization allows for ongoing views of continuity and change in the uses of and reactions to handwritten documents; indeed, many of the essays span nonstandard periodizations as they examine the textual "afterlives" of particular works being remediated from manuscript into print, or vice versa—and into the digital medium today. In each section, the focus is on handwritten texts and practices, but these can never be isolated from the broader multimedia context of eighteenth-century literature and twenty-first century scholarship.

The essays in part 1 question the association of manuscript with amateur, domestic, and apolitical production. Andrew O. Winckles focuses on communal religious practices in the scribal productions of Methodist women from the mid-eighteenth century to the early nineteenth century, showing the centrality of manuscript memoirs and letters—including some that have been misleadingly archived and catalogued—to what has been understood as a print-centric religious revival. While the second-generation male leaders of the movement attempted to use print to shut down women's preaching activities, women continued to successfully employ written and oral venues to publicize their spiritual experiences. Beth Fowkes Tobin looks to the arena of science and the development of natural history from the 1770s to the 1830s in the career of John Abbott, a naturalist who published his American nature prints thirty years before John Jacob Audubon but whose contributions are less well known because he remained in "the field," the state of Georgia, instead of returning to London. Tobin finds the Enlightenment scientific emphasis on the collection of specimens and of the manuscript notes describing them conflicting with the growing print-focused concentration of natural history, even as Abbot's thousands of manuscripts were highly valued and collected by professional naturalists into the nineteenth century.

Turning from influential scribal communities to key scribal genres, my essay opens a new view of one of the most examined eighteenth-century manuscript genres, the letter, to argue that close attention to archival correspondence undercuts conventional scholarly assumptions that the letter was a particularly private, feminine form. Looking at the correspondence circles surrounding two prominent diplomats, Charles Hanbury Williams and Henry Seymour Conway, I show how everyday letters subverted private-public and feminine-masculine epistolary norms. Michelle Levy uses another apparently intimate, personal form, the notebook—in this case, Dorothy Wordsworth's—to demonstrate the continuation of sociable manuscript practices into the Romantic period. Examining the affordances of the notebook form in facilitating writing, drawing, pasting in, and collecting texts and images, Levy argues that Wordsworth's notebooks were not solitary and inward-facing drafts but, rather, communal documents meant to be used and read by others. While the writings were not intended for print, extracts from the notebooks that circulated more widely contributed to Wordsworth developing a reputation as a writer during her own lifetime—but the twentieth-century remediation of the notebooks into print and particularly printed anthologies obscured their more sociable purposes. These essays reveal the continuation of what Love calls "scribal publication" and Ezell "social authorship" throughout the eighteenth century and into the nineteenth, showing how manuscript remained a preferred or necessary medium for many writers.

The essays in part 2 turn the spotlight on a theme that is also implicit in part 1: the intersection between manuscript and print media of production and publication in the long eighteenth century. Philip S. Palmer looks to print as a source of manuscript culture, identifying the genre of manuscript verse inscribed as paratext in printed books. By customizing books through adding commendatory verse, early modern readers were able to take on a number of roles, functioning simultaneously as writers, advertisers, and consumers. Manuscript also enabled readers to enter print publication themselves. Leith Davis and Kathryn R. King both look at the interaction between manuscript and print in periodical form. Davis shows Restoration-era news consumers relying on multimedia sources, in particular exploring how the formal features of the official manuscript newsletter worked in tandem with printed news sources to provide readers an account of the Revolution of 1688. King turns to affect theory to argue that the letters to the editor in a periodical such as Frances Brooke's the *Old Maid* (1755–56) preserved some of the ethical and aesthetic features associated with the scribal medium, a set of conventions that she calls the "script affect." The *Old Maid*'s community of reader-correspondents constituted a group of self-presented oddballs living outside of traditional conjugal family arrangements, who found voice through printed letters. Meanwhile, Colin T. Ramsey examines the print-centric narrative of American revolutionary politics, focusing on the scientific activities of Benjamin Franklin to reveal that it was necessary for that avatar of print culture to engage in traditional scribal, and in many ways anti-print, practices of scientific exchange for his work to be taken seriously. While Franklin printed widely, it was only by first circulating his theories on electricity in correspondence with noted English scientists, and by disavowing his desire to publish in the preface to the printed version, that his *Experiments and Observations on Electricity*,

Made at Philadelphia (1751) earned him entry to the Royal Society. As these essays show, even as the print marketplace expanded in the eighteenth century, readers expected printed texts to reference and incorporate the manuscript medium in varied, evolving ways.

Part 3 shows the usefulness of new interdisciplinary methods for the seemingly retro field of manuscript and archival studies. Emily C. Friedman details her creation of a digital database for manuscript novels, showing how this genre long associated with the rise of a mass print culture appeared in a multitude of handwritten forms throughout the century. Focusing on manuscript novels that were not intended for eventual print publication, Friedman argues that a variety of academic and institutional factors—including assumptions about the nature of eighteenth-century manuscript practices, definitional discrepancies, and incomplete or inaccurate archival cataloguing—have made such texts invisible to scholars, a fact that she works to remedy by reclassifying examples of the genre. Collin Jennings uses a computational approach to analyze early modern notebooks, particularly those that combine text with "notational features" such as lists and charts. By using a vector space model to identify lexical variation in printed texts, Jennings shows that works with a high degree of lexical variation—the unlikelihood that particular words will appear alongside one another—tend to incorporate notational features. Moving between digitized manuscript and printed notebooks, he shows how lexical variation often signifies the presence of script features in print. Brian Rejack focuses on an effort that takes advantage of the meeting points of manuscript studies and digital publication, the Keats Letters Project. Rejack retraces the postal history of a single letter by Keats, which crossed the Atlantic in the nineteenth century before being stolen from and ultimately recovered by the Historical Society of Pennsylvania in the twenty-first, to argue that eighteenth- and nineteenth-century letters continue to circulate today in a variety of ways. The Keats Letters Project does not provide a new edition of the letters. Rather, it offers commentary and connects readers to existing print and digital sources. Similarly, Marissa Nicosia explores the theoretical insights of her scholarly popular project *Cooking in the Archives: Updating Early Modern Recipes (1600–1800) in a Modern Kitchen*. By re-creating recipes from historical cookbooks, Nicosia argues, we can open up a new method for manuscript studies that helps us better understand early modern material history, collective writing, and concepts of taste. These approaches, combining in-depth archival work with digital and often popular engagement, open up new fronts for manuscript studies in the digital age.

Finally, Margaret J. M. Ezell, whose books *Social Authorship and the Advent of Print* (1999), *Writing Women's Literary History* (1993), and *The Patriarch's Wife: Literary Evidence and the History of the Family* (1987) were pioneers in this field—and are referenced extensively by this volume's authors—closes *After Print* with an epilogue considering the state of manuscript studies now. Ezell shows how the authors mount a collective argument against the idea of media obsolescence, revealing not only that media do not necessarily progress, but also that users retain "old" media for a variety of reasons: "As the essays in this volume clearly demonstrate, there was an extended transition period from handwritten copies to the new print opportunities in the post-1700 world, and, notably, there was a pattern of deliberate, strategic return to older media modes." *After Print* thus provides a timely new approach to eighteenth-century studies, offering a methodological and interpretive model for resituating some of the era's best-known printed works without privileging an established canon. The authors give the same attention and seriousness to the anonymous creator of a fragmentary manuscript novel as they do to writers as central to the narrative of eighteenth-century print culture as Pope, Franklin, and Wordsworth. This alignment both recovers important and illuminating texts and offers new, archivally informed ways to read canonical works.

As a closing example, let us consider the collection of letters, mentioned earlier, sent to Richard Steele as author of the *Tatler* and the *Spectator*, which are now part of the British Library's Blenheim Papers. The dozens of letters survive today because they were never printed, unlike the manuscript documents that would have been destroyed by the printer after being used for copy. The existence of this collection has long been acknowledged, but a scholarly understanding of the two periodicals as paradigmatic examples of early eighteenth-century print culture has obscured its nature and significance. While most scholarship assumes that the hundreds of letters included in the *Tatler* and *Spectator* were largely fake—that, is that they were written by Addison and Steele and not based on actual manuscript "originals"—the archival collection shows a robust interaction with readers, who responded to queries printed in the journals, asked their own questions, provided full essays, and furnished themselves with characteristic pseudonyms such as "Philogelus," "John Trusty," and "Alice Maybe." And these correspondents did not presume the primacy of print, often declaring their satisfaction in simply communicating with Isaac Bickerstaff or Mr. Spectator; as one wrote in 1709, "For the publicity of this Epistle . . . do with [it] as you think fit."[46] Indeed, some of the letters resist the print medium altogether; a facetious request from "the Dealers in Gold & Silver Lace" for Bickerstaff to reverse his prohibition on lace petticoats took the format of an official petition on a folio sheet with text running in multiple directions, while a flourishing, curlicue-embellished advertisement for a writing school provided excellent evidence of the instructor's abilities but could hardly be intended for printing in the periodical (see figs 1 and 2).[47] Many of the writers seem to have conceptualized their letters in the epistolary modes of reciprocity and exchange—even with one side of the relationship occurring in print.

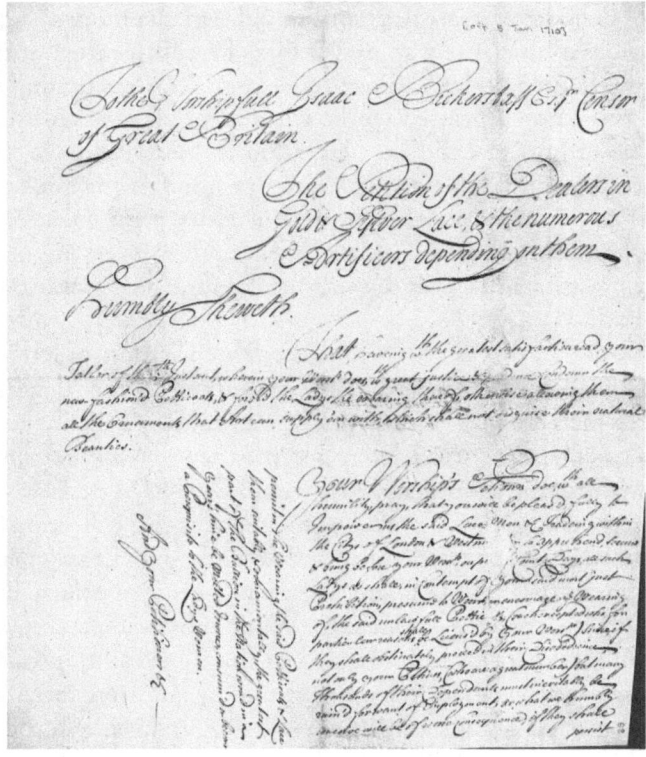

FIGURE 1. "Petition of the Dealers in Gold & Silver Lace, & the numerous Artificers depending on them" to "the Worshipfull Isaac Bickerstaff Esq.ʳ Censor of Great Britain." (Correspondence and Papers of Sir Richard Steele, after January 5, 1710, Add MS 61687, ff. 67ᵛ–68ʳ; © The British Library Board)

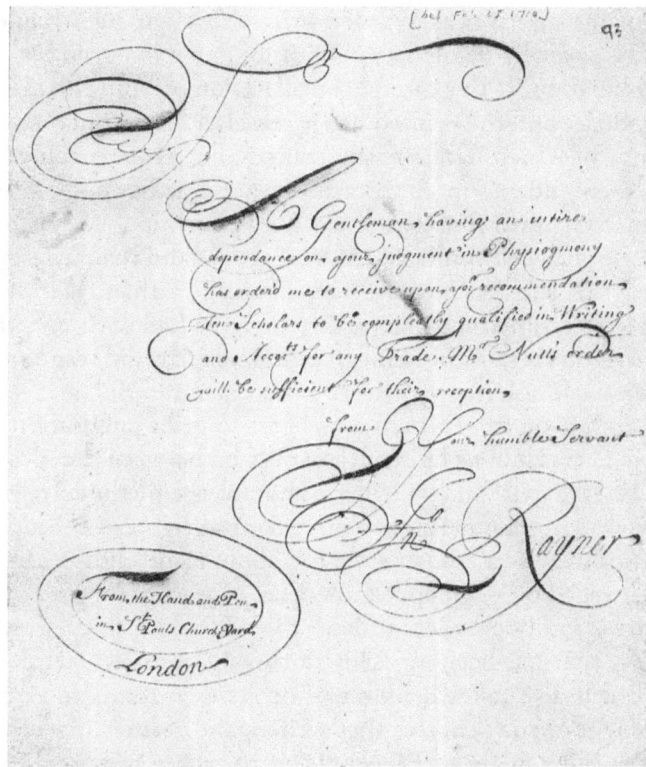

FIGURE 2. Letter from John Raymer to Sir Richard Steele. (Correspondence and Papers of Sir Richard Steele, before February 25, 1710, Add MS 61687, f. 93; © The British Library Board)

As a correspondent wrote in February 1710, "You have in your last Tatler taken notice of me in a manner so obliging that I can't omit expressing the Sense I have thereof: If you please to accept of my Gratitude in returns of this kind, I will endeavour to keep up a Correspondence with you as long as your Patience will allow me."[48] These letters eschewed a print-manuscript media hierarchy, assuming instead a scene of interactive circulation.

Our print-centric approach to periodicals, however, can obscure the multimediality at play—and thus obscure how common such interactions were. The influential model of Jürgen Habermas and Michael Warner has positioned the *Tatler* and *Spectator* as mass media that allowed for the creation of an anonymous print public sphere, specifically at the expense of manuscript; as Warner writes, through such venues print "came to be specially defined as publication, now *in opposition* to manuscript circulation."[49] But careful consideration of both the manuscript correspondence and the printed paper reveals a local London epistolary community in which letters easily transitioned from manuscript into print, then engendered more correspondence. Furthermore, the periodicals themselves often functioned as a kind of semipublic epistolary circle, as Steele and Addison included inside jokes and thanked the friends and colleagues, such as Eustace Budgell and Jonathan Swift, who had provided letters, hints, and essays. Together, the handwritten letters and printed periodicals show not only that readers really did respond to periodicalists' calls for correspondence, but also that they did not see a unidirectional transition from manuscript letter to print publication. Rather, they pursued continuous lines of transmission between the media.

As the essays that follow further elaborate, the methodology of *After Print* uncovers new knowledge about canonical eighteenth-century texts while demonstrating a fundamental fact about eighteenth-century printing: that it relied on ongoing, handwritten contact among readers, writers, printers, and booksellers to have the wide-scale impact on culture and society that has been so richly documented in eighteenth-century studies. But it also takes manuscript on its own terms to understand the ongoing, everyday choices that writers and readers made to create, consume, and circulate texts. Attention to manuscript reminds us of the actual complexity of any media system and helps to clarify the oft-noted media self-reflexivity of the eighteenth century, a time when many writers themselves denigrated print and undercut a developmental media model. By foregrounding the scribal medium in what has often been understood as the age of print, this collection offers a comprehensive picture of the lived experience and changing conditions of eighteenth-century media.

Notes

1. Defoe, *A Review of the Affairs of France*, 1:161.
2. Budgell, *Bee*, n.p.; Pope, *New Letters of Mr. Alexander Pope*, i–ii.
3. Macpherson, "Advertisement," 33; Boswell, *Life of Johnson*, 2:296.
4. Fielding, *The Journal of a Voyage to Lisbon*, 192.
5. One anecdote: in the Ossian case, Thomas Becket, the publisher of *Fingal*

and *Temora*, advertised in 1775, in an attempt to refute Johnson, "I hereby declare that the originals of FINGAL and other poems of Ossian lay in my shop for many months in the year 1762, for the inspection of the curious," and several people claimed to have seen the manuscripts. Quoted in Gaskill, "Introduction," 11.

6. Multigraph Collective, *Interacting with Print*, 11; Douglas, *Work in Hand*, 2; McDowell, *The Invention of the Oral*, 14.
7. Multigraph Collective, *Interacting with Print*, 11. While Paula McDowell analyzes "the problems inherent in the term 'print culture,'" she argues that the eighteenth century demonstrated a "perception" that it had become a "print society," and she focuses on how orality emerged through print: "reflection on the spread of *print* was a key factor in shaping our modern intellectual category of 'oral culture.'" McDowell, *The Invention of the Oral*, 7, 3.
8. As Caroline Levine explains, "affordance" is a term borrowed from design theory that has become widespread in media and literary studies. It "describe[s] the potential uses or actions latent in materials and designs": Levine, *Forms*, 6.
9. McKenzie, *Bibliography and the Sociology of Texts*, 13; McKenzie, "The Sociology of a Text," 334.
10. Justice, "The Social World of Authorship 1660–1714," 279.
11. Kernan, *Printing Technology, Letters, and Samuel Johnson*, 4, 8.
12. See also Johnston and Van Dussen, *The Medieval Manuscript Book*, and Clemens and Graham, *Introduction to Manuscript Studies*, both of which focus on medieval texts.
13. This is the more problematic because Steven May long ago dismantled the myth of the "stigma of print." See May, "Tudor Aristocrats and the Mythical 'Stigma of Print.'"
14. Love, *The Culture and Commerce of Texts*; Ezell, *Social Authorship and the Advent of Print*. Michelle Levy extends the chronology forward, arguing that the Romantic period saw a vital culture of manuscript authorship centered in the family, a phenomenon that "lies on the cusp between a vanishing manuscript culture and the dominance of print." Similarly, Sigurður Gylfi Magnússon and Davíð Ólafsson focus on the nineteenth century, showing how "lay scholars" in Iceland ensured that people had access to a wider array of texts than were available in print, which was controlled by the church. Levy, *Family Authorship and Romantic Print Culture*, 2; Magnússon and Ólafsson, *Minor Knowledge and Microhistory*, 2–3, 18.
15. Likewise, Arthur Marotti has focused on manuscript publication of lyric poetry in the sixteenth and seventeenth centuries, arguing that "the two systems of literary transmission [manuscript and print] not only competed but also influenced each other and, to a great extent, coexisted by performing

different cultural functions." However, he sees print as replacing manuscript as the norm for poetic writing by the Restoration: Marotti, *Manuscript, Print, and the English Renaissance Lyric*, 1, 68–69.
16. Ezell, *Social Authorship and the Advent of Print*, 111.
17. Justice, "Introduction," 5.
18. Schellenberg, *Literary Coteries and the Making of Modern Print Culture*, 17.
19. Raven, *The Business of Books*, 10.
20. Ibid.
21. Justice, "Introduction," 15.
22. Habermas, *The Structural Transformation of the Public Sphere*, 48–49.
23. Gilroy and Verhoeven, "Introduction," 3.
24. Dierks, *In My Power*, 4, xiii, xvii.
25. Bannet, "Printed Epistolary Manuals and the Transatlantic Rescripting of Manuscript Culture," 15.
26. Reiman, *The Study of Modern Manuscripts*, 38, 65.
27. Love, *The Culture and Commerce of Texts*, 32, 35–36.
28. David Allan has argued for the continuing importance of commonplace books in the eighteenth century, despite scholarly assumptions that their use died out or declined at the end of the Renaissance. Allan, *Commonplace Books and Reading in Georgian England*, 20–21 and passim.
29. DeMaria, *The Life of Samuel Johnson*, 262.
30. Suarez, "Towards a Bibliometric Analysis of the Surviving Record," 43. See also Raven, *The Business of Books*, 131.
31. Wahrman, *Mr. Collier's Letter Racks*, 20.
32. *Athenian Mercury*, vol. 4, no. 1, September 29, 1691, 1. This issue was accessed via the ProQuest British Periodicals database, which lists the publication as the *Athenian Gazette*.
33. Steele, *Tatler*, 1:63.
34. Stallybrass, "Little Jobs," 341.
35. Sherman, *Used Books*; Blair, "Errata Lists and the Reader as Corrector."
36. Blair, "Errata Lists and the Reader as Corrector," 37.
37. Multigraph Collective, *Interacting with Print*, 189.
38. Johns, *The Nature of the Book*, 2, 31–36. See also McDowell, *The Women of Grub Street*; McDowell, *The Invention of the Oral*; Piper, *Dreaming in Books*; Loughran, *The Republic in Print*.
39. McKitterick, *Print, Manuscript and the Search for Order*, 21–36, 59.
40. Ibid., 20, 33.
41. Cohen, *The Networked Wilderness*, 7, 11.
42. McKenzie, "Speech-Manuscript-Print," 87.
43. Duguid, "Material Matters," 72.
44. Guillory, "Genesis of the Media Concept," 321.

45. Zielinski, *Deep Time of the Media*, 10.
46. "To the Author of the Tatler," August 1709, Add MS 61687, Correspondence and Papers of Sir Richard Steele, British Library, London, f. 2.
47. "To the Worshipfull Isaac Bickerstaff Esq.ʳ Censor of Great Britain," after January 5, 1710, and John Raymer to Richard Steele, before February 25, 1710, Add MS 61687, Correspondence and Papers of Sir Richard Steele, British Library, ff. 67, 93.
48. "From the Trumpet Club," February 23, 1710, Add MS 61687, Correspondence and Papers of Sir Richard Steele, British Library, f. 90.
49. Warner, *The Letters of the Republic*, 8.

Works Cited

Allan, David. *Commonplace Books and Reading in Georgian England*. Cambridge: Cambridge University Press, 2010.

Bannet, Eve Tavor. "Printed Epistolary Manuals and the Transatlantic Rescripting of Manuscript Culture." *Studies in Eighteenth Century Culture* 36 (2007): 13–32.

Blair, Ann. "Errata Lists and the Reader as Corrector." In *Agent of Change: Print Culture Studies after Elizabeth L. Eisenstein*, edited by Sabrina A. Baron, Eric N. Lindquist, and Eleanor F. Shevlin, 21–41. Amherst: University of Massachusetts Press, 2007.

Boswell, James. *Life of Johnson*, edited by George Birkbeck Hill and L. F. Powell. 6 vols. Oxford: Clarendon, 1934–64.

Budgell, Eustace. *The Bee: Or, Universal Weekly Pamphlet*. London, 1733.

Clemens, Raymond, and Timothy Graham, eds. *Introduction to Manuscript Studies*. Ithaca, NY: Cornell University Press, 2007.

Cohen, Matt. *The Networked Wilderness: Communicating in Early New England*. Minneapolis: University of Minnesota Press, 2010.

Defoe, Daniel. *A Review of the Affairs of France*, edited by John McVeagh, 2 vols. London: Pickering and Chatto, 2003.

DeMaria, Robert, Jr. *The Life of Samuel Johnson: A Critical Biography*. Oxford: Blackwell, 1993.

Dierks, Konstantin. *In My Power: Letter Writing and Communications in Early America*. Philadelphia: University of Pennsylvania Press, 2009.

Douglas, Aileen. *Work in Hand: Script, Print, and Writing, 1690–1840*. Oxford: Oxford University Press, 2017.

Duguid, Paul. "Material Matters: The Past and Futurology of the Book." In *The Future of the Book*, edited by Geoffrey Nunberg, 63–101. Berkeley: University of California Press, 1996.

Ezell, Margaret J. M. *Social Authorship and the Advent of Print*. Baltimore: Johns Hopkins University Press, 1999.

Fielding, Henry. *The Journal of a Voyage to Lisbon, Shamela, and Occasional Writings*, edited by Martin C. Battestin. Wesleyan Edition of the Works of Henry Fielding. Oxford: Clarendon, 2008.

Gaskill, Howard. "Introduction." In *Ossian Revisited*, edited by Howard Gaskill, 1–18. Edinburgh: Edinburgh University Press, 1991.

Gilroy, Amanda, and W. M. Verhoeven. "Introduction." In *Epistolary Histories: Letters, Fiction, Culture*, edited by Amanda Gilroy and W. M. Verhoeven, 1–25. Charlottesville: University of Virginia Press, 2000.

Guillory, John. "Genesis of the Media Concept." *Critical Inquiry* 36, no. 2 (Winter 2010): 321–62.

Habermas, Jürgen. *The Structural Transformation of the Public Sphere: An Inquiry into a Category of Bourgeois Society*, translated by Thomas Burger. Cambridge, MA: MIT Press, 1991.

Johns, Adrian. *The Nature of the Book: Print and Knowledge in the Making*. Chicago: University of Chicago Press, 1998.

Johnston, Michael, and Michael Van Dussen, eds. *The Medieval Manuscript Book: Cultural Approaches*. Cambridge: Cambridge University Press, 2015.

Justice, George L. "Introduction." In *Women's Writing and the Circulation of Ideas: Manuscript Publication in England, 1550–1880*, edited by George L. Justice and Nathan Tinker, 1–16. Cambridge: Cambridge University Press, 2002.

———. "The Social World of Authorship 1660–1714." *Scriblerian and the Kit-Cats* 38, no. 2 (Spring 2006): 279–80.

Kernan, Alvin. *Printing Technology, Letters, and Samuel Johnson*. Princeton, NJ: Princeton University Press, 1987.

Levine, Caroline. *Forms: Whole, Rhythm, Hierarchy, Network*. Princeton, NJ: Princeton University Press, 2015.

Levy, Michelle. *Family Authorship and Romantic Print Culture*. New York: Palgrave Macmillan, 2008.

Loughran, Trish. *The Republic in Print: Print Culture in the Age of U.S. Nation Building, 1770–1870*. New York: Columbia University Press, 2007.

Love, Harold. *The Culture and Commerce of Texts: Scribal Publication in Seventeenth-Century England*. Amherst: University of Massachusetts Press, 1998.

Macpherson, James. "Advertisement." In *The Poems of Ossian: And Related Works*, edited by Howard Gaskill, 33. Edinburgh: Edinburgh University Press, 1996.

Magnússon, Sigurður Gylfi, and Davíð Ólafsson. *Minor Knowledge and Microhistory: Manuscript Culture in the Nineteenth Century*. New York: Routledge, 2017.

Marotti, Arthur F. *Manuscript, Print, and the English Renaissance Lyric.* Ithaca, NY: Cornell University Press, 1995.

May, Steven. "Tudor Aristocrats and the Mythical 'Stigma of Print.'" *Renaissance Papers* 10 (1980): 11–18.

McDowell, Paula. *The Invention of the Oral: Print Commerce and Fugitive Voices in Eighteenth-Century Britain.* Chicago: University of Chicago Press, 2017.

———. *The Women of Grub Street: Press, Politics, and Gender in the London Literary Marketplace 1678–1730.* Oxford: Oxford University Press, 1998.

McKenzie, D. F. *Bibliography and the Sociology of Texts.* Cambridge: Cambridge University Press, 1999.

———. "Speech-Manuscript-Print." *Library Chronicle of the University of Texas at Austin* 20, nos. 1–2 (1990): 87–109.

———. "The Sociology of a Text: Orality, Literacy, and Print in Early New Zealand." *Library* 6, no. 4 (December 1984): 333–65.

McKitterick, David. *Print, Manuscript and the Search for Order, 1450–1830.* Cambridge: Cambridge University Press, 2003.

Multigraph Collective. *Interacting with Print: Elements of Reading in the Era of Print Saturation.* Chicago: University of Chicago Press, 2018.

Piper, Andrew. *Dreaming in Books: The Making of the Bibliographic Imagination in the Romantic Age.* Chicago: University of Chicago Press, 2009.

Pope, Alexander. *New Letters of Mr. Alexander Pope, and Several of His Friends.* London, 1737.

Raven, James. *The Business of Books: Booksellers and the English Book Trade.* New Haven, CT: Yale University Press, 2007.

Reiman, Donald H. *The Study of Modern Manuscripts: Public, Confidential, and Private.* Baltimore: Johns Hopkins University Press, 1993.

Schellenberg, Betty. *Literary Coteries and the Making of Modern Print Culture, 1740–1790.* Cambridge: Cambridge University Press, 2016.

Sherman, William. *Used Books: Marking Readers in Renaissance England.* Philadelphia: University of Pennsylvania Press, 2008.

Stallybrass, Peter. "'Little Jobs': Broadsides and the Printing Revolution." In *Agent of Change: Print Culture Studies after Elizabeth L. Eisenstein,* edited by Sabrina A. Baron, Eric N. Lindquist, and Eleanor F. Shevlin, 315–41. Amherst: University of Massachusetts Press, 2007.

Steele, Richard. *Tatler,* edited by Donald F. Bond. 3 vols. Oxford: Oxford University Press, 1987.

Suarez, Michael F., SJ. "Towards a Bibliometric Analysis of the Surviving Record, 1701–1800." In *The Cambridge History of the Book in Britain, Volume 5: 1695–1830,* edited by Michael F. Suarez and Michael L. Turner, 39–65. Cambridge: Cambridge University Press, 2009.

Wahrman, Dror. *Mr. Collier's Letter Racks: A Tale of Art and Illusion at the Threshold of the Modern Information Age.* Oxford: Oxford University Press, 2012.

Warner, Michael. *The Letters of the Republic: Publication and the Public Sphere in Eighteenth-Century America.* Cambridge, MA: Harvard University Press, 1990.

Zielinski, Siegfried. *Deep Time of the Media: Toward an Archaeology of Hearing and Seeing by Technical Means.* Cambridge, MA: MIT Press, 2006.

PART I

Coteries, Communities, Collaborations

Manuscript Publication

"Pray for the Unworthy Scribbler"
The Textual Cultures of Early Methodist Women

ANDREW O. WINCKLES

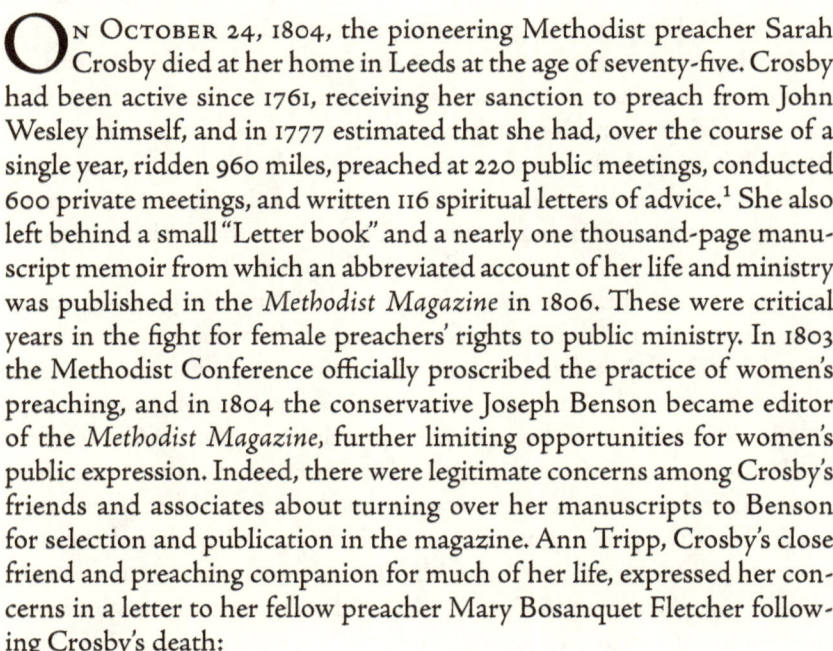

ON OCTOBER 24, 1804, the pioneering Methodist preacher Sarah Crosby died at her home in Leeds at the age of seventy-five. Crosby had been active since 1761, receiving her sanction to preach from John Wesley himself, and in 1777 estimated that she had, over the course of a single year, ridden 960 miles, preached at 220 public meetings, conducted 600 private meetings, and written 116 spiritual letters of advice.[1] She also left behind a small "Letter book" and a nearly one thousand-page manuscript memoir from which an abbreviated account of her life and ministry was published in the *Methodist Magazine* in 1806. These were critical years in the fight for female preachers' rights to public ministry. In 1803 the Methodist Conference officially proscribed the practice of women's preaching, and in 1804 the conservative Joseph Benson became editor of the *Methodist Magazine*, further limiting opportunities for women's public expression. Indeed, there were legitimate concerns among Crosby's friends and associates about turning over her manuscripts to Benson for selection and publication in the magazine. Ann Tripp, Crosby's close friend and preaching companion for much of her life, expressed her concerns in a letter to her fellow preacher Mary Bosanquet Fletcher following Crosby's death:

> I do indeed expect a trial respecting our Deceased Friends papers; May the 6 I recd a Letter from Mrs M[ortimer] informing me "*she*, & Mr Benson had recd the first experience & thought it should be shortened,

which could not be done without copying, that he had desird her to take out of the diary *small* paragraphs expressive of the state of her mind, & that I must draw up an account of the closing scenes; & he would insert it in the Magazine: that he would do all in his power to let me have any of the original papers (she sent him alterd with a pencil) back again." I wrote her my mind pretty freely upon it & have heard nothing since; But I can do nothing but commit the whole to God.[2]

Tripp's concerns were justified: the account of Crosby's life that was eventually published erases many important details of her public life and ministry. The manuscript itself disappeared in the nineteenth century and has yet to be recovered.[3]

Manuscript production and circulation practices such as Crosby's, along with their historical silencing, are one of the untold stories of women's participation in Methodism. Although the manuscript practices used by Methodist women were not original to them, they were adapted in intentional ways and for particular purposes within the context of the Methodist movement. These conventions had their origins in the earliest days of the movement (1738–40), when women from all social classes began organizing themselves into close-knit communities for mutual spiritual edification. It was in these communities that women learned and developed the types of discourse practices Vicki Tolar Burton has termed "spiritual literacy."[4] Women testified publicly about their spiritual experiences, read manuscript accounts aloud, and assisted illiterate sisters in the process of writing their own conversion and spiritual experience narratives. Such practices continued after the early days of the revival and even after John Wesley realized and used the immense power and potential of print to spread his message. Although Wesley did more than perhaps any British leader before him (with the possible exception of George Fox) to elevate women's voices in print within his religious movement, there is also abundant evidence that women relied particularly on manuscript networks as the primary means by which they publicly shared their experiences with one another and with other Methodists, male and female. In addition, these manuscript practices did not fade at the beginning of the nineteenth century but actually intensified as, in the wake of Wesley's death, it became difficult for women to get their writings into print or access public roles for themselves within Methodism.

However, these types of manuscript practices have been obscured by a narrative increasingly told of Methodism: that it was a movement founded on the power of print.[5] There is some truth to this argument. After all, at the time of Wesley's death the Methodist Book Room, which was responsible for printing and distributing official Methodist publications, contained nearly £4,000 worth of unsold stock, and there is little doubt that Wesley was a master of using the technology of print to spread his message throughout the British Isles and, eventually, the world.[6] Methodism was certainly a textual movement—one founded on the practices of reading, writing, and hearing the gospel—but print was only one of the technologies through which Methodist experience was mediated. When Methodist manuscripts have been noticed or written about, however, they mainly have been employed as primary source material in the service of larger historical arguments. At the same time these manuscripts, often by women, are considered almost exclusively private documents: daily records of inner experience; collections of spiritual sayings and letters published elsewhere; or (at most) semipublic letter exchanges between two individuals, useful primarily for what they tell us about the male correspondents. Very rarely are the manuscripts read as explicit and intentional public and published documents—as texts intended to be read by others for specific rhetorical purposes. While this type of scribal publication was nothing new, at least to the women who engaged in it, it does run counter to the prevailing narrative of technological "progress" from manuscript to print in the eighteenth century. The way these women's manuscripts have been handled by generations of scholars and archivists reveals assumptions about what an archive is and how it should be curated and read.

A case in point is the manuscript "Letter book" of the early Methodist preacher Crosby, now held in the Frank Baker Collection of Wesleyana and British Methodism at Duke University Libraries (see fig. 1). This text was first discovered by the Methodist scholar Frank Baker at a bookshop in Sheffield, United Kingdom, during World War II. The Duke Library catalogue identifies the manuscript volume simply as a "Letter book" and dates it to about 1760. This designation, which seems to have originated in Baker's own description, has long gone unchallenged in the few volumes that have used the manuscript as a primary source.[7] In his notes on the volume, Baker always refers to it as a "letter-book" and describes it as a "neat little duodecimo volume, calf-bound, gilt-tooled, and clasped, into which [Crosby] copied her most important correspondence."[8] Furthermore, although Baker clearly recognized the rarity and value of the volume, it was not prioritized for publication when he made his first

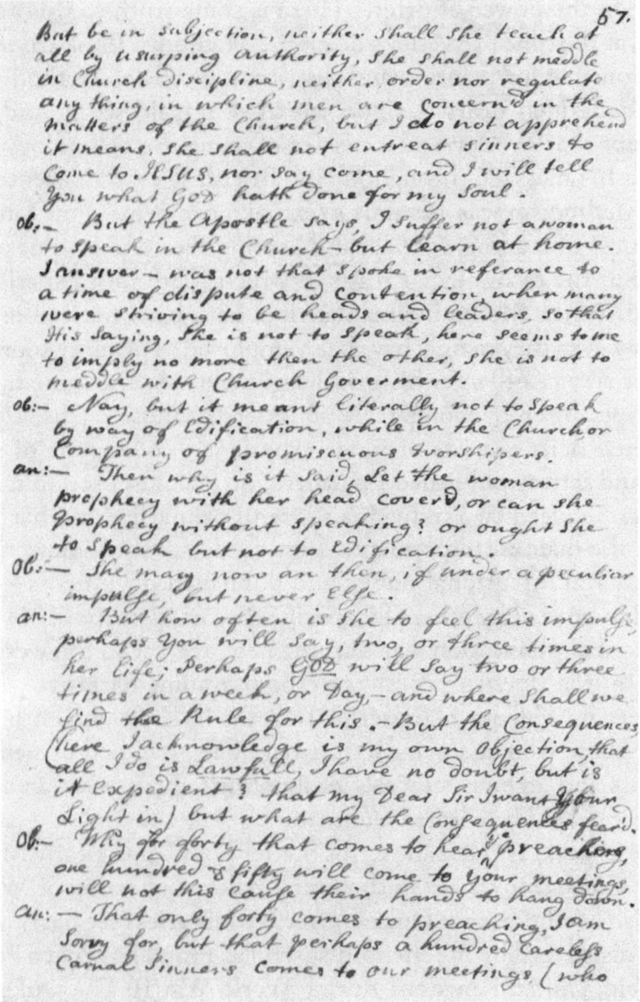

FIGURE 1. Page from Sarah Crosby's "Letter book." (Sarah Crosby Papers, 1760–1804, RUB Bay 3356, box 1, 57; David M. Rubenstein Rare Book and Manuscript Library, Duke University)

donation of materials to Duke. In a memo dated May 13, 1961, that is appended to a typewritten description of the manuscripts included in one of his first loans, Baker indicates that he is "not so anxious" about the publication of Crosby's manuscript as about others, generally related directly to the Wesleys.[9] This is understandable, given the importance of the Wesley manuscripts, many of which exist only in his collection, but it also provides a clue as to why Crosby's volume has been categorized exclusively as a letter book for so long.

However, there are reasons to doubt both the classification and dating of the text. To begin with, the selection of the letters and extracts in the volume is anything but random; also, it does not include simply her "most important correspondence." The content is too cohesive and organized for it to be a letter book—at least in the sense that it is not a straightforward record of outgoing and incoming correspondence. Instead, the text is selected and organized around issues relating to women's public ministries within Methodism. The letters are not simply presented chronologically but carefully arranged to highlight moments in which women intervened in public space. Central to the collection, both literally and figuratively, are Crosby's transcription of Mary Bosanquet Fletcher's 1771 letter to John Wesley justifying the practice of women's preaching, Wesley's reply recognizing Bosanquet Fletcher's "extraordinary call" to preach, and Crosby's correspondence with Wesley regarding her own preaching. But these are only the most notable examples. Almost every other letter in the collection also seems chosen to highlight the extent to which women such as Crosby felt called by God to preach and met with tremendous success in doing so. For example, in one letter Crosby writes at length about what she sees as her unique call from God and her faithfulness in following that call:

> I think I do use the little Strength I have in Instructg the Ignorant reclaiming the wicked relieving the Pain of those who suffer in body or mind. I am generaly some way or other imploy'd in some of these works. I am not conscious of any willfull omissions. . . . I do not think it was [not] for women to speak in public provided they speak by the Spirit of GOD, but at present I see myself just where I ought to be & just so imploy'd. I think we want more abundant life *here*. what a blessing it wd be if the People in general were [way] Simple & full of Love & yet free from enthusiasm and surely this is possible.[10]

Given this very specific content, it is difficult to imagine the volume as simply a private record of important correspondence. Material clues support this point: the ink and hand are consistent throughout, indicating that the book was written with the same ink over a short time span. By contrast, most letter books, diaries, and commonplace books from this period exhibit a wide variety of inks and nib sizes over the months or years they cover. Given that the letters included in the volume date from 1760 to the mid-1770s, it is odd that the ink or handwriting size should change so little. Furthermore, unlike in private letter books, these letters are in many cases heavily edited or redacted, sometimes with entire pages marked to the point that the writing underneath is illegible. This text was copied at one time and for a particular purpose. What appears to be occurring here is an instance of what Harold Love has called "scribal publication," the creation of a volume in manuscript that could then be circulated and read by various constituencies within Crosby's extensive social circle.[11]

If, therefore, the document is not a private letter book created over time but a discrete document produced in a specific time and place for a specific rhetorical purpose, then the date of 1760 does not bear close scrutiny. Crosby could not have transcribed letters written in 1777 at this earlier date. Given that the only evidence for dating the text to 1760 is the date on the endpaper (which, interestingly, is located below a faint date that begins 180?) and that this date is not necessarily or even likely in Crosby's own hand, it would be reasonable to assume that the manuscript was produced at a later date—likely the mid- to late 1780s or even the early 1790s. Further evidence for this later dating can be found in the watermark of the paper itself, which portrays Britannia seated on a chariot with a spear and scepter and bearing the inscription "Libertas et Natale Solum." This image, or similar ones, of Britannia appears on various watermarks in the Gravell database throughout the 1780s and '90s but rarely before this time. The inscription "Libertas et Natale Solum," however, is unique and does not appear in any online database, though the identical watermark does appear on an architectural drawing now held at Kedleston Hall in Derbyshire. Eleanor Shevlin has traced similar watermarks to paper produced by Harison and Company, at 18 Paternoster Row, during the late 1780s and early 1790s.[12] Harison had business ties in Derbyshire; Crosby lived most of her later life in Leeds, nearly seventy-five miles from Derby, but is known to have traveled in and through Derbyshire on her way to and from London and in the course of her travels. With these connections it seems likely that Crosby purchased the blank journal marked with the Harison watermark in Derbyshire during the mid-1780s and then used it to transcribe a selection of her letters, sermons, and spiritual experiences as a public record of her ministry.

That such an important text could have been misidentified for so long is not surprising given that manuscript texts, especially those by women, have often been accorded second-class status in the "age of print"—the assumption being that those who could print did and that manuscript culture was fading into an exclusively private sphere in the eighteenth century. However, as scholars such as Margaret J. M. Ezell and others have demonstrated, this was not the case. Ezell argues that "rather than being a nostalgic clinging to an outdated technology representing a fading aristocratic possession of the world of letters, the older practice of circulating scribal texts was instead a choice.... Indeed manuscript culture permitted and encouraged participation in literary life of groups of people whom print technology effectively isolated and alienated."[13] Furthermore, George Justice points out that the advent of mass print culture in the eighteenth century meant that writers had "more social and technological *choices* in the production and dissemination of their works," not that print triumphed over manuscript culture. In other words, "writers used manuscripts (or print technology, for that matter) because it suited their needs."[14] Elizabeth Singer Rowe, for example, "tactically" moved between manuscript and print publication throughout her career, in Kathryn R. King's words, to "take advantage of the dual possibilities of manuscript and print to advance her literary ambitions ... negotiating a series of positions for herself in the early eighteenth-century literary world."[15] In the case of the female Methodist preachers who are the subject of this essay, scribal publication of letters, diaries, and sermons provided a way to communicate within a defined community of faith, to justify their continued preaching activity, to preserve records of their spiritual experiences, and to circumvent the increasing controls over official Methodist publishing channels.

This approach to Methodist manuscripts not only changes how we read Crosby's text and others like it, but also suggests new purposes and audiences for scribal publication in the late eighteenth century. The later dating of the Crosby text is significant because the context of the Methodist movement from 1789 through the early nineteenth century was different from that between 1740 and 1760. In particular, there was less space for women's public discourse in Methodism. This manuscript, then, represents a turning point in that it looks back to and adapts the existing manuscript practices of the evangelical revival while looking forward to the new social and rhetorical realities that were coming into being within an increasingly centralized, conservative, and male-dominated post-Wesley Methodist institution. Methodist women's manuscript production and circulation practices thus provide a unique window into the shifting rhetorical spaces and discourse conditions of British religion and culture at the turn of the nineteenth century. To better understand what was at stake in these shifts, though—how they occurred and how women negotiated them—we must briefly glance back at how these manuscript practices developed within and were adapted to Methodism before we turn to the shifting discourse conditions of the turn of the century and how Methodist women used manuscript production, circulation, and preservation to establish a voice for themselves and their religious experiences outside the officially sanctioned Methodist media machine.

The Origins of Methodist Manuscript Culture

One of the distinctive innovations that Wesley introduced early on to Methodism was a system of single-sex classes and bands that worked to hold members accountable, encourage spiritual growth, and operate as community-action organizations. This idea originated in Bristol where, in 1742, the Methodist society divided itself into small groups of twelve to financially support the growing society and provide accountability among members. The idea spread, and Wesley recounted that he "called together all the Leaders of the classes . . . and desired, that each would make a particular inquiry into the behaviour of those whom he saw weekly."[16] The only requirement for becoming part of a class was a desire to "flee the wrath to come."[17] Members were examined quarterly to find out whether they were growing in faith; if so, they were issued with a "class ticket" for the next quarter.

The single-sex bands and select bands developed later on to accommodate those who were advancing further in the faith and were held to a higher standard of accountability. It was in this social space that many men and women came to experience God in new ways. Especially for women, these classes and bands provided an opportunity for community and an intellectual outlet that was unavailable to them elsewhere. As Phyllis Mack has pointed out, Methodist women "lived and worked in a relatively stable collective environment, where regular class and band meetings encouraged mutual discussion and mutual confession."[18] These meetings were the foundations for transformative relationships between women that would come to structure their interactions with early evangelical discourse practices. Despite the difficulty of recovering what went on in these communal spaces—to hear the voices of these women—I contend that we can read the textual scraps in archives as important media events that engendered more media production in the form of manuscript letters and spiritual experience accounts that circulated widely within single-sex networks and the movement at large through Wesley's networks of itinerant preachers. As Michael Warner has recently argued, "In a movement context that mixed printed and preached sermons with pamphlets and newspapers, performance and print were densely laminated together."[19] This type of discourse culture reveals the extent to which print, manuscript, and oral cultures were still not well differentiated. They all reflected mediated events.

For example, the associations of women that formed soon after the Wesleys' organizing in Bristol and London worked together within their communities to produce manuscript conversion narratives that were then sent on to John and Charles Wesley. These collections of manuscript texts are now held at the University of Manchester's John Rylands Library and represent one of the earliest and most comprehensive records of how women participated in and perceived the beginning of the revival. These records reveal how fluid and spontaneous the early days of the revival were and how central women's experiences were to the discourse practices and mediated experiences of the revival. In fact, these narratives center on the senses of hearing and touch as women go to "hear" different preachers and readings and then seek to incorporate these experiences into their internal spiritual lives. The narratives have not gone unnoticed by scholars of Methodism. Mack and Bruce Hindmarsh have used these letter collections as evidence for the importance of conversion narratives to the Methodist movement in general and to Methodist women in particular.[20] That said, the focus of their books is the content of the manuscripts, not the manuscripts as material objects produced and circulated within a defined spiritual community.

Indeed, perhaps the most interesting aspect of the letters in these collections is the material evidence they bear of having been produced collectively within a community of women. Several letters by different women are written in the same hand. For example, letters signed by Susannah Designe and Margaret Furnivall feature the same handwriting, while letters by Designe appear in both the Charles Wesley and John Wesley collections in different hands. Likewise, letters by Elizabeth Halfpenny, Naomi Thomas, and Elizabeth Saice to Charles Wesley are written in the same hand and open with the same phrase, and two of the three bear the same watermark. Almost all of the letters make reference to a group of women that seems to be organized around a Sister Robinson, who ran the class and band meetings in Bristol, and the content of these letters explicitly frames their conversion experiences in terms of the communal bonds that were established within the highly mediated atmosphere of early Methodism.

In fact, almost all of these women reveal their conversions as mediated experiences and social events—mediated especially through the process of hearing others speak or read selections from their private journals within the Methodist community. Variations on the verb "hear" occur more than two hundred times in the letters to Charles Wesley alone. Women structure their narratives around going to hear George Whitefield, John Wesley, and Charles Wesley, and moments of spiritual clarity often focus on hearing. Margaret Austin, for instance, recounted that "when you [Charles Wesley] was Reading your Journal and said the same Spirit that raisd Jesus from the dead shall quicken the Dead body. then I felt that Christ would finish what he had begun: the Monday following we heard another of your Journals."[21] Not only does this passage emphasize the extent to which early Methodism was an auditory experience, but it also points to some of the ways that manuscript texts and their public reading played an integral role in Methodist devotional practice. Oral and manuscript media were inherent to conversion experiences for these women, not simply a result of conversion. It was through hearing and then writing their spiritual experiences that women became Methodists. Furthermore, these manuscript conversion narratives were produced in a community—performed in band meetings and then, in the case of women who could not write, transcribed by the members who could. One of the letters to John Wesley, for example, includes narratives from Susannah Designe and Margaret Furnivell written in the same hand. Designe's elegant handwriting appears numerous times throughout the collection in letters to both of the Wesleys, indicating that she often acted as a scribe for this particular group of women. This practice not only allowed otherwise illiterate women entrance into a public sphere but also makes clear that, for early Methodist women, textual production and the performance of spiritual experience within a community were intertwined.

The Shifting Discourse Culture of Methodism

In 1803, the Methodist Conference—the governing body of the Wesleyan Methodists in the United Kingdom—officially proscribed the practice of women's preaching, stating, "We are of the opinion that in general they ought not" to preach because "a vast majority of our people are opposed to it," and "their preaching does not at all seem necessary; there being a sufficiency of preachers, whom God has accredited, to supply all places in our connexion with regular preaching."[22] This decision made official what had been occurring in practice—namely, a steady move away from the toleration of women's public roles in Methodism following John Wesley's death in 1791. While Wesley allowed women to preach, his successors were less enthusiastic. Whereas during the eighteenth century single-sex spaces often acted as launching points for the public ministries of women such as Sarah Crosby, after 1803 women's roles within Methodism were increasingly confined to private, domestic, and single-sex spheres. While many women continued to preach well into the nineteenth century—Sarah Mallett, for example, lived and preached in East Anglia until 1843—these preaching women became increasingly rare.[23]

More dramatic than the delimiting of women's public preaching roles, however, was the rapidly shrinking space for women's expression in important Methodist mouthpieces such as the *Methodist Magazine*. While Wesley, as editor of the *Arminian Magazine* (as the publication was then titled), encouraged women's submissions and printed many of their accounts and letters, his successors, particularly Joseph Benson, who became editor in 1804, did not. Instead, Benson preferred male-authored accounts of pious, holy, and domestic women. As Zecheriah Taft, husband of the Methodist preacher Mary Barritt Taft and a vocal proponent of women's preaching, pointed out in the introduction to his 1825 *Biographical Sketches of the Lives and Public Ministry of Various Holy Women*,[24] this decline in material by and about women active in ministry was no accident:

> A great deal of pains has been taken to preserve in printed records, some account of the labours and success of those *men*, whom God has honoured by putting them into the ministry; while many *females*, whose praise was in all the churches while they lived, have been suffered to drop into oblivion, and their pre-eminent labours, and success in the conversion of souls to remain as destitute of any public record as though they had never existed; or if any account of their exemplary piety is preserved, their public labours are either suppressed or passed over in silence. It is very easy to account for this, the great majority of Biographers and Editors of Magazines are enemies to females preaching, so that we have very little concerning their labours.[25]

This decline in opportunities for women's publication can be measured both quantitatively and qualitatively. After John Wesley's death, the number of experience accounts written by women in the *Arminian Magazine* plummeted even before the official proscription of women's preaching. Margaret P. Jones estimates that between the inception of the *Arminian Magazine* in 1778 and Wesley's death in 1791, each volume averaged sixty letters by women, and of the 132 autobiographical accounts published during these years, 40 percent were by or about women.[26] As I have argued elsewhere, these accounts tended to be first-person experience narratives that appropriated the genre and form of conversion narrative to transmit personal revelation more widely.[27] From 1791 to 1804, however, there was a dramatic change. The number of letters by women dropped—of 151 letters involving women, sixty-five were written by them and eighty-six were written *to* them as letters of spiritual advice—as did the number of autobiographical accounts. In these years, only fifteen accounts by women were published, six of which were sent by Mary Bosanquet Fletcher, and the percentage of overall material related to women fell precipitously as the *Arminian Magazine* began to publish more and more obituaries of male preachers.[28]

After 1804 it became even more difficult for women to get into print as Benson took over editorship of what was now called the *Methodist Magazine* and began to change its format. Under Benson's editorship, content by and about women was often altered. While the total number of pages in each volume began to increase, the number of pages dedicated to women decreased at the same time that what was included changed in both tone and content. While 235 lives and 155 short obituaries of women were published during the eighteen years of Benson's editorship, most were not firsthand narratives but, rather, edited posthumous accounts or biographies written by men that followed an increasingly standardized form that emphasized the subject's pious and domestic Christian womanhood. Overall, although Tolar Burton estimates that a quarter of the published accounts in the *Methodist Magazine* were about women, few were actually written by them.[29] These were largely what Felicity Nussbaum characterizes as "stories of chaste and upright women who lead and record unremarkable lives, their stories less eventful than those of their male counterparts."[30]

In addition, Benson changed the structure of the *Methodist Magazine*, organizing it under headings such as "The Grace of God Exemplified," where most women's accounts appeared and that linguistically shifted the focus from woman as subject (*I* experienced God's grace) to woman as object (the grace of God *was* exemplified). Benson also sought to control access to print circulation by making individual (male) preachers the official channels for submission to the magazine.[31] The combined effect of these changes to the *Methodist Magazine* was to limit the ways in which women could both access and represent themselves in print, leaving them to look elsewhere for means to mediate their spiritual experiences.

With avenues to print publication increasingly restricted, women such as Crosby relied on the manuscript communities that originated in the early days of the revival to publish and circulate their works. While the manuscript networks of the early revival had acted as a means for women to communicate their experiences with one another and the Wesley brothers, the discourse practices that sprang up within these textual communities became the primary channel through which women produced and circulated their works by the end of the eighteenth century. As Amy Culley writes, the Methodist "commitment to a collective writing practice and communal history must be understood in the context of hostility to women's preaching and its marginalisation within official histories of the movement."[32] In many ways, scribal publication was a more flexible and adaptable means of publication, and one that Methodist women had long used to communicate within social networks. To return to Crosby's "Letter book," for example, mounting a public defense of women's preaching was not the sole reason for producing this manuscript; it was also part of a larger project of creating alternative spaces for women's experiences and expression as the path to print narrowed. As Crosby writes, the space of the friendly spiritual letter—read first by its intended recipient and then by whomever the letter is shown to—allows her "some liberty or freedom of conversing with ... those that Love me & receive what I say," whereas in other situations she does not find "the same freedom to converse about myself with those whom I think dislike me or will not receive what I say."[33] Scribal publication of this nature allowed Crosby the space and liberty to speak freely; this space would become especially important to Crosby's younger preaching protégés, Mary Bosanquet Fletcher and Mary Tooth.

Mary Tooth's Manuscripts and the Archives

Crosby first met the young Mary Bosanquet around 1757 in London, where both were involved with the Methodist Society and Crosby was a class leader for young women. Bosanquet was the daughter of prosperous merchants of Huguenot descent and began attending the Methodist society when she was about eighteen years old. Crosby was her first class leader and quickly became a role model and type of "spiritual mother" for the young woman, even counseling her to turn down a favorable offer of marriage that had been arranged by her family. This decision exacerbated tensions with her parents, and when Bosanquet turned twenty-one her father asked her to leave the house. She subsequently moved to rented rooms in London, where she lived with Sarah Lawrence, her lifelong friend, servant, and fellow preacher. In 1762, Bosanquet, along with Lawrence and Sarah Ryan, another early preacher, moved to Leytonstone, Essex, where Bosanquet owned a house. Here they established their first community of women that acted as a sort of charitable organization—preaching, teaching, and assisting the poor, mainly children. Eventually, due to Ryan's failing health, they moved to Yorkshire and purchased a farm, Cross Hall, which became a base for Methodist women's charitable activities in the north of England. By this time, Crosby had moved back to Leeds and become a frequent guest at Cross Hall, helping foster the new religious community. Bosanquet in essence became a business manager for the everyday affairs of the farm, which was largely run by the poor and orphaned whom they welcomed into their doors. Ryan died shortly after their move in 1768, but Cross Hall became the center of an extensive community of women who lived and worked together during the late eighteenth century.[34]

In 1781, Bosanquet married the Methodist theologian, and Wesley's heir apparent, John Fletcher and moved with him to his parish in Madeley, Shropshire. Here she once again went about establishing her charitable and preaching ministries, gathering around her another formidable army of women. John Fletcher died in 1785, but Mary continued to live in the vicarage until her death in 1816. She wielded considerable influence in the community, even exercising a say over who was appointed curate in the parish. She held meetings almost every night of the week and traveled extensively, preaching to mixed audiences around the country. Her home in Madeley also acted as a hub for women engaged in public ministry. At various times Sarah Crosby, Sarah Lawrence, Elizabeth Ritchie, Susanna Knapp, Ann Tripp, Mary Barritt Taft, Martha Grigson, and Sarah Mallet lived with or visited Bosanquet Fletcher, and her correspondence with this network was extensive.

Perhaps the most important of the relationships Bosanquet Fletcher cultivated with Methodist women was with Mary Tooth. Despite her importance to the history of women in Methodism, not much is known about Tooth's early life except that she was born in Birmingham in 1778 and moved to Madeley in 1795 at the age of seventeen to work as a servant for a local woman. By 1799, after rejecting a proposal of marriage, Tooth was living in the vicarage, as well, and she recounted that only once during the next fifteen years of Bosanquet Fletcher's life were they parted for more than twenty-four hours. After Bosanquet Fletcher's death, Tooth continued her ministry in Madeley until her own death in 1845, preaching openly and actively throughout Shropshire long after most Methodist women had abandoned the practice.[35] In addition to her own preaching and writing activities, Tooth scrupulously preserved Bosanquet Fletcher's extensive collection of manuscripts. Indeed, Bosanquet Fletcher took intentional steps to protect her papers and those of the women in her network by entrusting them to Tooth after her death in 1815.[36] Bosanquet Fletcher's papers and Tooth's extensive collection of diaries, commonplace books, and letters make up the Fletcher-Tooth Collection, which now spans forty archival boxes at the Rylands Library, representing perhaps the single largest record of women's preaching and writing in the nineteenth century and demonstrating the extreme care Tooth took to ensure that the papers were preserved intact.

The Fletcher-Tooth Collection is filled with box after box of loose manuscripts and manuscript books that contain spiritual experience accounts and conversion narratives by women, copies of letters, and even manuscript sermons. Many of these manuscripts exist in multiple copies in various hands throughout the collection, bearing evidence of having been intentionally copied for preservation and circulation within the Fletcher-Tooth network. Crosby's "Letter book" predates this collection of material, but it is very much in the same vein and indicates that the Crosby-Fletcher-Tooth circle was already thinking along these lines prior to Wesley's death, using the familiar networks of Methodism and its class and band structure to circulate texts.

Indeed, Tooth's daily pocketbooks, which extend from 1799 through 1831, record her and Bosanquet Fletcher regularly collecting and publicly reading out selections from Wesley's *Journals*, Bosanquet Fletcher's diaries, Sarah Ryan's manuscript account, Hester Ann Rogers's spiritual *Account*, letters and narratives from the *Arminian Magazine*, and manuscripts produced by other women in their network at various towns surrounding Madeley. Both Tooth and Bosanquet Fletcher seem to have traveled a regular preaching circuit in much the same manner as male

Methodist itinerants. On November 7, 1813, for example, Tooth opened her sermon to a gathering in Grindel by remarking, "It is now my friends 10 months since I visited you here at Grindel," before proceeding to the substance of her sermon.[37] Other towns, such as Coalport, she seems to have visited almost quarterly.

The texts that Tooth and Bosanquet Fletcher "read out" at these various locations were collected from oral testimony, manuscript documents, or printed sources and then transcribed in a variety of forms and made easily portable as manuscript fragments that Tooth, Fletcher, and others could carry from town to town and have ready to present or incorporate into sermons in front of class or society meetings. These fragments were sometimes copied down in diaries or commonplace books, but they often were just that—fragments of loose paper that could be easily slipped into a pocket and carried. Take, as one example among many, the following excerpts from "The Account of Mrs. Planche," which was originally published in the *Arminian Magazine* in 1791:

> What a proof this that the eye of the Lord is over us, she [Mrs. Planche] had no human instructer, but God could speak to her by a dream & shewed her at this time what came to pass many years after, for when she was under great distress seeing herself fit only for hell, the Lord led her to a man, whom she knew to be him she had seen in her dream, who led her to look & find a savior from all her sins.
>
> She seems to have been led in the right way, many rest in the drawing of God, the visits as she calls them, that she had from the Almighty. but you see she was determined not to be satisfied without a clear discovery of the pardoning love of God. or in other words, without clear & open communion with her savior. from this it is that all our victory springs, when we get to be one spirit with the Lord then we can do all things thro' Him who strengtheneth us.[38]

Although the version of the narrative printed in the *Arminian Magazine* is much longer, Tooth abridged the text to highlight key passages. The four slips of paper are numbered to indicate the order in which they were to be read, and they could easily be stacked and fastened with a pin (see fig. 2). This method of transmission allowed the preacher to either read the narrative out as a standalone text or incorporate it into a larger sermon, which is what Tooth often did.

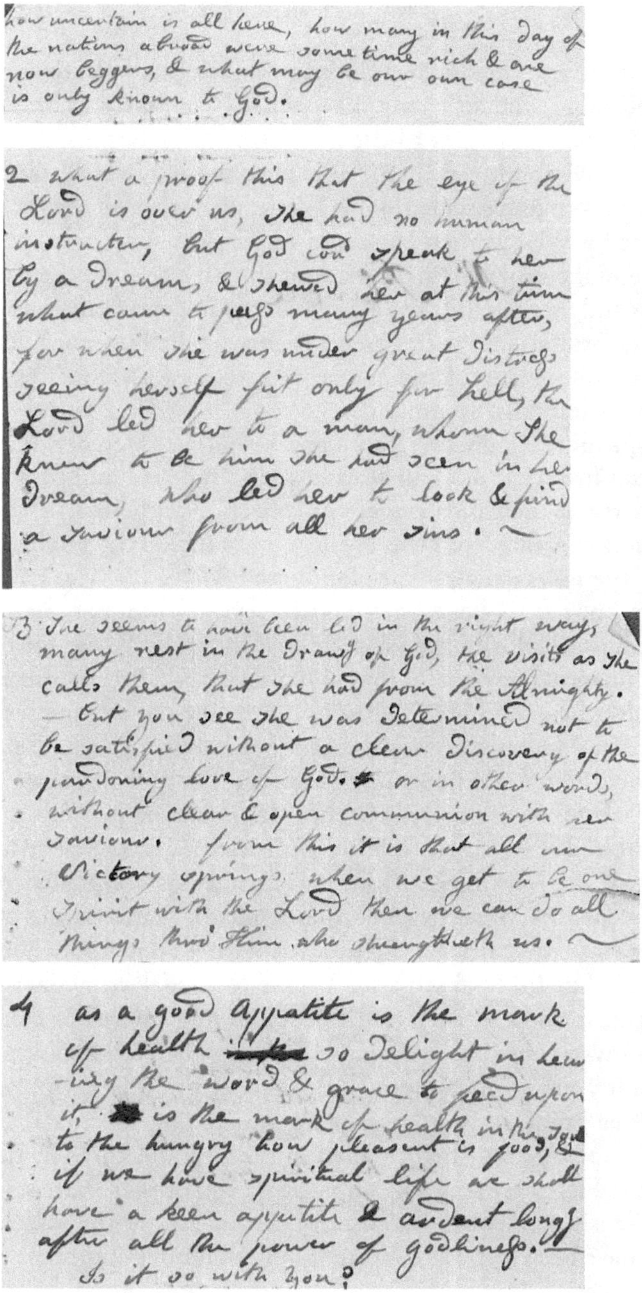

how uncertain is all here, how many in this day of the nations abroad were some time rich & are now beggars, & what may be our own case is only known to God.

2 what a proof this that the eye of the Lord is over us, she had no human instructor, but God could speak to her by a dream, & shewed her at this time what came to pass many years after, for when she was under great distress seeing herself fit only for Hell, the Lord led her to a man, whom she knew to be him she had seen in her Dream, who led her to look & find a Saviour from all her sins.

3 She seems to have been led in the right way, many rest in the Draught of God, the visits as she calls them, that she had from the Almighty. — But you see she was determined not to be satisfied without a clear Discovery of the pardoning love of God, or in other words, without clear & open communion with her Saviour. From this it is that all our Victory springs. when we get to be one Spirit with the Lord then we can do all things thro' Him who strengtheth us.

4 as a good Appetite is the mark of health so Delight in hear-ing the word & grace to feed upon it is the mark of health in the soul, to the hungry how pleasant is the food, & if we have spiritual life we shall have a keen appetite & ardent longs after all the power of godliness. Is it so with you?

FIGURE 2. Slips of paper containing fragments of "The Account of Mrs. Planche." (Fletcher-Tooth Collection, GB 133 MAM/FL/7; courtesy of the University of Manchester)

Thus, well into the nineteenth century a spiritual experience account by a Methodist woman—one that would be unlikely to be published in the *Methodist Magazine* of the day—was being retransmitted within networks of Methodist women.[39] Planche's account, which started out in manuscript as a letter sent to John Wesley in the 1780s, was transferred into print by Wesley, then back into manuscript by Tooth, and finally back into oral culture when Tooth read the narrative to other women in the 1820s and 1830s. While the content of the fragments may seem unimportant or utilitarian, the fragments themselves tell us much about how Methodist women circulated and remediated one another's experiences within the Methodist community.

Perhaps more significant, Tooth and Bosanquet Fletcher did not simply rely on material that had already been produced and printed. They also undertook their own project of collecting and circulating spiritual experiences separate from the Wesleys and outside the publication network of the increasingly male-dominated *Methodist Magazine*. These accounts appear to have been solicited by Bosanquet Fletcher and Tooth, transcribed, and then copied by a variety of hands for transmission within local networks or for oral performance. An account of the life of Mary Mathews, for example, was written down by Bosanquet Fletcher shortly after Mathews's death sometime in the late 1780s. This text exists in two different versions in the Fletcher-Tooth Collection. Mathews was an early follower of John Fletcher, despite being initially "prejudiced against him" due to his association with Methodism. Nevertheless, out of curiosity she went to hear him preach and was eventually converted. After Fletcher married Mary Bosanquet in 1781, Mathews was one of the first women to meet her. As Bosanquet Fletcher relates in her account of Mathews, "The first Sabath after I came to Madeley my dear husband brought me into the kitchen to the people saying 'I have not married this Wife for myself only but for you &c' she was much effected & found her heart greatly united to us both."[40] Bosanquet Fletcher then proceeds to give various proofs of Mathews's piety—including spiritual dreams and mystical experiences—before relating the circumstances of her death. Bosanquet Fletcher eventually published a few of these narratives in the *Methodist Magazine*, but manuscript circulation of the narratives appears to have been just as important as, if not more important than, their print publication.[41]

Finally, the Fletcher-Tooth Collection includes a set of Tooth's commonplace books that contain the sermons she preached between 1813 and 1818, a collection that includes not only sermons by other people that she "read out" but also her own carefully constructed discourses, which have never been published or systematically analyzed. Each volume also contains a detailed record of the places she preached during the period the volume covers and which sermon she preached at each location. These sermons often incorporate elements of women's spiritual narratives that she had collected in both manuscript and print, which were then employed to illustrate her points. Likewise, she seamlessly interwove her own explication of scriptural texts (the element of women's preaching that most offended the Methodist authorities) with snippets of other writers' discourses, indicating the depth and breadth of her reading.[42]

Each sermon follows a relatively consistent pattern: it begins with a greeting and address to her audience; moves on to the introduction of a theme and scripture passage, then a lengthy example from her manuscript collection or a print publication; and concludes with the application of the lesson to the listeners. For example, in a sermon Tooth preached at Stirchley in Shropshire on August 29, 1813, and again at Wenlock on October 1, 1815, she began in a familiar manner, indicating that her audience was acquainted with her, and then transitioned into the main topic of her message—whether or not her hearers were prepared to devote themselves wholly to God during the time they had:

> Well my friends a merciful God has once more given us an opportunity of meeting together in his name & I trust it will be to our edification that he may be glorified.... The spirit of God has expressly declared, "Whatsoever a man sows, that shall he also reap." Are you my friends, sowing to the flesh, or to the Spirit? Are you seeking to please yourselves? Or is it your constant endeavor to please that God in whose hand your breath is? Is any among you lovers of pleasure that is seeking your happiness in those things which are forbidden you by the unerring standard of right & wrong, the scriptures of Truth? Hear what those secret oracles declare, "He, or she, that liveth in pleasure is dead while they live."[43]

She then moved on to illustrate this point by example, weaving together scripture, interpretation, and other texts and quoting from *Death, A*

Vision (1766), by the Scottish Baptist minister John MacGowan, and *The Works of the Rev. Charles Buck* (1808), another dissenting theologian.

In another sermon, first preached on November 7, 1813, at Grindel, Tooth integrated the manuscript narrative of Mary Mathews into her address, thus remediating the spiritual experience of another Methodist woman who had been reached by Bosanquet Fletcher's ministry while encouraging her audience to follow in her footsteps: "Hoping it will be made an encouragement, to some of you to seek that God, who will be found of all them who come to Him with a sincere desire that they may walk in His ways; I will now read you an account of a woman that was brought to the knowledge of God by Mr Fletchers ministry. the account of her was wrote by my dear Mrs Fletcher, soon after her death. Mary Matthews [sic], has been from the beginning, a steady walker, & an ornament to the profession she made, of being a follower of Jesus."[44] Tooth went on to copy sections from each of the Bosanquet-Fletcher manuscripts into her sermon before concluding by reminding her audience that following Christ in the same manner as Mathews was not easy and that, as a result of her involvement with Methodism, "she had many trials in her family; & in the beginning of her Christian race much persecution. She was brought before Magistrates for receiving the Gospel into her house, but thro' all she stood. 'As an iron pillar strong; & steadfast as a wall of brass.'"[45] This type of preaching from example or quoting from the works of others seems commonplace today (indeed, it may account for why Tooth's sermons have been ignored for so long—they are not "original" enough), but it was unique in that Tooth relied primarily on teaching by example instead of simply explicating a scriptural passage.[46]

When Tooth did explicate scripture, or "take a text," she was careful about how she framed her rhetoric. For example, her "Sermon on Isaiah 43" is a copy of a sermon by Nathanael Culverwel, a seventeenth-century divine, which was published in a 1751 compendium of sermons and addresses titled *The Life of Christ the Pith and Kernel of All Religion*. However, just because this sermon is a copy does not mean that it and other texts like it in her "commonplace books" do not deserve our attention. While the text itself may not be new, its rhetorical context and its means of mediation were. Within a Methodist climate that viewed women's preaching with suspicion, Tooth's decision to rely on remediating other texts—print and manuscript, by men and women—allowed her to continue her public ministry long after other female preachers had ceased to itinerate. More important, Tooth was able to use her extensive collection of manuscripts to control her rhetorical situation for her own purposes.

Because so few manuscript sermons by women have survived—and none of them were printed—this element of Methodist experience has not received enough scholarly attention. Much work remains to be done on these manuscript volumes, but it seems clear that, like Crosby's "Letter book," these manuscripts have for much of their history been ignored or undervalued simply because they are nonstandard texts—public manuscripts produced in the age of print. As such, they are treated as copied material, commonplace books, or background source material.[47] However, the fact that these sermons had to be carefully preserved in manuscript and intentionally kept out of the hands of the male Methodist leadership is evidence of how much Methodist discourse culture had changed since the early days of the revival. Whereas early Methodist women such as Susannah Designe felt authorized to write their own narratives of empowerment within their spiritual communities and then send them to John or Charles Wesley, Tooth used manuscript circulation to circumvent official Methodist channels. Both women relied on manuscript media, but for diverging purposes.

This change in climate is illustrated in a letter from Sarah Mallett to Tooth. Mallett Boyce received a license to preach from the Methodist Conference in 1787, the only woman ever to receive official sanction, and over the course of her long life and ministry witnessed the change in attitude toward women's roles in Methodism. In a letter dated January 26, 1841, she took male preachers to task for relegating women to second-class status, writing, "Satan has always tried to hinder me—in my Lords Work—but could not—now he has set others to Work to do it that ought to have helped me—they own they cannot hinder me from publick speaking—because Mr. Wesley took me in as a preacher—but I am denied the pulpit—I may exhort in the meetings but take no text—I ask them—if God had ordered them to choose his instruments—and their work—and how—and w[h]ere—it was to be done."[48] By the 1820s, Methodism had begun to be defined by a more domestic, middle-class sociability. Though in some corners of society it continued to be a synonym for enthusiasm and radicalism, the official body of Methodism was becoming increasingly respectable. With these changes came a rapidly shifting discursive space for Methodist women, and in their return to transcribing, copying, and circulating the manuscript accounts of women and Methodists, especially outside publishing centers such as London, women such as Bosanquet Fletcher and Tooth reopened a space for varied religious voices.

Notes

A portion of this essay was originally published in Andrew O. Winckles, *Eighteenth Century Women's Writing and the Methodist Media Revolution: "Consider the Lord as Ever Present Reader"* (Liverpool: Liverpool University Press, 2019).

1. Sarah Crosby, "The Grace of God Manifested in an Account of Mrs. Crosby," *Methodist Magazine* 29 (1806): 418–23, 465–73, 517–21, 563–68, 610–17.
2. Ann Tripp to Mary Bosanquet Fletcher, June 13, 1805, GB 133 MAM/Fl/7/5/9, Fletcher-Tooth Collection, Methodist Archives and Research Centre, John Rylands Library, University of Manchester, Manchester, U.K.
3. Zecheriah Taft had access to the text as late as 1828, when he published the second volume of his *Biographical Sketches of Holy Women*, writing, "It will not be long, I hope, before the desire and expectation of the author and her confidential friends will be realized, and these documents receive that publicity, which their intrinsic excellence certainly merit": Taft, *Biographical Sketches of the Lives and Public Ministry of Various Holy Women*, 2:24.
4. Tolar Burton, *Spiritual Literacy in John Wesley's Methodism*.
5. See, e.g., Anderson, *Imagining Methodism in Eighteenth-Century Britain*; Krueger, *The Reader's Repentance*; McInelly, *Textual Warfare and the Making of Methodism*; Rivers, "John Wesley as Editor and Publisher."
6. Tolar Burton, *Spiritual Literacy in John Wesley's Methodism*, 235.
7. See, e.g., ibid., 163; Chilcote, *Early Methodist Spirituality*, 81.
8. Baker, "John Wesley and Sarah Crosby," 77.
9. Frank Baker to Donn Michael Farris, memorandum, May 13, 1961, Baker Collection Files series, 1955–2001, Frank Baker Papers, David M. Rubenstein Rare Book and Manuscript Library, Duke University, Durham, NC, box 1.
10. Sarah Crosby, "Letter book," RUB Bay 3356, Sarah Crosby Papers, 1760–1804, Frank Baker Collection of Wesleyana and British Methodism, Rubenstein Library, box 1, 38.
11. Love, *The Culture and Commerce of Texts*, 32.
12. Eleanor Shevlin, correspondence with the author, September 7, 2015.
13. Ezell, *Social Authorship and the Advent of Print*, 12.
14. Justice, "Introduction," 1, 5, emphasis added.
15. King, "Elizabeth Singer Rowe's Tactical Use of Manuscript and Print," 160.
16. Wesley, *The Works of John Wesley* (2007), 8:252–53.

17. Wesley, *The Works of John Wesley* (1989), 9:69.
18. Mack, *Heart Religion in the British Enlightenment*, 135.
19. Warner "The Evangelical Public Sphere."
20. Mack, *Heart Religion in the British Enlightenment*; Hindmarsh, *The Evangelical Conversion Narrative*.
21. Margaret Austin to Charles Wesley, May 19, 1740, GB 135 MAM/FL/1/12/9, Early Methodist vol. 1, Methodist Archives and Research Centre, John Rylands Library.
22. *Minutes of the Methodist Conferences*, 188–89.
23. Lloyd, *Women and the Shaping of British Methodism*, 116–18. While at one time more than sixty women were preaching in Britain, that number had fallen to just one woman, Elizabeth Bultitude, by 1850.
24. Significantly, this volume was *not* published by the official Methodist publishing house, saw only one edition (unusual for Methodist publications), and is now a rare text in its own right.
25. Taft, *Biographical Sketches of the Lives and Public Ministry of Various Holy Women*, 1:i.
26. Jones, "From 'The State of My Soul' to 'Exalted Piety,'" 275.
27. Winckles, "Excuse What Difficiencies You Will Find."
28. Jones, "From 'The State of My Soul' to "Exalted Piety,'" 281.
29. Tolar Burton, *Spiritual Literacy in John Wesley's Methodism*, 200.
30. Nussbaum, *The Autobiographical Subject*, 173.
31. Jones, "From 'The State of My Soul' to "Exalted Piety,'" 282–83.
32. Culley, *British Women's Life Writing*, 20.
33. Crosby, "Letter book," RUB Bay 3356, box 1, 38.
34. For more on the life and work of Mary Bosanquet Fletcher, see Mack, *Heart Religion in the British Enlightenment*; Krueger, *The Reader's Repentance*.
35. For more on the life of Mary Tooth see Corley and Blessing, "Speaking Out: Feminist Theology and Woman's Proclamation in then Methodist Tradition."
36. Krueger, *The Reader's Repentance*, 76–78.
37. Mary Tooth, "Sermon Preached at Grindel, Nov. 7, 1813," GB 133 MAM/FL/26, Fletcher-Tooth Collection, Methodist Archives and Research Centre, John Rylands Library.
38. "An Account of Mrs. Planche," GB 133 MAM/FL/7, Fletcher-Tooth Collection, Methodist Archives and Research Centre, John Rylands Library, published as "An Account of Mrs. Planche [Written by herself sometime before her death]," *Arminian* 14 (1791): 416–23.
39. For more on the content of Planche's narrative and ones like it in Wesley's *Arminian Magazine*, see Winckles, "Excuse What Difficiencies You Will Find."
40. "Account of Mary Mathews," GB 133 MAM/FL/7/33/3, Fletcher-Tooth Collection, Methodist Archives and Research Centre, John Rylands Library.

41. Jones, "From 'The State of My Soul' to 'Exalted Piety,'" 281.
42. In a letter to Sarah Crosby from 1769, John Wesley advised Crosby to "never take a text"—that is, explicate a passage of scripture—but instead to confine herself to "short exhortations with prayer." For more on the difference between the two, see Krueger, *The Reader's Repentance*.
43. Mary Tooth, "Sermon Preached at Stirchley, August 29, 1813," GB 133 MAM/FL/26, Fletcher-Tooth Collection, Methodist Archives and Research Centre, John Rylands Library.
44. Tooth, "Sermon Preached at Grindel," GB 133 MAM/FL/26.
45. Ibid.
46. Tolar Burton, *Spiritual Literacy in John Wesley's Methodism*, 157–58.
47. The exception to this is "Speaking Out," Corley and Blessing's excellent, but far from comprehensive, chapter in *Being Feminist, Being Christian*.
48. Sarah Boyce to Mary Tooth, January 26, 1841, GB 135 MAM/FL/1/12/9, Early Methodist vol. 1, Methodist Archives and Research Centre, John Rylands Library.

Works Cited

Anderson, Misty G. *Imagining Methodism in Eighteenth-Century Britain: Enthusiasm, Belief, and the Borders of the Self*. Baltimore: Johns Hopkins University Press, 2012.

Baker, Frank. "John Wesley and Sarah Crosby." *Proceedings of the Wesley Historical Society* 27, no. 4 (1949): 73–82.

Chilcote, Paul Wesley. *Early Methodist Spirituality: Selected Women's Writings*. Nashville: Kingswood, 2007.

Corley, Lisa Bernal, and Carol Blessing. "Speaking Out: Feminist Theology and Woman's Proclamation in the Methodist Tradition." In *Being Feminist, Being Christian: Essays from Academia*, edited by Allyson Jule and Bettina Tate Pederson, 127–56. New York: Palgrave Macmillan, 2006.

Culley, Amy. *British Women's Life Writing, 1760–1840*. New York: Palgrave Macmillan, 2014.

Ezell, Margaret J. M. *Social Authorship and the Advent of Print*. Baltimore: Johns Hopkins University Press, 1999.

Hindmarsh, D. Bruce. *The Evangelical Conversion Narrative: Spiritual Autobiography in Early Modern England*. Oxford: Oxford University Press, 2005.

Jones, Margaret P. "From 'The State of My Soul' to 'Exalted Piety': Women's Voices in the *Arminian/Methodist Magazine*, 1778–1821." In *Gender and Christian Religion: Papers Read at the 1996 Summer Meeting and the 1997 Winter Meeting of the Ecclesiastical Historical Society*, edited by R. N. Swanson, 273–86. Woodbridge, U.K.: Boydell, 1998.

Justice, George L. "Introduction." In *Women's Writing and the Circulation of Ideas: Manuscript Publication in England, 1550–1800*, edited by George L. Justice and Nathan Tinker, 1–16. Cambridge: Cambridge University Press, 2002.

King, Kathryn R. "Elizabeth Singer Rowe's Tactical Use of Manuscript and Print." In *Women's Writing and the Circulation of Ideas: Manuscript Publication in England, 1550–1800*, edited by George L. Justice and Nathan Tinker, 58–81. Cambridge: Cambridge University Press, 2002.

Krueger, Christine L. *The Reader's Repentance: Women Preachers, Women Writers, and Nineteenth-Century Social Discourse*. Chicago: University of Chicago Press, 1992.

Lloyd, Jennifer. *Women and the Shaping of British Methodism: Persistent Preachers, 1807–1907*. Manchester, U.K.: Manchester University Press, 2009.

Love, Harold. *The Culture and Commerce of Texts: Scribal Publication in Seventeenth-Century England*. Amherst: University of Massachusetts Press, 1998.

Mack, Phyllis. *Heart Religion in the British Enlightenment: Gender and Emotion in Early Methodism*. Cambridge: Cambridge University Press, 2008.

McInelly, Brett C. *Textual Warfare and the Making of Methodism*. Oxford: Oxford University Press, 2014.

Minutes of the Methodist Conferences, from the First, Held in London, by the Late Rev. John Wesley, A.M. in the Year 1744, vol. 2. London: Conference Office, 1812.

Nussbaum, Felicity A. *The Autobiographical Subject: Gender and Ideology in Eighteenth Century England*. Baltimore: Johns Hopkins University Press, 1989.

Rivers, Isabel. "John Wesley as Editor and Publisher." In *The Cambridge Companion to John Wesley*, edited by Randy L. Maddox and Jason E. Vickers, 144–59. Cambridge: Cambridge University Press, 2010.

Taft, Zechariah. *Biographical Sketches of the Lives and Public Ministry of Various Holy Women*, 2 vols. Peterborough, U.K.: Methodist Publishing House, 1992.

Tolar Burton, Vicki. *Spiritual Literacy in John Wesley's Methodism: Reading, Writing, and Speaking to Believe*. Waco, TX: Baylor University Press, 2008.

Warner, Michael. "The Evangelical Public Sphere: Printing and Preaching: What Is a Sermon?" Presentation, A. S. W. Rosenbach Lectures in Bibliography. University of Pennsylvania, Philadelphia, March 25, 2009.

Wesley, John. *The Works of John Wesley*, edited by Thomas Jackson, 14 vols. Grand Rapids, MI: Baker, 2007.

———. *The Works of John Wesley*, edited by Rupert E. Davies, 10 vols. Nashville: Abingdon, 1989.

Winckles, Andrew O. "'Excuse What Difficiencies You Will Find': Methodist Women and Public Space in John Wesley's *Arminian Magazine*." *Eighteenth-Century Studies* 46, no. 3 (Spring 2013): 415–29.

Collecting John Abbot's Natural History Notes and Drawings

BETH FOWKES TOBIN

JOHN ABBOT (1751–1840), a naturalist artist, made more than six thousand watercolor drawings of North American birds and insects. He was the first naturalist living in the United States to have his natural history artwork published in folio, preceding John James Audubon by two decades and Alexander Wilson by a decade. Abbot's drawings of butterflies and moths were engraved in London and published in a beautiful two-volume publication entitled *The Natural History of the Rarer Lepidopterous Insects of Georgia* (1797), in addition to appearing in Jean Alphonse Boisduval and John Eatton Leconte's *Histoire générale et iconographie des lépidoptères et des chenilles de l'Amérique septentrionale* (Paris, 1829–34).[1] However, the vast majority of his drawings were never printed, although they were highly prized by British, American, and French naturalists. Several prominent amateur and professional entomologists collected Abbot's drawings and field notes, regarding them as bearers of valuable information about the natural world. Abbot's career as an illustrator and naturalist spanned sixty years, from the 1770s to the 1830s, and thus offers a glimpse at how manuscript culture operated within the natural sciences. Despite the proliferation of scientific publications in the late eighteenth and early nineteenth centuries in the form of journal articles, zoological treatises, primers on taxonomy, and illustrated zoological books, naturalists continued to collect natural history manuscripts, including naturalists' field notes, journals, diaries, letters, and drawings.

Today we may assume the authority of print, especially in scientific matters; however, as this volume of essays argues, the notion that print eclipsed manuscript over the course of the eighteenth century is an oversimplification. David McKitterick has challenged the "assumed authority of print," demonstrating how the early modern printed book was a much less stable product than is commonly assumed: "The concept of printing is not necessarily one of fixity, of textual rest or (still less) of stability, but actually implies a process liable and subject to change as a result both of its own mechanisms and of the assumptions and expectations of those who exploit its technological possibilities."[2] For example, readers annotated and grangerized printed texts, remaking them in the process of encountering them. Printed books were made unstable by printing processes themselves: errors crept into publications with transposed plates, missing pages, and poorly colored illustrations. Printed books were not necessarily reliable sources of information, a fact of which naturalists and other scientific-minded people were well aware, despite their eventual embrace of print as a medium that could confer authority on them as experts in their field. Naturalists' desire to publish sat side by side with their veneration for manuscripts and the information they held.

Collecting naturalists' papers, correspondence, and notebooks was something that naturalists did because these materials often contained information that did not circulate in print. As Elizabeth Yale has convincingly documented, collecting manuscripts in the form of letters, notebooks, commonplace books, and annotated printed books was how naturalists in the early modern period gathered and organized information about the natural world.[3] Naturalists' papers, regarded as "storehouses of scientific and technical information," were collected as "raw material for the construction of natural knowledge."[4] This long-standing practice of naturalists collecting one another's manuscripts showed no sign of abatement in the last quarter of the eighteenth century and, in fact, became key to establishing a naturalist's authority as an expert. For instance, Sir Joseph Banks (1743–1820), who was the president of the Royal Society from 1778 to 1820, made himself the center of several naturalist networks by collecting naturalists' papers and, in particular, natural history illustrations. These papers, along with natural history specimens, made his library an invaluable resource for other naturalists, who needed to consult this ever-growing body of material before they could publish their findings. Johann Christian Fabricius (1745–1808), Europe's premier entomologist, had to travel to England from Copenhagen, Denmark, and from Kiel, Germany, several times to consult Banks's collection of manuscripts and specimens before publishing his important contributions to insect taxonomy, *Species Insectorum* (1781) and *Entomologia systematica* (1792–99).

Banks, acting as a gatekeeper to his storehouse of information, wielded access to his library as a mechanism to position himself at the center of the British Enlightenment's empiricist project of describing and classifying the natural world. The scale on which Banks operated is what distinguished him from his peers, who, as amateur and professional naturalists, also put collecting at the center of their engagement with the natural world. These naturalists, who collected manuscripts, drawings, and specimens, did not have the financial means to support the wide range of collecting that Banks engaged in, and as a result, they usually focused their energy on collecting within what have since become the distinct disciplines of botany, entomology, ornithology, and malacology. Dru Drury (1725–1804), a silversmith and amateur entomologist, for instance, possessed the largest insect collection in Britain in his era, while Margaret Cavendish Bentinck, Duchess of Portland (1715–1785), amassed the largest shell collection in Europe; in the process of building these collections, Drury and Cavendish acquired a significant cache of manuscript notes and drawings pertaining to their specialties. Sir James Edward Smith, a physician turned botanist, focused his attention on collecting Carl Linnaeus's books, papers, correspondence, and natural history specimens, items he bought from Linnaeus's widow at the urging of Banks in 1784. On the basis of possessing these materials, Smith founded the Linnean Society in 1788 and became its president and, in the process, a prolific writer and lecturer on Linnaean systematics and botany, composing many volumes including *English Botany* (1813, 36 volumes) and *English Flora* (1824–28, 4 volumes).[5]

Despite the rise of scientific print culture in the second half of the eighteenth century, manuscript material continued to be valued as a means to acquire knowledge about the natural world and to gain authority within natural history circles. This essay provides a case study of how and why one naturalist's papers—in particular, his notes on insects and his entomological drawings—were collected by amateur naturalists and professional scientists on both sides of the North Atlantic. Amazingly, several collections of Abbot's drawings and notes that were made during his lifetime have survived intact, traveling through time and space relatively unscathed and offering us the opportunity to explore collectors' motives for the acquisition and, in some cases, the exchange of manuscript drawings and notes. By examining these collections, some of which were "the byproduct of producing printed knowledge," and others of which were collected as entities possessing scientific (and aesthetic) value in and of themselves, we can surmise the principles of acquisition and selection that organized these manuscript collections.[6] Of course, we cannot know what has been lost, but we should be grateful that these clumps of papers—some carefully curated by their collectors and others less cared for—have survived.[7] This survey of five Abbot manuscript collections traces the paths that these drawings and notes took on their way to their collectors, and, if known, where they now reside, revealing much about the sociability of Enlightenment natural history and its cultures of collecting that were primarily the domain of talented and curious amateur naturalists.

Abbot's Drawings and Notes

Abbot, an Englishman, was twenty-five when he arrived in Georgia in 1776 with a plan to support himself as a natural history artist by collecting insect and bird specimens for London's natural history collectors and dealers. When Abbot left London for the American South, he fully expected to return after a few years with enough drawings to pursue a career as a published natural history illustrator. In his brief and unfinished memoir, he wrote that as a young man he had been inspired to go the Americas by seeing Mark Catesby's prints of New World flora and fauna and had hoped to join the ranks of distinguished natural history artists. However, Abbot never left the South, living the rest of his long life in rural Georgia, where he continued to draw and collect insects and birds into his eighties. In choosing to live in the "field," Abbot stepped off the career path pursued by most natural history artists, including Catesby, Wilson, and Audubon, who made sojourns into the field to sketch and collect specimens but returned to urban centers, where they oversaw the publication and promotion of their artworks. Unlike his fellow naturalist artists, Abbot put collecting and drawing insect specimens at the center of his life. He lived where he collected, moving inland and farther south to escape the deforestation and draining of swamps that accompanied the westward movement of small farmers and big planters. Abbot seems to have become something of a recluse, perhaps settling for a modest life surrounded by the things he loved to draw—Georgia's exceptionally diverse flora and fauna—or remaining from a conviction that he could do more valuable work in the field in Georgia than by returning to London or moving north to urban centers of natural history inquiry.

Whatever the reason, Abbot's decision to live in the field meant that no other contemporary natural history artist knew as much as he did about his subject matter. Abbot became the authority on North American arthropods, particularly butterflies, moths, beetles, spiders, grasshoppers, and dragonflies, and he collected information on their locales, foods, and life cycles. This information accompanied his drawings in the form of numbered lists, with the number corresponding to the drawing of an insect. For example, Abbot created hundreds of watercolor drawings of spiders. On small pieces of paper (approximately 3 × 5 inches), Abbot drew one spider on each piece, placing a few dots above the spider to convey the configuration of its eyes, the main physical characteristic that naturalists used to identify and classify species of spiders (see fig. 1). Above these dots and the image of the spider, Abbot wrote a number that corresponded to one on a list that made up his notes. On a separate sheet of paper he wrote next to that number a description of the spider: how, when, and where he caught it; what it ate; what its web looked like (if it had a web); how rare or common it was; and any interesting local knowledge about these species (see fig. 2). He commented, for instance, on the ingenious way in which the dirt dauber, a wasp, captures and paralyzes spiders, storing the spiders' immobile, living bodies in its mud-walled nest to serve as future food for the wasp's hatching larva. Several of his rarest spider specimens were in fact found in dirt daubers' nests.[8]

Abbot's watercolor drawings of spiders are examples of his incredible skill as a draughtsman and watercolorist. The minuteness of his subject matter did not deter him from giving these spiders his full attention. He recorded with precision in his life-size drawings the patterns on these spiders' abdomens, using paintbrushes consisting of only a few hairs to carry microscopic dots of watercolor to these small rectangles of paper. The care with which these little arthropod bodies were rendered conveys the respect that Abbot felt for his subject matter, and his notes reveal his enthusiasm and personal engagement with these creatures. Remarking on how nimble a spider was as it ran across the leafy forest floor as he chased it, Abbot endowed these spiders with agency and conveyed his own sense of wonder and joy in their presence.

Abbot's art grew out of his collecting practices of documenting, stabilizing, and transporting specimens. Drawing was a way to capture the features of color and contour that were distorted by death—beetles'

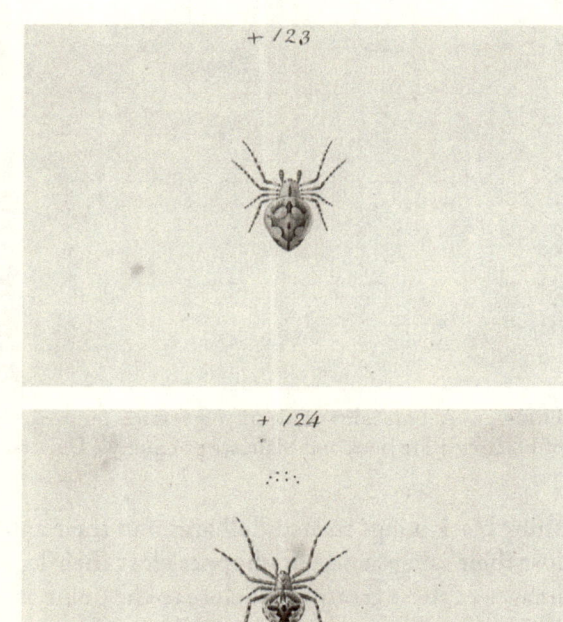
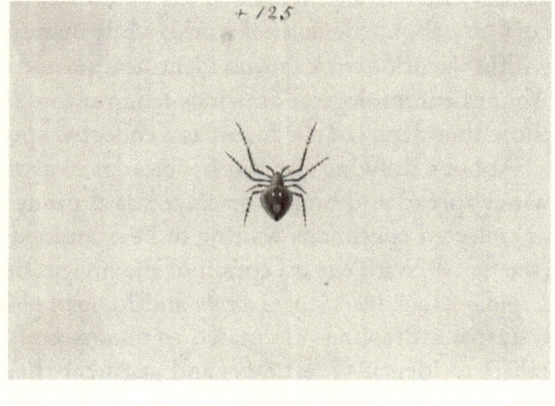

FIGURE 1. John Abbot's watercolor drawings of spiders, each on a roughly 3 × 5-inch piece of paper. (John Abbot, *Aranea*, ca. 1799, Rare Bk Folio QL458.42.A7 A2 1799; courtesy of Hargrett Rare Book and Manuscript Library/University of Georgia Libraries)

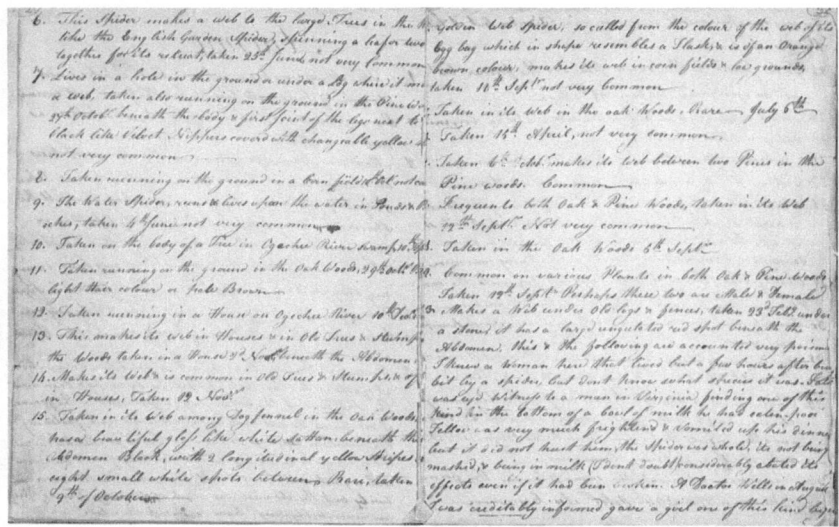

FIGURE 2. Abbot's notes of identifying features for particular spiders. (*Aranea*; courtesy of Hargrett Rare Book and Manuscript Library / University of Georgia Libraries)

shiny black wings turned dull gray and their antennae fell off, butterflies lost their wings, and grasshoppers lost their legs. Drawing and painting images of these creatures as close to the point of capture as possible minimized the forces of decay and allowed for the retention of information that was crucial to classification. Natural history drawings, as opposed to engraved or etched illustrations, functioned differently within the cultures of natural history and operated in very different regimes of value. The printed illustration in the eighteenth century was often consumed as a luxury item to signify its owner's wealth, elevated taste, and fashionable curiosity about the natural world, while manuscript drawings were used within scientific circles to aid identification and classification. The bulk of Abbot's entomological drawings fell into this second category, especially those that depicted the insect as a collected specimen.

Abbot's drawings of moths, cicadas, wasps, flies, and beetles, with wings spread and bodies displayed as if pinned, depicted their subjects as collected specimens waiting to be examined by an attentive audience (see fig. 3). With the exception of the images designed for publication in *Lepidopterous Insects of Georgia* and *Iconographie des lépidoptères*, Abbot's watercolor drawings circulated as manuscripts and were used by naturalists to identify specimens and augment their collections. His careful rendering of an insect's morphology was invaluable to these processes. Abbot's keen eye and knowledge of what the naturalist wanted to see made his drawings quite desirable. With his focus on a specimen's easily observable physical traits, such as the number of segments on a moth's antenna or the shape of a beetle's jaw, Abbot contributed greatly to the ongoing collaborative process of making natural knowledge.[9]

Natural history illustrations, however, could do more than merely support the taxonomic process. Drawings could shape how collectors saw their specimens, directing them to look at a specimen in a certain way and teaching them which anatomical elements to focus on and which patterns and colors to attend to. The tiny veins that crisscross an insect's wing, when depicted with the level of detail that Abbot put into his drawings of dragonflies, could persuade a collector that wing venation was important to the identification of these creatures. Moreover, illustrations offered collectors a substitute for the specimen that was stable and transportable.[10] Paper, ink, and watercolors may not seem like particularly durable media, but compared with actual specimens that were vulnerable to decay, paper technologies were much more stable and convenient to

FIGURE 3. Abbot's graphite and watercolor drawing of a cicada. ("Drawings of the Insects of Georgia, in America, 1792–1804," SB q A.1c Vol. 5, f. 46; courtesy of the Trustees of the Natural History Museum, London)

ship across seas and to carry around when visiting other naturalists who, as they tried to identify specimens, might have needed images to compare against their own collections.

Identifying specimens and classifying collections generated a vibrant manuscript culture, producing writing, often in the form of little scraps of paper to label specimens, notebooks filled with provisional lists and schemes for arrangement of species within genera and of genera within families, and letters to other naturalists filled with queries and conjectures.[11] Also central to this process of enumerating and classifying the natural world were the face-to-face encounters among naturalists who gathered informally and formally to examine one another's collections, to argue over the characteristics of specimens, to share the discovery of not-yet-described species, and to describe other distinguishing features and behavior of the animals and plants under discussion. This combination of handling specimens, examining them, talking and writing about them, making lists and jotting down notes, and consulting drawings was the primary method by which natural historical knowledge was generated in the eighteenth century.[12] From Georgia, Abbot was a vital participant in this manuscript culture of the sociable world of specimen-based natural history, contributing notes and drawings, as well as specimens, to the ongoing tasks of identification and classification.

Abbot's Networks of British Naturalists

Although he lived far from urban centers of natural history inquiry, Abbot was an active participant in several natural history networks, conveying his observations, drawings, and specimens to collectors and naturalists in London, Manchester, Paris, Zurich, Philadelphia, New York, and Boston. Among the most important of his clients was Dru Drury, who, in his quest to acquire exotic insects, had sponsored the voyages of several natural history collectors, most famously those of Henry Smeathman to Sierra Leone and John William Lewin to Australia.[13] Drury may have lent financial support for Abbot's voyage to Virginia and definitely sent letters of introduction to his contacts in the South, instructing them to help Abbot get started as an insect collector. Once Abbot had settled in Georgia after nearly two years in Virginia, where he failed to acquire enough exotic insects for his patrons, he was able to establish himself in the second half of the 1780s (post–Revolutionary War) as a key supplier of exotic insects for Drury and other London-based insect collectors. Drury's manuscript catalogue lists hundreds of insects Abbot sent from Georgia's swamps and woodlands; they were shipped in boxes of Drury's design that housed cork-lined drawers filled with pinned insects. The boxes contained false bottoms in which Abbot put his drawings and notes, hiding them from Custom Officials to avoid paying duties on these paper objects. A remnant of what must have been hundreds of drawings that Abbot sent to Drury remains in Harvard's Houghton Library. Drury's distinctive scrawl on the back of each drawing indicates his attempt to identify the insects represented in these drawings.[14]

Abbot had met Drury in the late 1760s when Abbot was in his mid-teens and just starting out as a natural history illustrator. Drury possessed "the best Collection of Insects both English and foreign of any one," and Abbot described his delight in making Drury's acquaintance: "I leave you to judge my pleasure and astonishment at the sight of his cabinets the first I had ever seen of the kind[.] He very politely offered to lend me insects to Draw, and we immediately became well acquainted. That hour may be said to have given a new turn to my future life." Inspired by Drury's vast collection of insects, Abbot acquired "a Mahogony [sic] Cabinet made of 26 drawers, covered with sliding tops of glass, it cost me 6 guineas & I began to collect with increasing industry."[15] Drury took Abbot under his wing, instructing him in entomology and inviting him to draw insects from his massive collection. Abbot benefited in multiple ways from being within Drury's circle of naturalists, artists, and specimen collectors. While drawing butterflies and moths in Drury's collection, Abbot was undoubtedly privy to Drury's negotiations with Moses Harris, who between 1766 and 1782 illustrated and colored the three volumes of Drury's beautiful book *Illustrations of Exotic Insects*, which was based on his insect collection.[16] Abbot learned from Drury's fraught engagement with Harris what a naturalist wanted to see in the illustrations of his specimens.[17] In addition, Abbot may have been tutored in Linnaean taxonomy and the principles of systematics by members of Drury's circle, which included the Duchess of Portland, who was also a knowledgeable collector of insects. Abbot had access to her butterfly and moth collections, from which he made several drawings, some of which have survived into the present.[18] Through Drury, Abbot met Smeathman, whose collecting trip to Africa was sponsored by a consortium organized by Drury and consisting of Banks, the Duchess of Portland, Dr. John Fothergill, and Marmaduke Tunstall, all keen natural history collectors. It was Smeathman who gave Abbot the idea of going abroad to collect natural history specimens.

Abbot wrote in his very brief autobiography, "This Mr Smeathman went to Africa on an intention chiefly to collect insects. . . . I now began to entertain thoughts of going abroad to collect foreign insects myself."[19] Under Drury's tutelage, Abbot's nascent interest in insects blossomed into a deeply committed engagement with collecting and drawing insects.

In the 1790s, Abbot developed a relationship with John Francillon (1744–1816), also a London jeweler and silversmith, who, like Drury, built a massive insect collection.[20] Francillon had become Abbot's primary client as Drury had become increasingly ill as he aged and had grown weary of maintaining his collections to the degree that he sent out queries to see whether anyone might be interested in buying his enormous insect collection. He died in 1804, and his son put his collections of specimens, books, and manuscripts up for auction. During this time of Drury's waning interest, Francillon became Abbot's friend and agent, brokering deals on behalf of Abbot with interested parties in Britain. Francillon had persuaded the Manchester Natural History Society, for instance, to purchase Abbot's bird drawings, but members complained that Abbot's style was old-fashioned. Abbot had learned to draw birds from George Edwards, and had mimicked Edwards' "stump and stare" pose of a taxidermized bird perched on a stick.[21] Francillon suggested to the society that it might prefer Abbot's insect drawings, and he may even have brokered the society's purchase of the spider drawings discussed earlier.[22]

In addition to buying thousands of insect specimens from Abbot, Francillon built a huge collection of Abbot's artwork.[23] Abbot sent him thousands of drawings over the course of two decades. Francillon took these drawings, which mostly consisted of one image on a small sheet of paper, and pasted them, usually two or three at a time, onto large sheets of wove paper. He also transcribed Abbot's notes onto the bottom of the paper and then bound the mounted drawings into seventeen volumes. Each volume contains a letterpress plate with the title date, and each is bound in red Moroccan leather with gold-embossed volume numbers on the spine. Francillon's manuscript collection contains nearly three thousand of Abbot's drawings. When Francillon died in 1816, all of his specimens were sold at auction, but fortunately this collection of drawings was bought by the British Museum in 1818 and saved from being broken up and dispersed. With the exception of the few letters mentioned earlier that are in the British Library, Francillon's personal papers and business archives cannot be traced, so we do not know the details of how these volumes came to be housed in what was the natural history section of the British Museum.[24]

Also during the 1790s, a period of tremendous creative productivity for Abbot, he partnered with Sir James Edward Smith, president of the Linnean Society, to produce the magnificent *Natural History of the Rarer Lepidopterous Insects of Georgia* (1797). For this book, Abbot did not portray the insects as collected specimens laid flat on a sheet of paper. Instead, he self-consciously imitated Maria Sibylla Merian's style, which included the host plant in the depiction of insects. Each of Abbot's folio drawings featured a butterfly or a moth, its caterpillar, pupae, and host plant, all drawn in the most elegant and graceful style while at the same time satisfying the taxonomic needs of naturalists. Abbot attended scrupulously to what had to appear on the page if the moth or butterfly, its caterpillar, and its host plant were to be identified using Linnaean classificatory systems.

Adherence to Linnaean taxonomy bound these two very different men in one united purpose: to display visually and describe verbally the physical characteristics of Lepidoptera and their host plants that were necessary to their identification and classification within Linnaean systematics. Smith's choice to collaborate with Abbot is quite remarkable since Smith was at the center of a botanical empire based on the acquisition of specimens and manuscripts, while Abbot resided literally and figuratively on the peripheries of this empire. Also remarkable is Smith's often-stated regard for and deference to Abbot's local knowledge, something that did not often apply to the specimen hunters on the ground, who were regarded generally as insufficiently knowledgeable to make valuable observations about the natural objects they gathered and recorded.[25] Smith remarked repeatedly throughout *Rarer Lepidopterous Insects* on Abbot's botanical and entomological knowledge and openly deferred to Abbot's opinion. Smith valued Abbot's drawings greatly, writing to a fellow botanist, Dr. Richard Pulteney, who was excited about the publication of the book: "In a few days a splendid work on the Rarer Lepidopterous Insects of Georgia will appear from the shop of Edwards in Pall Mall.... The original drawings were the most *perfect* things I ever saw" (see fig. 4).[26] This publication and collaboration with Smith is a measure of how much the British scientific establishment respected Abbot's activities as a naturalist and an artist.

In the wake of printing the book, Smith gave Abbot's beautiful drawings to the sickly daughter of an old friend, a teenage girl who had shown an aptitude for natural history. Smith's gesture is in keeping with his role as a promoter of Linnaean taxonomy and one who encouraged women

FIGURE 4. Abbot's original watercolor drawing "Humble-Bee Hawk-Moth," in his and James Edward Smith's *The Natural History of the Rarer Lepidopterous Insects of Georgia* (2 vols.; London, 1797). (QL551. G4S64 1797 vol. 1, TAB. XLIII; John Work Garrett Library, Johns Hopkins University)

and children to become botanizers and partake of the pleasures of collecting and cataloguing plants.[27] The gift of these beautiful watercolor drawings bound with the letterpress text of the book signals his appreciation of Abbot's artwork and demonstrates the sociability of the culture of natural history. As a gift, especially one given in such a manner, Abbot's drawings were removed from the marketplace as a byproduct of the book trade and were installed firmly within natural history's gift economy and its particular brand of sociality.

Abbot's Networks of American and French Naturalists

In the first decade of the nineteenth century, Abbot began to make connections with naturalists living in the northern United States, exchanging information, specimens, and drawings. He was sought out by Alexander Wilson (1766–1813), a prominent member of Philadelphia's American Philosophical Society who needed Abbot's guidance when it came to birding in Georgia and South Carolina. Wilson was determined to gather specimens of every bird species of the new American Republic but had little experience in the Southeast. Abbot took Wilson birding in the Savannah River Valley. Wilson wrote of his experience in a letter to William Bartram, his mentor: "There is a Mr. Abbot here, who has resided in Georgia thirty-three years, drawing insects and birds. I have been on several excursions with him. He is a very good observer, and paints well. He has published, in London, one large folio volume of the Lepidopterous Insects of Georgia. It is a very splendid work."[28] Wilson, referring to Abbot as a "mysteriously obliging and modest" man, acknowledged Abbot's ornithological expertise in his *American Ornithology* (1808–14).

Late in his life, Abbot corresponded with Harvard University's Dr. Thaddeus William Harris (1790–1856), who owned Abbot's drawings and possibly the Smith and Abbot book. They agreed to exchange specimens and information about birds and insects. Abbot was introduced to Harris by John Eatton LeConte (1784–1860), a retired U.S. Army major, topographical engineer, and founding member of New York City's Lyceum of Natural History. LeConte had become Abbot's main client in the United States by the early 1810s, receiving from him two thousand to three thousand drawings over the course of two decades.[29] They probably met in Savannah, which was not far from where LeConte's brother Louis LeConte, an amateur botanist and garden designer, owned a rice plantation. It was through John Eatton LeConte that Abbot gained access to centers of natural history inquiry in Boston, New York, and Paris.

In 1828, LeConte took Abbot's lepidopteron drawings to Paris, where he worked with the famous naturalist J. A. Boisduval on their co-authored book *Histoire générale et iconographie des lépidoptères et des chenilles de l'Amérique septentrionale* (1829–34). LeConte had asked Abbot to draw one species of butterfly on each piece of paper with two poses, one from above and one from the side; to include the caterpillar and its cocoon; and to omit the plants on which these caterpillars fed. Of the hundreds of drawings LeConte took to Paris, only sixty-three appeared in Boisduval and LeConte's beautiful small volume. LeConte left Abbot drawings with Boisduval when he returned to the United States.[30] These drawings were considered precious enough by Boisduval to keep for further use. Boisduval and Achille Guenée, a fellow lepidopterist, mined Abbot's drawings for images of caterpillars, using them for plate 2 of their multivolume *Histoire naturelle des insectes; species général des lépidoptères* (Paris, 1839–58).

Abbot's drawings continued to be used by lepidopterists as the basis for their publications' illustrations. Boisduval, for example, lent Abbot's drawings to the American lepidopterist Samuel H. Scudder (1837–1911), who used them for his mammoth publication *Butterflies of the Eastern United States and Canada* (1889). John Calhoun, a present-day lepidopterist who has carefully traced the publication of Abbot's lepidopteron drawings, has also tracked their usage after their initial publication. "In 1876, three years prior to his death," Calhoun writes, "Boisduval presented his library, ostensibly including these drawings, to good friend and fellow Parisian lepidopterist Louis M. A. Depuiset. Depuiset organized all of Boisduval's assorted illustrations sometime before his death in 1886."[31] Eventually these drawings found their way to the marketplace in the 1920s, when they were bought and disappeared into a private collection; they resurfaced in the 1960s at Sotheby's and were purchased by the University of South Carolina. Boisduval had also given to Scudder some of Abbot's drawings and his manuscript descriptions and elaborate lists of insects: "Dr. Boisduval was good enough to present me with three series of manuscript notes entitled 'Notes to the Drawings of Insects,' all written in Abbot's own hand, and comprising twenty-seven foolscap pages, rather closely written, and describing the changes of two hundred and one species."[32] Boisduval's gift of natural history drawings and manuscripts to various fellow lepidopterists who would appreciate them is typical of how manuscripts and objects of natural history inquiry circulated within naturalists' networks of exchange and knowledge production.

Collecting Practices

Two motives for collecting Abbot's drawings and notes can be inferred from the trajectories these various collections took. Drury and Francillon collected the drawings as part of building their insect collections. The manuscripts were key in providing them with information about the exotic insects they collected and helped them to identify their specimens and organize their collections. Smith, by contrast, was neither an insect collector nor an entomologist and was interested in accumulating Abbot's drawings and notes primarily as the raw material from which to produce a beautifully illustrated natural history book. Smith was amazingly successful in doing this, producing one of the era's most beautiful butterfly books. LeConte and Boisduval collected insects and worked on insect publications using the Abbot materials they had collected. However, the size of LeConte's collection of Abbot's drawings far exceeded his needs as a publisher of printed materials, which aligns his collecting practices more closely with the methods of natural history collectors, such as Francillon, whose focus was on the accumulation of specimens and related documentation.

Of the major collectors of Abbot's drawings and notes—Drury, Francillon, Smith, LeConte, and Boisduval—LeConte and Francillon stand out with collections of well over two thousand drawings each. To assess their methods as collectors of natural history manuscripts, it is helpful to employ Elizabeth Yale's distinction between amassing papers and collecting manuscripts. Collectors transform piles of papers into manuscripts and, ultimately, usable archives through their work of organizing, arranging, labeling, and storing paper documents.[33] The labor required to turn papers into an archive is extensive, often lasting decades and involving the employment of several hands. Francillon's careful curation of Abbot's manuscripts puts his collection at a remove from LeConte's accumulation of papers. Francillon invested energy and resources transforming Abbot's drawings and notes into a proper manuscript collection and, in the process, gave them a chance to weather time's forces of decay and indifference. LeConte's collection, meanwhile, became an unwelcome inheritance when he died; he left them to his son, John Lawrence LeConte, a prominent entomologist, who regarded his father's papers as remnants of an old-fashioned way of doing science. The elder LeConte was a generalist, interested in all aspects of natural history; his favorite subjects, judging by his publications and his own drawings, were butterflies and beetles, frogs and turtles, orchids and violets. His son, as a professional entomologist, worked hard to develop entomology as a distinct specialty within the natural sciences. As a taxonomist, he focused on classification and may have regarded collecting drawings as an inferior and outdated method for identifying and naming new species. For him, textual description was preferable to drawings and even to type specimens. Textual description, he thought, must be scientific—succinct, condensed, and abstract—and must erase the individual entomologist's voice as well as remove all traces of the process of naming and the narrative surrounding hunting for specimens. Abbot's descriptions of chasing nimble spiders would not be considered scientific enough for this new generation of professional entomologists.

Given this attitude toward specimens, drawings, and chatty notes, John Lawrence LeConte did not make the best legatee of his father's papers.[34] John Eatton LeConte's papers were scattered, John Lawrence probably giving away some of Abbot's drawings or, perhaps, swapping them for drawings or notes on beetles, his specialty.[35] Some of the more curated materials belonging to John Eatton LeConte—a bound volume of his own drawings of turtles and frogs, for instance—were sold shortly after the younger LeConte died in 1883. The appearance of John Eatton LeConte's materials in the 1880s rare book market suggests that John Lawrence LeConte had not made arrangements to preserve his father's papers in the archives of a natural history institution.[36] In contrast, Francillon's collection of Abbot drawings were pasted onto sheets of fine paper, labeled with Abbot's notes transcribed by Francillon himself, and bound in sturdy volumes that survived London's blitz and are available today for inspection at the Natural History Museum's library, where Abbot's drawings can still be called on to offer insight into questions concerning the identity, habitat, population, biology, and ecology of the insects of the American South—as well as into the material practices of late eighteenth- and early nineteenth-century study of the natural world.

To conclude, Abbot's drawings circulated among insect collectors, naturalists, and professional entomologists who regarded them as bearers of valuable information. Abbot's drawings could aid in organizing collections and cataloguing specimens, as well as provide models for printed illustrations. His drawings traversed the Atlantic when he shipped them to his English clients Drury, Francillon, and Smith, while LeConte was responsible for carrying Abbot's drawings to Paris in preparation for his co-authored volume with Boisduval. LeConte gave these drawings to Boisduval, who, in turn, gave some to the American Samuel Scudder; in the process, they recrossed the Atlantic, ending up in Boston, where they were joined by drawings (including Drury's) that the British Museum donated to the Boston Society of Natural History.[37] Moving through naturalists' networks as commodities, gifts, exchanges, and legacies, Abbot's drawings and notes offer an example of how natural history's manuscript culture was sociable, collaborative, collective, and key to the production of knowledge about the natural world.

Notes

1. Although LeConte generally spelled his name with a capital "C," and often with a space between "Le" and "Conte," he could not lawfully do so for his French publications because he was not an aristocrat.

2. McKitterick, *Print, Manuscript, and the Search for Order*, 3–4.
3. Yale, *Sociable Knowledge*.
4. Yale, "With Slips and Scraps," 10.
5. See Kennett's biography of Smith, *The Lord Treasurer of Botany*. For early eighteenth-century collecting of curiosities, see Delbourgo, *Collecting the World*.
6. Yale, "With Slips and Scraps," 3.
7. In focusing on these five manuscript collections (originally acquired by Drury, Francillon, Smith, LeConte, and Boisduval), I have for the sake of clarity left out other Abbot collections, some dating from the 1820s (when he was in his seventies) that seem to be more personal and decorative than scientific in their import. Also, I have omitted the marvelous collection of Abbot drawings made by William Swainson, a gifted illustrator and prominent naturalist with whom Abbot had hoped to publish butterfly and moth drawings. These are housed in the National Library of New Zealand. Swainson brought them to New Zealand when he emigrated there in 1841. These drawings have been reproduced in Neri, Nummedal, and Calhoun, *John Abbot and William Swainson*.
8. John Abbot, *Aranea*, ca. 1799, Rare Bk Folio QL458.42.A7 A2 1799, Hargrett Rare Book and Manuscript Library, University of Georgia, Athens.
9. For maker's knowledge, see Smith, "Art, Science, and Visual Culture in Early Modern Europe"; Smith et al., *Ways of Making and Knowing*.
10. Latour, *Science in Action*, 215–57.
11. Daston, "The Empire of Observation." See also Daston and Galison, *Objectivity*.
12. For natural history sociability and material practices, see Bleichmar, *Visible Empire*; Terrall, *Catching Nature in the Act*; Tobin, *The Duchess's Shells*. On the "affective socialscape of Enlightenment science," see Tobin, "A Naturalist's Notebooks," 145.
13. For Smeathman's career as a naturalist, see Coleman, *Henry Smeathman, the Flycatcher*.
14. Abbot drawings that Drury owned are part of the Houghton Library's collection of Abbot drawings: John Abbot, "John Abbot Notes and Drawings, 1766–1887," MS Typ 426–426.5, Houghton Library, Harvard University, Cambridge, MA.
15. Abbot, "Notes on My Life," bMs 1.41.1, Ernst Mayr Library, Museum of Comparative Zoology, Harvard University, Cambridge, MA.
16. The full title of Drury's book is *Illustrations of Natural History; Wherein Are Exhibited upwards of Two Hundred and Forty Figures of Exotic Insects, according to Their Different Genera* (London, 1770–82).
17. For Drury's tense relationship with his illustrator Moses Harris, see

Noblett, "Publishing by the Author." See also Tobin, "Butterflies, Spiders, and Shells."

18. The Library of the Carnegie Museum of Natural History possesses a few of Abbot's drawings of the Duchess of Portland's butterflies. They were part of Andrei Avinoff's collection of Abbot drawings, all of which date from Abbot's pre-America time in London, from 1767 to 1772.
19. Abbot, "Notes on My Life," bMs 1.41.1.
20. I do not think that it is a coincidence that jewelers were attracted to insect collecting since insects, especially beetles, can possess a gem-like appearance, and both insects and jewelry can partake of the aesthetics of shine, intricacy, and tininess.
21. Simpson, Jr., "Artistic Sources for John Abbot's Watercolor Drawings of American Birds."
22. John Francillon to John Leigh Phillips, November 1, 1805, Add MS 29533, Original letters of Naturalists, chiefly English, British Library, London, f.96^r-97^v.
23. Francillon collected nearly three thousand Abbot drawings. His collection, consisting of seventeen volumes, is titled "Drawings of the Insects of Georgia, in America, 1792–1804," and is held at the Zoology Library, Natural History Museum, London.
24. *The History of the Collections . . . of the British Museum*, 1: 23.
25. For the Royal Society's dismissive treatment of colonial naturalists, see Chaplin, "Nature and Nation"; Parrish, *American Curiosity*.
26. James Edward Smith to Richard Pulteney, May 1, 1797, GB-110/JES/MS238/17, Correspondence of Sir James Edward Smith, Linnean Society, London.
27. See Kennett, *The Lord Treasurer of Botany*; Tobin, "Domesticating the Tropics."
28. Alexander Wilson to William Bartram, 1809, reprinted in Wilson, *American Ornithology*, 1: xcvi.
29. Dow, "John Abbot," 71–72.
30. It is unclear how many drawings LeConte took with him to Paris or whether he left some or all these drawings with Boisduval when he returned to the United States.
31. Calhoun, "History of the Lepidoptera Illustrations in the Thomas Cooper Library."
32. Scudder, "John Abbot." One of Harvard's bound volumes of Abbot drawings that once belonged to the Boston Society of Natural History contains a note signed by Scudder saying he received these particular drawings as a gift from Boisduval: "Given me by Dr Boisduval." See Abbot, "John Abbot Notes and Drawings."

33. Yale describes this "process of transforming papers into manuscripts" as involving "cleaning them up and reordering them, transcribing sections that were difficult to read, and binding them into books arranged by genre or topic": Yale, *Sociable Knowledge*, 213.
34. For a brief overview of the drawings associated with Major John Eatton LeConte that were acquired by the American Philosophical Society in the 1950s, see Rehn, "The John Eatton Leconte Collection of Paintings of Insects." See also Calhoun, "John Abbot's 'Lost Drawings.'"
35. John Lawrence LeConte's cousin was Spencer Fullerton Baird (1823–87), who joined the Smithsonian as its first curator in 1850, becoming the second secretary of the Smithsonian Institution, from 1878 to 1887. I suspect that John Lawrence gave Baird a set of one hundred bird drawings by Abbot after his father's death in 1860; they are in the Smithsonian archives with Baird's handwritten notations on them.
36. *Catalogue of the Valuable Entomological Library of the late John L. Le Conte*, 17.
37. Asa Gray gave this volume to the Boston Society of Natural History "to compete their series of Abbott's Drawings now in their possession." He had received these drawings as a gift from John Edward Gray, curator at the British Museum, in 1869. This information is on a small piece of paper glued to the inside of the book cover signed, "Asa Gray, Cambridge January 1874." See Abbot, "John Abbot Notes and Drawings."

Works Cited

Bleichmar, Daniela. *Visible Empire: Botanical Expeditions and Visual Culture in the Hispanic Enlightenment*. Chicago: University of Chicago Press, 2012.

Calhoun, John V. "History of the Lepidoptera Illustrations in the Thomas Cooper Library, University of South Carolina." April 2003. Electronic resource, Irvin Department of Rare Books and Special Collections, University of South Carolina, Columbia.

———. "John Abbot's 'Lost' Drawings for John E. Le Conte in the American Philosophical Society Library, Philadelphia." *Journal of the Lepidopterists' Society* 60, no. 4 (2006): 211–17.

Catalogue of the Valuable Entomological Library of the late John L. Le Conte, M.D. of Philadelphia . . . to be sold . . . May 6th, 7th, and 8th, 1884. Philadelphia, 1884.

Chaplin, Joyce E. "Nature and Nation: Natural History in Context." In *Stuffing Birds, Pressing Plants, Shaping Knowledge: Natural History in North America, 1730–1860*, edited by Sue Ann Prince, 75–95. Philadelphia: American Philosophical Society, 2003.

Coleman, Deirdre. *Henry Smeathman, the Flycatcher: Natural History, Slavery, and Empire in the Late Eighteenth Century.* Liverpool: University of Liverpool Press, 2018.

Daston, Lorraine. "The Empire of Observation, 1600–1800." In *Histories of Scientific Observation,* edited by Lorraine Daston and Elizabeth Lunbeck, 95–101. Chicago: University of Chicago Press, 2011.

Daston, Lorraine, and Peter Galison. *Objectivity.* New York: Zone, 2007.

Delbourgo, James. *Collecting the World: Hans Sloane and the Origins of the British Museum.* Cambridge, MA: Harvard University Press, 2017.

Dow, Robert Percy. "John Abbot, of Georgia." *Journal of the New York Entomological Society* 22 (1914): 65–72.

Kennett, Tom. *The Lord Treasurer of Botany: James Edward Smith and the Linnean Collections.* London: Linnean Society, 2016.

Latour, Bruno. *Science in Action: How to Follow Scientists and Engineers through Society.* Cambridge, MA: Harvard University Press, 1987.

McKitterick, David. *Print, Manuscript, and the Search for Order, 1450–1830.* Cambridge: Cambridge University Press, 2003.

Neri, Janice, Tara Nummedal, and John V. Calhoun. *John Abbot and William Swainson: Art, Science, and Commerce in Nineteenth-Century Natural History Illustration.* Tuscaloosa: University of Alabama Press, 2019.

Noblett, William. "Publishing by the Author: A Case Study of Dru Drury's 'Illustrations of Natural History' (1770–1782)." *Publishing History* 23 (1988): 67–94.

Parrish, Susan Scott. *American Curiosity: Cultures of Natural History in the Colonial British Atlantic World.* Chapel Hill: University of North Carolina Press, 2006.

Rehn, James A. G. "The John Eatton Leconte Collection of Paintings of Insects, Arachnids and Myriopods." *Proceedings of the American Philosophical Society* 98, no. 6 (1954): 442–48.

Scudder, Samuel H. "John Abbot, the Aurelian." *Canadian Entomologist* 20 (1888): 150–54, 230–32.

Simpson, Marcus B., Jr. "Artistic Sources for John Abbot's Watercolor Drawings of American Birds." *Archives of Natural History* 20, no. 2 (1993): 197–212.

Smith, Pamela H. "Art, Science, and Visual Culture in Early Modern Europe." *Isis* 97 (2006): 83–100.

Smith, Pamela H., Amy R. W. Meyers, and Harold J. Cook, eds. *Ways of Making and Knowing.* Ann Arbor: University of Michigan Press, 2014.

Terrall, Mary. *Catching Nature in the Act: Réaumur and the Practice of Natural History in the Eighteenth Century.* Chicago: University of Chicago Press, 2014.

Tobin, Beth Fowkes. "Butterflies, Spiders, and Shells: Coloring Natural History Illustrations in Late Eighteenth-Century Britain." In *The Materiality of Color: The Production, Circulation, and Application of Dyes and Pigments, 1400–1800,* edited by Andrea Feeser, Maureen Daly Goggin, and Beth Fowkes Tobin, 265–80. Farnham, U.K.: Ashgate, 2012.

———. "Domesticating the Tropics: Tropical Flowers, Botanical Books, and the Culture of Collecting." In *Colonizing Nature: The Tropics in British Arts and Letters, 1760–1820*, edited by Beth Fowkes Tobin, 168–97. Philadelphia: University of Pennsylvania Press, 2005.

———. *The Duchess's Shells: Natural History Collecting in the Age of Cook's Voyages*. New Haven, CT: Yale University Press, 2014.

———. "A Naturalist's Notebooks." *Studies in Eighteenth-Century Culture* 45 (2016): 131–56.

Trustees of the British Museum. *The History of the Collections Contained in the Natural History Departments of the British Museum*, 2 vols. London: British Museum, 1904.

Wilson, Alexander. *American Ornithology; or, The Natural History of the Birds of the United States*, 3 vols. New York, 1828–29.

Yale, Elizabeth. *Sociable Knowledge: Natural History and the Nation in Early Modern Britain*. Philadelphia: University of Pennsylvania Press, 2016.

———. "With Slips and Scraps: How Early Modern Naturalists Invented the Archive." *Book History* 12 (2009): 1–36.

A "Female Accomplishment"?
Femininity, Privacy, and Eighteenth-Century Letter-Writing Norms

RACHAEL SCARBOROUGH KING

IN EIGHTEENTH-CENTURY studies, the letter's status as a feminine genre has often been taken for granted. Works from Ruth Perry's *Women, Letters, and the Novel* (1980) to Linda S. Kauffman's *Discourses of Desire: Gender, Genre, and Epistolary Fictions* (1986), Elizabeth Goldsmith's edited volume *Writing the Female Voice: Essays on Epistolary Literature* (1989), and Dena Goodman's *Becoming a Woman in the Age of Letters* (2009) have operated on the premise that there was a connection between women and letters that colored the expansion of letter writing and epistolary print that occurred in the period. Goldsmith writes, "Since the sixteenth century, when the familiar letter was first thought of as a literary form, male commentators have noted that the epistolary genre seemed particularly suited to the female voice," while Goodman argues that in the eighteenth century letter writing underwent a "regendering" that resulted in the "vision of a new, modern woman whose sensibility and maternal care are articulated through epistolary practice."[1] Feminist criticism, in seeking to recover a tradition of women's writing, focused on the letter as a site of female authority and resistance to patriarchal literary strictures. As Mary Favret sums up the scholarly discourse, "We have adopted this fiction which insists that the letter be read as a feminine space, and that the feminine be detached from *le monde* of business and cities, untainted by discussion of politics and philosophy. The world of women and the world of letters form a pastoral paradise."[2] Even those historicist studies that contextualize such associations often take contemporary commentators' pronouncements about the naturally feminine identity of letter writing as the era's accepted norm. Derived from paradigms of print culture and the epistolary novel, the conventional figure of the eighteenth-century letter writer is that of the solitary woman unbosoming herself to a friend or lover.

This essay resists such generalizations through attention to archives of diplomatic and political correspondence, which exist in enormous volumes in official records but which scholars often overlook because they do not support an ideal of the letter as, in Jürgen Habermas's terms, the space where "the individual unfolded himself in his subjectivity."[3] Such collections show that correspondents did not, for the most part, define their letters in gendered terms; neither did they see them as quintessentially personal, private, and oriented toward the expression of interiority. Instead, in texts that circulated among mixed-gender writers in a variety of social, political, educational, and commercial situations, individual letters frequently crossed what we now identify as public and private spheres and veered from the dry transmission of news to the sentimental outpourings of the heart. The letter was the primary forum for financial, political, and journalistic communication, as merchants exchanging trade information, diplomats on the continent, and "foreign correspondents" sending dispatches to newspapers all relied on the structural support of the post. Indeed, a large proportion of the eighteenth-century correspondence that remains in existence today pertains to the realms of business, diplomacy, and news, a numerical significance that can cast women's letters as exceptions rather than the rule. Of course, this is in part due to the systems in place for preserving such official correspondence and to the differing literacy rates for men and women, but it should give us pause when we instinctively turn to the image of the female letter writer. Konstantin Dierks sees the letter as the "common denominator of a new 'documentary culture'" in the eighteenth century and argues, "The widening encouragement for women to write letters was most often framed as a duty shared equally by both sexes, not as a duty imposed purely on women."[4] Manuscript archival correspondence bears out his assertion of the broad reach of letters.

Understanding letter writing as a wide-ranging literary activity therefore reveals the discrepancies between norm and practice that often appear when a particular genre is identified as "masculine" or "feminine." A view of eighteenth-century letters as private and feminine is, I argue, a back-formation that relies on Romantic-era and nineteenth-century redefinitions of the letter as the paradigmatic sentimental, personal, and amateur genre. It was only late in the eighteenth century that letter-writing norms consolidated around the presumed femininity of letters, and such dicta often came in the context of instructional works such as epistolary manuals and educational treatises. In 1771, for example, Dorothea Dubois, the author of *The Lady's Polite Secretary, or New Female Letter Writer*, wrote that "in every age, every nation, it has been a confessed maxim that women are born with talents peculiarly adapted for this path of literature—with a liveliness of imagination, and a facility of expression, unknown to the lords of the creation," while the author of *The Royal Letter Writer or Every Lady's Own Secretary* (1793) praised epistolary writing as the foremost "female accomplishment."[5] But it was in fact at this historical moment, when letters were becoming associated with women, that such writers began proclaiming their transhistorical feminine nature, thus revealing the prescriptive rather than descriptive nature of these epistolary manuals.[6] Earlier commentators rarely made such gendered comments and usually assumed a male rather than a female letter writer. In *Rambler* no. 152, Samuel Johnson asserted, "As letters are written on all subjects, in all states of mind, they cannot be properly reduced to settled rules, or described by any single characteristic.... Letters are written to the great and to the mean, to the learned and the ignorant, at rest and in distress, in sport and in passion."[7] Similarly, Hugh Blair noted, "Epistolary Writing appears, at first view, to stretch into a very wide field. For there is no subject whatever, on which one may not convey his thoughts to the Public, in the form of a Letter."[8] Eve Tavor Bannet has shown how epistolary manuals transitioned from addressing an elite audience to extending "letter-writing to all manner and ranks of people in late seventeenth- and eighteenth-century Britain and British-America."[9] Even in the late eighteenth century, most manuals continued to direct themselves toward would-be clerks and merchants, with titles such as *Every Man His Own Letter-Writer: Or, the New and Complete Art of Letter-Writing* (1782) and *The New and Complete British Letter-Writer; or, Young Secretary's Instructor in Polite Modern Letter-Writing* (1790). The pragmatic importance of correspondence meant that the letter genre retained a wide range of associations.

    Clarifying the status of the letter can thus illustrate more broadly the heterogeneous nature of eighteenth-century manuscript culture. This essay demonstrates the practical, nongendered character of much letter writing in the mid-eighteenth century, exploring how everyday writers both resisted and revealed norms by focusing on the epistolary circles surrounding two prominent politicians and diplomats: Charles Hanbury Williams (1708–1759) and Henry Seymour Conway (1721–1795). Both men, collections of whose letters are now held at Yale University's Lewis Walpole Library, held overseas posts requiring them to write regular news dispatches home, and both were voluminous correspondents. Diplomats were expected to convey continual updates on the news and gossip of their postings and to keep detailed records of their incoming and outgoing mail; as Jeremy Black writes, "Diplomats could be criticized severely if they failed to write sufficiently often or comprehensively."[10] But Williams's and Conway's letters, and those to and from their friends and family, do not hew cleanly to public-private, business-pleasure, or masculine-feminine divides. Instead, their contents frequently pivot from military news to intimate gossip, from orders for goods to emotional appeals, and from the objective to the sentimental. Similarly, the letters composed by male and female correspondents do not split in terms of subject matter or tone. Instead, both groups express a common set of assumptions about the purposes of communicating by letter and the conventions that should be followed in doing so.

In material terms, the letters also defy clear divisions among modes of correspondence. Bannet argues that letters were not seen as private because they would normally be read aloud upon receipt, and printed epistolary manuals both elicited writing in the form of readers' letters and represented letters as a transcription of natural speech. She outlines: "During its trajectory from one correspondent to another, the letter successively occupied each place on a continuum that ran from oral speech to the silent speech of manuscript (and thence potentially to print), from the silent speech of writing to vocalized writing or script speech—and back the same way when the speech or conversation that a letter stimulated in its reader or among the company at its point of reception produced a new letter."[11] This intermedial status also complicates the letter genre's gendered identity since, as Clare Brant points out, an assumption of the letter as a manuscript document has gone hand in hand with its feminine status: "The opposite of the feminised private body is assumed to be an ungendered public body, achieved through the decorporealising medium of print."[12] It is only by viewing the handwritten letter in the context of its oral and printed mediation that we can understand its complicated connection to notions of masculine and feminine writing.

But it is not just that letters crisscrossed media. Handwritten letters also displayed a variety of material textual formats. Williams's writings

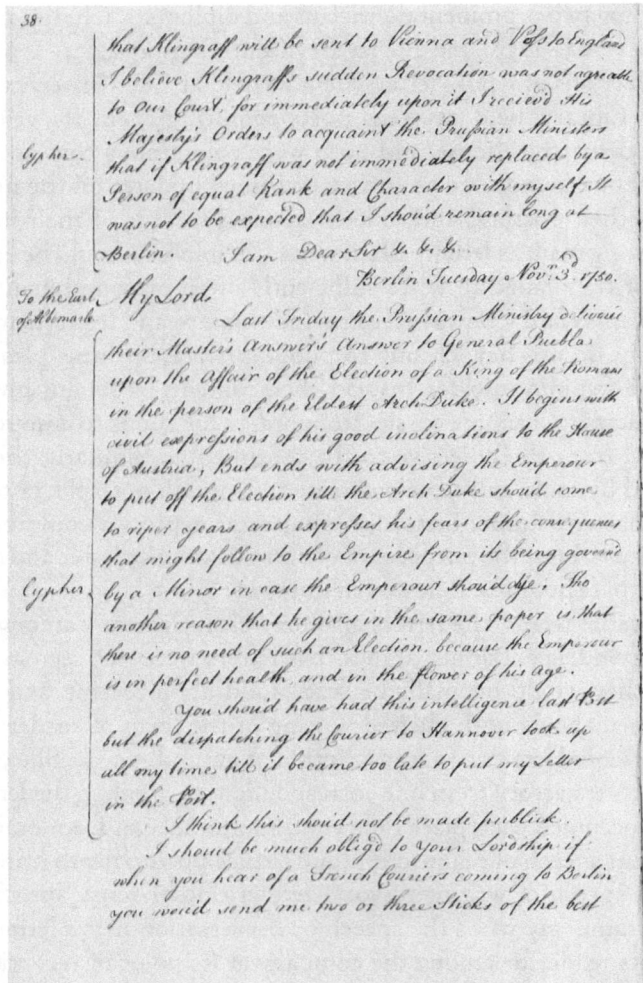

FIGURE 1. Page from Charles Hanbury Williams's letter book. (Sir Charles Hanbury Williams Papers, Mss. V. 14-10883, f. 38; courtesy of the Lewis Walpole Library, Yale University)

are preserved in a letter book, a folio volume featuring the copies he made of his outgoing mail (see fig. 1). Keeping a letter book was a common practice for diplomats and merchants, and in this case it means that the letters are clearly laid out, sequenced, and translated out of cipher when necessary. One of the books in the Walpole Library's collection covers his residence as ambassador in Berlin from 1750 to 1751. However, the letters in this official format do not merely record Williams's transaction of his diplomatic duties; they also cover a range of personal and emotional concerns. Meanwhile, Conway's letters employ the common epistolary format of a half-sheet quarto, which was made by folding a cut folio sheet in half to create a four-page booklet, with the final page left blank for an address panel (see fig. 2). This had become the standard format for personal letters by the mid-eighteenth century, as stationers sold pre-cut sheets of letter paper, sometimes gilded around the edges, for the purpose. The female writers in Williams's circle, including his daughter Frances Hanbury Williams (later Frances Capel, Countess of

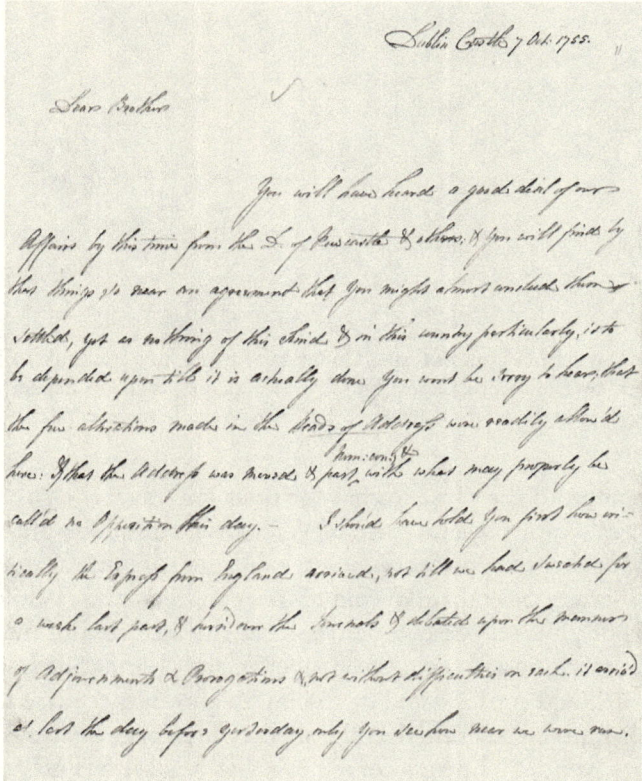

FIGURE 2. Letter from Henry Seymour Conway to Francis Seymour Conway. (Letters to Francis Seymour Conway, October 7, 1755, MS. Vol. 84, f. 11; courtesy of the Lewis Walpole Library, Yale University)

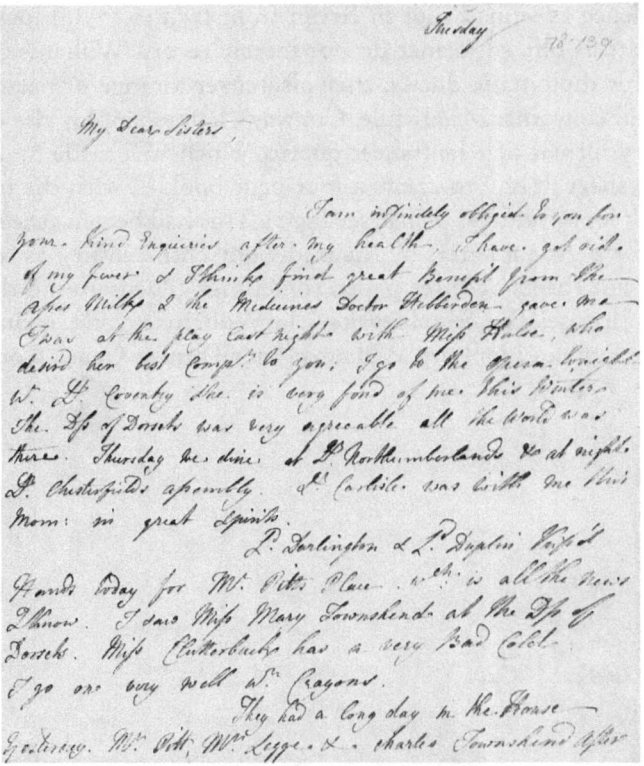

FIGURE 3. Letter from Frances Capel, Countess of Essex (née Hanbury Williams), to her sister-in-law Lady Anne Capel. (Sir Charles Hanbury Williams Papers, n.d. [after 1754], Mss. V. 78-11389, f. 139; courtesy of the Lewis Walpole Library, Yale University)

Essex), employed the same format for their letters (see fig. 3). But just as the bureaucratic physical form of Williams's letter book did not foreclose personal correspondence, neither did the personal appearance of Conway's letters leave them devoid of news and business. While certain standards of physical presentation, such as the inclusion of more white space when writing to a stranger or superior and clear dating to place letters in order, had consolidated by the mid-eighteenth century, the range of content contained within the folio sheet or four-page quarto continued to support Samuel Johnson's contention that "a letter has no peculiarity but its form."[13]

Rather than seeing diplomatic and political letters as an exception to the feminine, sentimental rule, then, it is important for scholars to consider the range of epistolary communication in the period if we are to fully understand what Habermas called the "century of the letter."[14] As Favret writes, "Rather than determine any single fiction of the letter's 'femininity,' we should trace the historically specific tensions between publication and correspondence, between the Post Office and letter-writing, and between the epistolary novel and other representations of the letter."[15] Letters may be among the best-documented aspects of eighteenth-century manuscript culture, with a flourishing field of epistolary studies producing important works such as Brant's *Eighteenth-Century Letters and British Culture*, Susan Whyman's *The Pen and the People: English Letter Writers, 1660–1800*, and Amanda Gilroy and W. M. Verhoeven's edited collection *Epistolary Histories: Letters, Fiction, Culture*. Most scholars, however, continue to focus on the letters of canonical authors and elite coteries, emphasizing the private details that can be "discovered" in the archive. But there is reason to believe that pragmatic letters had as great an impact on contemporary definitions of the letter genre as did women's personal letters. In fact, such letters may give us a clearer window into the period's epistolary sense, since they tended not just to include business and politics, but also to cross public and private spheres in their content, composition, and reception. Diplomatic correspondence is exemplary of the tendency of eighteenth-century letters to eschew the categories—feminine, private, and manuscript—to which a traditional view of manuscript circulation has assigned them.

News and Opinion in Men's and Women's Letters

When Charles Hanbury Williams arrived in Berlin in mid-1750 he understood that one of his primary tasks as a diplomat was to establish correspondence networks. His letter book records several examples of a quasi-form letter that he sent out to his fellow continental envoys updating them on his new status. As he wrote to Melchior Guy Dickens, ambassador in Saint Petersburg, "I wou'd not miss the first Opportunity of Notifying to you my Arrival at Berlin and of desiring you to favour me with your Correspondence, which is a thing I have long wish'd for and which will be of the greatest Importance to me in the carrying on his Majestys Business at this Court," while to Robert Murray Keith he noted, "I beg you wou'd not fail to let me hear how your great Work at Vienna goes on, and whatever happens here worth your knowing, shall be constantly communicated to you."[16] To George Keppel, Earl of Albemarle, he was more deferential, writing, "Tho' I have not yet had my first audience of the King of Prussia I wou'd not defer any longer acquainting your Excellency with my arrival, and offering you my Services both in my Private & Publick Capacity at this Court."[17] These letters have a largely phatic quality to them, working to establish a channel of communication rather than to convey particular pieces of information.[18] Williams represented letter writing as an integral element of the diplomat's duties; as he wrote to Albemarle in 1751, "Since last Wednesday night I have never been one moment without a pen in my hand."[19]

Alongside the maintenance of his epistolary network, Williams frequently figured the sending of news as his primary motive for writing, whether this was public news intended for dissemination at court and in the newspaper or private news for the individual recipient. His letters reveal a constantly shifting set of expectations regarding the borders between such public and private spheres; indeed, as Jennifer Mori points out, "There was little confidentiality to [diplomatic] dispatches, extracts from which might be presented to parliament, published in the *London Gazette*, or distributed amongst government departments."[20] Williams often deferred to his correspondents' judgment regarding further circulation of information, offering advice rather than instruction. As he wrote to Onslow Burrish in Munich regarding negotiations with the king of Prussia, "I think all this shou'd not be made publick. I write it purely for your Information and leave it entirely to your Discretion."[21] Writing to Dickens in late 1750 about his belief that he was soon to be recalled from his post, he concluded, "All this I write to you purely for your own Information giving you leave at the same time to communicate as much as you please of it in Secrecy to the Great Chancellor."[22] Several of the letters move in and out of cipher, indicating the varying levels of privacy contained in a single sheet; that is, even within a single letter Williams assigned items different degrees of confidentiality. He also often referred to printed materials within his written letters. In January 1751, he informed Dickens of "a paper handed about here said to be deliver'd by the Court of Petersbourg to Monsieur Wahrendorff the late Prussian Minister at that Court an Extract of it is also printed in the Amsterdam Gazette," adding in cipher, "But as I have not receiv'd it from your Hands I still continue to doubt whether it is genuine or not."[23] At other times he sent more official diplomatic news for use at Whitehall or in the foreign embassies. For example, in 1750 he enclosed several copies of a "Letter from the Great General of Poland to the King of Prussia," while in December 1750 he wrote to Dickens, "Monsieur Klingraff who was lately the King of Prussia's Minister in England is going Envoy from His Prussian Majesty to the Court of Vienna. And Monsieur Ammon who was lately the King of Prussia's Minister at the Hague is going or gone upon an extraordinary commission to Paris."[24] Diplomats were expected to keep track of their counterparts' movements, a form of news that again combined levels of personal and official activities.

At the same time, many of the missives transcribed in Williams's letter book include much more gossipy or intimate information than we might expect from bureaucratic documents. While the letters worked to establish channels of news transmission with fellow diplomats, they also drew on the conventions of friendship and sentimental correspondence. As he wrote to Keith, minister in Vienna, in a style that would accord with the advice of an epistolary manual, "I was glad to find by your Letter of the 24th of October: that you had not quite forgot that there was such a Person in the World as myself, And the true Esteem and Regard that I have for you made me uneasy for fear you shoud [sic] have taken a Resolution to put a Stop to our Correspondence; But your Letter has made me thoroughly easy." In the diplomat's voice, he added, "I shall not fail of continuing regularly to inform you of whatever happens at this Place worthy your Notice."[25] Later letters to Keith included more particular information. In one November 1750 letter he wrote of the new Prussian envoy to Vienna, "He is the ablest Foreign Minister in the King of Prussia's Service, but He is a very dangerous man. He never drops an unguarded word, & won't answer directly to the commonest question. He did all the harm He cou'd whilst He resided at our Court. His Birth is neither good nor bad." In a more intimate vein, he added cryptically, "If Madam Sternberg is at Vienna make my best compliments to her and tell her that I don't yet believe the Person in question is with Child, but if she is the Child was begotten last Shrove Tuesday."[26] Williams also used his diplomatic correspondence to obtain personally significant information; in October 1750, for example, he concluded a letter to Arthur Villettes at Geneva, "So much for publick Affairs. But there is a private one to which you are no Stranger, and which I am naturally very curious about, and of which nobody can inform me so well as yourself. Pray then send me word where Lord Essex"—Williams's future son-in-law, then on an extended Grand Tour—"now is, and which way I must write to him."[27] In addition to gleaning such information, he employed his letters to secure personal goods, as when he asked Albemarle, at the end of a letter detailing negotiations over the election of the Holy Roman Emperor, to "send me two or three Sticks of the best Rapee Snuff, you can get at Paris. I take a great deal and 'tis difficult here to get it good."[28] These official bureaucratic records ranged over a wide array of informational and material topics as diplomats performed their work alongside maintaining private relationships.

In some ways, it is to be expected that Williams's diplomatic correspondence would draw together personal and professional topics: diplomats relied on the postal system to stay in touch with both home and office, and the diplomatic residence abroad was simultaneously a private house and public workplace.[29] But comparison of Williams's letter book with the letters of his daughter, Frances Hanbury Williams, and a group of her female friends and relatives reveals the similarly border-crossing nature of middle- and upper-class women's correspondence, the variety of letter that has often been seen as the quintessential private missive in the eighteenth century. These letters also emphasize the importance of maintaining a channel of communication and of news transmission; include a range of information variously considered "public," "private," and "secret"; and assume that letters will be shared among a correspondence circle. They show that women, too, employed letters for a variety of pragmatic purposes beyond the expression of sentiment that is often assumed to be the sine qua non of women's correspondence.

This group of letters from the 1740s, also held at the Walpole Library, constitutes those written to Lady Anne Capel, sister of William Capel, Earl of Essex and, thus, future sister-in-law of Frances Hanbury Williams. The correspondence chains, like those of Charles Hanbury Williams, began with the women establishing the expectation to correspond; as another friend, Albinia Townshend, wrote to Capel in 1746, "I am very sorry that you have not had a letter from [name missing] as I know that you are so fond of her, but I think that perhaps, she has not received yours, & wonders as much that she has not heard from you." In the same letter she inquired, "You say nothing in your letter of when you heard from [name missing] do they continue writing as constantly as ever? Do they write longer letters than usual? I assure they do not to me."[30] At this early point in their epistolary relationship the writers worked to forge a secure connection, but as the correspondence grew they increasingly exchanged news that ranged from private gossip to public politics. Townshend attributed the best "news" to Lady Anne, writing in July 1746, "You do not, I suppose, expect news from me, who never know any, but what I learn from you, who have spies every where, & who know whatever happens to any of your friends, for my part I am astonish'd at it, & cannot imagine where you get your intelligence." In a later note she added, "I shall not attempt to send you news from hence, as you have always better intelligence than any body, & generally know better what passes at London when you are at Cashionbury [Cassiobury], than I do, even when I am upon the Spot," while in yet another she sent "a thousand thanks for your letter, which had more news in it than any I have read this great while, you seem to me to have heard lately from all parts of the world."[31] Townshend continually praised her correspondent's ability to supply news, which included information about a wide group of relatives, friends, acquaintances, and strangers.

At other times, however, Townshend attempted to hold up her end of the epistolary bargain, supplying her own news. In July 1746 she gave an eyewitness account of a trial of Jacobite rebels, blending sentiment and reportage to write: "I went very bravely, intending to have no sort of compassion for them, but no sooner did they appear than I felt my courage fail me. & the second day when the two Earls made their speeches I could not forbear crying. . . . I wish you had been at the Trials, for it is much the finest sight in the world." In the same letter she added, "I hear that Miss Jenny Conway is to marry Major Johnson, this is all the news that is stirring."[32] Frances Hanbury Williams likewise mixed together quotidian personal updates with political items, writing to Anne Capel, for example, "I hope Master Hyde continues well. My Sister & I had Miss Mansel with us all yesterday evening. The Appleby Election was carried by 83 Votes in Lord Thanet[']s Side. . . . I will not seal this till I get to Whitehall where I perhaps may hear some news." Elsewhere she offered details on parliamentary transactions, writing, "They had a long day in the House yesterday. Mr. Pitt, Mr. Legge & Charles Townshend after having spoke against the Treaties, were rather slow in moving out of the House & the Door was shut upon them so in numbering the Division they were set down amongst those who were for it. They say Mr. Pitt kept scratching at the Door to get out, like a Dog but to no Purpose."[33] Rather than confining themselves to domestic and sentimental topics, women in this circle were also transmitters of political news and rumor.

The correspondents, however, made little distinction among the varieties of knowledge they were discussing, classing hearsay, scandal, politics, and reports on London amusements such as the theater and Ranelagh Gardens alike as "news." Frances Hanbury Williams's just-cited report on the House debate followed a paragraph of information on her recent social engagements: "I was at the play last night with Miss Hulse, who desir'd her best Compliments to you; I go to the opera tonight with Lady Coventry she is very fond of me this Winter."[34] The letters' categories of public versus private information were similarly variable. Townshend more than once advocated burning the letters between her and Lady Anne after they had been read—although she did not specify what topics might be objectionable—but settled for the practice of washing off individuals' names. At the same time, all of the correspondents wrote group letters, composed their letters in the midst of company, and often expected that letters would be read aloud or recirculated. While Townshend wrote to "scold" Anne Capel for "shew[ing] Lord Essex all my letters," she added, "I am not afraid that my Lord Essex should repeat what he sees there." In the same letter she noted in a postscript that the "Miss Pelhams have sent me Lady Die [Diana Beauclerk]'s last letter to them."[35] Elsewhere she wrote, "The next letter you receive from Miss G— you may expect to have a post cript [sic] from me in," while another letter opened, "Though I am writing to you, My Dearest Lady Anne, yet I must begin my letter with thanking of Lady Die for her last."[36] After her marriage, Frances (Hanbury Williams) Capel addressed group letters to her "Dear Sisters" and revealed the social setting in which she might compose a letter, noting in one, "Excuse blots Evr'y body is talking in the room."[37] If, therefore, criticism has highlighted the "particularity of the I-you" address as central to the "epistolary pact" that creates conditions of intimacy and confidentiality,[38] the second-person plural "you" frequently at work in everyday writers' correspondence—as well as the "we" implied in collectively composed letters—complicates the calls for secrecy and discretion that characterize many of the letters. Both personal and political letters featured fluctuating expectations for privacy and collaborative communication.

Personalized Diplomacy

Henry Seymour Conway's letters to his brother, Francis Seymour Conway, Marquess of Hertford, likewise span a surprising range of personal and political functions. A military commander during the War of the Austrian Succession and member of the Irish Parliament, Henry Seymour Conway received requests from his brother, a high-ranking courtier and politician, for practical updates on military and political affairs.

But while Conway provided some such details, he also often expressed a lack of knowledge and turned instead to sentimental tropes in his correspondence. In June 1743, for example, he wrote to assure his brother of his safety following the Battle of Dettingen. Conway assumed that his family in London would already have read about the details of the battle, so he focused on personal affairs, writing, "before you receive this you will have heard of an action between us & the French. I know your goodness for me & therefore I know I ought not to lose the first opportunity of letting you know that I am safe & in good health," adding that the account he sent was "authentick tho' I shall not pretend to give you an accurate one."[39] During his posting as chief secretary for Ireland, Conway noted that his brother "made large demands on me for Irish news," but he more frequently sent emotional appeals, writing in December 1755, "You are vastly good & write often to me; for which I return you a thousand thanks tis really a perfect charity I assure you, & you cant imagine how well bestow'd to judge of it by my constant impatience to hear from you."[40] In May 1764, following his abrupt and highly publicized dismissal from all of his government posts, he wrote in flowery epistolary language, "It is a satisfaction in most situations certainly to communicate even ones griefs to those friends to whom one can do it in confidence but it is a pain when one thinks it must give them any."[41] At times during his Irish and continental postings Conway did supply hard news items—for example, writing in November 1762 about the surrender of Cassel and in December 1763 about parliamentary debates regarding John Wilkes's libels—but he as frequently treated his letters as means of emotional connection.

Conway's "news" therefore had much in common with that of the middle- and upper-class women's letters, which in turn shared many features with diplomatic correspondence, as discussed earlier. His letters blurred the borders between gossip and intelligence in language similar to that of Albinia Townshend and Frances Hanbury Williams. In 1761, when he was serving as groom of the bedchamber and colonel of the 1st Dragoons, he sent a long catalogue of London social affairs:

> Loo is reviv'd I think with its usual vivacity & our parties got in train again, in spite of parties & politicks: the D.ss of Grafton the D.ss of Bedford, &c &c, the Duke & D.ss of Marlborough are also become too players & sometimes of our parties.... Miss Pelham is ... less violent & distressed than usual, & poor La: Jane Scott is quite off the stage being sunk in a terrible nervous disorder; brought on they say by Lady

Molesworth's dreadful accident, who was her intimate friend. These are little Anecdotes but one must talk of something & great events do not so readily present themselves.

He added at the end of the letter: "All the world says his M[ajesty] goes to Germany; but I know as little of that as anything."[42] Instead of insider information, he frequently sent his brother printed materials or assumed his previous knowledge of news items, noting in October 1764, for example, "As the words of [the Duke of Devonshire's] codicil are got into the news-papers I need not send them to you."[43] When he had himself become the topic of newspaper debate following his dismissal from government service for voting against the ministry and in favor of Wilkes,[44] he sent updates on his affairs in the form of pamphlets and newspapers, which included letters to the editor concerning him. As he wrote in September 1764, "I can't finish politicks without telling you how disagreeably I have myself been the object of them, I believe I did mention before that several of the Ministerial papers & pamphlets took occasion to abuse me."[45] Like other male and female letter writers, Conway mixed together written and printed materials and surveyed a continuum of public and private information and feeling in his correspondence with his brother. It is difficult to classify any single letter as public, private, sentimental, corporate, professional, or feminized.

Functional letters of news, diplomacy, and politics, such as those of Charles Hanbury Williams and Henry Seymour Conway, demonstrate the dangers of drawing conclusions about the supposedly feminine character of letter writing based on either the prescriptive statements of epistolary manuals or the stylized correspondence of epistolary novels. The status of the letter as a "female accomplishment" was not in evidence in the masculine correspondence networks of diplomats and politicians. Likewise, the familiar letters of middle- and upper-class women—traditionally seen as the source and target of norms regarding feminine letter writing—show how much personal missives had in common with practical bureaucratic correspondence. The letters of the Anne Capel–Albinia Townshend–Frances Hanbury Williams circle took the same format as those of Henry Seymour Conway, a four-page half-folio booklet, and in each case this standard form for a familiar letter did not restrict the correspondents to personal topics. Similarly, the more official format of the bifolium, which Charles Hanbury Williams used for his letter book and which was also a common form for government letters sent in the mail, did not prevent him from including a variety of intimate concerns in his correspondence. Both physical layouts mixed together written and printed materials, as the writers enclosed, excerpted from, and commented on newspapers, pamphlets, books, and printed engravings. Williams and Conway wrote to their colleagues and family to accomplish specific political tasks, providing news on the outcome of battles or detailing parliamentary activity. But throughout the series, we see male correspondents offering emotional, introspective commentary and female writers collecting and circulating political updates, and vice versa. The utter lack of commentary within the letters on such seemingly gender-transgressive behavior suggests that it was, in fact, not subversive but expected.

If, in the late eighteenth century, letter-writing norms did increasingly assume a feminine facility for the genre, it remained the case that everyday letters constantly breached such boundaries. As the author of *The Preceptor* (1758) argued in favor of men's instruction in "those Letters which are most useful, and by which the general Business of Life is transacted,'" It is possible to pass many Years without the Necessity of writing Panegyrics or Epithalamiums; but every Man has frequent Occasion to state a Contract, or demand a Debt, or make a Narrative of some minute Incidents of common Life."[46] In *Northanger Abbey*, Jane Austen poked fun at the still-tenuous connection between women and letters, having her heroine, Catherine Morland, wonder, "doubtingly, 'whether ladies do write so much better than gentleman. That is, I should not think the superiority was always on our side.'" Her love interest, Henry Tilney, after declaring, "Every body allows that the talent of writing agreeable letters is peculiarly female," continues that "the usual style of letter-writing among women is faultless, except in three particulars," which, he continues, are "a general deficiency of subject, a total inattention to stops, and a very frequent ignorance of grammar."[47] As Clare Brant notes, in novels and prescriptive texts "women who wrote familiar letters were figures of epistolary contradiction, simultaneously lauded as 'naturally better' writers and disparaged as naturally disorderly."[48] This fact not only complicates the status of women's letters in the eighteenth century but also works to break down binary divisions between feminine and masculine writing. In the midcentury women's correspondence there is little discussion of those commonly held feminine epistolary defects, poor handwriting and spelling. Instead, Lord Essex deferred to his sister Lady Anne as an orthographic authority, writing, "I hope you will find no false spellings pray if you dont tell me of it in your next letter."[49] In these dozens of letters spanning two decades, the correspondents make no reference to expectations that men's or women's letters would hew to specific, separate literary standards.

Even as letter writers in print began to present the letter as the universally acknowledged feminine genre, therefore, the contents within those pages tied together male and female writers within expanding, entangled networks of epistolary intercourse. A more accurate description of epistolary practices, based on in-depth archival research, not only clarifies the status of this genre that has long been acknowledged as integral to key eighteenth-century narratives such as the rise of the novel and the emergence of the individual; it also illustrates the importance of a holistic view of the period's manuscript culture. By focusing on correspondence that does not fit our stereotype of letters as private and feminine, we can also see how letters that do fit this image—those of female friends gossiping with one another—similarly resist easy definition. As with manuscript texts more generally, letters continued to serve a variety of public, professional, and practical purposes in the long eighteenth century.

Notes

The archival research for this essay was supported by the Lewis Walpole Library's George B. Cooper Fellowship, for which I am grateful. I also thank Bethany Wong for her research assistance.

1. Goldsmith, "Introduction," vii; Goodman, *Becoming a Woman in the Age of Letters*, 10, 15.
2. Favret, *Romantic Correspondence*, 19, 21. "Until quite recently," Gilroy and Verhoeven add, "critical discourse has on the whole accepted female epistolary skill as a truth universally acknowledged, and has subscribed to the fiction of the feminine, private letter": Gilroy and Verhoeven, "Introduction," 3.
3. Habermas, *The Structural Transformation of the Public Sphere*, 48.
4. Dierks, *In My Power*, 12, 173.
5. Dubois, *The Lady's Polite Secretary*, 3; *The Royal Letter Writer or Every Lady's Own Secretary*, 1.
6. Roger Chartier notes that an "essential question raised by letter-writing manuals is that of their usefulness," while Eve Tavor Bannet shows how writers and readers adapted and remixed epistolary manuals to suit their purposes: Chartier, "Introduction," 4; Bannet, *Empire of Letters*, xi.
7. Johnson, *Rambler*, 45.

8. Blair, *Lectures on Rhetoric and Belles Lettres*, 2:297.
9. Bannet, *Empire of Letters*, 4.
10. Black, *British Diplomats and Diplomacy*, 8.
11. Bannet, *Empire of Letters*, 48.
12. Brant, *Eighteenth-Century Letters and British Culture*, 20.
13. Johnson, *Rambler*, 45.
14. Habermas, *The Structural Transformation of the Public Sphere*, 48.
15. Favret, *Romantic Correspondence*, 15.
16. Charles Hanbury Williams to Melchior Guy Dickens, July 11, 1750, and Williams to Robert Murray Keith, July 15, 1750, Mss. V. 14–10883, Sir Charles Hanbury Williams Papers (hereafter, Williams Papers), Lewis Walpole Library, Farmington, CT, ff. 1, 6–7.
17. Williams to George Keppel, Earl of Albemarle, July 14, 1750, Mss. V. 14–10883, Williams Papers, Lewis Walpole Library, ff. 9–10.
18. Roman Jakobson defines the phatic as one of the six primary linguistic functions. It pertains to "messages primarily serving to establish, to prolong, or to discontinue communication, to check whether the channel works ... to attract the attention of the interlocutor or to confirm his continued attention": Jakobson, "Linguistics and Poetics," 337.
19. Williams to Albemarle, January 30, 1751, Mss. V. 14–10883, Williams Papers, Lewis Walpole Library, f. 92.
20. Mori, *The Culture of Diplomacy*, 33.
21. Williams to Onslow Burrish, October 24, 1750, Mss. V. 14–10883, Williams Papers, Lewis Walpole Library, f. 34.
22. Williams to Dickens, December 30, 1750, Mss. V. 14–10883, Williams Papers, Lewis Walpole Library, f. 63.
23. Williams to Dickens, January 23, 1751, Mss. V. 14–10883, Williams Papers, Lewis Walpole Library, f. 75.
24. Williams to Albemarle, July 14, 1750, and Williams to Dickens, December 5, 1750, Mss. V. 14–10883, Williams Papers, Lewis Walpole Library, ff. 18, 46–47.
25. Williams to Keith, November 3, 1750, Mss. V. 14–10883, Williams Papers, Lewis Walpole Library, f. 35.
26. Williams to Keith, November 30, 1750, Mss. V. 14–10883, Williams Papers, Lewis Walpole Library, f. 43.
27. Williams to Arthur Villettes, October 6, 1750, Mss. V. 14–10883, Williams Papers, Lewis Walpole Library, ff. 30–31.
28. Williams to Albemarle, November 3, 1750, Mss. V. 14–10883, Williams Papers, Lewis Walpole Library, ff. 38–39.
29. Mori, *The Culture of Diplomacy*, 17.
30. Albinia Townshend to Lady Anne Capel, June 24, 1746, Mss. V. 78–11389, Williams Papers, Lewis Walpole Library, ff. 25, 29.

31. Townshend to Capel, July 17, 1746, n.d., and n.d., Mss. V. 78–11389, Williams Papers, Lewis Walpole Library, f. 35, ff. 71–72, f. 75.
32. Townshend to Capel, July 31, 1746, Mss. V. 78–11389, Williams Papers, Lewis Walpole Library, ff. 38–39.
33. Frances Hanbury Williams to Anne Capel, May 18 [no year], and Frances Capel, Countess of Essex (née Hanbury Williams), to Anne Capel, n.d. [after 1754], Mss. V. 78–11389, Williams Papers, Lewis Walpole Library, ff. 117, 139–40.
34. Frances Capel to Anne Capel, n.d. [after 1754], Mss. V. 78–11389, Williams Papers, Lewis Walpole Library, f. 139.
35. Townshend to Capel, n.d., Mss. V. 78–11389, Williams Papers, Lewis Walpole Library, ff. 61, 63.
36. Townshend to Capel, n.d., Mss. V. 78–11389, Williams Papers, Lewis Walpole Library, ff. 106, 111.
37. Frances Hanbury Williams to Anne Capel, n.d., Mss. V. 78–11389, Williams Papers, Lewis Walpole Library, f. 137.
38. Altman, *Epistolarity*, 117–18, 120.
39. Henry Seymour Conway to Francis Seymour Conway, June 30, 1743, MS. Vol. 84, Letters to Francis Seymour Conway (hereafter, Conway Letters), Lewis Walpole Library, f. 6.
40. Conway to Francis Seymour Conway, October 7, 1755, and December 18, 1755, MS. Vol. 84, Conway Letters, ff. 11, 13.
41. Conway to Francis Seymour Conway, May 1, 1764, MS. Vol. 84, Conway Letters, f. 26.
42. Conway to Francis Seymour Conway, March 21, 1761, MS. Vol. 84, Conway Letters, f. 23.
43. Conway to Francis Seymour Conway, October 17, 1764, MS. Vol. 84, Conway Letters, f. 29.
44. Towse, "Conway, Henry Seymour."
45. Conway to Francis Seymour Conway, September 9, 1764, MS. Vol. 84, Conway Letters, f. 28.
46. *The Preceptor*, xviii.
47. Austen, *Northanger Abbey*, 20.
48. Brant, *Eighteenth-Century Letters and British Culture*, 18.
49. William Capel, Earl of Essex, to Anne Capel, n.d., Mss. V. 78–11389, Williams Papers, Lewis Walpole Library, f. 189.

Works Cited

Altman, Janet Gurkin. *Epistolarity: Approaches to a Form*. Columbus: Ohio State University Press, 1982.

Austen, Jane. *Northanger Abbey.* Cambridge Edition of the Works of Jane Austen. Cambridge: Cambridge University Press, 2006.

Bannet, Eve Tavor. *Empire of Letters: Letter Manuals and Transatlantic Correspondence, 1688–1820.* Cambridge: Cambridge University Press, 2005.

Black, Jeremy. *British Diplomats and Diplomacy, 1688–1800.* Exeter, U.K.: University of Exeter Press, 2001.

Blair, Hugh. *Lectures on Rhetoric and Belles Lettres,* 2 vols. London, 1783.

Brant, Clare. *Eighteenth-Century Letters and British Culture.* Basingstoke, U.K.: Palgrave Macmillan, 2006.

Chartier, Roger. "Introduction: An Ordinary Kind of Writing: Model Letters and Letter-Writing in Ancien Régime France." In *Correspondence: Models of Letter-Writing from the Middle Ages to the Nineteenth Century,* edited by Alain Boureau, Cécile Dauphin, and Roger Chartier, 1–23. Princeton, NJ: Princeton University Press, 1997.

Dierks, Konstantin. *In My Power: Letter Writing and Communications in Early America.* Philadelphia: University of Pennsylvania Press, 2009.

Dubois, Dorothea. *The Lady's Polite Secretary, or New Female Letter Writer.* London, 1771.

Favret, Mary A. *Romantic Correspondence: Women, Politics and the Fiction of Letters.* Cambridge: Cambridge University Press, 1993.

Gilroy, Amanda, and W. M. Verhoeven. "Introduction." In *Epistolary Histories: Letters Fiction, Culture,* edited by Amanda Gilroy and W. M. Verhoeven, 1–25. Charlottesville: University of Virginia Press, 2005.

Goldsmith, Elizabeth C. "Introduction." In *Writing the Female Voice: Essays on Epistolary Literature,* edited by Elizabeth C. Goldsmith, vii–xiii. Boston: Northeastern University Press, 1989.

Goodman, Dena. *Becoming a Woman in the Age of Letters.* Ithaca, NY: Cornell University Press, 2009.

Habermas, Jürgen. *The Structural Transformation of the Public Sphere: An Inquiry into a Category of Bourgeois Society,* translated by Thomas Burger. Cambridge, MA: MIT Press, 1991.

Jakobson, Roman. "Linguistics and Poetics." In *The Routledge Language and Cultural Theory Reader,* edited by Lucy Burke, Tony Crowley, and Alan Girvin, 334–39. London: Routledge, 2000.

Johnson, Samuel. *The Rambler,* edited by W. J. Bate and Albrecht B. Strauss. Yale Edition of the Works of Samuel Johnson, vol. III. New Haven, CT: Yale University Press, 1969.

Kauffman, Linda S. *Discourses of Desire: Gender, Genre, and Epistolary Fictions.* Ithaca, NY: Cornell University Press, 1986.

Mori, Jennifer. *The Culture of Diplomacy: Britain in Europe, c. 1750–1830.* Manchester, UK: Manchester University Press, 2010.

Perry, Ruth. *Women, Letters, and the Novel.* New York: AMS Press, 1980.

The Preceptor: Containing a General Course of Education. London, 1758.
The Royal Letter Writer or Every Lady's Own Secretary. London, 1793.
Towse, Clive. "Conway, Henry Seymour (1719–1795)." In *Oxford Dictionary of National Biography.* Oxford: Oxford University Press, 2004. https://doi.org/10.1093/ref:odnb/6122.
Whyman, Susan. *The Pen and the People: English Letter Writers, 1660–1800.* Oxford: Oxford University Press, 2009.

Bookmaking and Archiving in Dorothy Wordsworth's Notebooks

MICHELLE LEVY

Aᴄᴄᴏʀᴅɪɴɢ ᴛᴏ Mark Bland, "Manuscripts are always witnesses to something other than the texts they preserve," and as artifacts that specially encode time, they often record their own histories more fully than do printed books.[1] Manuscripts tell histories of their making and use and other stories that print often obscures: of sociability and intimacy; of freedom of expression and censorship; and of the everyday domestic practices that were part of their period's writing culture. This essay explores these alternative histories by examining the blank notebooks that Dorothy Wordsworth filled over a period of four decades. Margaret J. M. Ezell has termed these manuscript documents "invisible books," neglected by scholars largely because of their textual complexity and physical messiness.[2] These books have also been rendered invisible because their readerships have not been well understood: as documents that often were not intended to be printed, they were usually presumed, at least by the early nineteenth century, to have been nearly audienceless. Careful attention to Wordsworth's notebooks challenges these assumptions, allowing a fuller understanding of the visibility and impact of writing that is often misunderstood because of its manuscript status.

One of Wordsworth's best editors and critics, Ernest de Selincourt, has described her as "probably the most remarkable and the most distinguished of English prose writers who never wrote a line for the general public."[3] In his editions and critical writing he advocates for her work to be better known to modern audiences while at the same time perpetuating the belief that her lifetime audiences were limited and her impact was narrow. Many scholars have embraced this view, such that Wordsworth has been characterized as an exemplary journal writer of the period, with journal writing understood as a largely solitary, self-oriented practice. However, many of her best readers—de Selincourt included—have long recognized that she did not write for herself alone. For Susan Levin, her "writing literally exists to serve a community," and for Pamela Woof, "In Dorothy's Notebooks generally we are aware less of solitude than of company, of the presence of one person or of more, of interaction, conversation, both intimate and casual. Her Notebooks preserve more than herself."[4] Yet the assumption remains that Wordsworth's manuscripts were essentially private documents.

Donald Reiman has delineated three categories of modern manuscripts based on their intended audiences: private manuscripts, meant only for the eyes of the writer or perhaps one or two more; confidential manuscripts, intended for a slightly wider but still constrained social audience; and public manuscripts, intended for a broad and indiscriminate readership, usually via print.[5] The belief that much of Wordsworth's writing was intended for one or two readers, at most, exhibits a lack of awareness of the larger middle ground of the sociable, the realm within which much of her writing circulated. This essay undertakes a further examination of her notebooks—the material objects in which her writing, in various genres and modes, is recorded—to determine both the nature and the extent of their sociability and to demonstrate the inseparability of social life from manuscript culture and of manuscript culture from the print realm.

This examination of the materiality of Wordsworth's notebooks also calls attention to many of the distinct affordances of her chosen communications media, handwritten script, and chosen material support, bound blank notebooks. Notebooks not only enabled shared modes of book production, but they also encouraged multimodality, encoded temporality, and facilitated archiving in ways that demand closer examination. We understand, intuitively, that methods of inscription are constrained by the material forms and properties of various tools and surfaces, such as wood, glass, stone, and copper. Opportunities and limitations also present themselves to those who use pen and pencil, scissors and glue, within the pages of a bound notebook. According to Lisa Gitelman, blank books "were for writing, or at least for incremental filling in, filling up."[6] A blank notebook can be contrasted with printed blanks, "the blank dedicatory spaces" found in gift books, receipts, and, later, letterhead, all of which invite handwriting while limiting the possibilities for interaction by demarcating a space in which writing should take place, framing its orientation on the page and prescribing its content.[7] Although Gitelman notes that "most blank books would have worked however modestly to mold, to direct and delimit expression," they offer far more freedom than printed blanks.[8] Blank notebooks invite the incorporation of multiple registers, authors, hands, and genres; they can include original and copied material, drawing and writing, drafting and fair copying. Without rule lines or margins, pages can be turned into surfaces inviting the incorporation of other media, of print and engraving and drawing. Within blank notebooks the norms of the printed codex are not strictly enforced: users frequently begin blank books at both ends, remove pages as required, and rotate the book to write, draw, or paste in multiple directions as serves their needs. Blank notebooks are thus typically sites of multimodality—of drawing and writing but also of cutting, folding, pasting, and sewing.

Fundamentally, as well, a bound notebook can provide an enduring container for material—one that has a far greater likelihood of survival than loose sheets or scraps of paper. As Gitelman writes, the essence of the blank notebook is its "fillability," allowing, as we shall see, its blank spaces and pages to be manipulated for a wide range of purposes.[9] In addition to enabling users to write, draw, and affix items, pages within a notebook allow for material to be stored; loose sheets and pressed flowers, even if not attached to pages, can be held within the notebook form. The blank book thus allows for a double archival function, facilitating the incorporation of both textuality and graphicality via its blank spaces and of extraneous material via its structure of blank pages and binding.

Because it invites handwriting and incorporates artifacts that can accumulate over time, the manuscript notebook records temporality in a way that is markedly different from that of print. Whereas in the mechanized process of print production an entire sheet is printed at once, handwritten words are produced letter by letter, a process of accretion that remains visible to later readers. Print captures and reproduces a text at a static point in time and regularizes textuality through its presentational logic, whereas handwriting can deposit layers of emendation—layers that cannot easily be entirely obliterated and that often, as we shall see in Wordsworth's notebooks, are deliberately retained. Even when handwriting cannot be recovered because of heavy cancellations or because paper has been torn or cut or pasted over, a record of transformation remains, memorializing the process of loss. Its archival function means that documents can be added (and removed) over time, producing a similar accumulation (and loss) of layers. In these ways, the manuscript artifact situates itself in time, a feature that is readily apparent and potentially recoverable to subsequent viewers.

The writing that emerges in Wordsworth's notebooks also forces reassessments of the boundaries between the draft and fair copy and of the romanticization and privileging of the former over the latter that has been central to scholarship on modern manuscripts—that is, those produced in the print era. Contemporary scholars such as Marta Werner celebrate the modern draft manuscript in part because it reflects the originary, creative power of the author. For Werner, a scholar of Emily Dickinson's poetry, the exemplum of modern manuscripts is the draft, not the fair copy. A draft manuscript, she contends, "belongs most essentially to the realm of the private: it offers a living record of 'the writer at grips with his or her own traces' . . . , and, more importantly, documents the 'secret [life] of writing, the back and forth of the text in the process of creating itself.'"[10] For Werner, the draft offers our best glimpse into the life of writing, securing our access to the creative process—one that, at least in Dickinson's case, is almost always solitary.

In Wordsworth's notebooks, however, we find not a single writer but a community of writers and readers, and not a secret scene but a collective one in which texts are almost always socially created and oriented toward an audience. The notebooks produced in the Wordsworth family exhibit a model of shared literary and, indeed, book production, as Dorothy, William, and others shared notebooks and worked in conjunction with one another. The notebooks also reveal traces of the practices that surround and support writing, from reading to copying, drawing, and scribbling. Wordsworth's notebooks destroy the illusion that literary creation occurs only within a sacred and private space, as a result of the undivided concentration of an individual writer. The line between drafts and fair copies blurs, as fair copies are transformed into drafts and drafts, into fair copies. The value of the fair copy also comes into focus, to Wordsworth personally and to her wider literary community, as we find evidence that her fair copies were beloved as instruments of friendship and sources of beauty, worthy of preservation and ornamentation.

Most of Wordsworth's notebooks are held by the Wordsworth Trust in Grasmere, where (or nearby to where) they were written and she lived from 1800 until her death in 1855, with her brother and his family. Although this archive contains some loose sheets, mostly in the form of letters and some separate copies of various works, the vast majority of her writing that survives was collected in notebooks. A careful study of the notebooks enables us to view her varying practices and how the material support of the blank notebook allowed for the neat and the untidy, the orderly and the chaotic, the draft and the fair copy, to exist side by side. Intentionality is layered and complex, as within a single notebook she can write for herself, write for others, and write for publication. At once, her notebooks partake in the professional practices of her brother and the domestic practices of their household and social circle, with the boundaries between the two realms emphatically blurred.

Dorothy Wordsworth's Manuscript Notebooks

Although Wordsworth's address to a domestic audience has long been recognized by her editors and closest readers, her supposed absence from the print record has been a lingering source of discomfort for many of the feminist scholars who have celebrated her achievements as a writer.[11] Susan Levin exemplifies these tensions: one of the scholars primarily responsible for recovering and promoting Wordsworth's writing, she has also characterized it as "weirdly idiosyncratic" and as failing to "engage the world in the usual manner," and Wordsworth as "constantly denigrat[ing] herself and her talent," a "process [that] reflects [her] guilt and torment."[12] Summarizing Wordsworth's current reception, Patricia Comitini similarly observes that "whether characterizing her as a domestic subject, novice writer or helpmate, scholarship has focused primarily on her failure to realize herself, develop her talent, or establish her own home."[13] What these understandings share, at least in part, is the predominant scholarly assumption that print constitutes the appropriate means for disseminating works of literary merit. This approach ignores what Ezell has demonstrated so persuasively in relation to early modern female writers—that they had compelling reasons for circulating literature in handwritten, as opposed to printed, form.[14] With Wordsworth we find that these reasons persist, such that her use of manuscript circulation should be understood as an option rather than a limit, an opportunity instead of a failure. Furthermore, by underestimating both the extent and the influence of manuscript circulation, we continue to view

Wordsworth's use of manuscript as a failure rather than a choice, and a choice that provided her with a broad scope for literary activity, prestige, and recognition.

By returning to the physical notebooks in which her writing was both produced and disseminated, we can appreciate her writing as neither idiosyncratic nor frustrated but, rather, as participating in long-standing traditions of manuscript culture. My argument extends even further to make the claim that, in our attempts to slot Wordsworth's writing (and her notebooks) within generic or aesthetic categories believed to be intrinsic to either print or manuscript, we fail to give due attention to its (their) embeddedness within complicated material and social practices. Her habits of composing, collecting, copying, sharing, and reading—activities that she almost always engaged in with others—were continuous with long-established habits of manuscript culture that extended back generations. These practices inevitably, however, intersected with print, and this intermingling is observable in every aspect of domestic bookmaking within the Wordsworth household, as family labor was pooled in the production of both public and social writing. Thus, within the notebooks we find various readerships imagined, for which the separate categories of private, social, and public are often inadequate.

This essay adopts Rachel Feder's call for an "archival reading" of Wordsworth as a means of rematerializing her writing. When we read her journal entries, edited, excised, corrected, and otherwise prepared for print, we encounter editorial creations, distinct products of a modern print consciousness. As Feder notes, Wordsworth's writings "become denatured and dematerialized when removed from the textual corpus that they and their implied authors inhabit."[15] Nevertheless, unlike Feder, who positions Wordsworth as seeking to "transcend, ironize, and imitate print culture," my aim is to resituate Wordsworth's manuscripts within the material and social realm in which her writing was produced and circulated, one in which script and print are in dialogue and not necessarily in tension.[16] In my view, the seemingly experimental or idiosyncratic forms her writing takes, in terms of their multimodal and temporal play, and her tolerance for indeterminacy owe more to her ongoing adaptation of manuscript practices than to any deliberate or even unintentional resistance to print norms and conventions.[17]

The notebooks record acts of creation and archiving, of drafting but also of revising and recopying; as Woof observes, the notebooks are "for practising expression as well as for recording" and "for preservation."[18]

They manifest a suite of activities that surround creation—the reading, copying, scribbling, conversing, and collecting out of which writing is born. In this regard, the categorization of her notebooks as "commonplace books" and their contents as "journals" or "travel narratives" masks the more complex and imbricated writing practices that take place on their pages. Wordsworth's status as a manuscript author who wrote for herself and her brother has been cemented by the *Grasmere Journals*, which are usually treated as the pinnacle of her literary achievement: excerpts from Wordsworth's *Grasmere Journals* were the first text by a woman of the Romantic period to be included in the *Norton Anthology of English Literature* (in the third edition of 1974).[19] The editing of the journals to present an unbroken record of Wordsworth's affective life and perspicacious observations on her natural surroundings further reinforces ideas about the essential privacy and inwardness of manuscript culture.

An examination of the notebooks from which the *Grasmere Journals* have been constructed tells a different story. To begin, the journal entries are taken not from a single notebook, but from a series of four (Wordsworth Trust DCMS 20, 25, 19, and 31), which are intermingled with heterogeneous material that upsets received understanding of the journals as a sequential narrative of her feelings and observations.[20] The first three inexpensive, store-bought paperbound notebooks—DCMS 20, 25, and 19—were first used in Germany during the winter of 1798–99. In addition to the journal entries from Grasmere, written between 1800 and 1803, the notebooks include material from this earlier visit to Germany, consisting of notes, accounts, fragments of essays and verse by William Wordsworth in his own hand, and other miscellaneous items. These notebooks were therefore communal, used by Dorothy and her brother over a period of several years, for a variety of purposes. As Woof speculates, Wordsworth likely returned to these notebooks in 1800, realizing that there were many empty and hence unused pages (a necessary act of thrift in an age when paper was an expensive commodity). This practice of using a notebook for multiple purposes continues in the fourth notebook, DCMS 31, which does not have material originating in the visit to Germany but does include drafts of William's poetry. In addition, the so-called Rydal Journals (largely unpublished today), dating from 1824 to 1835, are contained within fifteen notebooks that are similarly interspersed with other material. The *Grasmere Journals* are, however, always presented without this other material, creating an impression of generic integrity that the notebooks do not bear out.

Attention to the physical notebooks contradicts other misperceptions. When regularized for presentation in print, and even more so when edited and selected for anthologies, the journal entries appear to conform to the model of modern manuscripts described by contemporary scholars, as drafts firmly situated with the private sphere. But a closer examination challenges some of these assumptions of privacy. Although often written in haste, the journals are not drafts: there are few corrections and revisions except those made in the first moment of writing, and there is no evidence in the journals or elsewhere that she intended to rework the material. Nor, of course, are they fair copies, being neither fair nor copied from any previous document. Further, though punctuated by moments of intense feeling, during Wordsworth's lifetime the journal entries did not, per Werner, "belong to the realm of the private," as she anticipated that they would be read and used by others. Indeed, her first entry, of May 14, 1800, explains that she began her journal during one her brother's absences, "because I shall give Wm. pleasure by it when he comes home again."[21] Thereafter, she kept her journals to be read and used by William and others within the family. She also kept them to organize her thoughts and observations and as a record of everyday life—of weather, chores, walks, visitors, food, reading, and letters received and sent.

Wordsworth preserved the notebooks for more than five decades, and near the end of her life, she (or someone within the family with authority to show them, such as Mary Wordsworth) allowed for substantial excerpts (of about ten printed pages) to be included in *Memoirs of William Wordsworth*, published by the poet's nephew in 1851. As Mary Ellen Bellanca has shown, these extracts, along with substantial selections from Wordsworth's *Recollections of a Tour Made in Scotland*, were sufficient to establish a considerable public reputation for her during the second half of the nineteenth century.[22] The scholarly failure to recognize Wordsworth's standing as an author whose writing circulated in both manuscript and print during her lifetime stems at least in part from the assumption that she did not write for the public and hence that her writing could not be widely known. It reinforces the belief that there was a sharp divide between manuscript and print, a belief that is further eroded by the understanding that, in fact, several of Wordsworth's poems and many excerpts of her prose narratives were printed in her lifetime, in her brother's poetic works and in other collections.[23]

At the same time, Wordsworth's editors have contributed to the understanding of her journals as reflecting a private sanctuary, saturated by interiority. Her late Victorian editor, William Knight, fomented this view in his published edition of the *Grasmere Journals* (first printed in 1897) by removing references to illness and bodily functions; to housework such as baking, laundry, and gardening, discussion of which constitutes a large portion of the notebooks; and to her unseemly though penetrating observations about drunken priests and battered wives.[24] In this way, Wordsworth's writing is stripped of both the social and the material conditions in which she lived. The result, abetted by editors of modern anthologies who excerpt only short entries, sometimes based on Knight's expurgated edition, accentuates Wordsworth's reputation as, in effect, a Romantic poet, much like Percy Shelley's "nightingale, who sits in darkness and sings to cheer its own solitude with sweet sounds."

The remediation of Wordsworth's journals into print and their entry into the canon, as it were, perpetuates misunderstandings about her writing and, more broadly, about literary manuscript culture of the late eighteenth and early nineteenth centuries. Returning to the journals, within their notebooks we find a wider range of imagined readerships and a different implied relation to the print realm. We also find a wider range of textual models, for which notions of fixity, inherited from print, are largely inapplicable. As we have seen, however, Wordsworth's journal entries both record and embody daily habits—an interweaving of literary, domestic, and social practices that were highly valued by the Wordsworths and their wider community. A careful examination of DCMS 120 enables a richer understanding of Wordsworth's writing practices, and the high esteem in which her writing was held.[25]

Wordsworth's Commonplace Book

DCMS 120 accentuates Wordsworth's use of the blank notebook as a space for drafting, collecting, and preserving heterogeneous material. Although cataloged as a "commonplace book," the notebook offers only a modest, and in no way a systematized, account of her reading. Of sturdier construction than DCMS 19 and some of the other notebooks she used for her journals, this notebook served an archival function in several respects, one of which was to compile material she read and copied. She also used it to collect both drafts and fair copies of nearly all of her poems, some written in her hand and some copied by others. She included poetry and prose written by others, also in a variety of forms. She collected this material both through the act of directly copying onto pages in the notebook and by pasting loose sheets into the notebook pages.

The notebook's label survives to provide details about where it was purchased: in Boulogne Sur Mer at a bookseller and binder known as Griset Fils Ainé. In November 1820, the Wordsworths spent ten days in Boulogne, a town situated at one of the narrowest crossings of the English Channel and thus one that catered to English tourists. They were stationed there after their ship ran aground on the first attempt at the crossing, an incident that is perhaps best known for William Wordsworth's unchivalrously stripping off his clothes to save himself, "thinking," in Dorothy Wordsworth's words, "it would be impossible to save his wife and me."[26] Stranded for many days before attempting another crossing, Wordsworth purchased a notebook that would be filled, in more ways than one, for at least the next sixteen years. Part workbook for her verse, part poetic miscellany, part commonplace book, and part scrapbook, the notebook embodies what Ezell terms "messy" manuscript volumes, domestic literary artifacts that have been largely invisible to modern scholars precisely because of their refusal to conform to print norms.

DCMS 120 defies contemporary scholarly expectations in numerous ways: it starts at each end, a feature that Ezell describes as "a doubling of the matter in an inverted format" resulting in "a practice alien to print technology ... and disorienting for modern readers."[27] As with all draft manuscripts, corrections, revisions, and errors remain visibly apparent in layers, as Wordsworth worked and reworked her own poetry. Time is thus encoded on the pages in a way that is distinctive to the scribal medium. The white space within the manuscript is also unevenly distributed, with some pages left entirely blank, some barely written on, and others crammed with writing; there are pages cut or torn or patched, all contributing to a lack of uniformity that is indicative of the book's being filled over time, without a predetermined plan. Text appears multidirectionally and cross-written in the notebook; there are sheets pasted in horizontally that must be folded out; and the entire book must be manipulated and rotated throughout for proper reading. There are no navigational tools—no tables of contents, indices, signatures, attributions, or page numbers—and very few titles. Legibility, regularity, and reusability are all compromised.

In many ways, the notebook is impenetrable to us—illegible in places, with missing pages, unknown hands, and unidentified scraps copied and clipped from print and manuscript sources. It is a book without a narrative, without coherence. Nevertheless, DCMS 120 had profound importance to Wordsworth. In it she collects most of her own poetry, and we observe her returning to her poems years later, rereading, revising, and recopying them. She includes fair copies of her poems made by others, demonstrating that her poetry (like the notebook itself) was shared with a group. She annotates her poems with emphatic markings in pencil—a preferred writing tool later in life—adding another stratum to their textual archeology. The tolerance of variation and, indeed, messiness—the willingness to allow for corrections to remain visible, for draft and fair copies to remain side by side—enables a revisiting of past versions and, with them, of past selves, very much a Wordsworthian theme at the core of Wordsworth's, as well as her brother's, poetics. Wordsworth also includes poetry and prose by others, thus placing the contents within, to borrow Jon Mee's memorable phrase, a conversable world.[28]

Stephen Gill has commented on William Wordsworth's "creative revisiting"—in particular, the "poet's continual return not to his past but to his past in past writing." A similar process seems to be at work in DCMS 120, as well as in the other notebooks.[29] Sally Bushell, also addressing William Wordsworth's manuscripts, argues that we should avoid taking a "hermeneutic approach to draft materials, applying traditional methods of interpretation to subtle changes of wording over time," as this approach "tends to produce a teleological view of ever-improving communication, with publication as the point of completion and validation."[30] Such a strategy is particularly inappropriate for Dorothy Wordsworth, who did not often revise with publication in mind, although, like her brother, she constantly revised and wrote for an audience, often a considerable one.

DCMS 120 thus demands a different reading strategy from that to which we are acculturated by print alone, for the writing within its pages frustrates any attempt to impose a telos of textual improvement. The notebook contains nearly all of Wordsworth's original verse, but she frequently allows for the coexistence of differing versions of the same poem, thereby embedding textual multiplicity, an effect that is apparent even within individual poems. In these poems, Wordsworth writes queries to herself as she questions whether to make a change without fixing on a decision. For example, in "Grasmere—A Fragment" she includes marginal and interlinear penciled revisions that are at variance with each other, without deciding on any particular reading (see fig. 1).[31] The two line choices—"And lodged in many a sheltered chink" and "There, too,

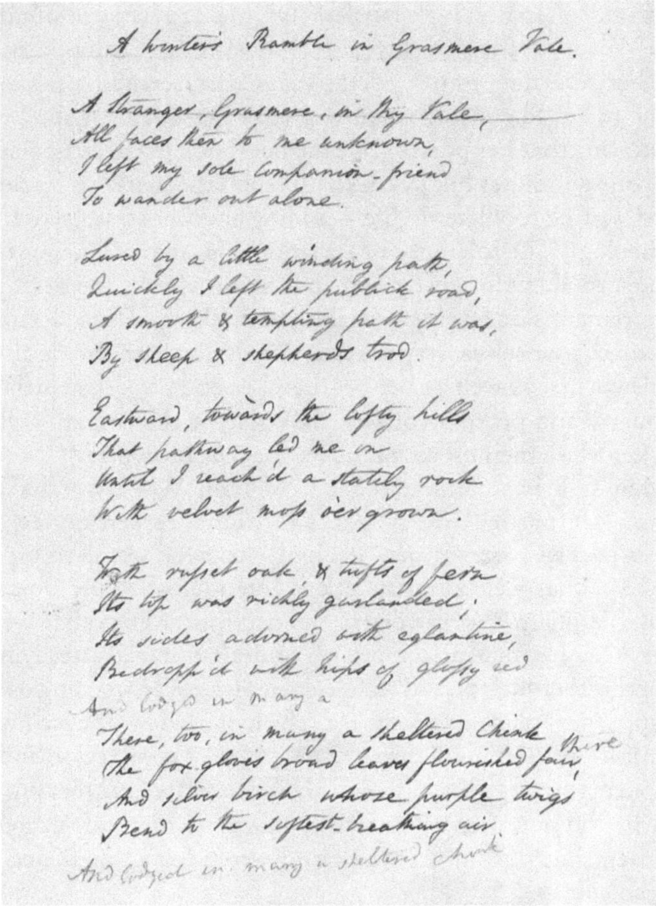
A Winter's Ramble in Grasmere Vale.

A Stranger, Grasmere, in thy Vale,
All faces then to me unknown,
I left my sole companion-friend
To wander out alone.

Lured by a little winding path,
Quickly I left the publick road,
A smooth & tempting path it was,
By sheep & shepherds trod.

Eastward, towards the lofty hills
That pathway led me on
Until I reach'd a stately rock
With velvet moss o'er grown.

With russet oak, & tufts of fern
Its top was richly garlanded;
Its sides adorned with eglantine,
Bedropp'd with hips of glossy red
And lodged in many a
There, too, in many a sheltered Chink
The fox-gloves broad leaves flourished fair, there
And silver birch whose purple twigs
Bend to the softest-breathing air
And lodged in many a sheltered chink

FIGURE 1. Dorothy Wordsworth's penciled-in revisions to "Grasmere—A Fragment." (DCMS 120.15, f. 20; Wordsworth Trust, Dove Cottage, Cumbria)

in many a sheltered chink"—hover spectrally around the poem. Similar examples abound in copies of her verse throughout the notebook. By permitting different iterations of her poems to rest side by side, Wordsworth demonstrates a "versioning" approach to textuality, retaining and archiving different versions of the same text. She also participates in what Sharon Cameron has identified as Emily Dickinson's refusal to choose between variants. Both Dickinson's and Wordsworth's manuscripts evince "the difficulty of enforcing a limit," with completion being "another limit extended temporally as well as spatially by the proliferation of the variants."[32]

Another example of Wordsworth's tolerance for not choosing can be found in the multiple copies of individual poems within the commonplace book. In figure 2, we see the final four stanzas of a draft of "Lines Intended for My Niece's Album" on the verso, followed by a tipped-in fair copy of the same poem, renamed "To Dora Wordsworth," in Sara Hutchinson's hand.[33] Many draft manuscripts similarly capture a form of Microsoft Word's "Track Changes" function, as layers of revision accumulate on top of each other. These multiple versions of individual poems, marked with pen and pencil and overwritten with pasted additions, are attentive to various audiences. Wordsworth's conception of textuality is therefore not teleological but "capable of being in uncertainties, mysteries, doubts," to quote John Keats's famous concept of negative capability.[34]

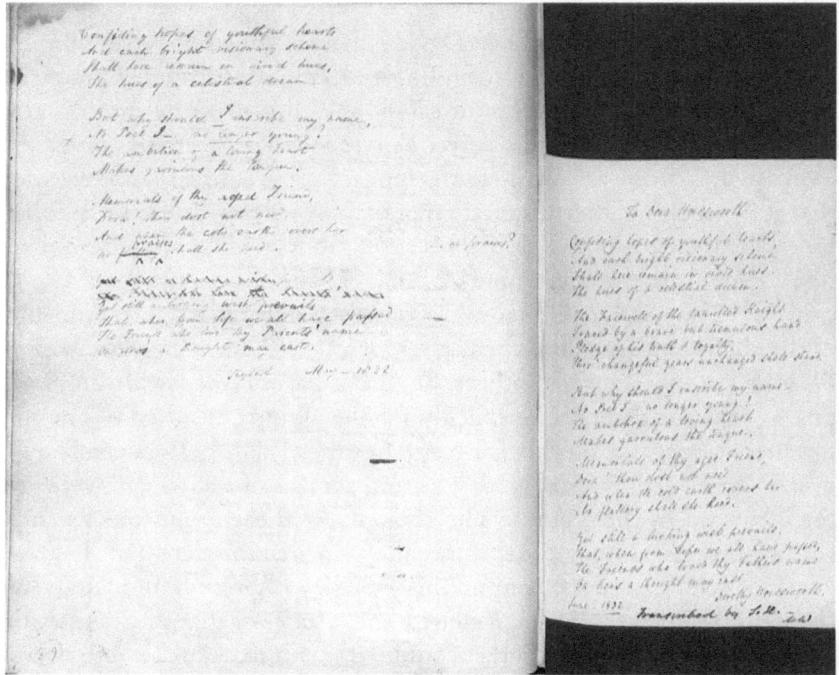

FIGURE 2. Multiple versions of the same poem in Wordsworth's commonplace book: "Lines Intended for My Niece's Album" (verso) and "To Dora Wordsworth" (tipped in, in Sara Hutchinson's hand). (DCMS 120.23, f. 28ᵛ, and DCMS 120.24, inserted between f. 28 and f. 29; Wordsworth Trust, Dove Cottage, Cumbria)

While Wordsworth's manuscripts rebut our understanding of the handwritten draft as a space of unfolding authorial genius, they also undermine the myth of solitary creation. Wordsworth began at one end of DCMS 120 with an act of oral transcription, headed "26 June 1830—Sunday Evening—Dictated by William Wordsworth to D. Wordsworth Pen."[35] Two years later she recopied the poem fair, explicitly memorializing the act of recopying by annotating the poem, "Recopied August 2nd 1832."[36] The inscriptions to both copies join brother and sister together in shared acts of textual production, of listening and recording, and of revising and recopying. The social circle extends beyond brother and sister, as Wordsworth uses the notebook to gather together material written, copied, and drawn by others. In the fair copy of "To Dora Wordsworth" written by Sara Hutchinson, for example, the words "Transcribed by S. H." appear to have been added subsequently, in a different hand, in an act possibly motivated by a desire to acknowledge and mark the affective labor of copying (see fig. 2).

DCMS 120 also reflects what David Allan has shown to be the vibrant commonplace culture of Georgian England, embodying a set of practices that transform into the album or scrapbook culture of the early Victorian period.[37] The notebook serves as a repository for items copied by Wordsworth from various manuscript and print sources, another way that it is used to gather disparate material. Wordsworth even copies an excerpt from her friend Mary Barker's commonplace book (which in turn had copied from the commonplace book of "Isabella, Countess of Glencairn").[38] Thus, in DCMS 120 we witness the sharing and intermingling of the commonplace books themselves, practices that strongly imply that DCMS 120 was shown to others. On other pages, Wordsworth drafted poems that she composed explicitly for the albums of others—one for her niece Dora, and another for Edith Southey.[39] For both poems, however, Wordsworth instructed that several stanzas of each poem were *not* for inclusion in the albums. The reasons for these exclusions are not readily obvious, although such annotations do demonstrate that she (like Mary Barker) shared her commonplace book with friends and family; at the same time, her exclusion of some stanzas suggests that she was able to exercise control over what copies could be taken and circulated by others.

Finally, markings in the notebook provide evidence of Wordsworth's own rereading, a process possibly but not necessarily accompanied by rewriting. In her study of William Wordsworth's manuscripts, Bushell identifies at least three different temporalities of rereading: immediate, short term, and long term, with the long term being motivated "out of pleasure (a desire to read [or rewrite] a work again), as an act of reassurance (a return to a familiar, much-loved text), [or] as an act of self-recovery (re-visiting our own past selves through a text read at an earlier time)."[40] In the following examples, we see how all three motivations are bound together, as Wordsworth rereads to resituate herself within the temporal frame of a specific poem. In penciled additions to "Lines Intended for My Niece's Album," she adds underlining to the phrase "no longer young" to provide emphasis or mark the additional passage of time since the poem was originally written, or both.[41] She also uses penciled marginal notes to adjust the pronouns in the stanza: in the poem, she refers to herself as "*thy* aged friend" and to the time "when the cold earth covers *her*." In her markings—I would not call them revisions—she returns the poem to the more intimate, if morbid, first person, imagining the moment when "the cold earth covers *me*." With these penciled additions demarcating acts of rereading as opposed to revision, Wordsworth directly invokes her mortality to repersonalize the poem. In a final example from this notebook, she uses pencil annotation as a means of echoing her own voice in the poems. In "Irregular Stanzas: Holiday at Gwerndovennant" she recopies, twice, the expression "Trust me," from the first line, once again emphasizing the passage of time: that "Too soon your hearts shall own / The past is all that is your own."[42] Sharon Cameron observes of Dickinson's variants that many appear to place her both within and "outside the ostensible boundaries of the poem."[43] Wordsworth occupies the same double or multiple positionality, as an older self encircles a younger one in poems that themselves thematize the passage of time.

 The physical notebook provides what Jacques Derrida has termed a "structure of archivization," allowing Wordsworth to collect and conserve most of her original poetry, in multiple versions and in various states, alongside other material that held meaning for her.[44] According to Jared Curtis, "[William] Wordsworth and his amanuenses were 'hoarders,' savers of paper generally, of notebooks, both commercial and handmade, and of loose manuscripts of the poet's writings, and were reluctant to let it escape from their hands even after a work they contained had been published."[45] Evidence of this recycling of texts and scraps of paper can be found in DCMS 120, an excellent repository both for notes and scraps. The bound notebooks Wordsworth made or bought provided an ideal material support for her to revisit her poems, not only for the purpose of correcting, improving, or sharing them but also to experience them anew.

She also collected them with other material, investing them with new contextual meanings. DCMS 120 reveals the sociable and bookmaking practices inherent in the Wordsworths' writing lives, as Dorothy transcribed both her own and others' writing and invited others to transcribe and read her writing.

The scene of writing that emerges within Wordsworth's commonplace book is not that of the solitary genius, or even the solitary tinkerer, as it is apparent that many others were invited into the pages of her notebook as authors, transcribers, and readers. Attention to the complexity and range of handwritten forms within a single notebook undermines the attempt to separate draft from fair copy and to distinguish the intimate scene of writing from the sociable scene of both creation and dissemination. A holistic approach to the notebook also helps us to see the inadequacy of existing generic categories (journal, commonplace book) for manuscript documents.

Wordsworth's Tour Notebooks

Wordsworth's travel notebooks, though more generically stable than DCMS 120, provide an even more fully realized example of the sociability inherent in her bookmaking processes, as well as of the interactivity between the cultures of manuscript and print. For Ernest de Selincourt, Wordsworth's *Recollections of a Tour Made in Scotland* holds "the supreme place ... among Dorothy's writing," a position established in part "by the existence of no less than five [complete] manuscripts."[46] Based on a six-week, 663-mile journey through the Scottish Lowlands and Highlands undertaken from August to September 1803, the first extant manuscript (DCMS 50) is a two-volume transcript made by her friend Catherine Clarkson, which was taken from an original that has not survived. This copy, bound in green leather with custom titles, was highly cherished. Clarkson explained, in a note affixed to the end of her two-volume, 250-page transcription:

> This copy of my beloved friend's journal was begun at Grasmere the beginning of September and finished at Patterdale this day (the 1st of November 1805). When I began the work I scarcely indulged the hope of finishing it myself, my health being so indifferent that every little exertion of mind or body fatigued me exceedingly; but instead of a difficult task I have found it the easiest and pleasantest employment

that I have ever engaged in; and though the possession of such a treasure makes me very happy, yet I am sincerely sorry that my work is ended.... C.C.⁴⁷

Clarkson's inclusion of this note provides a simultaneous record of the act of copying and the pleasure she took in the activity. Neither tedious nor menial, transcription for Clarkson was deeply meaningful, even curative. In both this and a subsequent copy, Clarkson involved others in the creation of the book. Her husband, Thomas Clarkson, drew the title page, and George Hutchinson, Mary Wordsworth's brother, drew the half-titles on this page and throughout the volumes.

Wordsworth created an additional copy of *Recollections* (DCMS 55 MS. C i]), as did Sarah Hutchinson (DCMS 55 MS. C ii]). Both are illustrated with elaborate titles and half-titles by George Hutchinson (see fig. 3). The title page to DCMS 55 MS. C i) also features Samuel Taylor Coleridge's inscription, demonstrating that the book was copied for and given to him. In this way, the physical acts of copying, illustrating, inscribing, and gift giving drew women *and* men into the process of domestic bookmaking, as together they produced a book that Wordsworth "addressed to her friends," written for "a few ... who, it seemed, ought to have been with us."⁴⁸ The use of blank notebooks to create beautiful books that rival what was possible in letterpress and engraving further destabilizes the distinction between the two copying technologies, demonstrating how the entire communication circuit could be, as it were, domesticated.⁴⁹

Over the next two decades, Wordsworth continued to work on *Recollections*, producing two additional copies, DCMS 54 and DCMS 97. DCMS 54 began as a fair copy taken from Clarkson's copy, with the addition of tables of contents and hand-drawn maps.⁵⁰ Wordsworth's additions provide navigational tools that have both a practical purpose—to orient the readers of her narrative—and an aesthetic one, as the maps interrupt blocks of text while also uniting them within a single medium: the same hand both writes and draws. Sometime in 1822, however, about seventeen years later, Wordsworth returned to this copy of *Recollections*, transforming the fair copy into a draft through revision. While the double archival structure of the blank book therefore allows for different modes of textuality to emerge, it also challenges the binary between drafts and fair copies, showing how easily fair copies could be transformed into drafts. DCMS 54 also bears an inscription: "Dora Wordsworth, from her aff[ectiona]te Father J Wordsworth. Nov 1 1866." The inscription marks

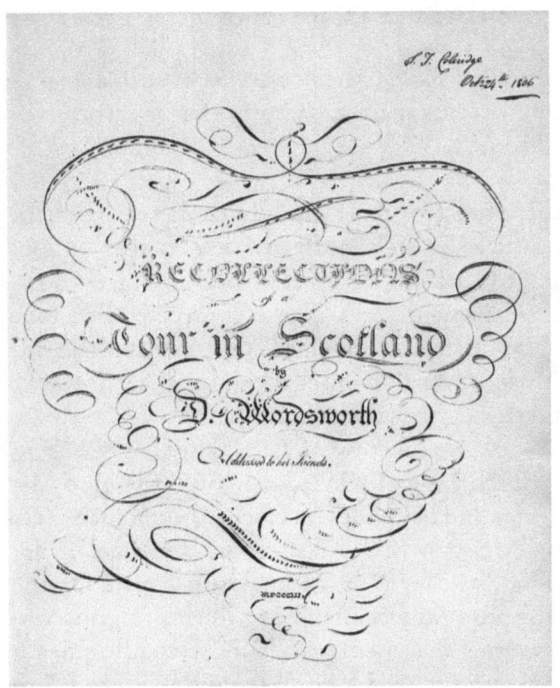

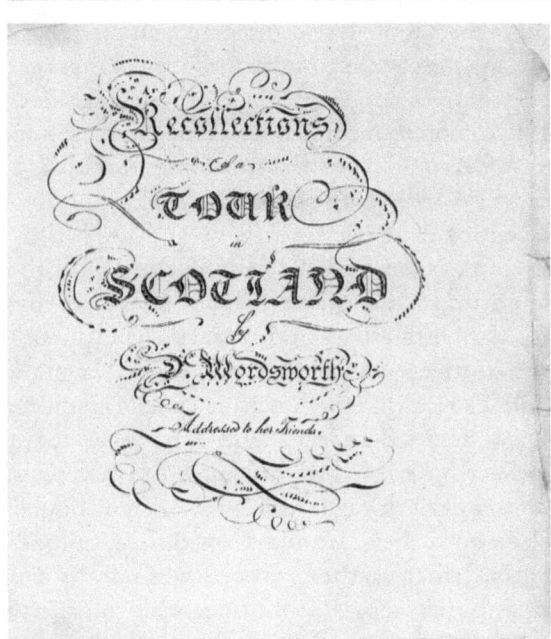

FIGURE 3. Two copies of Wordsworth's *Recollections of a Tour in Scotland*, with illustrated title pages by George Hutchinson. (*Dorothy Wordsworth's Scotch Tour*, DCMS 55 MS. C i) and DCMS 55 MS. C ii), in Sara Hutchinson's hand; Wordsworth Trust, Dove Cottage, Cumbria)

an intergenerational example of "regifting," as the book was passed down from the poet's eldest son (John) to his daughter more than sixty years after the narrative was first composed.

The image in figure 4 displays all of the copies of *Recollections* discussed earlier. The variability in the physical containers—in the spines and binding and size of the books—demonstrates the range of materials with which Wordsworth worked. Figure 5 shows the inside of one of four additional handmade packages dating from about 1821, in which Wordsworth revised her *Recollections* yet again, apparently with a view to print publication (DCMS 97). Here, Wordsworth created a paper wrapper, with loose sheets and gatherings included for each of the four volumes, a kind of deconstructed notebook. As can be seen, the materiality of these books ranges greatly—from flimsy, handmade folders containing sheets and gatherings to purpose-bound leather books with customized labels and linen covers. The capaciousness of the notebook form is evident; some pages reflect what Mark Bland has called the "presentational language of print," while others reveal the workshop of textual transformation.[51] These notebooks were shared labors of love. Yet it is wrong to assume they existed strictly within a domestic economy. At various moments, Wordsworth was encouraged to contemplate—and appears to have contemplated—publication for *Recollections*.

FIGURE 4. Various copies of *Recollections of a Tour in Scotland*. (From top to bottom: DCMS 55 MS. C ii), 1803, 1806; DCMS 55 MS. C i), 1803, 1806; DCMS 54, 1805–1806, 1822; DCMS 50, 1803; Wordsworth Trust, Dove Cottage, Cumbria)

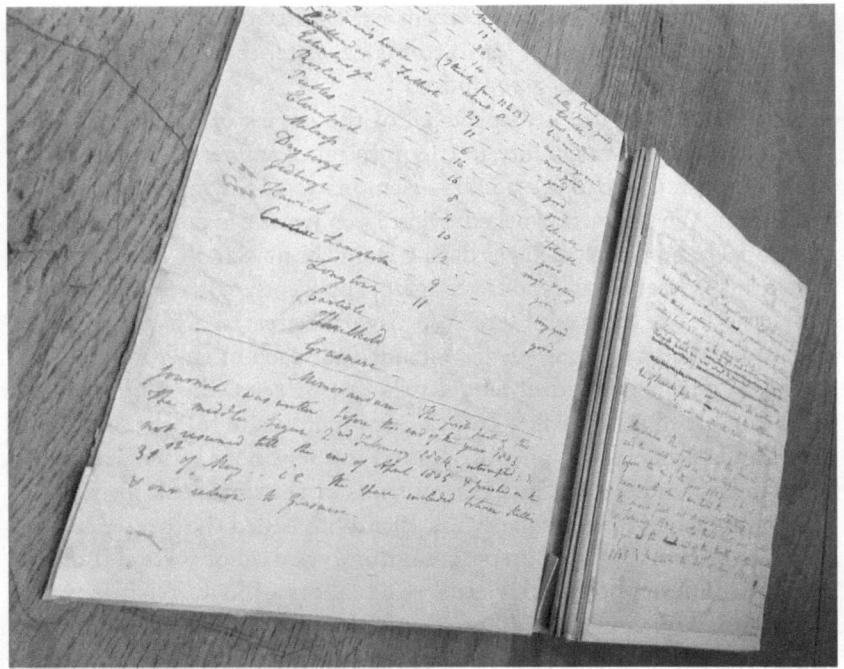

FIGURE 5. Opening of one of four handmade collections of gatherings and loose sheets containing *Recollections of a Tour in Scotland*. (DCMS 97.1; Wordsworth Trust, Dove Cottage, Cumbria)

A subsequent work, Wordsworth's *Journal of a Tour of the Continent* (DCMS 90), originated in a visit to Europe in 1820 (when the DCMS 120 notebook discussed earlier was purchased). Unlike *Recollections* and unusually for her, this text survives only in one fair copy. This notebook, like the others, demonstrates the collaborative processes of bookmaking; it represents what is probably the most lavishly prepared of all of her manuscripts. Wordsworth's fair copy manuscript of the tour is interleaved with tipped-in prints, bought for her by her friend Henry Crabb Robinson, who also annotated the manuscript. As she did not have the prints when drafting her manuscript, the fair copy appears to have been rebound with these images, which she carefully selected to illustrate various scenes. The print in figure 6 provides one example: on the verso is her description of the Cathedral of St. Michael and St. Gudula in Brussels and her lament that it "has been most unworthily treated.—Mean shops and dwelling places being built up against its very walls"; on the recto is the print (supplied by Robinson) representing these "mean" structures.[52] This page and the entire notebook demonstrate how script can emulate print conventions, with the neatness of Wordsworth's handwriting borrowing the "principal advantages of type (its legibility, regularity, and reusability)."[53] She also uses page numbers, running heads, and catchwords to create a manuscript page that closely echoes the print conventions of the day.

At the same time, Wordsworth's manuscript page cuts against the fixity of print. Just as she incorporated print via extra-illustration, she preserved within the notebook a record of how the writing had changed over time. At one point, she included a note correcting the original information about the Palace at Bruchsal, beginning, "I have since learned."[54] Rather than simply correcting the information in making a fair copy, she preserved the earlier (and erroneous) information. This willingness to acknowledge the evolution of a text is one of the ways in which the logic of manuscript differs from that of print. An analogy would be to a printer including both errors and their corrections in a new edition. More akin

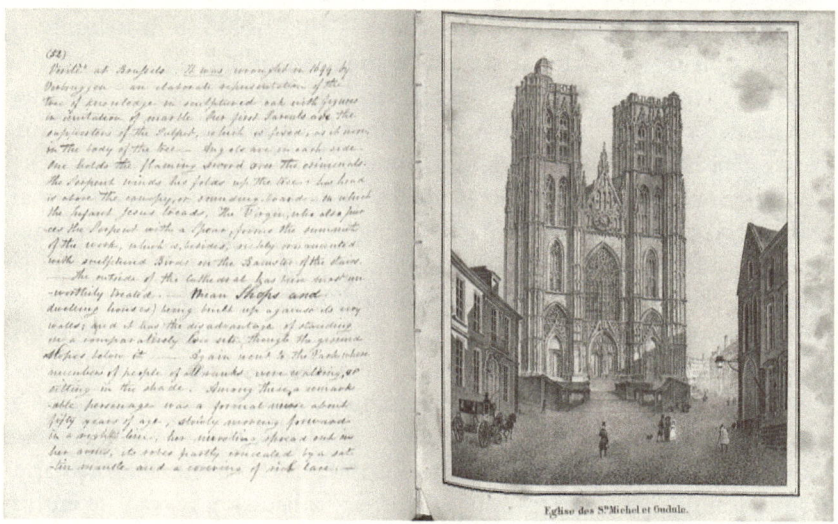

FIGURE 6. Wordsworth's description of the Cathedral of St. Michael and St. Gudula in Brussels, with a tipped-in print of the cathedral. (*Dorothy Wordsworth's Journal of a Tour on the Continent*, DCMS 90, 52–53; Wordsworth Trust, Dove Cottage, Cumbria)

to the blogging convention of showing strikethrough, which preserves the original text that has now been overwritten, Wordsworth elected to retain these textual layers and make them visible to her readers.

Textual indeterminacy was, in fact, a signal feature of both of the Wordsworths' working methods. As *The Excursion* went to press in 1814, Dorothy Wordsworth expressed great relief. "We are all most thankful," she wrote, "that William has brought his mind to consent to printing so much of this work; for the MSS. were in such a state that, if it had pleased Heaven to take him from this world, they would have been almost useless."[55] Wordsworth's writing, like her brother's, inhabited this world of textual flux, though it would be manifestly unfair to say that the state of her manuscripts renders them "almost useless." In her notebooks we find time encoded through her use of alternatives both within and between individual copies of the same work. She also used the physical space of the notebooks to extend a spatial limit through insertions and tipped-in illustrations that thicken her books.

Wordsworth's notebooks remind us of the capaciousness of the notebook form: that it can be used to create exquisite presentation-quality volumes that showcase fair copying and illustration, as well as to hold the messier, more disorderly practices of note taking, excerpting, revising, and sketching. The materiality of the codex—the "book" in "notebook"—provides an organizational structure that can be adopted (when one page is written after another in logical sequence) or abandoned as needed (when material is collected in more haphazard fashion), accommodating both linear narrative and random accumulation. Thus, Wordsworth used her notebooks to store polished works; collect miscellaneous material; and perform the work of writing, drafting, revising, copying, reading, and rereading. To make visible this textual and bookmaking labor, we must return to the material notebooks. Scholarly encounters with and uses of Romantic-period manuscripts have tended to reinforce the central importance of the draft, as attention to literary manuscripts of the period has had as its object the study of textual history and the reconstruction of literary genius. *The Cornell Wordsworth* (devoted to the works of William Wordsworth) provides one salient example. In the profusion of manuscript facsimiles that it reproduces, this critical edition reveals its enthusiasm for the draft by offering, as its reading texts, the "earliest complete form" of the poet's works.[56] Although the original plan for the series was to create a set of facsimiles (and transcriptions) of entire notebooks, the editors elected to proceed poem by poem, an editorial approach that, however attentive to the needs of readers, inevitably fails to preserve the integrity of the notebook view and the scene of writing it manifests. If *The Cornell Wordsworth* had proceeded along the lines originally imagined, our understanding of the Wordsworths' writing and bookmaking practices would have been fundamentally altered. As witnesses to scenes of literary production that confound notions of individual genius and reorient understandings of Romantic-era literary culture, the notebooks of Dorothy Wordsworth, as well as those of her contemporaries, warrant our closer attention.

Notes

This essay is reproduced in part from chapter 2 of my monograph, *Literary Manuscript Culture in Romantic Britain*, Edinburgh University Press, 2020.

1. Bland, *A Guide to Early Printed Books and Manuscripts*, 9.
2. Ezell, "Invisible Books," 53–69.
3. Wordsworth, *Journals of Dorothy Wordsworth* (1970), 1:v.
4. Levin, *Dorothy Wordsworth and Romanticism*, 6; Woof, "The Uses of Notebooks," 10.
5. Reiman, *The Study of Modern Manuscripts*, 65.
6. Gitelman, *Paper Knowledge*, 21.
7. Piper, *Dreaming in Books*, 127.
8. Gitelman, *Paper Knowledge*, 22.
9. Ibid, 21.
10. Werner, "Reportless Places," 62.
11. For Dorothy's appearances in print during her lifetime, see my discussion on p. 93.
12. Levin, *Dorothy Wordsworth and Romanticism*, 3–4.
13. Comitini, "More than Half a Poet," 307.
14. Ezell, *Social Authorship and the Advent of Print*.
15. Feder, "The Experimental Dorothy Wordsworth," 543.
16. Ibid., 542.
17. Feder claims that Wordsworth's writing "function[s] as a site of intertextual and generic experimentation": ibid., 541.
18. Woof, "The Uses of Notebooks," 4, 10.
19. Abrams, *Norton Anthology of English Literature*, 2:263–83.
20. These notebooks contain entries for the period May 14, 1800, to January 16, 1803, with a gap, between DCMS 20 and 25, from December 23, 1800, to October 9, 1801: Dorothy Wordsworth, *Dorothy Wordsworth's Grasmere Journals*, DCMS 19, 20, 25, 31, Wordsworth Trust, Grasmere, Cumbria, U.K.

21. Wordsworth, *Journals of Dorothy Wordsworth* (1970), 1:37.
22. See Mary Ellen Bellanca, "After-Life-Writing: Dorothy Wordsworth's Journals in the Memoirs of William Wordsworth," *European Romantic Review* 25, no. 2 (March 2014): 201–18.
23. For a discussion of William's use of his sister's writing (as well as that of Mary Wordsworth and Sara Hutchinson) in his print publications, see Levy, *Family Authorship and Romantic Print Culture*, 123–42, esp. 124–25, 139. Two of Dorothy's prose narratives were also included in various editions of her brother's *Guide to the Lakes*.
24. See Wordsworth, *Journals of Dorothy Wordsworth* (1897). Pamela Woof describes Knight as "a far from reliable textual editor": Woof, "The Uses of Notebooks," 3. For a discussion of Knight's editing practices, see Woof, "The Alfoxden Journal and Its Mysteries."
25. Wordsworth, *Dorothy Wordsworth's Commonplace Book*, DCMS 120, Wordsworth Trust.
26. "My brother, thinking it would be impossible to save his wife and me, had stripped off his coat to be ready to swim": Wordsworth, *Journals of Dorothy Wordsworth* (1970), 2:333–34.
27. Ezell, "Invisible Books," 60.
28. Mee, *Conversable Worlds*.
29. Gill, *Wordsworth's Revisitings*, 10, 12.
30. Bushell, "From *The Ruined Cottage* to *The Excursion*," 75.
31. Dorothy Wordsworth, "Grasmere—A Fragment," DCMS 120.15, Wordsworth Trust, f. 20.
32. Cameron, *Choosing Not Choosing*, 6, 14.
33. Dorothy Wordsworth, "Lines Intended for My Niece's Album," DCMS 120.23, and "To Dora Wordsworth," DCMS 120.24, Wordsworth Trust, f. 28^r, inserted between f. 28 and f. 29.
34. Rollins, *The Letters of John Keats*, 1:193–94.
35. Dorothy Wordsworth, "26th June 1830," DCMS 120.2, Wordsworth Trust, f. 1^r.
36. Ibid, f. 13^v.
37. Allan, *Commonplace Books and Reading in Georgian England*.
38. Dorothy Wordsworth, "Extracts from the Common-place Book of Isabella Countess of Glencairn," DCMS 120.10, Wordsworth Trust, ff. 8^r–11^v. In addition to Mary Barker's commonplace book, Sara Hutchinson curated a poetic miscellany titled "Sara Hutchinson's Poets," Mary Wordsworth produced her own *Tour of the Continent*, and her niece kept a poetic album.
39. Wordsworth, "Lines Intended for My Niece's Album," DCMS 120.23, and "Lines Intended for Edith Southey's Album," DCMS 120.25, Wordsworth Trust, ff. 29^r–31^v.
40. Bushell, "From *The Ruined Cottage* to *The Excursion*," 78.

41. Wordsworth, "Lines Intended for My Niece's Album," DCMS 120.23.
42. Dorothy Wordsworth, "Irregular Stanzas—Holiday at Gwerndovennant—May 1826," DCMS 120.14, Wordsworth Trust, ff. 15ᵛ–18ᵛ.
43. Cameron, *Choosing Not Choosing*, 24.
44. Derrida, *Archive Fever*, 17.
45. Curtis, "The Cornell Wordsworth: A History," 7. This essay was previously posted on the Cornell University Press website, but is currently unavailable.
46. These are DCMS 50, 55 MS. C i), 55 MS. C ii), 54, and 97 (see figs. 4–5).
47. Wordsworth, *Journals of Dorothy Wordsworth* (1970), 1:viii.
48. Dorothy Wordsworth to Catherine Clarkson, January 1806, cited in ibid., 1:vii.
49. For Robert Darnton's theory of the "communication circuit," see Darnton, "What Is the History of Books?" 65–83.
50. Dorothy Wordsworth, *Dorothy Wordsworth's Scotch Tour 1803*, MS. B, DCMS 54, Wordsworth Trust.
51. Bland, *A Guide to Early Printed Books and Manuscripts*, 68.
52. Dorothy Wordsworth, *Dorothy Wordsworth's Journal of a Tour on the Continent*, DCMS 90, Wordsworth Trust, 52–53.
53. Bland, *A Guide to Early Printed Books and Manuscripts*, 118.
54. Wordsworth, *Dorothy Wordsworth's Journal of a Tour on the Continent*, DCMS 90, 2:158.
55. Dorothy Wordsworth to Catherine Clarkson, April 24, [1814], in Knight, *Letters of the Wordsworth Family from 1787 to 1855*, 2:26.
56. Curtis, "The Cornell Wordsworth," 5.

Works Cited

Abrams, M. H., ed. *Norton Anthology of English Literature*, 3d edition, 2 vols. New York: Norton, 1974.

Allan, David. *Commonplace Books and Reading in Georgian England*. Cambridge: Cambridge University Press, 2014.

Bland, Mark. *A Guide to Early Printed Books and Manuscripts*. Malden, MA: Blackwell, 2013.

Bushell, Sally. "From *The Ruined Cottage* to *The Excursion*: Revision as Rereading." *Wordsworth Circle* 45, no. 2 (Spring 2014): 75–83.

Cameron, Sharon. *Choosing Not Choosing: Dickinson's Fascicles*. Chicago: University of Chicago Press, 1992.

Comitini, Patricia. "'More than Half a Poet': Vocational Philanthropy and Dorothy Wordsworth's *Grasmere Journals*." *European Romantic Review* 14 (September 2003): 307–22.

Darnton, Robert. "What Is the History of Books?" *Daedalus* 111, no. 3 (Summer 1982): 65–83.

Derrida, Jacques. *Archive Fever: A Freudian Impression*, translated by Eric Prenowitz. Chicago: University of Chicago Press, 1998.

Ezell, Margaret J. M. "Invisible Books." In *Producing the Eighteenth-Century Book: Writers and Publishers in England, 1650–1800*, edited by Pat Rogers and Laura Runge, 53–69. Newark: University of Delaware Press, 2009.

———. *Social Authorship and the Advent of Print*. Baltimore: Johns Hopkins University Press, 1999.

Feder, Rachel. "The Experimental Dorothy Wordsworth." *Studies in Romanticism* 53, no. 4 (Winter 2014): 541–60.

Gill, Stephen. *Wordsworth's Revisitings*. Oxford: Oxford University Press, 2011.

Gitelman, Lisa. *Paper Knowledge: Toward a Media History of Documents*. Durham, NC: Duke University Press, 2014.

Knight, William, ed. *Letters of the Wordsworth Family from 1787 to 1855*, 3 vols. New York: Haskell House, 1969.

Levin, Susan M. *Dorothy Wordsworth and Romanticism*. New Brunswick, NJ: Rutgers University Press, 1987.

Levy, Michelle. *Family Authorship and Romantic Print Culture*. Basingstoke, U.K.: Palgrave Macmillan, 2008.

Mee, Jon. *Conversable Worlds: Literature, Contention, and Community 1762 to 1830*. Oxford: Oxford University Press, 2011.

Piper, Andrew. *Dreaming in Books: The Making of the Bibliographic Imagination in the Romantic Age*. Chicago: University of Chicago Press, 2009.

Reiman, Donald. *The Study of Modern Manuscripts: Public, Confidential, and Private*. Baltimore: Johns Hopkins University Press, 1993.

Rollins, H. E., ed. *The Letters of John Keats*, 2 vols. Cambridge: Cambridge University Press, 1958.

Werner, Marta L. "'Reportless Places': Facing the Modern Manuscript." *Textual Cultures* 6, no. 2 (2011): 60–83.

Woof, Pamela. "The Alfoxden Journal and Its Mysteries." *Wordsworth Circle* 26, no. 3 (1995): 125–33.

———. "The Uses of Notebooks: From Journal to Album, from Commonplace to Keepsake." *Coleridge Bulletin* 31 (2008): 1–18.

Wordsworth, Dorothy. *Journals of Dorothy Wordsworth*, 2 vols., edited by Ernest de Selincourt. Hamden, CT: Archon, 1970.

———. *Journals of Dorothy Wordsworth*, 2 vols., edited by William Knight. London: Macmillan, 1897.

PART II

The Manuscript-Print Interface

Paratextual Readers
Manuscript Verse in Printed Books of the Long Eighteenth Century

PHILIP S. PALMER

MANUSCRIPT VERSE inscribed in printed volumes is a widespread yet highly diverse phenomenon of early modern book culture. The genre is dominated by rhyming ownership inscriptions, which were perhaps taught in school and tend to follow a set formula that gives the owner's name, country, and city/town, followed by a line of devotional sentiment.[1] Presentation copies of printed books might also contain manuscript verses from an author or gift giver to the recipient. In the case of both gift and ownership inscriptions, verses typically emphasize the book as a piece of private property to be secured or exchanged rather than as a text to be read. There are also scores of examples of rhyming devotional texts and prayers, ribald and jesting verses, and specific subgenres such as the satirical epitaph. Manuscript verse in printed books thus seems to form an individual, self-contained, and idiosyncratic body of material evidence.

But the inspection of thousands of seventeenth- and eighteenth-century books reveals certain forms besides the rhyming inscription and similar subgenres. In this essay I explore one of the more interesting of these forms, manuscript commendatory verse, which consists of handwritten verses about or addressed to authors and frequently inscribed by readers at the front of printed book-copies.[2] Many of these poems address other readers, often in recommendation of the author. They also hold an implicit relationship to printed commendatory verses and early modern paratexts more generally.

Understood as "thresholds of interpretation," to borrow the subtitle of Gérard Genette's influential book, manuscript commendatory verses operated alongside printed paratexts to frame texts for readers.[3] But as Helen Smith and Louise Wilson have argued, Genette's study of paratexts does not account for the historical specificity of early modern books or readers and thus simplifies a cultural phenomenon that could be quite complex in practice. As Smith and Wilson write, paratexts "are not immutable instructions to the reader." Rather, they enact "a series of flexible and mutable relationships, as well as spaces which offer themselves for imaginative engagement."[4] The mere existence of manuscript commendatory verses establishes that readers also saw these paratextual spaces as sites of "imaginative engagement," where readers could become connected to authors and other readers in previously unforeseeable ways.

Besides being paratextual elements of printed books, manuscript commendatory verses borrow conventions from the larger genre of printed commendatory verse. Franklin B. Williams Jr. observes the rise and fall of commendatory verse, which he associates more with the sixteenth and early seventeenth centuries than the long eighteenth: the "vogue [for commendatory verses] reached its peak about 1650. . . . By about 1700 the sophisticated literary world had assumed a condescending attitude, and in the eighteenth century the practice lapsed into unimportance."[5] While Williams's article traces printed commendatory verse as a history of the "puff piece," more recent scholarship has remarked on the genre's role as paratext. According to Wayne Chandler, author of the only book-length study of the genre, printed commendatory verses have "three primary paratextual functions"—namely, "to advertise the book to book-buyers; to advertise the author(s) to patrons and book-buyers; and to influence the interpretation of the book by any readers."[6] But Chandler also describes how difficult it is to gauge the effect of commendatory verse on readers' interpretation of a commended volume, what he calls the "subject work": "In this present study I must work backward, starting not with the reader but with the material, the commendatory poems themselves. From that material I must reason how publishers and writers imagined and hoped readers to react."[7]

But what happens if we consider not printed puffs but manuscript commendatory verses written by readers? These texts are at once readers' responses to a subject work, including its paratexts, and original paratexts of their own. In adding manuscript commendatory verses, annotators actively participated in customizing the paratextual matter of their books. Through such interventions readers thus adopted complex roles within early modern book culture, functioning as advertisers (of commended books), authors (of commendatory verses), and readers (of texts and paratexts) all at once. Clearly, Chandler's emphasis on a division between "publishers and writers" and "readers," or Genette's focus on paratext as the expression of authorial intention, are not sufficient models for understanding how and why early modern readers added handwritten commendatory verses to their books.

As texts typically found on endpapers, moreover, manuscript commendatory verses are physically precarious elements subject to the vagaries of rebinding. And unlike other instances of early modern manuscript content intentionally removed from early printed books—for example, whitewashed or trimmed marginalia—no physical signs typically remain that such verses ever existed. At least with visibly illegible marginalia one knows the marginalia existed and were once legible (and perhaps could be made legible again via multispectral imaging). Manuscript verses on endleaves lost through rebinding, meanwhile—unless carefully documented by binders or conservators—leave no trace whatsoever.[8] Such verses and notes often constitute "hidden" collections at rare book libraries, in that catalogue records do not always draw attention to their existence or describe their content. Specimens of manuscript commentary verse in printed books, in other words, are rare and difficult to find, and due to their difficult accessibility, scholars have not typically included these texts in discussions of commendatory verse and paratextual matter in the early modern period. Because of this ephemerality, moreover, manuscript commendatory verse highlights key issues related to material survival, digitization, and the book-copy as archive.

In the following case study of a group of early modern annotated volumes—accomplished during a shelf survey of early printed books held at the William Andrews Clark Memorial Library, University of California, Los Angeles—I catalogue and discuss some of the many approaches readers brought to their writing of manuscript commendatory verse.[9] Anonymous or historically obscure, the readers who added these verses are not famous writers; thus, their work has little biographical import. Rather, these versifying readers and their poems offer broader insights into questions of reading, annotation, and book ownership in the early modern period.

Manuscript Verse in Coryats Crudities (1611)

Before turning to books printed in the late seventeenth century, I want to briefly discuss the case of Thomas Coryate's European travelogue *Coryats Crudities* (1611), which features one of the richest corpora of printed and manuscript paratextual matter surviving from the period. In illustrating the complex interactive potential of early modern print-manuscript paratexts, Coryate's travelogue and its material histories offer a way to understand the function of manuscript commendatory verse that can, in turn, be applied to books from later in the century. *Crudities* recounts Coryate's five-month journey through Europe in the early seventeenth century and has long been known for its eccentric prose style, its author's penchant for self-fashioned celebrity, and its numerous descriptive milestones in the history of English travel writing (e.g., being the first English travel book to mention both forks and umbrellas). *Crudities* is also well known for its dozens of prefatory mock-commendatory poems, written by some of the period's leading poets and wits, including Ben Jonson and John Donne, and printed with the first edition of the book.[10] The resulting collection of satirical "Panegyricke Verses," which occupies the first hundred or so printed pages of *Crudities* and presents Coryate as a buffoonish (if also learned) traveler, prompted many seventeenth-century readers to add imitative manuscript verses and satirical marginalia to their own copies of the travelogue. Some of this marginalia directly imitated the extensive side- and footnotes printed with the "Panegyricke Verses" (see fig. 1).

The printed glosses often amplified the jesting content of the verses, and the manuscript imitations of the notes performed a similar function. In many cases, it seems, such manuscript interventions were participatory in nature: readers sought to join the panegyrists in ridiculing Coryate and, by doing so, vicariously enjoy the culture of literary sociability such ridicule entailed. In turn, these manuscript additions served a paratextual function in annotated book-copies of the travelogue: what they offer is not simply a reaction or response to *Crudities* but, rather, a new text through which the author and his book might be interpreted.[11] The physical placement of these verses in surviving copies of *Crudities*—typically at the front of the volume, among the printed verses, or on blank pages preceding the start of the main travelogue—further underscores their role as "thresholds of interpretation" in that both modern and early modern readers would likely have encountered these manuscript additions

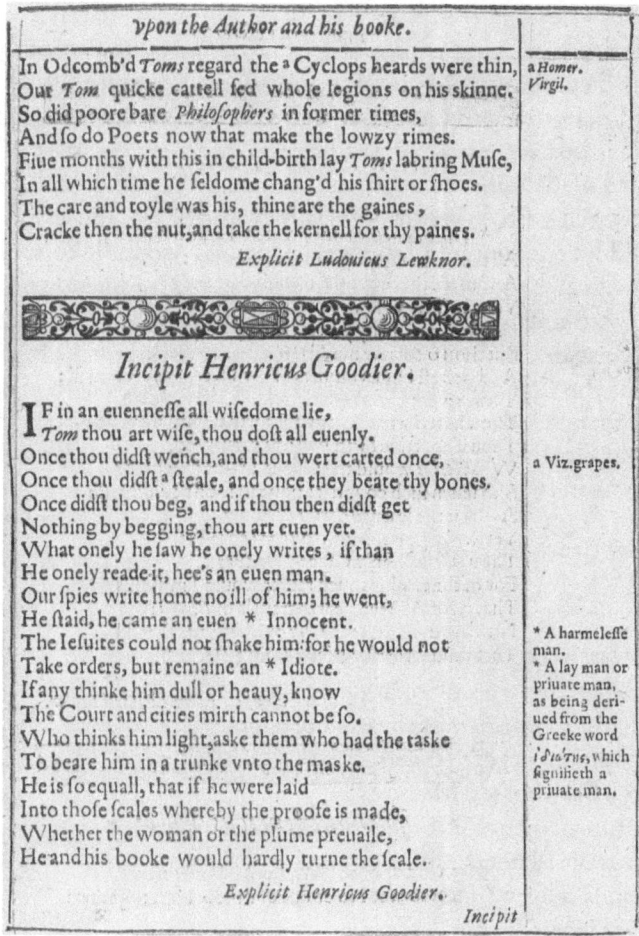

FIGURE 1. "Panegyricke Verse" by Henry Goodyear, in Thomas Coryate, *Coryats Crudities* (London, 1611). (PR 2237 .C61 *, sig. c6ʳ; William Andrews Clark Memorial Library, University of California, Los Angeles)

grouped with other, more established paratextual features, such as printed commendatory verse and prefatory prose.

Of the seventy-nine book-copies of *Coryats Crudities* I have inspected for manuscript additions and other copy-specific features, a small but significant portion—ten copies, or 13 percent—bear contemporary manuscript verses of the kind described earlier.[12] Yet what is remarkable about these verses—and, indeed, about the larger body of manuscript marginalia found in surviving copies of *Crudities*—are the distinct patterns of style and content they appear to follow. Such patterns suggest these verses and marginalia did not have merely incidental connections to the printed text but were part of a concerted effort on the part of readers and owners of *Crudities* to augment the text with additional, handwritten paratextual matter, resulting in a hybrid print-manuscript paratext that would be encountered by later readers. An example of such manuscript verses can be found in one of five copies of *Crudities* owned by Yale University's Beinecke Rare Book and Manuscript Library, a copy that also contains (in a different hand) satirical manuscript marginalia alongside one of the "Panegyricke Verses." The manuscript poem in question, which appears on the blank page facing the opening of the travelogue proper, was clearly composed after Coryate's untimely death while traveling in Asia in 1617. It reads:

Vpon y^e death of y^e aforsayd travelinge
    Thomas of Odcomb dying in his travailes

Thou sacred sceptick of each worthyes shrine
Odcombian foot=post Coriat peregrine,
Who hadst y^e worlds vast theatre ore=gone
for expedition, next to Phaeton:
Had y^y 4 fiery horses, Memory,
wth ~~burninge~~ ^winged^ Eloquence, hott Industry,
And flagrant Phantasie, bein governed
By reasons reins wth judgment managed.
For want whereof y^y microcosme, (as his
great world was once:) to dust consumed is.
I cannot but those flattering Gnathos blame,
wch beinge alive y^{ee} praysed: but dead, disclaime.
Vngratful miscreants, like ~~ye compeditors~~ ye company
Thy monumental wardrup wch did fly.
Me thinks y^{ey} might in right retaliat
An Epitaph vpon Tom Coriat
And once adorne his hearse, who lent
To y^{em} so many a worthy monument.
Tis pitty his ~~tombe~~ should ly vncelebrate
y^t did at tombstons glory propagate.

Wherefore to keepe his merits alwayes safe
(reader) accept y^{is} for his Epitaph ...

An Epitaph ./
Here rests restlesse Tom who died
[N]ot wth strong ale at whitsuntide,
[N]or by ye spruck Venetian whore,
[Nor R]henish Hogs head, or German bore.
[Bu]t having traveled many a nation,
[Fe]ll sicke & died of observation.
[H]e Labourd much, body & mind.
[Thi]s volums witnesse left behind
[F]rom head to foote he was a man
[L]ett envious fame say what she can.[13]

Reading this poem in concert with the "Panegyricke Verses" printed with *Crudities* (e.g., the poem by Henry Goodyear reproduced in figure 1) reveals their affinities of style and content. Like so many of the other panegyrists, the anonymous versifier comments on several frequently discussed episodes of Coryate's travelogue, such as his tireless transcriptions from European tombs and monuments, his humorous mishaps among Venetian prostitutes and German farmers, and his infamously louse-ridden traveler's cloak ("ye company / Thy monumental wardrup wch did fly"). Most of these episodes are represented visually as part of *Crudities*' engraved title page, which depicts a handful of sensational incidents from Coryate's journey. In fact, many of the poets responsible for the "Panegyricke Verses" appear to have based their interpretation of *Coryats Crudities* solely on the engraved title page and its accompanying set of "Opening and Drawing Distichs," which are explanatory couplets written by Laurence Whitaker and Ben Jonson and keyed to alphabetic labels on the engraving. The anonymous composer of the Yale copy's manuscript verses is no different in that he focuses primarily on the travelogue's more famous episodes—that is, those most often mentioned by the mock panegyrists and depicted on the engraved title page. One aspect of this poem that sets it apart from the others collected in *Crudities* is its concluding epitaph, the ostensible purpose of which is the commemoration of Thomas Coryate's career as a traveler and antiquarian epigrapher ("who did at tombstons glory propagate"). Responding perhaps to the profusion of satirical Coryate references found in drama and poetry from the mid- to late seventeenth century, the composer of "Vpon ye death" refuses to let Coryate be forgotten and "ly vncelebrate," being maligned, as it were, by the unfriendly words of "flattering Gnathos" and "Vngratful miscreants."[14]

Besides being slightly more sympathetic to Coryate than most readers of *Crudities*, the writer responsible for "Vpon ye death" is also keenly aware of his poem's physical placement in the volume. "Aforsayd" in particular signals that these verses *follow other verses* about Coryate and thus occupy a meaningful place within the larger context and sequence of the printed book. "Aforsayd" implies that readers of the manuscript verses have already read one hundred-plus pages of printed poetry about Coryate—the "Panegyricke Verses"—and are only now arriving at "Vpon ye death," which is thus the last set of verses before the prose travelogue itself begins. And although the physical placement of the verses here could be said to be opportunistic—since sig. ^{2}D3^v is a blank page—they also signal quite conspicuously their position in a greater sequence of poems about Coryate. What is more, the manuscript poem addresses the reader directly in the last line before the epitaph: "(reader) accept y^{is} for his Epitaph." While certainly a literary convention, this address to the reader nonetheless indicates an intended audience for the verses—namely, other readers of this particular book-copy. Crucially, such audience recognition relates to the book not as a physical object or piece of private property—as is the case with presentation-copy dedicatory verses or rhyming ownership inscriptions—but as a text packaged in and informed by paratext: interpreting the text of *Crudities* requires wading through more than a hundred pages of mock panegyrics, with the manuscript poem that concludes the sequence being only the last, and perhaps most important, of the book's prefatory paratextual elements.

The case of *Coryats Crudities* and its manuscript verses presents a strong connection between printed and handwritten paratextual poetry, with the former being an obvious inspiration for the latter. While such a causal link between print and manuscript paratexts does not exist in many other cases of printed books bearing manuscript verse, there is evidence nonetheless that these verses hold paratextual functions in the books they inhabit. Turning now to other cases of manuscript verses addressed to the author and found in printed books of the mid- to late seventeenth century, I consider how annotating readers composed such verse with the genre of printed commendatory poetry in mind, even if the annotated books in question did not contain such poems themselves. Commendatory verse had become such a convention of print that, even when such verse began to fall out of print convention in the second half of the seventeenth century, readers started to create their own.

Manuscript Commendatory Verse and the Eighteenth-Century Reader-Annotator

Playful manuscript verses about an author do not always appear in volumes that also contain printed panegyric. In a copy of Thomas Fuller's *Good Thoughts in Bad Times, Together with Good Thoughts in Worse Times* (1649), an early reader named Stephen Jay inscribed a set of verses "On the authour Mr Tho. Fuller" (see fig. 2):

> Fuller, then FVLLER, who can pencill out
> The Character of verity, & doubt?
> Diuine Apelles! thou art not content,
> Vnlesse thou hast the grace of rauishment:
> For whoso stare's on this Imagery,
> Must surfet with excesse of Joy, & dye!
> Fortune, noe sooner miracles had wrought
> But straight they were digested in thy thought.
> Thy hand stands ready Vsher to thy mind,
> And act's with credit what hee hath design'd.
>   Gett hence, you petty Limners, Rags of art.
>   I blush to see how FVLLER makes you start!
>   Stephen Jay![15]

As in numerous pun-filled poems riffing on Thomas Coryate's name and hometown of Odcombe, the author's name in Jay's verses prompts a rather obvious pun in the question "Fuller, then FVLLER, who can pencill out / The Character of verity, & doubt?"[16] Unlike the mock commendatory verses in *Coryats Crudities*, however, the authorial praise in Jay's poem seems genuine and sets Fuller apart from inferior writers—those "petty Limners" and "Rags of art." Written during the height of the English Civil War, Fuller's *Good Thoughts* is a collection of meditations and wisdom that was first published in Exeter in 1645; it was "intended partly to console those whose lives were being torn apart by the war."[17] In the absence of a firm date it is difficult to know whether Stephen Jay wrote his verses during the Civil War or after the Restoration; such historical context could help illuminate the meaning of these lines. Yet as with the

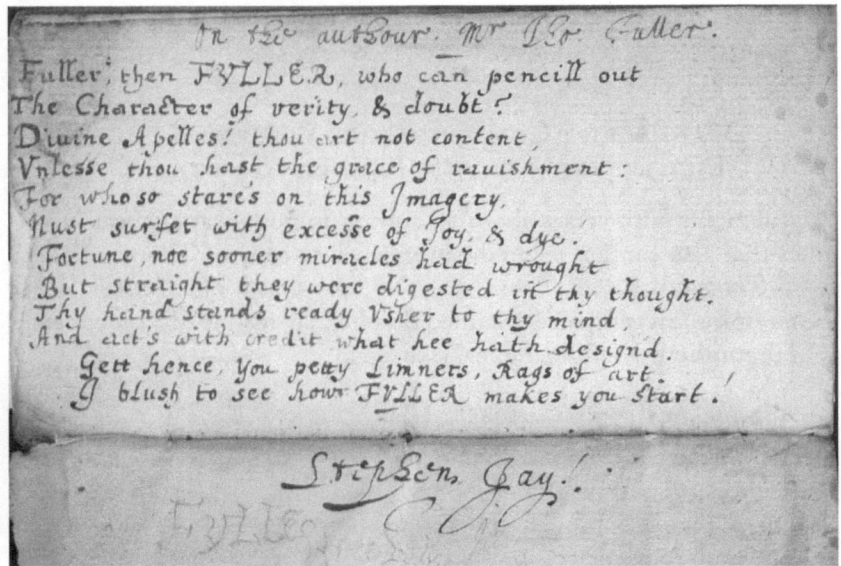

FIGURE 2. Manuscript verses by Stephen Jay, "On the Author Mr. Tho. Fuller," in Thomas Fuller, *Good Thoughts in Bad Times, Together with Good Thoughts in Worse Times* (London, 1649). (PR 3461.F8 G6 1649 *; William Andrews Clark Memorial Library, University of California, Los Angeles)

Thomas Coryate poem discussed earlier, the physical placement of Jay's verses in the volume reveals something about their probable function in this particular book-copy—a manuscript paratext that introduces the reader to the author and his book. But if in *Coryats Crudities* it was the large group of printed "Panegyricke Verses" that inspired readers to inscribe manuscript poetry in its margins, in Fuller's *Good Thoughts* there do not exist similar printed paratexts for readers to imitate. In fact, it seems likely instead that Stephen Jay borrowed the genre of commendatory verse from other books and adapted it to his reading of Fuller's *Good Thoughts*, which, in terms of paratextual matter, contains a prose dedication to Anne Villiers, Lady Dalkeith, but no commendatory verses. Jay's original manuscript poem therefore displays his understanding not only of commendatory verse as a genre but also of prefatory paratextual matter as a conspicuous feature of printed books.

Such an arrangement also appears in a privately owned copy of Richard Allestree's *The Causes of the Decay of Christian Piety* (1671). This copy bears commendatory manuscript verses written by two different seventeenth-century readers: an unidentified person with the initials "H. K." and another owner named Anthony Hartley (see figs. 3–4):[18]

> Good Christian Reader, doe not thou this booke;
>   with prejudice, or passion overlook.
> Nor spend too hasty judgment: unprepar'd.
>   here's somthing in it worth thy best regard.
> ffirst tast the fruit of it, but seek not thou
>   the Orchard, not the plant, from whence it grew
> But say, tis Manna sent thee from aboue,
>   the Causes of all Mischeifes to remoue.
> Though here no Author doth his name express,
>   yet more doe thou esteem of it, not less.
>   ffor by concealing of it wee may scan,
>   hee sought the praise of god, but not of man.
>   H. K.

> The Book of
>   Antho: Hartley 1676
>
> Being much Esteemed of
> by its owner:
> And praiseth god for the great
> Abilities & industrious Endeauours
> of its Composer:
>
> Awake my muse & let all people see
> Causes decay; of Christian piety.
> Causes in wch, both sin, & sorrow lyes
> Causes whereby; most mischeifes doe arise
> Causes from whence, such banefull mischief spring
> Mischief wch certain, will damnation bring,
> The cause of all these causes writte onely
> That piety may grow, & mischief dye
> Read here & learn; this book will you direct
> Tavoyde ye cause; of such mischeifs effect
> Aplaud ye Author, for his gratefull works
> Wch shewes ye cause; where mischief vices lurks
> And gives such counsel that not onely wee

May reape the fruite, but our posterity
But why subscribed, is ^not^ here his name
Best knowne himself; but certainly his fame
Is not the lesse but more; for in a word
His honours not from man; but from the lord
His painfull labours let all Christian men
Sing forth their praise; Concluding says Amen
          per A:H:[19]

Based on paleographical evidence, it seems likely that the first of the two poems, the one signed "H. K.," was written earlier than the second poem, by Anthony Hartley. There is also evidence that one of the poems influenced the other, as they discuss the author's anonymous identity in similar terms.[20] From the perspective of both readers, Allestree's *The Causes of the Decay* is an exceptional text, being "much Esteemed of by its owner," Anthony Hartley, and having "something in it worth thy best regard," according to "H. K." Both writers have the ostensible goal of encouraging their Christian peers to read Allestree's book. The poem by "H. K." addresses the "Good Christian Reader" directly, while

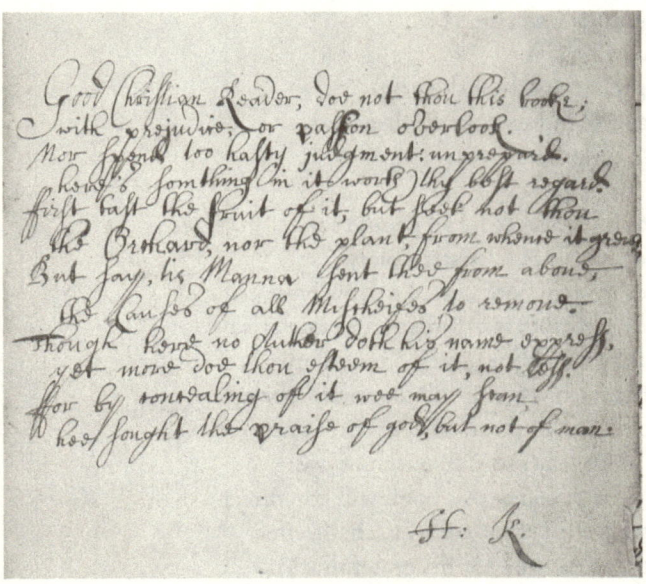

FIGURE 3. Manuscript verses by "H.K.," in Richard Allestree, *The Causes of the Decay of Christian Piety* (London, 1671). (Private collection of the author, New York)

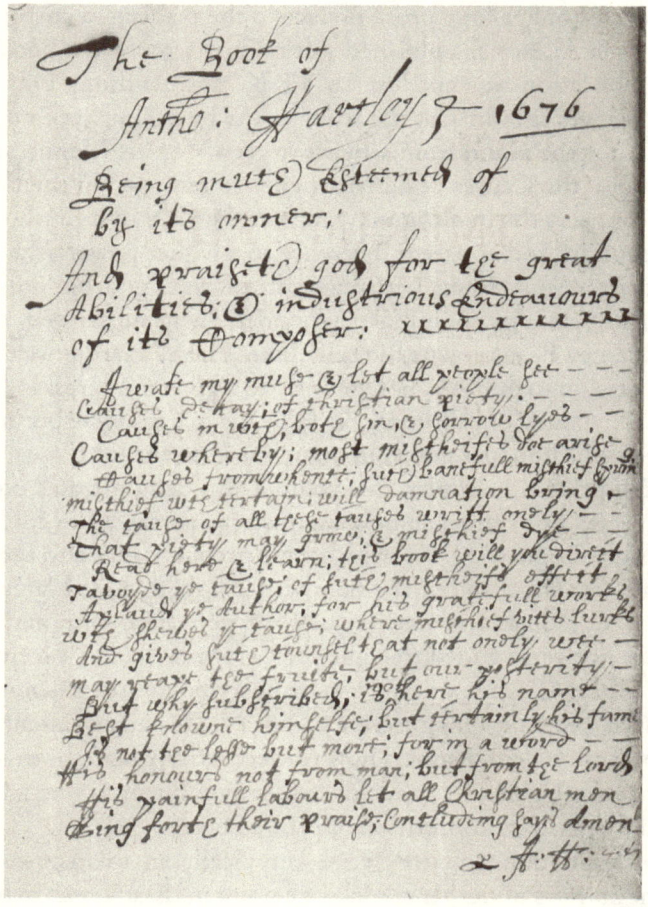

FIGURE 4. Manuscript verses and inscription by Anthony Hartley, in Richard Allestree, *The Causes of the Decay of Christian Piety* (London, 1671). (Private collection of the author, New York)

Hartley's address to his muse involves a concomitant request to "let all people see / Causes decay; of Christian piety." Hartley goes on to address readers directly when he enjoins them to "Read here & learn."

The case of this book-copy further illuminates the phenomenon of readers adding manuscript verse to their printed books, especially in the absence of preexisting printed commendatory poems. As an anonymously published book, in fact, *The Causes of the Decay* seems an unlikely candidate to include commendatory verse about its author. The printed book contains only a long prose preface to the reader—a customary arrangement in Allestree's published work. Furthermore, the book's anonymous publication was not lost on "H. K." and Anthony Hartley. For "H. K.," readers should "tast the fruit" of the book "but seek not . . . the Orchard, not the plant, from whence it grew," for "tis Manna sent thee from aboue, / the Causes of all Mischeifes to remoue." In the final lines "H. K." connects the book's anonymous authorship to its author's intellectual humility and apparent deference to a higher power: "ffor by concealing of it wee may scan, / hee sought the praise of god, but not of man." In a similar vein, Anthony Hartley ponders "why subscribed, is ^not^ here his name / Best knowne himself." Like "H. K.," Hartley ascribes Allestree's decision to publish anonymously to a greater interest in heavenly than earthly fame: "but certainly his fame / Is not the lesse but more; for in a word / His honours not from man; but from the lord."

Lacking printed examples, this volume also demonstrates how manuscript verses can influence new manuscript verses. One could argue that the verses signed "H. K.," which were probably added to the volume before any others, inspired the handwritten poem added later by Anthony Hartley. Such a scenario recalls the derivative form and content of manuscript verse added to copies of *Coryats Crudities*, except that in the case of the Allestree volume it is manuscript paratexts—not printed ones—that beget new manuscript paratexts. This arrangement is fascinating because it demonstrates how readers actively read the manuscript additions of other readers and subsequently influenced one another in their handwritten customization of printed books.

Manuscript commendatory verse is typically an amateur enterprise, and some authors of the genre make it a point in these verses to highlight their lack of learning and intellectual sophistication. A heavily marked-up students' copy of Joseph Moxon's *A Tutor to Astronomie and Geographie* (1670), for instance, has an original poem "Didicated to Joseph Moxon" written by a "T. P.," who, based on a title-page signature, was named Thomas Ponton and owned the book around 1750 in Thorney, Cambridgeshire. The verses praise Moxon and his book while also characterizing Ponton as someone of "Low" intellectual ability (fig. 5):

Didicated to Joseph Moxon. by T. P.
Well has't thou done Brave Moxon to Impart,
so good a peice of Geographic Art.
By thy Bright genious, may be understood.

The works of Earth & sea by the All'seeing good.
Goodness to thee, who hath Inspirid thy Sence,
To make thy works so great & ^so^ Emence.
Thy stile is Easy, most ^and^ fitted for ^the^ Low,
And for thy pains my thanks I do Bestow.[21]

In the second half of the seventeenth century, Moxon (1627–91) published dozens of scientific works marketed to common readers; *A Tutor to Astronomie and Geographie*, translated from William Bleau's *Institutio astronomica*, was Moxon's first scientific text to address a broad popular audience.[22] As Thomas Ponton writes in his verses, Moxon's "Easy" style, which is "fitted for the Low," is a major reason that *Tutor* is "so good a peice of Geographic Art." Ponton's sentiment matches other paratextual advertisements for the book's accessibility, such as the title page's claim that it has been "set forth . . . so plainly and methodically that the meanest Capacity may at first reading apprehend it." Moxon's preface to the reader further explains *A Tutor*'s approach to its subject matter:

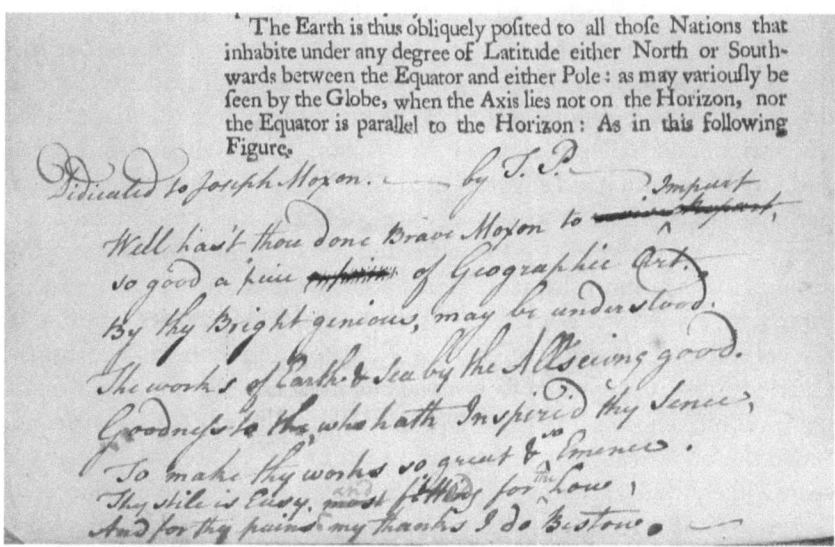

FIGURE 5. Manuscript verses by Thomas Ponton, "Didicated to Joseph Moxon," in Joseph Moxon, *A Tutor to Astronomie and Geographie* (London, 1670). (QB 41 .M93 1670 *, sig. E4ᵛ; William Andrews Clark Memorial Library, University of California, Los Angeles)

> My aim in this book hath been to make the Use of them [the globes] very plain and easie to the meanest Capacities.... I write not to expert Practioners [sic], but to Learners; to whom Examples may prove more Instructive than precepts. Besides, I hope to encourage those by an ample liberal plainness to fall in love with these Studies, that formerly have been disheartened by the Crabbed brevity of those Authors that have (in Characters as it were) rather writ Notes for their one Memories, than sufficient Documents for their Readers Instructions.[23]

In their celebration of Moxon's ability to help less sophisticated readers understand astronomy and geography, Ponton's verses confirm the efficacy of the goals set out in *A Tutor*'s preface.

But one could argue that the verses do not merely constitute a reader's reaction to or appraisal of Moxon's *Tutor* but, rather, amount to an advertisement—a framing paratext—for the book. Borrowing the earlier form of commendatory verse, which by 1750 had fallen out of fashion, Ponton composes a verse tribute to an author whom he ostensibly admires, inscribing the lines on the blank space of a page near the front. That other readers likely encountered Ponton's verses is borne out by the dense layering of inscriptions, doodles, diagrams, and other manuscript notes found throughout the beginning of the volume, which are illustrative of the book's social life among early modern English students. Several diagrams and sets of notes added to the book (including calculations for "A Horizontal Dial") are signed by a William Toola, whose unpracticed and juvenile round hand suggests he read Moxon's *Tutor* as a young man, perhaps as a student. And since Toola calculated his "Horizontal Dial" "for Thorney," we know that Ponton and Toola owned the book in the same place at around the same time, although it is impossible to determine who owned the book first.[24] Other signatures and inscriptions in the volume include those of Eleanor Kingston and Thomas Morton—married in 1747, according to a title-page manuscript note—and Samuel Shelton, whose signatures have been carefully obliterated with ink. Since the book was heavily used and read in the eighteenth century, it seems likely that at some point later readers would have encountered Thomas Ponton's commendatory verses on Joseph Moxon, just as Ponton would have encountered the numerous manuscript additions added by previous readers. If the material added by Morton and Toola is somewhat predictable—marriage records are not rare and mathematical scratchwork in such volumes is quite common—Ponton's poem would have been a much more atypical manuscript addition to the book. What makes these verses so fascinating is not only that Ponton appears to be the exact kind of reader Moxon aimed to reach with his *Tutor*, but also that Ponton then took it upon himself to advertise the book for other unsophisticated readers. If we might call the "Learners" in Moxon's preface his "ideal readers"—in that those are the people he hopes will read his book—then this particular copy showcases the specific historical practices of early modern "Learners" while also demonstrating readers' tendency to address one another and provide paratextual guidance outside the author's writing and influence. Simultaneously functioning as commendation, reader response, and paratextual advertisement, Ponton's verses underscore the complex roles readers can adopt in the books they annotate.

A final example of manuscript commendatory verse from the Clark Library dates to the 1660s and showcases a female reader responding to a medical treatise. This copy of William Kemp's *A Brief Treatise of the Nature, Causes, Signes, Preservation from, and Cure of the Pestilence* (1665) is signed "Mary Evans her Book Giuen By ye Author" on the title page; another inscription, on an endleaf excised from its original position and pasted onto the inside front cover of the rebound book, reads, "Mary Downing her Booke December 15 1665." Since the inscriptions seem to have been written by the same hand, it is possible that Mary Evans and Mary Downing are the same person and the two signatures reflect a change in her last name due to marriage. Two additional manuscript texts in this hand appear in the book: a recipe for raspberry cream and a set of verses "In Authorum" (fig. 6). The poem reads:

In Authorum

Though yet my muse ner usheul was to Booke
yet whilst I did with full contentment Looke
on this choyse peice fraught soe full with delight
I found it harder to forbare then wright
Admireing much thy Choyse and better part
Whoe Docter both for soules and boodys Art
And in Darke seasons showst thy kinder Light
As stars in Gloomy nights doe shine most bright
When physically you this worke Begin

you strike at the roote of all Diseases: sin
Then choyser meanes and Remedies you find
To ease the Body and Compose the mind
As if ^in^ your *owne you could all pleasures finde: Tis true.*[25]

Mary Evans/Downing foregrounds her mean intellectual capacity by describing herself as "ner usheul ... to Booke," both as a way to magnify the perceived greatness of Kemp's text and to adopt a rhetorical pose of affected modesty. In her verses Evans/Downing touches on some of the themes raised in Kemp's own paratextual remarks, found in an address "To the Reader" at the end of the book. There Kemp repudiates the charlatans who purport to sell their patients fantastical remedies such as phoenix eggs and Jason's Golden Fleece, emphasizing instead his focus on practicality and honest plain dealing: "My directions are plain and familiar, and easie to be understood by an ordinary capacity; ... I had rather communicate [them] for the good of the people of my Native Country, than to have gotten an Estate, by giving them a hard Name, to keep them

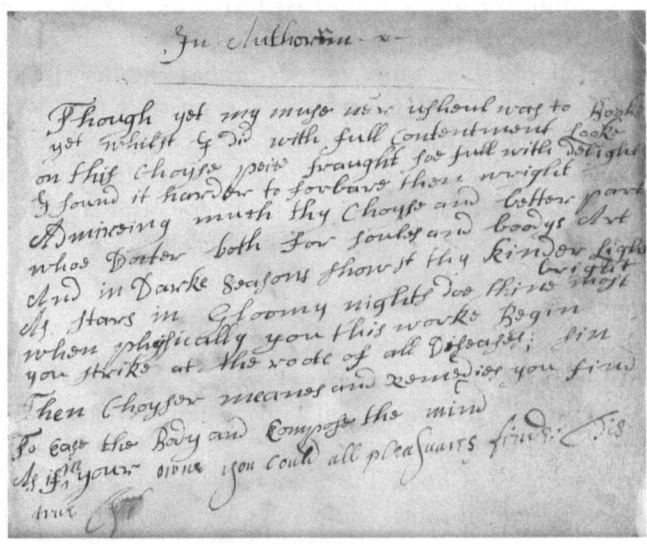

FIGURE 6. Manuscript verses by Mary Evans/Downing, "In Authorum," in William Kemp, *A Brief Treatise of the Nature, Causes, Signes, Preservation from, and Cure of the Pestilence* (London, 1665). (RC 171 .K32 *; William Andrews Clark Memorial Library, University of California, Los Angeles)

secret, and having them sold for my private advantage, (as the Custome now is) at an Apothecaries or Stationers shop."[26] Understanding the necessity of practically instructing people to treat plague victims, Kemp designed his treatise not for a readership of Latin-fluent experts but for people like Evans/Downing and other infrequent readers, much like the audience for Moxon's *Tutor*. Despite her limited education and reading, Mary was "fraught soe full with delight" from reading Kemp that she "found it harder to forbare then wright." These lines do not produce the choicest poetry, though the description of Dr. Kemp as a "kinder Light" amidst the "Darke seasons" of England's 1665 plague year is both apt and poignant. The verses also remark on the effectively structured content of Kemp's *Brief Treatise*, which progresses from a broad discussion of sin to a detailed catalogue of "choyser meanes and Remedies" meant "to ease the Body and Compose the mind." The reader's reluctance to commit pen to paper is overcome, in other words, by the "contentment" and "delight" afforded by Kemp's writing.

Despite the apparent hierarchies of literacy embodied by Evans/Downing and Kemp, the lines of influence and inspiration embodied in these manuscript verses are complex. Evans/Downing received a presentation copy of Kemp's *Brief Treatise* directly from the author at the height of England's infamous plague of 1665. Presumably not long after receiving the book, she added original commentatory verses to its blank endleaves; one might read her verses as a gesture of gratitude expressed toward the author, who generously gave her a book of exceeding practicality during 1665's "Darke seasons." However, the last line of her commendatory poem is interesting because it was written partially by Evans/Downing and partially by someone else. Predominantly written in what is clearly a lighter brown ink and different hand, the line reading "As if in your owne you could all pleasures find" was originally left unfinished by Evans/Downing (only "As if your" is in her hand). The anonymous scribe responsible for the final line added the further approbatory comment "Tis true." At some point after Mary wrote her lines on Kemp, therefore, another person read both the manuscript verses *and* the printed book—presumably viewing the two as part of the same textual package—and decided to augment those verses with a final line and statement of approbation. In this second act of manuscript addition to the volume, one reader is prompted by the customized paratext of an earlier reader to contribute new material to the book. What this case demonstrates is not only that readers could enhance their books with unique manuscript paratexts of their own, but also that other readers would react to and riff on such paratexts in their own annotation and inscription activities. Reader-generated manuscript paratexts could have a demonstrable impact on other readers and how they engaged with printed books, particularly, it seems in these cases, in vernacular, "popular" books of science and medicine.

Material and Digital Histories of Manuscript Commendatory Verse

Earlier I mentioned the precarious material lives of manuscript commendatory verses, being texts often inscribed on endleaves and thus susceptible to loss. While the lines added to *Coryats Crudities* and Moxon's *Tutor* would be secured against such oblivion because of their placement in blank spaces within the text, it is a small miracle that the verses by Mary Evans/Downing, "H. K.," Anthony Hartley, and Stephen Jay remain. Due to the accidents of time and circumstance, the verses in Kemp's *Treatise* and Allestree's *Causes of the Decay* have fortuitously survived their host books' apparently rough material lives. When the Clark's copy of Kemp's *Treatise* was rebound in the twentieth century, two scraps of paper with manuscript writing by Evans/Downing were preserved: the binder pasted one of her inscriptions onto the new front pastedown while also tipping in a soiled piece of paper bearing the raspberry cream recipe and the lines composed "In Authorum." Rebinding may have irrevocably disrupted the book-copy's original bibliographical context, but at least in this case a small and revealing piece of that context was preserved. The copy of Fuller's *Good Thoughts* annotated by Stephen Jay survives in its original binding in quite good condition—perhaps a sign that the book was little read. The copy of Allestree's *The Causes of the Decay*, meanwhile, is falling apart and exceedingly grubby in appearance; luckily, a note penciled in the book exhorting later owners to "Preserve these leaves," referring to the endleaves annotated by "H. K." and Anthony Hartley, has been dutifully followed. Shabby and unbecoming, this book-copy nonetheless retains for scholars a useful piece of material evidence and a rare example of manuscript commendatory verse from the period.[27]

If barriers exist for the material survival of this manuscript genre, they also exist for its discovery among library catalogues and other collections of metadata. It is well known that not all library catalogue records contain copy-specific notes on the provenances, bindings, and manuscript annotations of printed books. When they do, however, manuscript verses are not always classified differently from other types of manuscript notes. They are often identified with the term "ms. notes," for instance, making it impossible to distinguish in the metadata among a broad range of possible manuscript interventions. When such verses are identified as "ms. verses," "ms. verse," or "ms. poem," furthermore, it is rare to find any additional information in the record, such as a transcription or categorization of the verse. As outlined earlier, there are many types of manuscript verse in early modern printed books that ought to be distinguished, but due to cost and time constraints, it is unlikely that catalogue records will draw such distinctions.

The situation for researchers, then, is difficult: manuscript verses already do not survive in vast numbers, and when they do, they are not always easy to find. In searching for such books at the Clark Library I was fortunate that several catalogue records mentioned "manuscript poems"; in the cases of the Kemp and Fuller volumes, the records say that these verses relate to authors.[28] But the copy of Moxon's *Tutor* annotated by Thomas Ponton has no copy-specific notes; nor does the annotated copy of *Coryats Crudities* held at Yale. The manuscript commendatory verse in those books was discovered only because of the work of larger surveys: a copy census of *Coryats Crudities* (during which I examined every page of more than seventy-five copies of the book) and my shelf survey of early modern printed books at the Clark.

Because they have only marginal importance in relation to other early modern manuscript texts, handwritten verses in printed books typically are not viable candidates for digitization initiatives, which tend to privilege printed books *or* manuscripts but rarely the hybrid volumes that combine the two. While manuscript cataloguing and digitization are starting to include such mixed-media work, the dominant digital archives of early modern print—Early English Books Online (EEBO) and Eighteenth-Century Collections Online (ECCO)—are woefully inadequate for researching the complex histories of book-copies. While it may be common to encounter EEBO or ECCO texts bearing signs of provenance or historical use, in many cases that material evidence has been rendered illegible or unusable due to the generally poor quality of reproductions in these resources. And since bindings and endpapers are customarily absent from EEBO and ECCO facsimiles, it is impossible to use such databases systematically to find evidence for the social life of early books. When EEBO and ECCO do yield such evidence, it is almost invariably lacking in the crucial bibliographical context afforded by bindings and endleaves.

In our EEBO/ECCO–dominated scholarly research environment, it would be useful to keep in mind that early modern printed books can be considered manuscript archives of their own. As repositories of marginalia, inscriptions, reading notes, handwritten binders' waste, and laid-in manuscripts, early printed books serve the crucial secondary function of preserving manuscript texts for later scholars and readers. At a time that the EEBO or ECCO copy of a given early modern book threatens to stand in for *all* of that title's physically distributed book-copies, scholars would do well to remember how different a book can become in the hands of a proactively annotating reader-owner. And since this is also a time of diminished library budgets and surreptitious deaccessioning, administrators would do well to remember that each and every printed book could potentially contain a unique manuscript archive. It is the duty of scholars and librarians to ensure that such micro-archives become documented and discoverable, for by ignoring or marginalizing the ephemeral manuscript content of early print and focusing entirely on the texts they bear, we run the risk of sending the wrong message about so-called duplicate copies of early modern books.[29]

The examples of manuscript commendatory verse discussed here reveal how clever early modern readers could be in their interpretation and appropriation of printed paratexts. Whether by imitating printed mock commendatory verse or addressing elements raised by an author's preface, these readers looked to the forms and conventions of print, as well as to the habits of other readers, when customizing their books in manuscript. Hardly limited to commonplace rhyming inscriptions picked up in the schoolroom, manuscript verse inscribed in early modern print reveals the capacity and imagination of readers to respond to their books creatively, as texts not so much complete as endlessly open to refashioning.

Notes

1. A typical example, taken from a seventeenth-century Bible, reads, "Elizabeth White / it is my name and England is my nation / Bridgewater square my dwelling place / and Christ is my Salvation": *The Holy Bible, Containing the Old Testament and the New*, 1657, BS185 1657.C2 *, William Andrews Clark Memorial Library, University of California, Los Angeles.
2. For distinctions among "book," "book-copy," and "edition," see Dane, *What Is a Book?* 7–11.
3. Genette, *Paratexts*.

4. Smith and Wilson, "Introduction," 14. One of their main criticisms of Genette targets his overemphasis on the role of authors and authority in determining paratextual meaning: "The chapters in this book are united by their challenge to Genette's repeated assertion that the meaning and function of the paratext are determined by 'the author and his allies'... and that paratexts operate as a way of establishing and securing authorial intention": ibid., 7–8.
5. Williams, "Commendatory Verses," 3–4. Williams also wrote a reference book on dedications: see Williams, *Index of Dedications and Commendatory Verses*. Williams's overview of the historical rise and fall of commendatory verse must be qualified by the fact that the bulk of his research for "Commendatory Verses" and the *Index* stops at 1641.
6. Chandler, *Commendatory Verse and Authorship in the English Renaissance*, 6.
7. Ibid., 3, 14.
8. For the historical reception of annotated book-copies as "dirty books," subject to now-questionable practices such as whitewashing and trimming, see Sherman, *Used Books*, 151–78.
9. I conducted this shelf survey at the Clark Library from August 2014 to February 2015. I inspected some fourteen thousand individual volumes (printed books published before 1820) and found about five hundred books with significant manuscript annotation (i.e., annotation beyond ownership autographs and inscriptions, nineteenth- and twentieth-century biographical/bibliographical notes, and doodles/pen trials). Annotated books thus amount to 3.5 percent of the volumes surveyed.
10. For a reading of the "Panegyricke Verses" in *Crudities* as a "print event" fostering literary sociability among London elites, see O'Callaghan, *The English Wits*, 102–27.
11. See Palmer, "The Progress of Thy Glorious Book."
12. These copies are held at the Beinecke Rare Book and Manuscript Library, Yale University, New Haven, CT (two copies); the Morgan Library and Museum, New York City; Brandeis University, Waltham, MA; the Folger Shakespeare Library, Washington, DC; the Newberry Library, Chicago; the Royal Academy of Music, London; the National Library of Wales; and the Museum of London. An untraced copy also was sold on eBay in 2010.
13. Thomas Coryate, *Coryats Crudities* (London, 1611), Osborn pb57, sig. ^{2}D3^v, Beinecke Rare Book and Manuscript Library. In copies of *Crudities*, ^{2}D1–^{2}D3 consists of a gathering inserted into D^8 after D1. Although paleographical evidence is inconclusive for dating the verses, their almost complete absence of secretary letterforms suggests a date in the second half of the seventeenth century.
14. For more on print and manuscript collections of epitaphs in the seventeenth century, see Williams, "Manuscript, Monument, Memory."

15. Thomas Fuller, *Good Thoughts in Bad Times, Together with Good Thoughts in Worse Times* (London, 1649), PR 3461.F8 G6 1649 *, Clark Library.
16. Williams points out that "punning is frequent" in commendatory verse: Williams, "Commendatory Verses," 10.
17. Patterson, "Fuller, Thomas."
18. This is perhaps the Anthony Hartley who was a Glassman of Saint Andrew Holborn, City of London, and whose will in the Prerogative Court of Canterbury is dated August 1, 1681.
19. Richard Allestree, *The Causes of the Decay of Christian Piety* (London, 1671), private collection of the author.
20. Richard Allestree (1621/2–81) was most famous for his devotional book *The Whole Duty of Man* (1657), which was published anonymously (just like his later devotional manuals, including *The Causes of the Decay*, which attributes its authorship to "the Author of the Whole Duty of Man"). The author's identity remained a secret in the seventeenth century, although there is now a consensus that Allestree was responsible: Spurr, "Allestree, Richard."
21. Joseph Moxon, *A Tutor to Astronomie and Geographie* (London, 1670), QB 41.M93 1670 *, Clark Library.
22. Bryden, "Moxon, Joseph."
23. Moxon, *A Tutor to Astronomie and Geographie*, sig. A3^r.
24. Based on handwriting, it seems reasonable to conclude that Toola owned the book before Ponton (whom we know signed the book in 1750), although the evidence is inconclusive.
25. William Kemp, *A Brief Treatise of the Nature, Causes, Signes, Preservation from, and Cure of the Pestilence* (London, 1665), RC171.K32 *, Clark Library. The added emphasis reflects material written in a different hand, presumably by a different person.
26. Kemp, *A Brief Treatise of the Nature*, sig. N2^v.
27. The book's condition also made it attainable for this author, who purchased it on eBay several years ago at an affordable price.
28. This is true only of the catalogue cards, however. The online catalogue records do not yet reflect this copy-specific information.
29. For a compelling recent discussion on the research value of duplicate books, see Eckert and Grandison, "The Almanac Archive."

Works Cited

Bryden, D. J. "Moxon, Joseph (1627–1691)." In *Oxford Dictionary of National Biography*. Oxford: Oxford University Press, 2004. https://doi.org/10.1093/ref:odnb/19466.

Chandler, Wayne A. *Commendatory Verse and Authorship in the English Renaissance.* Lewiston, ME: Edwin Mellen, 2003.

Dane, Joseph A. *What Is a Book? The Study of Early Printed Books.* South Bend, IN: University of Notre Dame Press, 2012.

Eckert, Lindsey, and Julia Grandison. "*The Almanac Archive*: Theorizing Marginalia and 'Duplicate' Copies in the Digital Realm." *Digital Humanities Quarterly* 10, no. 1 (2016). http://www.digitalhumanities.org/dhq/vol/10/1/000240/000240.html.

Genette, Gérard. *Paratexts: Thresholds of Interpretation,* translated by Jane E. Lewin. Cambridge: Cambridge University Press, 1997.

O'Callaghan, Michelle. *The English Wits: Literature and Sociability in Early Modern England.* Cambridge: Cambridge University Press, 2010.

Palmer, Philip S. "'The Progress of Thy Glorious Book': Material Reading and the Play of Paratext in *Coryats Crudities* (1611)." *Renaissance Studies* 28, no. 3 (June 2014): 336–55.

Patterson, W. B. "Fuller, Thomas (1607/8–1661)." In *Oxford Dictionary of National Biography.* Oxford: Oxford University Press, 2004. https://doi.org/10.1093/ref:odnb/10236.

Sherman, William H. *Used Books: Marking Readers in Renaissance England.* Philadelphia: University of Pennsylvania Press, 2008.

Smith, Helen, and Louise Wilson. "Introduction." In *Renaissance Paratexts,* edited by Helen Smith and Louise Wilson, 1–14. Cambridge: Cambridge University Press, 2011.

Spurr, John. "Allestree, Richard (1621/2–1681)." In *Oxford Dictionary of National Biography.* Oxford: Oxford University Press, 2004. https://doi.org/10.1093/ref:odnb/395.

Williams, Claire Bryony. "Manuscript, Monument, Memory: The Circulation of Epitaphs in the 17th Century." *Literature Compass* 11, no. 8 (August 2014): 573–82.

Williams, Franklin B., Jr. "Commendatory Verses: The Rise of the Art of Puffing." *Studies in Bibliography* 19 (1966): 1–14.

———. *Index of Dedications and Commendatory Verses in English Books before 1641.* London: Bibliographical Society, 1962.

Mediating the "Sudden & Surprising Revolution"
Official Manuscript Newsletters and the Revolution of 1688

LEITH DAVIS

O**N NOVEMBER 5, 1688**, William of Orange landed his formidable force of forty thousand troops in Torbay, Devonshire.[1] Over the next six weeks, he marched to London and took control of the English government as James II fled to France. After a lengthy and contentious meeting of the Convention Parliament, William was proclaimed king of England in February 1689, with his wife, Mary, as queen. Scholars of the "Glorious Revolution," as it was later termed, have identified the important role that print played in these events, drawing attention to William's strategic use of printed texts at a time of strict official control over the press. Lois Schwoerer, for example, affirms, "By the time of the [1688] Revolution, English people were well accustomed to the public airing in print of political and religious commentary and ideas that were sharply critical of the government. This background of experience with the print media was an important part of the context within which the Revolution unfolded."[2] Joad Raymond, too, argues that the use of print was crucial to the success of the Revolution: "By 1688, the year of the Glorious Revolution, it was self-evident that any attempt to generate public support for a political initiative, party or position, would have to exploit the persuasive powers of the press."[3] Coming from the Dutch Republic, with its long history of a tolerant press,[4] William was well aware of the power of printed propaganda and used it to his advantage, publishing, among other works, *The Declaration of His Highnes William Henry by the Grace of God Prince of Orange, &c. of the Reasons Inducing Him, to Appear in Armes in the Kingdome of England* (1688).[5] Initially printed at The Hague, then shipped secretly to "key locations across England and Scotland," the *Declaration* was released "simultaneously at all these places," as well as at locations in mainland Europe, when William's fleet set sail.[6] In Jonathan Israel's view, "The Prince of Orange's *Declaration* was one of the greatest and most decisive propaganda coups of early modern times."[7]

Yet while there is certainly evidence to support the argument that William's use of the press to disseminate his political aims constituted a new media moment in England, other media, too, contributed to the communication of political news and ideas. As Ian Atherton reminds us, "most news" was still spread "by word of mouth" at this time, and there is indeed evidence that news about the upheaval in London was shared and passed on to the provinces by travelers.[8] Ballads and songs about the political changes taking place also played their part in both communicating information and channeling affect. Gilbert Burnet, for example, commented retrospectively on the unifying effect that the singing of "Lilliburlero" had for the opponents of James.[9] Likewise, manuscript materials also conveyed crucial information about political events in the autumn of 1688. Letters containing news about the campaign were sent between correspondents, then often copied and recirculated to other correspondents. Writing to his father-in-law Daniel Fleming on October 12, 1688, for example, Edward Wilson shared "the talk of these talkative times" regarding a petition to the king by seventy gentlemen of Yorkshire.[10] Nine days later, Alexander Faringdon sent Fleming copies of letters from his mother and a friend in London regarding the news and rumors in the capital.[11] Within the metropolis, coffeehouses provided physical spaces where the population could consume printed and written information, creating what Barbara Shapiro describes as "a kind of multiplier effect for the volume and velocity of available political information and opinion."[12]

To understand the unfolding of the Revolution, then, we need to attend to a media ecology that includes "voice, sound, image, and manuscript writing," as well as print.[13] As Shapiro suggests, "Real people ... do not learn from any single genre. They know what they know through a melange of sources, and not only by reading and having heard about distant matters but also through seeing and participating directly in the world around them."[14] In a similar vein, James Raven argues that putting too much "emphasis upon print and 'the book' threatens to isolate their study from a broader cultural history in which communication operated at multiple levels and in which the relationship between text and audience was often influenced by other modes of social interaction."[15] Although William's printed *Declaration* was a crucial intervention through which confidence in his cause was created and affirmed, the influence of the document was also amplified by its remediation in oral and manuscript media; the *Declaration* was performed orally in locations of political and religious significance such as Exeter Cathedral, and references to it in ballads and political songs added to its impact. It is significant that in attempting to dry up the flow of information and speculation about political events in late October 1688, James II issued a proclamation not just against printed material but against "divers evil disposed Persons" who "make it their business by Writing, Printing, or Speaking, to defame Our Government with false and seditious News and Reports."[16] His intervention was aimed at the entire mediascape, not just at printed copies of the *Declaration*.

In this essay, I want to encourage a wider focus on the mediation of events in the Revolution by considering the role of one particularly important but understudied nonprint genre that helped to communicate news in the fall of 1688: the official manuscript newsletter produced by the authority of the government. Initiated after the Restoration and sent by the secretary of state's offices to a limited number of recipients at home and abroad, including government diplomats overseas, official manuscript newsletters were "confidential" documents, in Donald Reiman's classification.[17] Given the regulations prohibiting the sharing of domestic political information through other media, including the attempted suppression of unofficial newsletters,[18] these official manuscript newsletters provide an invaluable source of information about the pressures faced by James's government. An examination of official manuscript newsletters during this delimited time period also gives us general insight into how the genre was understood and employed.[19] As we will see, there were formal properties associated with the genre of the official manuscript newsletter, properties that were tacitly understood by writers and readers at the time but that are sometimes difficult for us to discern because they combine elements that we now think of as distinct. Written behind closed doors by a cadre of clerks in the secretary of state's offices, official manuscript newsletters combined business, political, and personal connections, blurring the lines between public and private spheres. Derived from oral, manuscript, and printed sources, they traveled to their recipients along with other manuscript materials and printed works, and they amplified as well as corrected information provided in the printed gazettes with which they were sent. When they arrived at their destinations, they were collated and compared, sifted and sorted as pieces in a larger puzzle of information gathering within complicated diplomatic networks, then sometimes copied and sent out again with additional commentary. In the work that follows, I seek both to understand more about the Revolution through a close study of the official newsletters produced during this time and to learn more about the genre through a consideration of how official newsletters represented the era's extraordinary political events. This examination will contribute to a more comprehensive perspective on the media ecology at the time of the 1688 Revolution, as well as a more specific understanding of the affordances of official manuscript newsletters within that media ecology.

Histories and Archives of Official Manuscript Newsletters

The origins of the official manuscript newsletter system in Britain can be traced to the circulars sent out in the 1630s from the offices of the two secretaries of state: that of the Northern Department (responsible for overseeing interests connected with the Protestant northern European states) and that of the more prestigious Southern Department (whose mandate included the Catholic states in southern Europe).[20] As Ian Atherton suggests, however, the genre of the official newsletter changed significantly over the subsequent thirty years, largely because it adopted characteristics of the printed newsbooks of the early 1640s. After the Restoration, it was the news writer Henry Muddiman who developed the form of the official newsletter "to a point of efficiency, both in its contents and its circulation, that it had never reached before."[21] Muddiman also produced four printed newsbooks between 1659 and 1666. His newsletter had a circulation of approximately 150 and was not only sent out to subscribers but also distributed to coffeehouses and sold on market days in locations such as Norwich.[22] As James Sutherland notes, Muddiman "sent out his news-letters from his own office at the Seven Stars in the Strand near the New Exchange, but invariably headed them 'Whitehall.'"[23] The responsibility for producing official newsletters was eventually taken over by Joseph Williamson, although Muddiman did keep up an unofficial newsletter service. Williamson also assumed responsibility for producing the *London Gazette*, the printed newspaper produced "by authority."[24] In his varying official capacities over the next fifteen years (as undersecretary and then secretary of state), the highly efficient Williamson constructed an intricate network of news and intelligence gathering that involved both the newsletter service and the *London Gazette*. Whereas Muddiman's newsletter audience had been diverse, Williamson's was selective, designed for maximum information and efficiency. He relied on what we would now call the civil service abroad, sending newsletters crafted by his office to English diplomats in far-flung locations in expectation of receiving information from them in return.[25] Williamson was dismissed from his position as secretary of state in 1679, but the official manuscript newsletter system that operated in the fall of 1688 was essentially the same as it had been in Williamson's time. In fact, several of Williamson's former employees, such as Robert Yard and Owen Wynne, were still working in the offices of the secretaries of state when news of the Prince of Orange's amassing of troops became the focus of concern.

Official newsletters dating from this time period are scattered in a number of archives in Europe and North America. For the purposes of this essay, I consulted materials sent from the offices of the two secretaries of state to two English diplomats stationed in Europe during the time period: Sir Richard Bulstrode in Brussels (which was the responsibility of the Southern Department) and Edmund Poley in Sweden (which was under the purview of the Northern Department). Bulstrode was a Royalist soldier and lawyer who, after serving time in prison for major theft, converted to Catholicism, was forgiven by Charles II, and was appointed resident ambassador at Brussels when James II assumed the throne in 1685.[26] Poley was a career diplomat who served as envoy-extraordinary to Sweden during the fall of 1688.[27] The Carl Pforzheimer Collection of English Manuscripts at the Harry Ransom Center, University of Texas, Austin, contains 1,469 official manuscript newsletters sent to Bulstrode from the Office of the Secretary of State for the Southern Department. I consulted fifty-eight letters written between August 24, 1688, and February 1, 1689. Twenty-seven were written in French, the official language of diplomacy; twenty-one in English; and ten in both French and English.[28] A number of these bear the signature of Williamson's protégé, Robert Yard. The British Library holds seventeen official manuscript newsletters sent to Poley in Stockholm (by the secretary of state for the Northern Department) between September 28, 1688, and March 19, 1689, which are signed variously with the names of John Cooke, Owen Wynne, Humphrey Griffith, Rowland Tempest, and Richard Warre. I also consulted the additional material included with the Poley Papers: two newsletters from Holland regarding the landing of William of Orange's troops in England; two letters from Sir Gabriel de Sylvius, resident ambassador at Copenhagen; one letter from Richard Bulstrode; and forty-one letters from Sir Peter Wyche, resident ambassador at Hamburg.

The official manuscript newsletters sent to Bulstrode and Poley provide a comprehensive account of the events of the Glorious Revolution from the perspective of the offices of James's two secretaries of state. They give us a sense of the shared features of the genre of the official manuscript newsletter, including their multimodal and multimediated character, as well as the differences between particular newsletters that were effects of their creation by individual writers in different offices. The additional materials in the Poley collection suggest the "extensive" reading that an envoy's office would employ to gather information.[29] Moreover, the letters from Wyche, in particular, demonstrate the horizontal connections involved in the circulation and consumption of official manuscript newsletters; Wyche received newsletters from London in less than a week, copied and added to them, then sent them on to Poley, whose newsletters from London took approximately three weeks in transit.[30] Wyche's letters also indicate how material from the newsletters was reproduced and recontextualized in subsequent iterations. Together, these materials demonstrate the important role of manuscript sources in the late seventeenth-century news media.

Newsletters as Sites of Multimodal Connectivity

Official manuscript newsletters sent to Bulstrode and Poley fulfilled several different functions. On the one hand, they were government and business documents. Comments by correspondents confirm the expectation established by Williamson that news would be traded for news. In a letter to Bulstrode dated October 29, 1688, for example, Robert Yard wrote, "And now you must give me leave to tell you that the news papers are somewhat barren containing nothing but what is in the Brussels Gazettes; pray lett the Secretary favour me with what passes in yr owne parts, at least what is fitt for me to know."[31] Two weeks later, he again asked for more extensive reports: "Pray Sir favor me with an account of the news from yr parts for of late I have onely had the papers from Vienna, especially since the scene of war is now removed to Germany."[32]

Envoys were also expected to promote the views sent to them through the newsletters, as Peter Wyche indicated when he suggested that Poley use the news sent from Whitehall to "disabuse [the] Court where you are [which] may have suckt in ye poyson" regarding the story of the illegitimacy of the Prince of Wales.[33]

Although they operated as professional transactions among government officials, manuscript newsletters depended on the cultivation of human relationships. They used general protocols for eighteenth-century letter writing, as outlined by Eve Tavor Bannet.[34] Writers to both Bulstrode and Poley employed the language of courtesy in their newsletters, referring to themselves as "your servant" and to the letters sent by their correspondents as "favours." While an unidentified clerk would have transcribed the newsletters that Peter Wyche sent out, Wyche himself always formally signed his letters with the phrase "Yr most obedient and most humble servant," produced in his own distinctive block handwriting (fig. 1). By signing his own letters, Wyche capitalized on what Harold Love and Arthur Marotti describe as "script's greater power of projecting the individuality of the inscriber."[35] Newsletters frequently began by acknowledging the receipt of an earlier letter, tacitly reinforcing the sense of intimacy and obligation as well as confirming the ongoing relationship involved in the newsletter writing process. John Cooke commenced his letter of October 19, 1688, to Poley, for example, by noting, "Your last favour of Sept. 19 came to my hands the 15th instant for which I returne you my thanks."[36] Official manuscript newsletters even included the occasional personal note, as, for example, a reference to Bulstrode's earlier illness in a letter dated November 5, 1688.[37] The establishment of ongoing

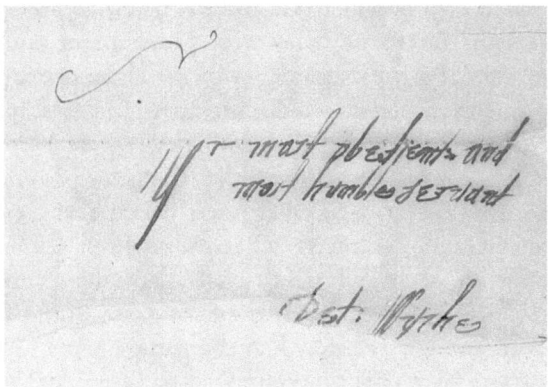

FIGURE 1. Manuscript newsletter with Peter Wyche's signature. (Poley Papers, October 5, 1688, Add MS 45731, f. 10; © The British Library Board)

relationships meant that correspondents felt freer to request additional "favours" when necessary, and, given the events of late 1688, there was a constant desire for more news in the hopes of obtaining a fuller picture of the threat to the nation.

The sudden dismissal of Robert Spencer, 2nd Earl of Sunderland, as secretary of state for the Southern Department at the end of October demonstrates how newsletter personnel moved between offices, working to establish new personal connections but also seeking to maintain old ones in case they might still be useful. In a farewell letter written on October 30, 1688, Wynne informed Poley that the current secretary of state for the Northern Department, Charles Middleton, Earl of Middleton, had taken over Sunderland's position in the Southern Department office and that it was Middleton's "pleasure & favour to me that I follow him" in making the shift of offices. Wynne conflated his office with the geographical location it oversaw as he conveyed his regrets to Poley that "I shall both quitt *this Province you are in* & shall loose the Honour as well as Satisfaction of yo. kind & obliging Letters." He commended the "honest Gentlemen" who would be writing to Poley in the future from the Northern office but also concluded by assuring Poley of his continued services if required: "When you shall see fit to honour me with any Commands of yours none shall more readily obey them to the extent of my power than ... Your most humble and obedient Servant, O. Wynne."[38] From his new position in the Southern Department, Wynne also wrote to Bulstrode, inquiring after his health and offering him "my little service."[39]

As these letters suggest, there was not a clear split between professional and personal concerns in the manuscript newsletters. Writers sought to sustain positive relationships, as the maintenance of strong social-personal relationships also encouraged a steady flow of information. Conversely, the fact that manuscript newsletters were written between individuals over a period of time contributed to the strengthening of individual social connections. Newsletters sent from Peter Wyche to Poley, for example, suggest how a strong personal connection could build up over a number of years. Wyche had news from the letters he received from Whitehall copied and sent on so Poley would receive it earlier than in letters sent directly to him from London. The letters from Wyche include the superscript "Whitehall" to indicate the authoritative source of their contents, but they are written in a cramped hand and unevenly spaced on the page, with material often squeezed into the margins, so they differ visibly from official newsletters sent out by the secretary of state's office (see fig. 2).

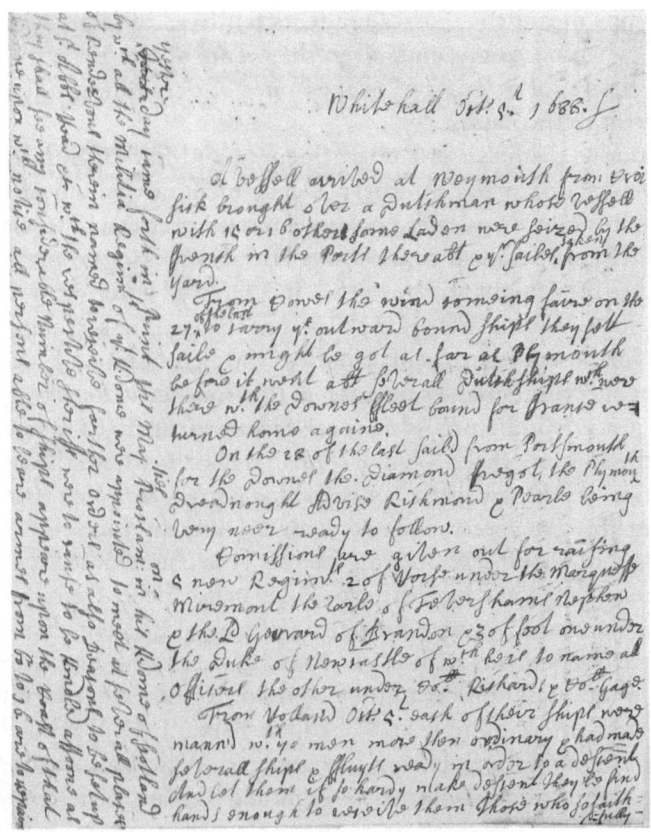

FIGURE 2. Manuscript newsletter from Peter Wyche to Edmond Poley. (Poley Papers, October 5, 1688, Add MS 45731, f. 11; © The British Library Board)

Wyche's letters also contain additional commentary, including his impressions of and reactions to events. His personal relationship with Poley allowed Wyche to express his thoughts more freely, as he clearly anticipated a sympathetic reader. In his letter of October 5, 1688, for example, he fulminated: "To what an height hath ye [Prince of Orange] brought things? to see the King and himself fighting in the feild one against the Other; Which (I'm sure) Heaven cannot see unconcernedly, no more than the sun could [see] Atreus' banquet [that] he made to his Brother. As a Plott discovered, hath seldom or never succeeded, soe one layd with soe horrid circumstances is to cry for Vengeance which consideration maintains me in some quietness & makes me not too disturbedly expect the great event."⁴⁰ As the reference to Atreus's banquet illustrates, Wyche often waxed poetic in his letters to Poley, drawing analogies between contemporary events and episodes from classical literature, the Bible, or more recent history. He recontextualized the material from the official newsletters from Whitehall by adding both more information (on the wars in Europe) and more affect. As we will see, the unfolding of events in the fall of 1688 would produce more such reactions, not only from Wyche, but also from the writers in the secretaries of states' offices.

Newsletters as Sites of Multimediation

In addition to connecting individuals in a variety of ways, official manuscript newsletters served as sites of multimediation, operating in relation to and as vectors for other media. Newsletters in both the Bulstrode and Poley collections suggest a complex connection between official manuscript newsletters and printed newspapers.⁴¹ On the one hand, there is a clear distinction between the news presented at the time in the only official newspaper, the *London Gazette,* and the news contained in the newsletters. As Harold Love indicates, "Much more could always be said in a letter than could be uttered in print."⁴² Because of the licensing laws and the government's concern to minimize the publicizing of political information, the *London Gazette* contained little information about the gathering threat from the Dutch in the fall of 1688. The issue of September 27, 1688, for example, noted only that the Prince of Orange had returned to The Hague and that the States of Holland, "who were adjourned for 2 or 3 days, assembled again on Wednesday" to discuss "the matter about the Prohibition of French Commodities."⁴³ It was not until the beginning of October that the *Gazette* provided news about the full extent of the threat:

> The great Preparations, that have been making here [in the Hague] for some time, are continued with extraordinary diligence. The Recruits that are ordered to be made will amount to 12000 Men: And 1300 of the Troops of *Brandenburgh, Lunenburgh,* and *Hesse Cassel,* are taken into the Service of this State: The Fleet lies now off of *Goeree;* and the Camp has been so ordered, that from thence they can send, as they do, the Troops to *Texel, Zealand, Helvoet Sluys,* and *Rotterdam,* to be embark'd; and all things will be ready for them to set sail the next week, with an Intention to invade *England.*⁴⁴

Although the *Gazette* subsequently included information about James's many attempts to restore confidence in his government and reprinted his official proclamations, it gave little indication about the nature or extent of the threat to the state.

In contrast to the silence of the *London Gazette*, manuscript newsletters were buzzing with concern about the Dutch as early as the end of August 1688. A newsletter to Bulstrode written on August 24, 1688, for example, reads, "Wee are here somewhat alarmed at the dutch preparations not being able to imagine what designe they can have . . . but whatever is to be the King will be in a posture not to fear them, for his Majesty has ordered 10 men of war more to be immediately fitted out and they will be ready in a very short time."[45] The Dutch ambassador, Arnout van Citters, continued to deny that the forces were being amassed for a strike against England, and an August 31, 1688, newsletter informed Bulstrode of decreasing anxiety regarding the prince's intentions: "the apprehensions we had here of the dutch preparations begin to dwindle and perhaps our new Equipage may thereupon slacken."[46] By the end of September, however, it was clear that the Dutch intended military action toward Britain. As Wyche wrote to Poley on October 5, "Tho in yr last favour off the 19th past, you seem to believe the Invasion from Holland is less to be credited, or that there are reasons to expect the best; yet yr letters receiv'd this morning will doubtless (as mine have done) acquaint you that the design is now clear to our Master who expects hourly the execution of it and will venture his Royal Person to repell it."[47] As Wyche's comments suggest, information in the manuscript newsletters during the unsettled period of fall 1688 was subject to constant revision, as one letter or enclosure could change the recipient's perspective on the situation completely.

Although there were differences in the kind and volume of information that was included in the newspaper versus the manuscript newsletter, the relationship between the two media was complex. Newspapers were included with newsletters in both the outgoing and incoming mail of the offices of the secretaries of state. Clerks would glean material from the incoming foreign newsletters and newspapers for inclusion in the upcoming issue of the *London Gazette* and, correspondingly, mail out current copies of the *Gazette* along with their own newsletters. Writers of the Bulstrode and Poley newsletters frequently referred their recipients to the information included in enclosed issues of the *Gazette*. A letter dated August 27, 1688, for example, told Bulstrode, "Vous verrez dans la Gazette la declaration que le Roy fit vendredy passé... touchant la convocation du Parlement" (You will see in the *Gazette* the declaration that the King made last Friday to his Council... regarding the convening of Parliament), while on October 12, 1688, John Cooke directed Poley to "see what the Gazette says, how many outlandish mails are in answer."[48] While the newsletters supplemented the information contained in the newspapers, the newspapers also were used as supplements to or shorthand for the news in the letters.

In addition to illustrating the intersections between official manuscript newsletters and the newspaper form, the Bulstrode and Poley collections demonstrate the complex relationship between manuscript newsletters and other nonprint media. The oral origin of much information contained in the newsletters is evident in expressions commonly used, such as "it is said" and "we hear" (or, for the letters written in French, "L'on dit que"). John Cooke's newsletter to Poley on October 19, 1688, suggests the multiple ways in which orality and aurality informed the news he sent:

> Though the Dutch Fleet has been long *talkd of*, as ready *tis said* to give us a visit, yet hitherto *we do not hear* they have made a descent anywhere, nor that they have yet appeared upon our coast. But if they intend an attempt upon us, *as it is generally said and believed* they do, it cannot be many days before they be obliged to let us know this meaning... Monsr. Van Citters the Dutch [Ambassador] wayted upon his [Majesty] yesterday... Those who pretend to have learnd something from the [Ambassador] himself, *say* it was to give his [Majesty] an account why the States arm'd so powerfully by Sea & Land at this time.[49]

As this example intimates, orality was never far from the surface of the manuscript newsletters.

Foreign letters were also frequently mentioned in the Bulstrode and Poley papers, giving us a glimpse into the communications networks on which the dissemination of news depended. As Rachael Scarborough King suggests, "Letters gave newsletters and newspapers their early facticity and authority."[50] By the end of October 1688, when anticipation about the Dutch invasion had reached its height, there was a sudden dearth of news due to adverse weather conditions that prevented letters from being sent on the packet boats. Newsletter writers reacted variously to the interruption in the exchange of news at this crucial stage. John Cooke wrote to Poley, with a mixture of exasperation and relief, "This same wind that hinders us from our transmission [of] letters, doth also (for so long at least) keep our enemies from approaching our coast."[51] Instead of presenting actual news, writers speculated about the intervention of providence in preventing the Dutch fleet from sailing and about the damage that was rumored to have been done to the Dutch ships by the storms. Despite the fact that there was no news, manuscript newsletter writers kept up their schedules, if only to point out the fact that they had no news. On October 19, 1688, Wyche wrote regretfully to Poley to say, "I have nothing for you, not a word being come hither this day from England & tis probable the letters may not currently come over [from] Holland."[52] The manuscript newsletters, like their print counterparts, the newspapers, were periodical forms that were expected to be produced regularly, regardless of what content was available.

Items written after November 5, 1688, highlight the manuscript newsletters' dependence on another manuscript genre: "express" letters carried within the nation by messengers on horseback. The newsletter of November 9, 1688, that informed Bulstrode of the invasion by William of Orange illustrates the updating of information that each newly arrived express provided: "On Monday last towards the Evening the Dutch began to land, and on Tuesday they were all come ashore, and their Parties began to advance towards Exeter. The last Express came from thence last Wednesday night or Thursday morning who brought an account that the Enemy were then within 9 or 10 miles from that citty."[53] A number of post-invasion newsletters show signs of having been finished at the last minute before posting to include information from the latest express.[54] Bulstrode's correspondent, for example, wrote on November 23, 1688, about halfway through a letter in which he recounted other news. "*Je viens d'aprendre a cet moment* que les avant guards du Prince d'Orange estaient avances a 20 milles de Salisbury" (*I have just learned at this minute* that the advance guards of the Prince of Orange have advanced to twenty miles outside of Salisbury).[55] The manuscript newsletters, unlike the oral and print sources on which they relied and to which they were connected, represented the chronological arrival of new news through inscription.

John Sommerville has argued that the regular publication of newspapers in the early modern era contributed to an alteration in ideas of time, encouraging an understanding of history as a series of present moments displacing each other in a linear fashion.[56] But as the periodicity of manuscript newsletters suggests, in the fall of 1688 manuscript documents, too, portrayed the events of the Revolution as a series of progressive present moments as they consolidated the information provided by oral information, letters, and printed works into continual updates. As we have seen, however, correspondents were conscious of the logistics of communication: the weather affecting packet boats, the changing information that came with each express, and the time lag between when events took place in England and when they became known in the rest of Europe. The consequences of this time lag were particularly evident during the rapid advance of William's troops. In his letter to Poley of November 27, Wyche noted that he had received Poley's letter from November 14, in which Poley discussed news sent from Whitehall on November 9, just after William's troops arrived. Wyche replied with information he had received from Whitehall dated November 20, "the freshest [that] could be."[57] While they were writing down and trading perspectives on the events of the Revolution of 1688, writers and readers of official newsletters were also aware that knowledge at any point was incomplete, provisional and subject to re-interpretation.

Narrating the Downfall of a Regime

As the autumn progressed and the news grew direr for the government forces, newsletter writers increasingly offered their personal perspectives on events. Mere formalities gave way to the language of affect. In his letter of October 12, 1688, to Poley, John Cooke lamented:

> I do not know that ever any nation was so distracted with suspicion & suspense as ours is at this time; and that which surmises to be the strangest thing of all, the Invasion now apprehended has two faces, which a man would think incompatible in one & this same subject; that is, to be friendly & driedfull, wellcome & abhored: yet so it appears to different persons & parties. My reason has always look't upon it as an attempt impossible, because against all justice, honour, and morall honesty; but since we have no assurances of the contrary, and all forain intelligence runs in this same stream, I cannot till now to defend my self any longer from believing it.[58]

Never one to hold back his sentiments, Wyche grew even more emotional as he wrote to Poley on October 19, 1688, that a "solemn fast to implore a blessing on the Princes designe" had been held in the provinces, adding. with his characteristic outrage, "Was God ever soe blasphemed or mocked?"[59]

The manuscript newsletters from early November, when William landed, until December 12, when James II attempted to flee to France, indicate just how quickly the regime crumbled. A letter to Bulstrode written on November 9 observed optimistically, "All things here are God be thanked very quiet and there does not yet appear any disposition in the people that can give the Prince of Orange any great Encouragement."[60] By November 12, the writer noted some signs of trouble, commenting that "the Boys and Rabble made last night some disturbance as they have done severall times before, to pull down as they pretend the Popish Chappells" and indicating that the "Insolency of the Rabble does not indeed look well." Even at this point, however, he concluded positively, "I doubt not but they will be prevented from committing any disorder by the militia that will be constantly kept up for a guard in the Citty and the troops that will be left here in the Kings absence."[61] By November 19, however, the letters had taken on a darker tone, as the writer conveyed the information about the removal of the Prince of Wales to Portsmouth, adding that "cett resolution" (this resolution) was revealed only "quelques heures avant son depart" (a few hours before his departure).[62] As desertion followed desertion and the Prince of Orange's army drew closer to London, letters became longer as writers were hard-pressed to include all the details of the collapse of support for James. Wyche's letters suggest how "melancholy a state" the kingdom was in at this point, as he sent on news from Whitehall to Poley: "Why I am (as I ought loyally to be) in great perplexity & unfit for all Conversation, you are to find in ye Inclosed receiv'd this morning, [which] are to tell you the Pr[ince of Orange] is Master of his designe."[63] The writer of a December 7, 1688, letter to Bulstrode similarly lamented, "These sort of melancholy news come so thicke upon one another that they are enough to confound the most constant mind."[64] The newsletter itself became a material embodiment of the collapse of the regime: although this letter began in ordered and elegant handwriting, suggesting a "spatialisation of thought" similar to that found in printed works, it ended in a blur of "expressive irregularity" without even a signature, as the writer hurriedly scrawled, "You must Excuse me that I doe not send you this likewise in french wee are in such a hurry of businesse that hardly have time to write this" (see fig. 3).[65]

The final blow for the network of newsletter writers and readers was the news of the departure of King James. The official newsletter sent to

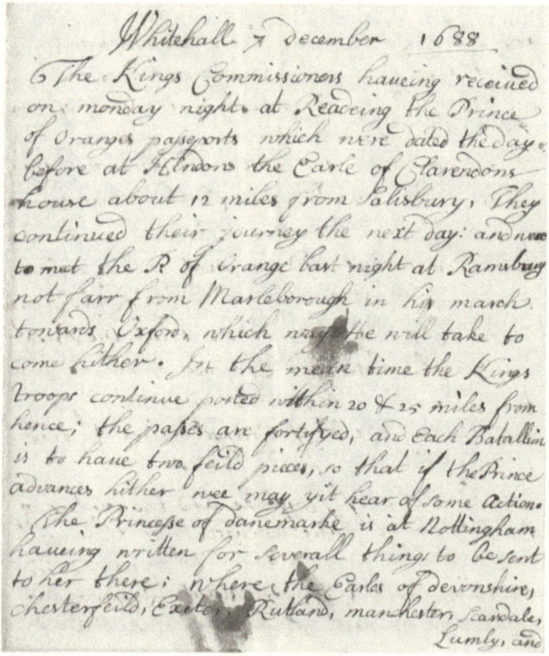

FIGURE 3. First and final pages of a manuscript newsletter sent to Sir Richard Bulstrode. (Carl H. Pforzheimer Collection of English Manuscripts, December 7, 1688, PFORZ-MS-1866, MS. 103c, box 10, folder 7; Harry Ransom Center, University of Texas, Austin)

Whitehall 7 december 1688

The Kings Commissioners haueing receiued on monday night at Reading the Prince of Oranges passports which were dated the day before at Hindon the Earle of Clarendons house about 12 miles from Salisbury. They continued their journey the next day: and were to meet the P. of Orange last night at Ramsbury not farr from Marleborough in his march towards Oxford, which way he will take to come hither. In the meane time the Kings troops continue posted within 20 & 25 miles from hence; the passes are fortifyed, and each Battallion is to haue two feild pieces, so that if the Prince advances hither wee may yit hear of some Action. The Princesse of Danemarke is at Nottingham haueing written for severall things to be sent to her there; where the Earles of devonshire, chesterfeild, Exeter, Rutland, manchester, Scarsdale, Lumly, and

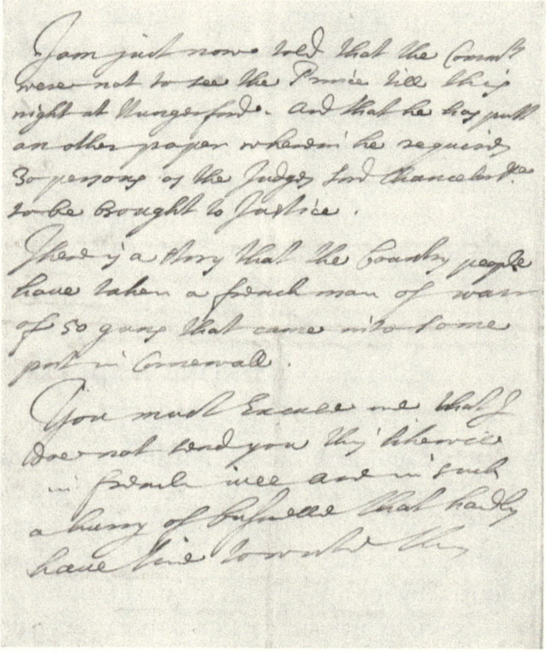

I am just now told that the Comm:rs were not to see the Prince till this night at Hungerford. And that he has putt an other prayer wherein he requires 30 persons as the Judges Lord Chancelor &c. to be brought to Justice.

There is a story that the Country people haue taken a french man of warr of 50 guns that came into some port in Cornewall.

You must Excuse me that I doe not send you this otherwise in french wee are in such a hurry of busynesse that hardly haue time to write this

Poley from Whitehall on December 12, 1688, read simply: "His Majesty who appeared very cheerful on the 10th at night at supper withdrew himself in person early on the 11th & left us" and concluded, "The Prince of Orange lays this night in Windsor."[66] A letter sent to Bulstrode on December 14 also informed him of James's flight and provided the additional unsavory details that the king's party was mistaken by the "Inhabitants of Feversham" for "some persons that were endeavouring to escape" and was pillaged and then returned to shore and escorted back to London. The newsletter ended with the understated editorial comment, "A sudden & surprising revolution indeed."[67]

James's departure prompted a meeting of the Lords Spiritual and Temporal, who drew up an official declaration that they presented to William requesting his assistance in procuring a "Free Parliament, to rescue Us, with as little Effusion, as possi[b]le, of Christian blood from the imminent Dangers of Popery and Slavery."[68] William arrived at St. James's Palace on December 18, 1688, and James left London a second time early that morning, this time successfully crossing to France. The diplomatic volte-face that accompanied the rapid regime change is indicated in the newsletter to Bulstrode written on December 28, as the writer celebrated the Revolution. Noting that the quick alteration might seem "bien suprenante" (quite surprising) to outsiders, he suggested that those familiar with the constraints under which the English had suffered for several years and the "mecontentement si universel" (discontent so universal) were not at all astonished to see how things changed so quickly at the first opportunity.[69] Although the formal qualities of the genre remained the same, and many of the personnel in the secretaries of states' offices kept their positions for a time at least, the official manuscript newsletters—remaining the mouthpiece of the government—necessarily reflected the position of the new regime.

A Shifting Media Ecology

In addition to constituting a change of regime, the period after William's arrival in London witnessed a shift in the media ecology as, in the ensuing confusion, enforcement of the licensing laws became impossible. The day of James's initial departure from London, December 11, 1688, also saw the publication of the *Universal Intelligence*, an unlicensed newspaper produced by John Wallis. In the next four months, as R. B. Walker notes, "at least eight newspapers and three journals of opinion commenced publication."⁷⁰ In the vacuum of information following William's arrival at London, newsletters lost their currency as newspapers vied with one another to share the most current domestic news. The editor of the new *London Courant* commented on the problem, observing, "The greater the itch of curiosity after News hath been here of late, the less has the humour been gratified. Insomuch, that a modest enquiry where his Majesty, or his Royal Highness the Prince of Orange was, or what they were doing, could scarce be resolved, till the news had been exported and imported in a Foreign News-Letter."⁷¹ The *Courant* suggests that the roles of manuscript newsletters and the newspaper had reversed, with the newspapers now providing the most immediate access to domestic information. It was to be a short-lived reversal, however, as by February 1689 William had reinstituted the prepublication censorship laws that would remain in place until the lapse of the Licensing Act in 1695.

As the number of unlicensed newspapers expanded after William's arrival, there was a corresponding dearth of official manuscript newsletters being sent out from the secretary of state's office from December to March—at least for those being sent abroad. The Poley Papers collection contains only one letter sent directly from Whitehall between December 4, 1688, and March 1, 1689. There are also more gaps in the letters sent to Bulstrode, with only one included that was written between December 31 and January 14, and then only six more until March 1689. A letter sent to Poley on February 16, 1689, by Richard Warre (a tardy response to a letter Poley had sent a month earlier) commented on the uncertainty in the offices of the secretaries of state at this point: "I know not yet what my fortune may be, but if I continue in their office, I [shall] always be glad to receive your commands and be ready to serve you."⁷² Comments in letters sent from Wyche confirm the lack of official correspondence. On December 25, for example, Wyche indicated that he had received "noe letters from Whitehall."⁷³ He was still awaiting letters on January 3, 1689, when the only news regarding England he had to send on to Poley was from the *Haarlem Gazette*.⁷⁴ Finally, on March 19 Wyche shared the news of his dismissal: "Ime just now told that some of this company have letters that orders are giving by ye irresistible present authority to recall in general all ye forraine Ministers: a new Broom Sweeps clean, & ye Correspondence to be held, & allyances to be made must be ye business of his own creatures."⁷⁵

The diplomats' letters in the early part of 1689 provide a strong indication of the personal relationships that had developed between them over the course of their professional careers. Bulstrode shared his despondency regarding the situation in a letter to Wyche written on January 9, 1689: "This day I receivd yrs of ye 3rd Inst., & must beg yr pardon that I have been soe long silent, having been fitter for some time past to write in tears then Inke; upon ye deplorable state of our Royale master." Although he suggested, "I am well satisfied since their Majesties are safe," he also outlined his own sad "particulars" in his letter: "I have above 2500 sterling now in arrears & God knows what will become of me, and what way I shall pay my debts here; my allowance from ye king being my all, having noe estate, being a younger Brother's Son."[76] Interestingly, Wyche appears to have sent this letter on to Poley, anticipating a sympathetic reception. But while the letters sent among government officials suggest that personal relationships would outlast changes of situation, the aftermath of the Revolution of 1688 also offers an opportunity to see the different political inclinations of those who contributed to the intelligence of the secretaries of states' offices. Bulstrode would remain loyal to James, following him into exile at the court at St. Germain; Wyche also stayed in Europe, shifting to provide intelligence to James's appointed secretary of state. But while Poley, too, felt the sweep of the "new Broom" as he lost his diplomatic position in spring of 1689, he later managed to reinvent himself as one of William's "creatures."[77]

In *Social Authorship and the Advent of Print*, Margaret J. M. Ezell asserts that "the latter part of the seventeenth and the first part of the eighteenth century still lack a clear description of the nature of manuscript literary activity, much less a theory of nonprint literary culture."[78] I would add to this observation that part of the task of understanding nonprint literary culture includes obtaining a wider perspective on the field of manuscript culture in general and understanding how manuscript culture worked in relationship to oral and print media. By focusing on a particular genre of manuscript culture, official manuscript newsletters, within the specific time frame of the Revolution of 1688, this essay has contributed to that wider mapping of manuscript within the dynamics of the long eighteenth-century media ecology. As I have argued, as multimodal forms of social communication that bear the traces of the other media involved in their production, dissemination, and reception, official manuscript newsletters represent a complex mixture of public and confidential, personal and professional, and literary and nonliterary elements. Moreover, an examination of the newsletters sent to Bulstrode and Poley in the fall of 1688 tells us much about how the events of the

Glorious Revolution were portrayed and understood. Although official manuscript newsletters did not promote revolutionary politics per se in the same way that the Prince of Orange's *Declaration* did, by providing periodic and chronological (albeit at times disrupted) commentary on events, they represented the fall of James's government as a steadily unfolding—and, by the end, an inevitable—narrative of the "sudden & surprising" revolution.

Notes

1. Jardine, *Going Dutch*, 4. For detailed accounts of the Glorious Revolution, see Harris, *Revolution*; Pincus, *1688*.
2. Schwoerer, "Liberty of the Press and Public Opinion," 220.
3. Raymond, *Pamphlets and Pamphleteering in Early Modern Britain*, 25.
4. See Briggs and Burke, *A Social History of the Media*, 47–48.
5. *The Declaration of His Highnes William Henry*. The *Declaration* asserts William's aims to "Preserv[e] the Protestant Religion" and restore "the Lawes and Liberties of England, Scotland and Ireland" by calling "a FREE AND LEGALL PARLIAMENT." It also calls into question the legitimacy of the recent birth of Prince James Edward Stuart.
6. The *Declaration* was written by Gaspar Fagel, William's English-trained Dutch adviser, with the help of Gilbert Burnet, a Scottish Episcopalian lawyer in exile at The Hague since the Restoration: Jardine, *Going Dutch*, 29.
7. Israel, *The Anglo-Dutch Moment*, 14.
8. Atherton, "The Itch Grown a Disease," 40. See also Fox, *Oral and Literate Culture in England*.
9. Burnet, *History of His Own Time*, 792.
10. *The Manuscripts of S. H. Fleming, Esq. of Rydal Hall*, 215.
11. Ibid., 216.
12. Shapiro, *Political Communication and Political Culture in England*, 53.
13. Siskin and Warner, "This Is Enlightenment," 7. While it may be true that, as Clifford Siskin and William Warner assert, print came to take "center stage" among other media in the eighteenth century, it is only by examining the entire media ecology that we understand how print culture rose to prominence within it.
14. Shapiro, *Political Communication and Political Culture in England*, 1.
15. Raven, "New Reading Histories, Print Culture and the Identification of Change," 268.
16. *By the King*.
17. Reiman defines confidential manuscripts as those "not intended for the eyes of a wide and diverse readership, but addressed to a specific group of indi-

viduals all of whom either are personally known to the writer or belong to some predefined group that the writer has reason to believe share communal values with him or her": Reiman, *The Study of Modern Manuscripts*, 39. I am grateful to Michelle Levy for this reference.

18. On October 6, 1688, James II ordered "the suppression of news letters at coffee houses and other publick places": Luttrell, *A Brief Historical Relation of State Affairs from September 1678 to April 1714*, 467.

19. Atherton comments, "Of all the genres of manuscript news, newsletters are particularly suitable for analysis for three reasons. First, they survive in relatively large numbers (whereas few manuscript news diaries are extant). Second, they are datable, whereas manuscript separates or 'pocket Manuscripts'—transcripts of treaties, trials, parliamentary proceedings and such like—often circulated many years after they were first written. Finally, most newsletters were signed and addressed, allowing us to study some of the intersections and relationships between writer and reader": Atherton, "The Itch Grown a Disease," 40.

20. For a similar account of the history of commercial newsletters, see King, "The Manuscript Newsletter and the Rise of the Newspaper." Peter Fraser suggests that "after 1676 an increasing volume of unlicensed newsletters appeared, purveyed by professional newswriters, which the Secretaries strove to suppress together with the unlicensed printed journals that appeared with the Popish Plot." As he indicates, both secretaries of state "had an interest and responsibility" in newsgathering and intelligence, with their "two systems" working "independently in friendly or sometimes hostile rivalry": Fraser, *The Intelligence of the Secretaries of State and Their Monopoly of Licensed News*, 2–3.

21. Sutherland, *The Restoration Newspaper and Its Development*, 6. Muddiman served Sir Edward Nicholas when he was secretary of state for the Southern Department and was the first editor of the government-approved newspaper the *Oxford Gazette* (which changed its name to the *London Gazette* when the Court returned to London after the plague). See also Marshall, "Sir Joseph Williamson and the Conduct of Administration in Restoration England"; Muddiman, *The King's Journalist 1659–1689*.

22. Atherton, "The Itch Grown a Disease," 53.

23. Sutherland, *The Restoration Newspaper and Its Development*, 6.

24. Fraser, *The Intelligence of the Secretaries of State and Their Monopoly of Licensed News*, 2. Atherton notes that Williamson "tried to take over Muddiman's newsletter," but when that failed, he began his own: Atherton, "The Itch Grown a Disease," 54.

25. Fraser notes that "the consuls in important locations received a weekly newsletter from Whitehall, as did all ambassadors and envoys abroad, and

certain other correspondents": Fraser, *The Intelligence of the Secretaries of State and Their Monopoly of Licensed News*, 6.
26. Davies, "Bulstrode, Sir Richard (1617–1711)."
27. Poley had the good fortune to be related through marriage to a previous secretary of state, Henry Bennet, Earl of Arlington, who had had helped him during his earlier diplomatic career at Brandenburg, Regensburg, and Frankfurt: see Handley, "Poley, Edmund (1655–1714)."
28. At the beginning of the period in question, there are letters French and English with the same date, and, presumably, included in the same dispatch.
29. Atherton suggests that "newsletters had to be read *extensively*" in large volume because "the best reports might be uncertain, temporary judgments in need of later confirmation or denial": Atherton, "The Itch Grown a Disease," 45.
30. Fraser, *The Intelligence of the Secretaries of State and Their Monopoly of Licensed News*, 64–65.
31. "Newsletter from the Office of Sir Joseph Williamson, Whitehall, London, to Sir Richard Bulstrode, Brussels," October 29, 1688, PFORZ-MS-1849, MS. 103c, Carl H. Pforzheimer Collection of English Manuscripts (hereafter, Pforzheimer Collection), Harry Ransom Center, University of Texas, Austin, box 10, folder 6.
32. "Newsletter from the Office of Sir Joseph Williamson, Whitehall, London, to Sir Richard Bulstrode, Brussels," November 12, 1688, PFORZ-MS-1854, MS. 103c, Pforzheimer Collection, Harry Ransom Center, box 10, folder 7.
33. Peter Wyche to Edmond Poley, November 16, 1688, Add MS 45731, Poley Papers, British Library, London, f. 56.
34. See Bannet, *Empire of Letters*.
35. Love and Marotti, "Manuscript Circulation and Transmission," 57–58.
36. John Cooke to Edmond Poley, October 19, 1688, Add MS 45731, Poley Papers, British Library, f. 20.
37. "Newsletter from the Office of Sir Joseph Williamson, Whitehall, London, to Sir Richard Bulstrode, Brussels," November 5, 1688, PFORZ-MS-1851, MS. 103c, Pforzheimer Collection, Harry Ransom Center, box 10, folder 6.
38. Owen Wynne to Edmond Poley, October 30, 1688, Add MS 45731, Poley Papers, British Library, f. 36.
39. "Newsletter from the Office of Sir Joseph Williamson, Whitehall, London, to Sir Richard Bulstrode, Brussels," November 12, 1688, PFORZ-MS-1856, MS. 103c, Pforzheimer Collection, Harry Ransom Center, box 10, folder 7.
40. Wyche to Poley, October 5, 1688, Add MS 45731, Poley Papers, British Library, f. 10.
41. Fraser indicates the intimate connection between Muddiman's newsletters and the *Gazette* when he writes, "Muddiman's newsletters were regularly

printed in the Haarlem and other gazettes, in exchange for which Castelyn and others supplied the Secretaries with their own newsletters, from which the 'copy' for the *London Gazette* was largely derived": Fraser, *The Intelligence of the Secretaries of State and Their Monopoly of Licensed News*, 6.
42. Love, *The Culture and Commerce of Texts*, 10.
43. *London Gazette*, no. 2385, September 27, 1688.
44. Ibid., no. 2386, October 1, 1688.
45. "Newsletter from the Office of Sir Joseph Williamson, Whitehall, London, to Sir Richard Bulstrode, Brussels," August 24, 1688, PFORZ-MS-1823, MS. 103c, Pforzheimer Collection, Harry Ransom Center, box 10, folder 5.
46. "Newsletter from the Office of Sir Joseph Williamson, Whitehall, London, to Sir Richard Bulstrode, Brussels," August 31, 1688, PFORZ-MS-1827, MS. 103c, Pforzheimer Collection, Harry Ransom Center, box 10, folder 5.
47. Wyche to Poley, October 5, 1688, Add MS 45731, f. 10.
48. "Newsletter from the Office of Sir Joseph Williamson, Whitehall, London, to Sir Richard Bulstrode, Brussels," August 27, 1688, PFORZ-MS-1824, MS. 103c, Pforzheimer Collection, Harry Ransom Center, box 10, folder 5; John Cooke to Poley, October 12, 1688, Add MS 45731, Poley Papers, British Library, f. 12.
49. Cooke to Poley, October 19, 1688, Add MS 45731, f. 20, emphasis added.
50. King, "The Manuscript Newsletter and the Rise of the Newspaper," 414.
51. Cooke to Poley, October 2, 1688, Add MS 45731, Poley Papers, British Library, f. 12.
52. Wyche to Poley, October 19, 1688, Add MS 45731, Poley Papers, British Library, f. 22.
53. "Newsletter from the Office of Sir Joseph Williamson, Whitehall, London, to Sir Richard Bulstrode, Brussels," November 9, 1688, PFORZ-MS-1852, MS. 103c, Pforzheimer Collection, Harry Ransom Center, box 10, folder 6.
54. As King points out, newsletters could accommodate information written at the last minute: King, "The Manuscript Newsletter and the Rise of the Newspaper," 424.
55. "Newsletter from the Office of Sir Joseph Williamson, Whitehall, London, to Sir Richard Bulstrode, Brussels," November 23, 1688, PFORZ-MS-1860, MS. 103c, Pforzheimer Collection, Harry Ransom Center, box 10, folder 7, emphasis added.
56. Sommerville, *The News Revolution in England*. For alternative perspectives on how newspapers altered concepts of time, see Claydon, "Daily News and the Construction of Time in Late Stuart England"; Woolf, "News, History, and the Construction of the Present in Early Modern England."
57. Wyche to Poley, November 27, 1688, Add MS 45731, Poley Papers, British Library, f. 65.

58. Cooke to Poley, October 2, 1688, Add MS 45731, f. 12.
59. Wyche to Poley, October 19, 1688, Add MS 45731, f. 22.
60. "Newsletter from the Office of Sir Joseph Williamson, Whitehall, London, to Sir Richard Bulstrode, Brussels," November 9, 1688, PFORZ-MS-1852, MS. 103c, Pforzheimer Collection, Harry Ransom Center, box 10, folder 6.
61. "Newsletter from the Office of Sir Joseph Williamson, Whitehall, London, to Sir Richard Bulstrode, Brussels," November 12, 1688, PFORZ-MS-1855, MS. 103c, Pforzheimer Collection, Harry Ransom Center, box 10, folder 7.
62. "Newsletter from the Office of Sir Joseph Williamson, Whitehall, London, to Sir Richard Bulstrode, Brussels," November 19, 1688, PFORZ-MS-1857, MS. 103c, Pforzheimer Collection, Harry Ransom Center, box 10, folder 7.
63. Wyche to Poley, December 1688, Add MS 45731, Poley Papers, British Library, f. 81.
64. "Newsletter from the Office of Sir Joseph Williamson, Whitehall, London, to Sir Richard Bulstrode, Brussels," December 7, 1688, PFORZ-MS-1866, MS. 103c, Pforzheimer Collection, Harry Ransom Center, box 10, folder 7.
65. Love and Marotti, "Manuscript Circulation and Transmission," 58.
66. Newsletter to Edmond Poley, December 14, 1688, Add MS 45731, Poley Papers, British Library f. 83.
67. "Newsletter from the Office of Sir Joseph Williamson, Whitehall, London, to Sir Richard Bulstrode, Brussels," December 14, 1688, PFORZ-MS-1868, MS. 103c, Pforzheimer Collection, Harry Ransom Center, box 10, folder 7.
68. *London Gazette*, no. 2409, December 13, 1688.
69. "Newsletter from the Office of Sir Joseph Williamson, Whitehall, London, to Sir Richard Bulstrode, Brussels," December 28, 1688, PFORZ-MS-1872, MS. 103c, Pforzheimer Collection, Harry Ransom Center, box 10, folder 7.
70. Walker, "The Newspaper Press in the Reign of William III," 695.
71. Quoted in Sutherland, *The Restoration Newspaper and Its Development*, 23. The reception of English news from foreign newsletters had been commonplace in earlier years when the dissemination of domestic news was prohibited.
72. Richard Warre to Poley, February 16, 1689, Add MS 45731, Poley Papers, British Library, f. 112.
73. Wyche to Poley, December 25, 1688, Add MS 45731, Poley Papers, British Library, f. 90.
74. Wyche to Poley, January 3, 1689, Add MS 45731, Poley Papers, British Library, f. 92.
75. Wyche to Poley, March 9, 1689, Add MS 45731, Poley Papers, British Library, f. 126.
76. Richard Bulstrode to Wyche, January 9, 1689, Add MS 45731, Poley Papers, British Library, f. 95.

77. Although Poley was recalled to London, where he petitioned to receive his unpaid salary, he returned to Europe in 1691, serving first William, and then Anne, in a diplomatic capacity before finishing his career as a lawyer in London: Handley, "Poley, Edmund (1655–1714)."
78. Ezell, *Social Authorship and the Advent of Print*, 22.

Works Cited

Atherton, Ian. "'The Itch Grown a Disease': Manuscript Transmission of News in the Seventeenth Century." In *News, Newspapers, and Society in Early Modern England*, edited by Joad Raymond, 39–65. London: Frank Cass, 1999.

Bannet, Eve Tavor. *Empire of Letters: Letter Manuals and Transatlantic Correspondence, 1680–1820*. Cambridge: Cambridge University Press, 2006.

Briggs, Asa, and Peter Burke. *A Social History of the Media: From Gutenberg to the Internet*, 3d ed. London: Polity, 2009.

Burnet, Gilbert. *History of His Own Time, Volume 1: From the Restoration of Charles II to the Settlement of King William and Queen Mary at the Revolution*. London, 1724.

By the King: A Proclamation. London, 1688.

Claydon, Tony. "Daily News and the Construction of Time in Late Stuart England, 1695–1714." *Journal of British Studies* 52, no. 1 (January 2013): 55–78.

Davies, J. D. "Bulstrode, Sir Richard (1617–1711)." In *Oxford Dictionary of National Biography*. Oxford: Oxford University Press, 2004. https://doi.org/10.1093/ref:odnb/3930.

The Declaration of His Highnes William Henry by the Grace of God Prince of Orange, &c. of the Reasons Inducing Him, to Appear in Armes in the Kingdome of England. The Hague, 1688.

Ezell, Margaret J. M. *Social Authorship and the Advent of Print*. Baltimore: Johns Hopkins University Press, 1999.

Fox, Adam. *Oral and Literate Culture in England, 1500–1700*. Oxford: Clarendon, 2009.

Fraser, Peter. *The Intelligence of the Secretaries of State and Their Monopoly of Licensed News, 1660–1688*. Cambridge: Cambridge University Press, 1956.

Handley, Stuart. "Poley, Edmund (1655–1714)." In *Oxford Dictionary of National Biography*. Oxford: Oxford University Press, 2004. https://doi.org/10.1093/ref:odnb/68401.

Harris, Tim. *Revolution: The Great Crisis of the British Monarchy*. London: Penguin, 2007.

Israel, Jonathan. *The Anglo-Dutch Moment: Essays on the Glorious Revolution and Its World Impact*. Cambridge: Cambridge University Press, 1991.

Jardine, Lisa. *Going Dutch: How England Plundered Holland's Glory*. London: Harper, 2008.
King, Rachael Scarborough. "The Manuscript Newsletter and the Rise of the Newspaper, 1665–1715." *Huntington Library Quarterly* 79, no. 3 (Autumn 2016): 411–37.
Love, Harold. *The Culture and Commerce of Texts: Scribal Publication in Seventeenth-Century England*. Amherst: University of Massachusetts Press, 1998.
Love, Harold, and Arthur Marotti. "Manuscript Circulation and Transmission." In *The Cambridge History of Early Modern English Literature*, edited by David Loewenstein and Janel Mueller, 55–80. Cambridge: Cambridge University Press, 2003.
Luttrell, Narcissus. *A Brief Historical Relation of State Affairs from September 1678 to April 1714*, vol. 1. Oxford, 1857.
The Manuscripts of S. H. Fleming, Esq. of Rydal Hall. London, 1890.
Marshall, Alan. "Sir Joseph Williamson and the Conduct of Administration in Restoration England." *Historical Research* 69, no. 168 (February 1996): 18–41.
Muddiman, J. G. *The King's Journalist 1659–1689: Studies in the Reign of Charles II*. London: John Lane, 1923.
Pincus, Steven. *1688: The First Modern Revolution*. New Haven, CT: Yale University Press, 2014.
Raven, James. "New Reading Histories, Print Culture and the Identification of Change: The Case of Eighteenth-Century England." *Social History* 23, no. 3 (October 1998): 268–87.
Raymond, Joad. *Pamphlets and Pamphleteering in Early Modern Britain*. Cambridge: Cambridge University Press, 2003.
Reiman, Donald. *The Study of Modern Manuscripts: Public, Confidential and Private*. Baltimore: Johns Hopkins University Press, 1993.
Schwoerer, Lois. "Liberty of the Press and Public Opinion, 1660–1695." In *Liberty Secured? Britain Before and After the Glorious Revolution*, edited by J. R. Jones, 199–230. Stanford, CA: Stanford University Press, 1992.
Shapiro, Barbara. *Political Communication and Political Culture in England, 1558–1688*. Stanford, CA: Stanford University Press, 2012.
Siskin, Clifford, and William Warner. "This Is Enlightenment: An Invitation in the Form of an Argument." In *This Is Enlightenment*, edited by Clifford Siskin and William Warner, 1–33. Chicago: University of Chicago Press, 2010.
Sommerville, C. John. *The News Revolution in England: Cultural Dynamics of Daily Information*. Oxford: Oxford University Press, 1996.
Sutherland, James. *The Restoration Newspaper and Its Development*. Cambridge: Cambridge University Press, 1986.

Walker, R. B. "The Newspaper Press in the Reign of William III." *Historical Journal* 17, no. 4 (December 1974): 691–709.

Woolf, Daniel. "News, History, and the Construction of the Present in Early Modern England." In *The Politics of Information in Early Modern Europe*, edited by Brendan Dooley and Sabrina A. Baron, 80–118. London: Routledge, 2002.

Manuscript, Print, and the Affective Turn

The Case of Frances Brooke's *The Old Maid*

KATHRYN R. KING

THE PERIODICAL-ESSAY genre cycled through its life span in roughly half a century. It seemed to leap into being in 1711–12 with the success of Joseph Addison and Richard Steele's *Spectator*, but by midcentury it had already begun its death by absorption into the roomy miscellaneity of the magazine format.[1] At every stage the genre reveled in its here-and-nowness, regarding itself as "entirely new and original."[2] The *Female Spectator* (1744–46), *Rambler* (1750–52), *World* (1753–56), *Connoisseur* (1754–56), and *Old Maid* (1755–56), to name some of the more important essay papers from the century's middle years, prided themselves on mirroring—with humor and élan—the fashions, fooleries, and serious public concerns of the moment. In other words, the periodical essay was a "thoroughly eighteenth-century phenomenon" and an essential feature of the nation's public life.[3] It stands at the nexus of a number of rises central to the story told today of the expansion of print culture—the rise of journalism, of the literary marketplace, of coffeehouse sociability, of the professional author, and, not least, of the Habermasian bourgeois public sphere. But it is not always remarked that this self-consciously up-to-date genre bears unmistakable traces of the manuscript culture that flourished in the seventeenth and early eighteenth centuries.

The assertion made some years ago by the editors of *English Manuscript Studies* that by the turn of the eighteenth century the "printing press did finally, and unquestionably, prevail" will stir little outright disagreement these days,[4] but subsequent work in the field of manuscript studies has taught scholars to distrust the triumphalist overtones of a word such as "prevail." The best work in recent years proceeds from an understanding that "each new technology does not replace the previous one. Rather, it augments it, and offers alternatives." Everywhere these days one comes upon reminders that "different cultures and media must inevitably exist side by side."[5] David Fairer approaches Alexander Pope's moment as one in which "the cultures of manuscript and print overlapped and engaged with each other as never before."[6] Such a perspective informs work on genres in addition to poetry, including prose fiction.[7] The coexistence of script and print "in multiple and complex ways" is a theme in Clare Brant's magisterial study of epistolary culture in the eighteenth century; the relationship between the two media is "simultaneous not sequential."[8] Margaret J. M. Ezell and Rachael Scarborough King consider in separate articles the script-print interaction in pre-*Spectator* periodicals, pointing out that Peter Anthony Motteux's *Gentleman's Journal* (1692–94) and John Dunton's *Athenian Mercury* (1691–97), respectively, use features such as reader correspondence to infuse the print medium with something of the familiar feel of sociable literary practices within coterie manuscript circles.[9] As these last examples suggest, scholarship on periodicals from a manuscript studies perspective has focused largely on the *Spectator* and its late-seventeenth-century precursors. Absent work on the periodical in its later iterations, it is easy to assume that a genre so firmly embedded in the culture of print had, by midcentury, shed its associations with manuscript culture. In fact, though, the script-print interface was alive and well in the 1750s, as can be seen vividly in the *Old Maid*, a periodical essay that appeared more than four decades after the conclusion of the *Spectator*.

This essay takes up aspects of the script-print interplay in the *Old Maid*, the weekly essay paper edited by Frances Brooke from November 15, 1755, to July 24, 1756—a periodical that offers fascinating instances of what Brant has called "crossing-points between print and script."[10] In recent years, the *Old Maid* has attracted a small but enthusiastic band of admirers who laud the appealing voice and breezy authority of "Mary Singleton, Spinster," the fictive editor who cheerfully admits to being on the verge of old age: she is nearly fifty.[11] (Brooke herself was a thirty-one-year-old married woman when she launched a periodical with an old maid at the editorial helm—"An odd attempt for a woman," she concedes.)¹² I, too, find Singleton delightful, but I want to direct attention to a device that, although less discussed, adds significantly to the distinctiveness of the periodical: the implied community of readers that emerges out of the interchange between the editor and her reader-correspondents. Many of the letters in the *Old Maid* are fictitious; some probably are real. Some were written by Brooke herself; others unquestionably were written by known contributors.[13] Together they create the impression of a kind of "club" of reader-correspondents. While the club fiction is far from unusual in the periodical essay, the set of correspondents assembled for the *Old Maid* is an unusually odd lot. Of greatest interest to me are the sex-gender outliers—single folk, women and men—who live outside or apart from sanctioned "he-and-she" conjugal families and households and who, in a couple of telling cases, are themselves frustrated periodical essayists. It is as if sociable exchange with an editor who insouciantly declares herself a spinster-sans-regret offers these outsiders a place and voice in a kind of weekly companionship of print.

To shape this argument, I have taken the unusual step, at least in periodical studies, of drawing on perspectives afforded by affect theory. This influential, if at times opaque, branch of theory seeks to steer humanist study away from the so-called linguistic turn ushered in by poststructuralism and toward study of pre- or paralinguistic phenomena tied to sensations, feelings, emotions, and their neuroscience and even toward the autonomic nervous system: affect and the affected body.[14] The affective turn has inspired, among other things, investigations into "ethico-aesthetic spaces that are opened up (or shut down) by a widely disparate assortment of affective encounters with, for example, new technological lures."[15] The new technology that concerns me in the eighteenth-century context is the periodical press, and, using Brooke's *Old Maid* as my case study, I show that ethical and aesthetic spaces associated with the older script medium were not shut down in the midcentury's print-oriented media environment. Pockets of residual affect persisted in spaces often figured by "hands" of various sorts: the writing hand, the process of writing by hand, handwritten materials. The discussion that follows identifies key crossover moments in the *Old Maid* in which the intensities and resonances associated with one or another kind of hand create a zone of *in-betweenness* in which sensations, feelings, and emotions—that is, affect—pool up, swirl, and find representation in the text, often in connection with an affected body.[16] It reads these moments, finally, in relation to the affect-oriented cultural materialism developed earlier by Raymond

Williams, especially the useful and well-known concept of "structures of feeling." In addition to challenging the misleading print-manuscript division, the affective turn taken in this essay lights up pockets of sensibility, sensation, and queerness that present themselves for analysis once we are able to set aside the Habermasian view, under assault but still widely accepted, that the periodical essay is first and foremost the product and prime begetter of rational critical discourse.

THE SCRIPT AFFECT

The loving description of the fictional Hartingley family manuscripts in *Old Maid* no. 28 (May 22, 1756) helps establish the nature of the residual feelings, meanings, and values associated with script in the media environment in which the periodical was conceived. The bound manuscript volumes that form the topic of the issue, two of prose pieces and four of poetry, "most beautifully and correctly written,"[17] correspond to the kinds of seventeenth-century family compilation volumes Ezell has described.[18] These compilations recall the amateur literary practices of the precommercial era; they also partake in a poignant story of love, loss, and grief. As Mary Singleton narrates, Dr. Hartingley, a landowning clergyman, had prepared them for a beloved daughter who died young; he now bestows them on a surrogate daughter. The volumes are "an incomparable treasure" imbued with almost sacred values: one is a "temple" (237). Drenched in nostalgic feeling and bespeaking continuity with an aristocratic tradition that values learning, the arts, and polite studies, these handwritten texts stand in implicit but strong contrast to the "nearly instant replay of human experience" that the London press is able to deliver.[19] They affirm deep and cherished personal and familial connections ratified, in effect, by the intensities of reverential feeling they arouse in Singleton, who must struggle to suppress her tears.

The Hartingley manuscripts, identified on their bindings as "MSS *English Classicks*," serve for the *Old Maid*'s eidolon and readers as reminders of moral and aesthetic values threatened by the commodification of literature (235). Unlike the "trite and common" passages endemic to compilations sponsored by booksellers, the selections in the Hartingley poetry miscellanies—"most judiciously chosen, from the best poems extant in our language" (235)—reflect cultivated taste. The verses have "absolute value": they hark back to a more discerning (and less demotic) past and offer a rebuke, in Harold Love's phrase, to "the promiscuously purchasable page created by print."[20] They are a bridge to a time when people of taste and discrimination used handwritten compilations to preserve the very best that had been written, regardless of its marketability. In Williams's terms, they represent an alternative or oppositional version of "what literature is (has been)" against "the pressures of incorporation" into consumer culture. They embody a rival set of residual values.[21]

Affect theory would have us attend to the way handwriting as an extension of the body impinges on the emotional life of an observer. It is often noted that the "thingness" of the typographic page tends to erase the physical presence of the author. The handwritten page, bearing as it does intimations of the presence of another body, has the opposite effect: the inked trace of an actual hand, living or once living, is able to "create affective resonances" that may be "independent of content or meaning."[22] These resonances often manifest as, or tap into, desire for connection with the absent other, even, or perhaps especially, if that desire cannot be fulfilled. For example, the autobiographical heroine of Jane Barker's *A Patch-Work Screen for the Ladies* (1723) is overwhelmed with sorrow when she sees the "Hand-writing, by way of Remarks" of a beloved dead brother in his books: the sight "always caus'd a new Flux of Tears."[23] Likewise, tears start to Singleton's eyes as she gazes at the handwritten pages of the Hartingley manuscripts. These pages are resonant with bodily presence—annotations in Dr. Hartingley's hand and drawings and decorations designed and executed by Mrs. Hartingley.[24] The sight of these elaborately handcrafted volumes produces in Singleton a recognition of the "approaches" of "grief" (235). We see here an instance of that "special kind of inward attention" that, according to John Mullan, induces a "concern with feeling as articulated by the body" characteristic of sentimental fiction in its commitment to the "true communication of feelings."[25] The melancholy episode of the Hartingley family manuscripts shows the shaping influence of the emerging discourse of sensibility and looks forward to future developments in the novel of sentiment, a sterling example of which, by the way, is Brooke's own *The History of Lady Julia Mandeville* (1763).

The Sociable Periodical

Such attention to manuscript texts was a recurring theme in the printed periodical. The eidolon of the *Connoisseur*, Mr. Town, imagines his weekly essay as a kind of manuscript passing through multiple hands in the coffeehouses and picking up traces of that contact along the way. "I have considered every speck of dirt as a mark of reputation, and have assumed to myself applause from the spilling of coffee, or the print of a greasy thumb," he writes.[26] The periodical essay was, in fact, an immensely sociable genre, and, like with manuscript materials circulating from hand to hand within amateur networks, scholars believe that its format drew readers into interactive communities akin to the literary coteries that had flourished in the previous century. Ezell analyzes Motteux's *Gentleman's Journal* as an early instance of a professional journalist's use of the coterie effect, as it might be called, to enhance the appeal of a commercial undertaking. She summarizes her findings: "Through the use of the letter form and the inclusion of interactive literary forms, the *Gentleman's Journal* established a literary environment of friendly community, founded on mutual literary exchange, only adapted for commercial purposes to a group of readers who are unknown to each other."[27] Reader correspondence was a fixture in periodicals of all sorts from the 1690s,[28] and it is thought that the "familiar genre of the letter" served to ease the transition from amateur to professional, script to print by signaling "the importance of building reading communities that would engage in ongoing exchange and interaction."[29] Periodicals provided a platform that served "more than novels, pamphlets, or poetry to encourage discourse with and among [their] readers."[30] By midcentury the cultivation of reader involvement in the ongoing life of a periodical was so institutionalized that even Samuel Johnson, no friend to readers' contributions, felt obliged to submit to what he considered the charade of soliciting submissions for the *Rambler*, to the bewilderment of at least one would-be contributor.[31]

Brooke followed time-honored practice in the *Old Maid*. The first issue ended with an appeal for correspondence from "all the ingenious of both sexes" (8), and subsequent issues directed readers to send letters to Millar's in the Strand. It is worth noting that neither Brooke nor her predecessor, Eliza Haywood, sought a specifically female audience, as is often said. In the *Female Spectator*, Haywood sought to be "as universally read as possible," and her eidolon later affirmed, "I do not confine myself to Sexes."[32] Over its two-year run, the *Old Maid* relied increasingly on letters from subscribers—whether actual or concocted it is impossible to know—and many appeared over men's names. Early on, in *Old Maid* no. 1 (November 15, 1755), Singleton made a show of appealing to women, especially "ladies of her own order," by playfully urging other "antiquated virgins" to "rail at the men with all their might, provided they are silent as to the faults of their own sex" (8), but there is some disingenuousness here. The first letter to reach print, in the fourth issue, of December 6, 1755, was from a man named Stentor, possibly Brooke's own satiric creation, an unemployed coffeehouse habitué who bumptiously offered to talk up Singleton's periodical in the coffeehouses. His astonishment at her "daring attempt to stand on [her] own legs," to say nothing of the success enjoyed by the *Old Maid* without benefit of his stentorian puffs, amounts to a cheeky piece of self-promotion (24).

In addition to readers' letters, the *Old Maid* used role-playing of various sorts to craft the illusion of an amateur coterie community. The editor contrived to give the impression that her materials originated in manuscript circles. "Ode to Health," in *Old Maid* no. 3 (November 29, 1755), came with a false provenance: the editor was informed by a gentleman that the ode was "wrote by one of my own sex" who "never yet appeared in print, and with great reluctance and fear consented to suffer this to be conveyed to me for that purpose" (20). "Ode to Health" was written by Brooke herself; it would soon be printed under her name.[33] The *Old Maid* featured recurring fictional correspondents—the Antigallican, for example, who in a series of three letters played out an increasingly tedious joke about bare-breasted English women lining up on the coast to repel French invaders by distraction. (The bosom-obsessed Antigallican was a friend of Brooke's, the clergyman Richard Gifford.) Other contributors played the impersonation game. John Boyle, Lord Cork (known today as Lord Orrery), was by turns Sarah Whispercomb, Sir Harry Hyacinth, Mary Singleton herself, and others—not that the *Old Maid*'s first readers had reason to suspect his hand in these roles.[34]

Finally, the *Old Maid* promoted a familiar relationship between the editor and her implied readers in part by casting Singleton as someone like themselves—a bit lazy, perhaps, and far from a writer by profession—and by making much of their shared Englishness. Brooke was a marketplace writer seeking to make a go of it in a crowded periodical field; that she opted to "buz[z] among the other insects for a while" was owing entirely—so she claimed—to the "generous approbation and favor which some essays of mine in manuscript, met with from some persons whom it is an honor to please" (1).[35] She spends her time, as she wrote in *Old Maid* no. 21 (April 3, 1756), "very inoffensively blotting paper, and wearing out my small remains of spirits and eyesight in the service and for the amusement of my fellow citizens" (182). A public-spirited woman who writes for the good of her country, she cleverly authorizes the undertaking in a way that combines her Englishness and her female nature: "In defiance of all criticisms I will write: every body knows an English woman has a natural right to expose herself as much as she pleases"—the ironic reference is to the recent fashion for scandalous memoirs by women—and "I should think it giving up the privileges of the sex to desist from my purpose" (2). Like ordinary mortals, she has trouble summoning the energy to write. She confesses to having, for a month past, "nodded in my elbow chair, pored over the *News-Papers*, half-slumbered over my knitting, without taking a pen in hand" (218). In taking leave of her readers in the final number—*Old Maid* no. 37 (July 24, 1756)—she braids her patriotic love of liberty with her supposed feminine volatility: "I am tired of the confinement of writing every week, whether I chuse it or not; a slavery not at all agreeable to the volatile spirit of woman" (303). Repeatedly, Singleton underscored her kinship with her readers: they were all lovers of their country, slaves to no confinement. In such moments the readership of *Old Maid* was artfully imagined as a literary coterie writ large, in print, on a national scale.

Epistolary Communities

Dunton's *Athenian Mercury*, the precursor of so many eighteenth-century periodicals, has been described as a "deeply-woven text, that interacted with, and was influenced by, the social circumstances of its own particular community of readers."[36] The description applies to *Old Maid*, but the particular community projected by the readers' correspondence consists to a remarkable degree of odd folk—real or imagined, volunteer or commissioned—who represent themselves as isolated and ignored, if not invisible, in the midcentury print world and who declare themselves eager to claim kinship with its old maid editor. The previous decade had seen a small flurry of female eidolons—all of them unmarried, interestingly—starting with Haywood's rather stern Female Spectator, then veering into such streetwise and carnivalesque female pretenders as Christopher Smart's Mary Midnight and Bonnell Thornton's Madam Roxana Termagant and her niece and successor, Priscilla Termagant. These cross-dressed editors were satiric creations, and morally dubious ones at that.[37] Brooke's creation of a respectable, empathetic, and proudly spinster eidolon was something new: it was as if the immensely likeable Mary Singleton made it safe to be quirky; just a bit queer. The letter writers, some of them old maids themselves, professed that Singleton enabled them to find a public outlet for their thoughts, feelings, and desires. An unnamed correspondent, a "*well-wisher*" who addresses Singleton as "the natural patroness of distressed virginity," appeals for support for a subscription to benefit an ingenious woman who had fallen upon hard times, identifiable as Ann Ockley, daughter of the author of a history of the Saracens (156). (This is one of the few instances in which it seems likely that the letter writer is speaking *in propria persona*.) "Abigail Easy," fearful that Singleton might be "some fellow who had taken the petticoat for a disguise," comes to be convinced that the editor of the *Old Maid* is indeed "one of the sisterhood" (191–92). The hilariously hyper-nosy "Sarah Whispercomb," one of Orrery's funniest creations, is a "terrible gibbeted example of curiosity" who regards the periodical as a "kind of confessional chair to our whole sex" to which we "may come to you veiled, and freely unburthen ourselves of our sins" (200, 204). "Cana Greypate," a spinster herself, pays tribute to Singleton: "Your maidenship has opened a channel, through which my thoughts may flow" (64). Bachelors were welcomed in *Old Maid* no. 6 (December 20, 1755): "Tom Bumper," a "jovial old Bacchanalian Bachelor" would be at home in a host of periodicals, but it is hard to imagine another venue that would suit so perfectly the aging Cambridge fellow Virginius, a self-styled "*Old Maid of the masculine gender*" (41, 43). The periodical-essay genre has given us any number of "clubs" of memorably quirky characters, but I know of nothing quite like the epistolary weave of sex-gender outliers created by Brooke in the *Old Maid*, a network of correspondents that would seem to imply the existence of stories and experiences, needs and desires, that go untold and possibly unrecognized in other periodicals.

The letter from the aging spinster Cana Greypate in *Old Maid* no. 9 (January 10, 1756) is crafted with a subtlety that repays close analysis. The letter uses "feeling as articulated by the body," in Mullan's phrase, to project a rather jaundiced view of the possibility of fulfillment for single women—a report, it is pleasing to note, undercut by the aptly named Marian Doubtful, who, in the letter that follows, questions whether marriage really represents "the highest earthly felicity any woman can arrive at" (68).[38] Greypate addresses Singleton as "my good sister virginity," but it is soon evident she wants little to do with the sisterhood. She deeply resents the preference of Oxford students for "a pack of ignorant, idle, giddy girls" and hankers to trade in her single state for a husband. Greypate, interestingly, is also a would-be public essayist, long ambitious to "entertain the public with periodical lucubrations upon some plan like your's" (64). Her letter opens periodical-essay style with the virtually de rigueur account of the author—although, oddly, Greypate likens it to the biographical sketch prefacing the works of a deceased author, a hint, perhaps, of her blighted aspirations. Soon she will lose control over her hand and, with it, periodical convention. A postscript apologizes for the profusion of inkblots on the page; they are due to the "tremor" Greypate has "been in from vehemency of passion" (65).[39] Blots suggest stains or disfigurement; the blotted page figures the intensity of her inner disorder. Brant has observed that in erotic fiction of the period, and earlier, "References to blots and smudges evoked emotions too powerful for the writer's body to control. Imaged through a falling tear or trembling 'hand', these excitements wrought effects visible in script, invisible in print." In fiction—in which category I would place Greypate's letter—this loss of control is "strategic," a device for "recovery of the moment of writing [that] helps establish a dynamic of time and place in which erotic drives predominate."[40] When a handwritten letter is converted into print, the involuntary bodily motions that almost inevitably leave a trace on the page—the shaking of a hand, for example—are lost to view. By rendering the blots "visible," Brooke (assuming it was she who personated Cana Greypate) called attention to the disruptive desires that an unfulfilled woman struggles to suppress.[41] The latter's loss of control over her hand, in at least two senses of the word, is simultaneously a loss of control over the conventions of the genre. She is an essayist no longer; instead, she becomes an almost parodic version of a Richardsonian epistolary heroine, trembling and unable to bring her letter to a close. "As women they say never know how to make an end of talking, so the pen, I think, is not easily wrested out of their hands," Greypate writes (66). Her postscript proceeds in a stuttering succession of add-on comments that, taken together, suggest the force of her deep, but frustrated, craving for human connection.

Cana Greypate stands as the mirror image of Mary Singleton. She is a compulsive writer who cannot lay down her pen but is unable to launch a periodical; Singleton is an accomplished essayist who lazes away whole weeks unable to put pen to paper. Greypate is emotionally disfigured by her yearning for marriage or, more specifically, the dignity she believes marriage confers on women (a comment, arguably, on the damage inflicted by what today would be called heteronormativity); the genial and easygoing Singleton is in love with the liberty and peace of mind that come with the single state. Together they show something of how Brooke is able to create a multilayered picture of women's single life that approaches but then turns away from familiar "old maid" stereotypes to reveal the complex humanity of a figure ridiculed and all too readily dismissed by her culture. Greypate finally brings her letter to a close with a question that amounts to a plea for admission to Singleton's literary circle: "Do you desire to hear any more from me?" In response Singleton expresses "fellow feeling" and invites Greypate to write again (66, 69). The print medium, in this exchange, not only gives voice to the previously voiceless but, in something of the manner of social media today, seems also to hold out the promise of new channels of connection.

Greypate has a male counterpart in Virginius, the old Cambridge Fellow in issue no. 6 and a similarly frustrated writer who for twenty years has failed to wedge one of his own productions into print. He has repeatedly submitted letters to various magazines—the *Gentleman's, London,* and *Universal* magazines; he has applied to Mother Midnight (fictive editor of Smart's *Midwife, or, The Old Woman's Magazine*) and Dr. Hill (Sir John Hill, author of the "Inspector" column in the *London Daily Advertiser*); he has seen even his riddles rejected. He is, in short, a print-world failure. When he first learns about the *Old Maid*, he feels an immediate affinity with its editor, sensing "something extremely *apposite* and *proper* in a correspondence to be settled between us" (41). After all, he reasons, an "old Fellow" is basically "*an Old Maid of the masculine gender,*" and, continuing this ironic line of thought, since one old maid is pretty much like another, "be the *gender* what it will," it follows that "there must be a certain *similarity* of *temper* and of *manners* between us" (41). From an affect theory perspective, it is interesting that his somewhat mysterious sense of connection with Singleton arrives in the form of a scarcely articulable bodily sensation: "I was affected in a very unusual manner: I immediately perceived a great *fullness* in myself, though I had eaten nothing but my *bare commons*" (40). This sense of corporeal repletion is an example of what affect theorists call a prelinguistic intensity or force, a sensation that precedes or exists just outside language. Considering himself under the influence of "*Sybil* herself," he finds utterance in a line from Virgil announcing the return of the Golden Age—"*Iam redit redeunt* VIRGO *et* SATURNIA *regna*"—but has no words of his own (40). In the episode of the Hartingley family manuscripts discussed earlier we saw that the sight of these prepared-by-hand volumes, linked to feelings of love and loss, produced tears that Singleton struggled to suppress. This is not far from the "vehemency of passion" that caused Greypate's hand to shake in the act of inscribing words on the page. In such moments, we glimpse a record of bodily movements related to what affect theory calls the interplay between "image-event" (script) and the "expression-event" (the affected body), out of which are generated the intensities and resonances that in these instances seem tied to a basic human desire for connection and belonging.[42]

Queer Folk?

While newspapers, pamphlets, and other forms of early journalism promised novelty, wonder, and surprise, as Paul Hunter has stressed, the periodical essay offered these elements and more. It used the device of the editorial persona—Isaac Bickerstaff, Mr. Spectator, Mr. Town, Mary Singleton—to provide a distinctive, unified, and (usually) predictable point of view, conferring comfort on "readers who could know what to expect."[43] This is not to deny Rachael King's point that the "insistent heterogeneity and multi-vocality" of early epistolary periodicals "offered readers a stake in the texts through the possibility to challenge the editors on matters of fact, politics, and literary style."[44] Rather, it is to bring into focus the interactive nature of periodical communities later in the century, as they were inflected by new cultural emphases on sensibility and inwardness. By virtue of its development of something like a brand identity, any given periodical paper—the *Connoisseur*, for example—could expect its contributors to take on roles within implicitly understood parameters, as our Virginius well knew. "Being a mortal enemy to the *modern Vertù*," he explains, "it would be ridiculously absurd in me to assume the character of a Connoisseur" (40). The *Old Maid*, even more than other papers, encouraged idiosyncrasy and difference. True, Brooke took on a wide range of public issues, and some of the best work on the *Old Maid* has investigated Brooke's civic and political engagements.[45] But as we have seen, she also used the weekly paper to admit into print voices drawn from the ranks of those who perceived themselves as isolated, alone, forgotten, and disrespected—queer folk such as Sarah Whispercomb, for whom the *Old Maid* serves as a "kind of confessional chair to our whole sex"; a male old-maid Cambridge fellow who finds a kindred spirit in Mary Singleton; a gray-pated spinster who attains in print the fellow feeling absent in her life, as well as a "channel" for her thoughts.

Much has been said in recent scholarship about the incorporeality of the print-world author. Manushag Powell has written brilliantly about the bodiless nature of the eidolon, a word that conjures "a spectral or insubstantial figure, as indeed a purely rhetorical projection of an author's editorial ego must be," since an author exists, "materially speaking, only in paper and ink."[46] But Brooke uses first-person narrative and novelistic technique to offset the tendency of print to erase bodily sensations and movements: Greypate narrates the tremor in her hand; Virginius records an inexplicable somatic event. Singleton herself is a quasi-novelistic character endowed with corporeal being: she dons spectacles, nods over her knitting, and lifts—or drops—her pen. With deft assurance, Brooke creates a fiction of affective bonds between editor and reader-correspondents, projecting an image of epistolary fellowship that complicates considerably the notion of the "rational-critical public debate of private persons with one another" still imagined by some scholars to define the essential nature of the periodical essay.[47]

Ezell observes that amateur manuscript culture in the seventeenth and early eighteenth centuries "permitted and encouraged participation in literary life of groups of people whom print technology effectively isolated and alienated."[48] She has in mind amateur provincial readers and writers at some distance from the London print publishing centers, forerunners of the Melissas and Fidos who, starting in the 1730s, found a home for their coterie verse in the poetry columns of the *Gentleman's Magazine*.[49] Many of the correspondents in the *Old Maid* belong to the category of the isolated and alienated, but less for geographic reasons than by virtue of feelings that place them beyond, outside, or estranged from the culture of "his and hers." Queer scholarship has shown that in the eighteenth century, "many people lived outside heterosexual dyads for all or part of their adult lives," as Susan Lanser reminds us, and she challenges students of the period to search out the pockets of queerness that heteronormative assumptions have screened from view in the seemingly straight archives.[50] Cana Greypate and Virginius write to Singleton from nonheteronormative spaces. Both, interestingly, are frustrated periodicalists who report, in handwritten letters, a longtime craving to see their thoughts in print. Both can be said to have their being, and perhaps their yearning for belonging, in a zone of in-betweenness partly enabled by the coexistence of script and print at midcentury. Further investigation of this zone may tell us more about, in Lanser's words, "heteronormativity and its discontents" in the eighteenth century.[51]

IMPLICATIONS

Study of the affective turn in Brooke's *Old Maid* represents a new direction in the "ripening" field of periodical studies.[52] Work on the periodical essay has tended to stress its relation to public sphere issues such as the formation of public opinion and a national public, as well as its place within the (somewhat besieged) model of separate public and private spheres. More recently, scholars have taken up the eidolon as a focus for recognizably modern performances of authorship. These approaches have added immeasurably to our appreciation of a vital if still understudied eighteenth-century genre. My discussion has drawn attention to representations of the sensations, emotions, and bodily movements that would figure importantly in the literature of sensibility in the second half of the century and that, within the *Old Maid*, are entwined in suggestive ways with an affect associated with hands and handwritten texts. Taken together, these affective elements partake of those "dynamic interrelations, at every point in the process, of historically varied and variable elements" that Raymond Williams has taught us to recognize as structures of feeling.[53] Moments of script-print fusion in the *Old Maid* share a space with bodily feelings and movements that relay something of the lived experience of the coexistence of a relatively intimate manuscript-based culture and a more impersonal print-based commercial media culture. Affect flows backward toward the intimacy and presence of handwritten texts (as contrasted with the mass-produced "thingishness" of the typographically rendered page) and simultaneously, and somewhat paradoxically, forward toward print-based forms of communication that enable new kinds of mediated companionship, new communities of belonging.

Williams's model of the dominant, residual, and emergent elements found in the structures of feeling at any given moment in the social material process has shaped much of this discussion. While the press was the dominant communication technology in the eighteenth century, handwritten texts and manuscript culture continued to exert a strong influence within the new media landscape. Manuscript and its affective contours belong to the category of the residual. Expressions of the residual—a lovingly embellished manuscript volume of verse, for example—may be found "at some distance from the effective dominant culture," as is the case with the Hartingley family manuscripts discussed earlier, but, crucially, such residual elements continue to be "some part of [dominant culture], some version of it."[54] To term something *residual* is emphatically not to imply that it is retrograde, peripheral, archaic, or spent: the residual "is still active in the cultural process, not only and often not at all as an element of the past, but an as effective element of the present."[55] I stress the point because Williams is so helpful in grasping the complexity of cultural change within the socio-literary environment and, more specifically, because it is just such a grasp that is needed to get past the unhelpful plotline that links the "rise" of print with the inevitable "fall" of manuscript. To take the view urged by Williams—the view that emergent, dominant, and residual elements must be thought together, as part of a jostling and commingling whole—is to recognize that the multimedia communication environment in the eighteenth century is far too dynamic and complex to be reduced to a linear narrative of rise and fall. To approach manuscript as a residual, and therefore still effective, element is to understand the story of print and manuscript as one of crossover and fusion that opens up new veins for study in the periodical essay at midcentury—which, if the *Old Maid* is any indication, is a genre that engages sensibility as well as rationality, affect as well as manners and morals, and queerness as well as the more familiar bourgeois domestic values.

Notes

1. The *Spectator* had recognizable precursors in John Dunton's *Athenian Mercury* (1691–7) and Daniel Defoe's *Review* (1704–13), as well as the more miscellaneous *Tatler* (1709–11), but it was perceived then, as now, as inaugurating a new literary tradition. An alternative origin story is that contemporaries regarded the periodical essay as a "modern variant of a tradition of urbane moral history writing that had originated in ancient Athens": Squibbs, *Urban Enlightenment and the Eighteenth-Century Periodical Essay*, 4.
2. *Connoisseur* no. 24 (July 11, 1754), 139. References are to Richard Baldwin's 1754 edition.
3. Powell, *Performing Authorship in Eighteenth-Century English Periodicals*, 2.
4. Beal and Griffiths, "Preface," viii.
5. McKitterick, *Print, Manuscript and the Search for Order*, 20.
6. Fairer, *English Poetry of the Eighteenth Century*, 1.
7. See Eicke, "Jane Barker's Jacobite Writings"; King, "Elizabeth Singer Rowe's Tactical Use of Print and Manuscript."

8. Brant, *Eighteenth-Century Letters and British Culture*, 9.
9. Ezell, "The *Gentleman's Journal* and the Commercialization of Restoration Coterie Literary Practices"; King, "Interloping with My Question-Project." For the social uses of script in the seventeenth century more generally, see Love, *The Culture and Commerce of Texts*, esp. chap. 5; Ezell, *Social Authorship and the Advent of Print*, esp. chap. 1.
10. Brant, *Eighteenth-Century Letters and British Culture*, 8.
11. For Brooke's Singleton persona, a well-contextualized starting point is Prescott and Spencer, "Prattling, Tattling and Knowing Everything."
12. The foundational study of the *Old Maid* is McMullen, *An Odd Attempt in a Woman*.
13. McMullen, *An Odd Attempt in a Woman*, 25–29, establishes some of the contributors: John Boyle, the 5th Earl of Cork and Orrery; Richard Gifford (the "Antigallican"); Brooke's husband, John Brooke; and the journalist and playwright Arthur Murphy.
14. I do not claim more than preliminary knowledge of affect or its theorization. Points of entry into the field that I can recommend are Shouse, "Feeling, Emotion, Affect"; Leys, "The Turn to Affect." See also nn. 15 and 42 in this chapter.
15. Gregg and Seigworth, "An Inventory of Shimmers," 7–8.
16. Ibid., 1.
17. Brooke, *Old Maid*, 235. The parenthetical page number references are to the 1764 revised edition. This issue was written by Orrery.
18. See Ezell, *Social Authorship and the Advent of Print*, 25–44.
19. Hunter, *Before Novels*, 167.
20. Love, *The Culture and Commerce of Texts*, 146.
21. Williams, *Marxism and Literature*, 123.
22. Shouse, "Feeling, Emotion, Affect," para. 14.
23. Jane Barker, *A Patch-Work Screen for the Ladies*, the second book in Barker, *The Galesia Trilogy and Selected Manuscript Poems of Jane Barker*, 84.
24. An Anne Finch poem, "O King of Terrors," is "distinguished by several beautiful ornaments in Indian Ink" (237).
25. Mullan, *Sentiment and Sociability*, 16. For the *Old Maid*'s strategic alignment with the sentimental novel, see Italia, *The Rise of Literary Journalism in the Eighteenth Century*, 174–77.
26. *Connoisseur* no. 29 (August 15, 1754), 172.
27. Ezell, "The *Gentleman's Journal* and the Commercialization of Restoration Coterie Literary Practices," 330.
28. For an overview of reader-letters in late seventeenth- and early eighteenth-century periodicals, see Berry, *Gender, Society and Print Culture in Late-Stuart England*, 35–43.

29. King, "Interloping with My Question-Project," 135.
30. Powell, *Performing Authorship in Eighteenth-Century English Periodicals*, 138.
31. Peter Sabor gives an account of Lady Bradshaigh's perplexity in "Women Reading and Writing for *The Rambler*," 177–80.
32. *Female Spectator* no. 1 (April 24, 1744), no. 7 (November 3, 1744), in King and Pettit, *Selected Works of Eliza Haywood*, 18, 260.
33. *Virginia, A Tragedy*, includes two other odes first printed in the *Old Maid*.
34. Orrery's contributions were identified by "Philo Boyleus" in *Gentleman's Magazine* no. 43 (December 1773), 583–84, and confirmed by annotations in his own hand in a bound volume of the original issues of the *Old Maid* in the Thomas Fisher Rare Books Library, University of Toronto. See McMullen, *An Odd Attempt in a Woman*, 25–26.
35. This passage, from *Old Maid* no. 2 (November 22, 1755, 11), is part of a section originating in a skirmish with the *Connoisseur's* Mr. Town that was removed in 1764: Brooke, *Old Maid*, 1.
36. Berry, *Gender, Society and Print Culture in Late-Stuart England*, 35.
37. For an overview of literary cross-dressing at midcentury, see Powell, *Performing Authorship in Eighteenth-Century English Periodicals*, 115–30.
38. Mullan, *Sentiment and Sociability*, 16. "Doubtful" continues in Johnsonian cadences: "I cannot but think a single life must be much less disagreeable, than a state of perpetual union, with one, who is perhaps so far from being the object of love and esteem, that he can excite no emotions but those of loathing and contempt" (68).
39. The original issue misprints "terror" for "tremor."
40. Brant, *Eighteenth-Century Letters and British Culture*, 8.
41. In 1764 Brooke credited herself with *Old Maid* no. 9, in which Greypate's letter appears.
42. The language in this sentence is indebted to Massumi, *Parables for the Virtual*, 26.
43. Hunter, *Before Novels*, 176.
44. King, "Interloping with My Question-Project," 122.
45. See Wild, "'Prodigious Wisdom"; Schellenberg, *The Professionalization of Women Writers in Eighteenth-Century Britain*.
46. Powell, *Performing Authorship in Eighteenth-Century English Periodicals*, 50.
47. Habermas, *The Structural Transformation of the Public Sphere*, 43. For the periodical letter as a public sphere discourse focusing on the *Spectator*, see Polly, "A Leviathan of Letters."
48. Ezell, *Social Authorship and the Advent of Print*, 12.
49. See Barker, "Poetry from the Provinces."
50. Lanser, "Of Closed Doors and Open Hatches," 274.
51. Ibid., 277.

52. Powell, "New Directions in Eighteenth-Century Periodical Studies," 240.
53. Williams, *Marxism and Literature*, 121.
54. Ibid., 123.
55. Ibid., 122.

Works Cited

Barker, Anthony. "Poetry from the Provinces: Amateur Poets in the *Gentleman's Magazine* in the 1730s and 1740s." In *Tradition in Transition: Women Writers, Marginal Texts, and the Eighteenth-Century Canon*, edited by Alvaro Ribeiro and James G. Basker, 241–56. Oxford: Clarendon, 1996.

Barker, Jane. *The Galesia Trilogy and Selected Manuscript Poems of Jane Barker*, edited by Carol Shiner Wilson. Oxford: Oxford University Press, 1997.

Beal, Peter, and Jeremy Griffiths. "Preface." *English Manuscript Studies 1100–1700* 1 (1989): vii–ix.

Berry, Helen. *Gender, Society and Print Culture in Late-Stuart England: The Cultural World of the Athenian Mercury*. Aldershot, U.K.: Ashgate, 2003.

Brant, Clare. *Eighteenth-Century Letters and British Culture*. Bashingstoke, U.K.: Palgrave Macmillan, 2006.

Brooke, Frances. *The Old Maid. By Mary Singleton, Spinster*. Revised edition, London, 1764.

Colman, George, and Bonnell Thornton. *The Connoisseur. By Mr. Town, Critic, and Censor-General*. London, 1754.

Eicke, Leigh A. "Jane Barker's Jacobite Writings." In *Women's Writing and the Circulation of Ideas: Manuscript Publication in England, 1550–1800*, edited by George L. Justice and Nathan Tinker, 137–57. Cambridge: Cambridge University Press, 2002.

Ezell, Margaret J. M. "The *Gentleman's Journal* and the Commercialization of Restoration Coterie Literary Practices." *Modern Philology* 89, no. 3 (Feb. 1992): 323–40.

———. *Social Authorship and the Advent of Print*. Baltimore: Johns Hopkins University Press, 1999.

Fairer, David. *English Poetry of the Eighteenth Century, 1700–1789*. London: Longman, 2003.

Gregg, Melissa, and Gregory J. Seigworth. "An Inventory of Shimmers." In *The Affect Theory Reader*, edited by Melissa Gregg and Gregory J. Seigworth, 1–27. Durham, NC: Duke University Press, 2010.

Habermas, Jürgen. *The Structural Transformation of the Public Sphere: An Inquiry into a Category of Bourgeois Society*, translated by Thomas Burger. Cambridge, MA: MIT Press, 1991.

Hunter, J. Paul. *Before Novels: The Cultural Contexts of Eighteenth-Century English Fiction.* New York: W. W. Norton, 1990.
Italia, Iona. *The Rise of Literary Journalism in the Eighteenth Century: Anxious Employment.* London: Routledge, 2005.
King, Kathryn R. "Elizabeth Singer Rowe's Tactical Use of Print and Manuscript." In *Women's Writing and the Circulation of Ideas: Manuscript Publication in England, 1550–1800,* edited by George L. Justice and Nathan Tinker, 158–81. Cambridge: Cambridge University Press, 2002.
King, Kathryn R., and Alexander Pettit, eds. *Selected Works of Eliza Haywood,* set 2, vol. 2. London: Pickering and Chatto, 2001.
King, Rachael Scarborough. "'Interloping with My Question-Project': Debating Genre in John Dunton's and Daniel Defoe's Epistolary Periodicals." *Studies in Eighteenth-Century Culture* 44 (2015): 121–42.
Lanser, Susan S. "Of Closed Doors and Open Hatches: Heteronormative Plots in Eighteenth-Century (Women's) Studies." *Eighteenth Century: Theory and Interpretation* 53, no. 3 (Fall 2012): 273–90.
Leys, Ruth. "The Turn to Affect: A Critique." *Critical Inquiry* 37, no. 3 (Spring 2011): 434–72.
Love, Harold. *The Culture and Commerce of Texts: Scribal Publication in Seventeenth-Century England.* Amherst, MA: University of Massachusetts Press, 1998.
Massumi, Brian. *Parables for the Virtual: Movement, Affect, Sensation.* Durham, NC: Duke University Press, 2002.
McKitterick, David. *Print, Manuscript and the Search for Order, 1450–1830.* Cambridge: Cambridge University Press, 2003.
McMullen, Lorraine. *An Odd Attempt in a Woman: The Literary Life of Frances Brooke.* Vancouver: University of British Columbia Press, 1983.
Mullan, John. *Sentiment and Sociability: The Language of Feeling in the Eighteenth Century.* Oxford: Clarendon, 1988.
Polly, Greg. "A Leviathan of Letters." In *The Spectator: Emerging Discourses,* edited by Donald J. Newman, 105–28. Newark: University of Delaware Press, 2005.
Powell, Manushag N. "New Directions in Eighteenth-Century Periodical Studies." *Literature Compass* 8, no. 5 (May 2011): 240–57.
———. *Performing Authorship in Eighteenth-Century English Periodicals.* Lewisburg, PA: Bucknell University Press, 2012.
Prescott, Sarah, and Jane Spencer. "Prattling, Tattling and Knowing Everything: Public Authority and the Female Editorial Persona in the Early Essay-Periodical." *British Journal for Eighteenth-Century Studies* 23 (2000): 43–57.
Sabor, Peter. "Women Reading and Writing for *The Rambler.*" In *Women, Popular Culture, and the Eighteenth Century,* edited by Tiffany Potter, 168–84. Toronto: University of Toronto Press, 2012.

Schellenberg, Betty A. *The Professionalization of Women Writers in Eighteenth-Century Britain.* Cambridge: Cambridge University Press, 2005.

Shouse, Eric. "Feeling, Emotion, Affect." *M/C Journal* 8, no. 6 (December 2005). http://journal.media-culture.org.au/0512/03-shouse.php.

Squibbs, Richard. *Urban Enlightenment and the Eighteenth-Century Periodical Essay.* Basingstoke, U.K.: Palgrave Macmillan, 2014.

Virginia, A Tragedy, with Odes, Pastorals, and Translations. By Mrs. Brooke. London, 1756.

Wild, Min. "'Prodigious Wisdom': Civic Humanism in Frances Brooke's *Old Maid*." *Women's Writing* 5, no. 3 (1998): 421–36.

Williams, Raymond. *Marxism and Literature.* Oxford: Oxford University Press, 1977.

Becoming Dr. Franklin

Benjamin Franklin's Science, Manuscript Circulation, and "Anti-Authorship" in Print

COLIN T. RAMSEY

Early in his *Autobiography*, Benjamin Franklin remarks, "Prose writing has been of great Use to me in the Course of my Life, and was a principal Means of my Advancement."[1] The statement has both literal and figurative dimensions: much of Franklin's wealth derived from his success as a printer, and he wrote a significant amount of the content for some of the most lucrative products of his own press, such as the *Poor Richard* almanacs and the newspaper the *Pennsylvania Gazette*. But this assertion is also a broader expression of Franklin's sophisticated understanding of his own practice of using written discourse to create a variety of self-promoting personae over the course of his life.[2] Writing was key to Franklin's construction of what Mitchell Breitwieser has described as his "representative personalities."[3] Perhaps because Franklin was such a successful printer, scholars have typically focused on his printed texts when considering the ways he used writing to manage his image, often arguing that he was uniquely dependent on the medium of print for his "advancement." Among the most influential articulations of this argument is that of Michael Warner, who in his still frequently cited *Letters of the Republic* argues that Franklin's modernity was defined by his exploitation of the apparent incorporeality of printed discourse. Following the model of a print "public sphere" articulated by Jürgen Habermas, and with what Rolf Englesing described as an eighteenth-century "reading revolution" providing implied historical context, Warner concludes that Franklin was "preeminently the republican man of letters" precisely because he was "the citizen of print."[4]

But as important as printing was to Franklin's "advancement" in life, he also understood that the medium of manuscript could sometimes be an even better tool for influencing how readers perceived his authorial personae.[5] In the context of his early scientific writing, for example, Franklin used both print and manuscript to disseminate his ideas, but it was manuscript that proved the essential medium through which his scientific work first earned the serious attention it deserved and his ambition demanded. Circulating his science in manuscript helped Franklin overcome his geographic and social disadvantages—he was a colonial printer and was thus considered rather lowly—as he attempted to enter the genteel world of Enlightenment natural philosophy. To demonstrate how this was so, in the essay that follows I compare Franklin's use of print publication and manuscript circulation to disseminate some of his most important early scientific work, for it was through this science that Franklin transformed himself from a colonial printer, a "mere mechanic," into a celebrity participant in the Republic of Letters, the feted "Dr. Franklin" and winner of the British Royal Society's Copley Medal. More specifically, I compare Franklin's circulation of his printed pamphlet *An Account of the New Invented Pennsylvanian Fire-Places* (1744) to his reliance on manuscript circulation to disseminate his now much more famous work, *Experiments and Observations on Electricity, Made at Philadelphia* (1751). The first work was a pamphlet Franklin printed to explain the scientific theories behind his improved heating stove, and the latter a detailed explanation of Franklin's experiments with and theories about electricity. However, Franklin limited the latter work to manuscript circulation for a considerable period of time. He agreed to print *Experiments* only after it had been effectively "scribally published," to use Harold Love's phrase for the phenomenon of manuscript publication.[6] Franklin's differing media choices and dissemination strategies for these two scientific works suggest he learned it was necessary to communicate his scientific ideas in manuscript, at least initially, if he was to have his work seriously reviewed by the transatlantic community of natural philosophers. Moreover, the form in which the printed version of *Experiments* did ultimately appear—with a paratext that emphasized the priority of the work's earlier circulation in manuscript—was essential to Franklin's establishment of credibility as a scientific author.

An Account of the New Invented Pennsylvanian Fire-Places: The "Errata" of Science in Print

Given the state of what we now call science in the early eighteenth century, it is not surprising that Franklin's earliest forays into scientific experimentation concerned what might be described as proto-thermodynamics. The behavior of air when energized had been a core subject of experimental study since the mid-sixteenth century, marked by Robert Boyle's 1660 account of his "air-pump," *New Experiments Physico-Mechanical, Touching the Spring of the Air and Its Effects*. As work by Boyle and others became widely available in print, artisans in London and other cities, such as Philadelphia, formed a growing segment of the audience for this literature. Eric Foner has argued that the distinct training and labor conditions typical to the artisan trades explain why these "mechanics," as they were sometimes called, were attracted to the new science. As Foner puts it, "The very nature of craft work required dexterity with tools, mastery of physical materials, and a technical knowledge which often stimulated a further interest in science."[7] Franklin, an artisan printer, was thus fairly typical for having an interest in science and experimentation; what was unusual was the degree of his scientific ability and ambition.

Understandably, access to a steady supply of scientific texts was important to Franklin's scientific development, and he leveraged his social and business networks to that end. As a young man Franklin cofounded the Junto, a group of mostly artisan men who came together to form a kind of autodidactic debating society. A particular advantage of the Junto was that its members were able to share funds to purchase books, an arrangement that developed into one of the first subscription libraries in British North America: the Library Company of Philadelphia. The Library Company frequently purchased works on natural philosophy, and Franklin consumed this literature with relish.[8] He began to see a connection between a routine subject of such texts—the behavior of air when energized by heat—and his long-standing interest in medicine and the prevention of disease.[9] By the early 1740s, Franklin had become convinced that cold and drafty rooms significantly contributed to illness, so he applied his theories on convection to a new heating stove design that warmed rooms more efficiently than other devices in common use. He completed his design in the winter of 1739–40 and named it the "Pennsylvanian Fire-Place." Franklin had his friend Robert Grace, an ironmonger and fellow member of the Junto, cast the iron plates to build the stoves, and Grace was soon doing so regularly. Franklin advertised the stoves in the *Pennsylvania Gazette* and sold them out of his print shop.[10]

Not long after sales began, Franklin wrote a pamphlet to explain the scientific theories behind his design, the 1744 *Account of the New Invented Pennsylvanian Fire-Places*. *Account* features two distinct stylistic registers—one pragmatic, even folksy, and the other erudite and technical. However, perhaps as a consequence of the text's sometimes informal tone, the scholarly view has long been that *Account*'s chief purpose was to advertise stoves. For instance, Leo Lemay notes, "Franklin wrote *Account* to promote the stove," while the editors of *The Papers of Benjamin Franklin* call it a "promotion brochure" that "encouraged [the stove's] sale."[11] Yet the text itself challenges this narrow view. Although at times humorous and informal, it is also scientifically sophisticated: it is replete with detailed references to other scientific literature, for instance, including some lengthy quotations in the original Latin, and it offers detailed descriptions of several experiments, inviting readers to replicate those experiments to test Franklin's evidence for his theoretical claims. Moreover, Franklin disseminated the work far beyond the geographical sphere of potential stove buyers in and near Philadelphia. He sent copies to several leading natural philosophers around British North America, and he was supportive when they sent it to others in Europe. All of this strongly suggests that *Account* was a much more ambitious project than a simple advertisement for a heating appliance. In important ways, it was a scientific treatise.

Account markedly reflects the experimental approaches popularized by Boyle and others that had become normalized by Franklin's time, and it draws on the previous scientific literature on air and heat. Franklin references Nicholas Gauger's *Mechanique de fue* (1713), for instance, a work translated into English by John Theophilus Desaguliers as *Fires Improved* (1715). Such references suggest Franklin self-consciously saw his pamphlet as contributing to this particular body of scientific literature. Indeed, Desaguliers seems to have been especially important to *Account*.[12] Franklin recognizes "the ingenious and learned Dr. Desaguliers, to whose instructive Writings, [he] acknowledges himself [to be] much indebted."[13] It may even be that Franklin hoped his pamphlet would attract Desauliers's personal attention, given the man's substantial scientific influence as one of the leading *virtuosi* of the British Royal Society. In particular, Franklin describes at length an experiment from Desaguliers's pamphlet *Physico-Mechanical Lectures: or An Account of What Is Explain'd and*

Demonstrated in the Course of Mechanical and Experimental Philosophy (1717). The experiment employed an air-pump and a bird, and Franklin notes Desaguliers's result approvingly: the bird lived when placed in a bottle filled with air that had passed through hot iron, but it died in a bottle of air that had passed through heated brass, proving that hot iron does not emit noxious fumes.

Franklin also provides instructions for a series of experiments of his own design, again following the models established by Boyle and Desaguliers. Early in *Account*, Franklin explains:

> Tis necessary to understand well some few properties of Air and Fire, vis. 1. Air is rarified by *Heat*, and condens'd by *Cold*; i.e. the same Quantity of Air takes up more Space when warm than when cold. This may be shown by several very easy Experiments. Take any clear Glass Bottle ... place it before the Fire, and as the Air within is warm'd and rarified, part of it will be driven out of the Bottle; turn it up, place its Mouth in a Vessel of Water, and remove it from the Fire; then, as the Air within cools and contracts, you will see the Water rise in the Neck of the Bottle, supplying the Place of just so much Air as was driven out.[14]

In providing this experiment, Franklin offers observational evidence for the physical principles that underlie his stove design. In so doing, he demonstrates his mastery of the accepted experimental principles used by members of the Royal Society—that is, he provides the sort of "virtual witnessing," what Steven Shapin and Simon Schaffer describe as the "production in a reader's mind of an image of an experimental scene," that scientific texts were expected to feature in support of their claims.[15] After providing additional experiments along the same lines, Franklin concludes this section of the pamphlet with a summary of his theoretical principal, noting, "Air rarified and distended by Heat, is specifically lighter than it was before, and will rise in other Air of greater Density.... Body or Matter of any sort is said to be *specifically* heavier or lighter than other Matter, when it has more or less Substance or Weight in the same Dimensions."[16] The inclusion of so much material of this sort makes plain that *Account* is as much a scientific treatise—one in a tradition of the scientific literature Franklin had been reading for some time—as a text written to sell stoves. In fact, we might consider the stove itself something of an experimental proof of concept that could confirm the validity of Franklin's broader theories about convection while also demonstrating the pragmatic usefulness of those theories. That is to say, Franklin's "fireplace" may have been something akin to Boyle's original air pump: an experimental apparatus that helped prove the validity of theoretical models, albeit, in Franklin's case, an apparatus that had the practical benefit of more efficient home heating.

However, regardless of its scientific content—and to say nothing of Franklin's personal ambitions for the work—Desaguliers did not read *Account*, having died in early 1744. Moreover, even if Desaguliers had lived long enough to read a copy, the text's form—a printed pamphlet—was problematic for a scientific work, especially one printed by its own colonial author. Desaguliers probably would have responded to Franklin's work in a manner similar to how the natural philosophers who did read it responded: in their view, it was not serious science to be examined and formally tested but simply a novelty. It was an interesting text, written by an "ingenious man," but one prosaically focused on home heating. Part of the difficulty Franklin faced lay in a general ambivalence toward scientific authorship in print during the early modern period. Adrian Johns has argued that this ambivalence stemmed from the widespread piracy of printed scientific texts—"piracy" covering a range of unauthorized printing practices—and associated fears about the loss of authorial, and thus reputational, control. For instance, printers often produced scientific texts without a review by or the approval of their original authors and, even if a printing had been authorized, printers sometimes issued altered additional copies for public sale far in excess of the original, authorized run. In addition, printers sometimes produced unauthorized abridged and summarized editions of scientific texts, works known as "epitomes," as well as unauthorized translations.[17] As Johns notes, such "piratical practices made [scientific] authorship intensely problematic. How could a gentleman ... natural philosopher become an author?" One common suggestion was that "gentlemen should abjure the vocation altogether" because "to become an author [in print] one had to subject oneself to tradesmen ... [who] had their own views."[18] As Johns summarizes the ambivalence of genteel scientific authors toward their work appearing in print, "The good name of a gentleman could never rest safe" in the power of printers and booksellers.[19]

There were two main techniques for coping with this ambivalence. One was to eschew print altogether, relying wholly on manuscript circulation to publicize one's work, as Johns points out both Isaac Newton and Boyle sometimes chose to do. But this was far from a perfect solution: texts circulated in manuscript were not absolutely secure from unauthorized printing, and even if manuscript circulation did sometimes constitute a form of publication, the quicker and broader reach afforded by print could in some cases be desirable. Thus, the other common solution was explicitly to inscribe into printed texts a posture that Johns calls "anti-authorial," an approach that "resulted in enhanced credibility" for scientific authors who did appear in print. That is to say, gentleman natural philosophers would include statements as part of their printed texts that deemphasized their authorization of that very printing, sometimes even going so far as to deny they had authorized any such printing at all.[20]

Abnegation of one's own authorship in print was in keeping with broader social expectations for scientific authors: that they be modest and public spirited rather than self-interested, and that they always remain "gentlemanly."[21] Boyle himself took such an anti-authorial stance in the printed work that made his air-pump apparatus famous. The title page of his *New Experiments* asserts the work was first "Written by way of Letter To the Right Honorable Charles Lord Viscount of Dungarvan." Boyle also included a prefatory note, "To the Reader," in which he remarked, "If it be demanded why I publish to the World a Letter . . . [I answer] I could not without quite tyring more then [sic] one Amanuensis, give out half as many Copies of them as were earnestly desired, that I could not civilly refuse them," adding, "Intelligent Persons in matters of this kinde perswaded me, that the publication of what I had observed touching the Nature of the Air, would not be useless to the World."[22] Boyle's paratext apologizes for print by casting the act of printing as a kind of secretarial service. It claims that since his own assistants could not keep up with the demand for manuscript copies, printing saved gentleman readers the labor of having to make their own. Likewise, one of Franklin's specific models for *Account*, Desaguliers's *Physico-Mechanical Lectures*, also included an anti-authorial paratext. At the beginning of *Physico-Mechanical* there is a prefatory note marked "To the READER" that makes a claim similar to that of Boyle: that Desaguliers only printed his work to save others the labor of copying by hand, and at their specific request: "The following Papers, being only Minutes of my Lectures for the use of such Gentlemen who have been my Auditors, were printed at their Desire; to save the trouble of Writing them over for every Person."[23] Thus we can see even that figures as deeply embedded within the community of Enlightenment natural philosophers as Boyle and Desaguliers considered it necessary to frame their printed texts in an anti-authorial manner.

This background suggests that if Franklin did see *Account* as a work of serious science, which the text itself strongly implies, he was mistaken in choosing, first, to print it without having earlier circulated it in manuscript, and, second, to not include any anti-authorial paratexts with the printed pamphlet. While Franklin had been cultivating a network of scientific correspondents for a number of years when he wrote *Account*, there is no evidence that he circulated any part of the work in manuscript prior to printing it, nor did *Account* include any introduction, preface, or note to readers that would frame the pamphlet, even fictitiously, as having earlier been circulated in manuscript, or even any claim that Franklin was at all reluctant to see the work printed. Indeed, the fact that Franklin printed the pamphlet himself, in his own shop, would make any such anti-authorial veneer especially difficult to assert. In 1744, Franklin was still a working printer, and as such he was deeply and obviously embedded within exactly the "craft community" that genteel natural philosophers hesitated to engage for fear of damaging their credibility and reputations. The title page of *Account* prominently features Franklin's brand trademark as a printer: "Philadelphia: Printed and Sold by B. Franklin. 1744" (see fig. 1).[24] Thus, *Account*'s title page actually highlights how Franklin had collapsed the roles of scientific author and commercial printer into a single, presumptuous entity, significantly reducing his work's credibility in the process.

It is thus not surprising that readers did not generally respond to *Account* as a work of serious science, even if some were enthusiastic about Franklin and his stove. When Franklin sent *Account* to a number of his regular scientific correspondents, they tended to respond to it as a curiosity rather than as a treatise of experimental science. For example, Franklin cultivated a correspondence with Cadwallader Colden—a Scottish physician who was the lieutenant governor of New York—as early as 1742, and he duly sent Colden a copy of *Account* once he had printed it.[25] Colden was himself a regular correspondent with many well-known British and continental natural philosophers, including the Dutch botanist Johann Gronovius, to whom he forwarded a copy of Franklin's pamphlet. Colden's description of the work in his letter to Gronovius is revealing. He mentioned Franklin's pamphlet only at the very end of a letter otherwise focused almost exclusively on Colden's prior exchanges with a third

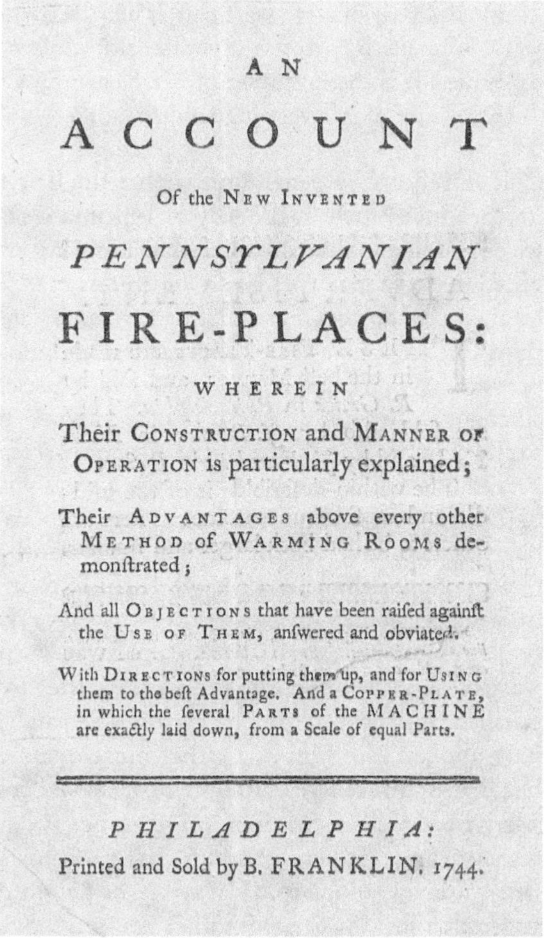

> AN
> # ACCOUNT
> Of the New Invented
> ## *PENNSYLVANIAN*
> # FIRE-PLACES:
> WHEREIN
>
> Their CONSTRUCTION and MANNER OF OPERATION is particularly explained;
>
> Their ADVANTAGES above every other METHOD of WARMING ROOMS demonstrated;
>
> And all OBJECTIONS that have been raised against the USE OF THEM, answered and obviated.
>
> With DIRECTIONS for putting them up, and for USING them to the best Advantage. And a COPPER-PLATE, in which the several PARTS of the MACHINE are exactly laid down, from a Scale of equal Parts.
>
> ---
>
> *PHILADELPHIA:*
> Printed and Sold by B. FRANKLIN. 1744.

FIGURE 1. Title page of Franklin's 1744 *An Account of the New Invented Pennsylvanian Fire-Places*. (Franklin 381 Ac2 1744; General Collection, Beinecke Rare Book and Manuscript Library, Yale University)

correspondent of substantial scientific reputation, Carl Linnaeus. At the conclusion of this letter, we find a brief mention of the enclosed copy of Franklin's pamphlet:

> You cannot expect much new in Literature from this part of the world. I send with this [letter] a curious & new invention for warming a room with a small fire more effectually than can be done by a large fire in the common method & is free of the inconveniencies which attend the Dutch and German Stoves; because by this contrivance there is a con-

tinual supply of fresh warm air. It may be particularly usefull to you & Dr. Linneus, by preserving your health while it keeps you warm at your studies. It is the invention of Mr. Benjamin Franklin of Philadelphia, the printer of it, a very ingenious man.[26]

Colden reflected a general sense that the British American colonies did not produce much in the way of legitimate scientific literature, and, by way of compensation, he offered an amusing alternative: Franklin's pamphlet, the "curious" work of an "ingenious man." The pamphlet was entertaining, perhaps even useful, but it was not "new [scientific] Literature." Even Colden, one of Franklin's earliest and most supportive patrons, appears to have all but ignored *Account*'s sophisticated scientific content, focusing instead on the text's utilitarian value: better home heating. Typical to the rhetorical style of Enlightenment correspondence, Colden framed Franklin's work as supportive of the always wished-for good health and happiness of the letter's recipient, the "fireplace" serving as material emblem that concretized the metaphoric warmth of friendship with which Colden closed the letter. Yet, while the author Franklin was "ingenious," his science, *qua* science, was either unseen or ignored.

"Ingenious" is a particularly important word in this context. While it was an adjective of approbation among the *virtuosi* of the Royal Society, at this stage in Franklin's career his scientific correspondents appear to have applied it to him in a rather more qualified way, underscoring that he was not himself yet a full member of that community. For instance, in a letter to William Strahan in December 1743, Colden described having met a printer (it was Franklin) the previous summer, a man who was "the most ingenious in his way ... of any in America." In his response to Colden in May 1744, Strahan guessed Colden had met Franklin and noted that Franklin was already known to him for the quality of his printing, agreeing that Franklin was, indeed, "a most ingenious Man in his Way." As Leo Lemay notes, both Colden and Strahan were simultaneously offering high praise for and condescension toward Franklin, the qualifier "in his way" marking Franklin's status as a colonial printer rather than as a gentleman of the metropole, a person in whom genius would be both more expected and capacious.[27]

As this exchange of letters suggests, Franklin faced a number of challenges as a scientific author. A colonial printer, Franklin was a "leather apron man" and thus decidedly not a "gentleman." To be sure, this social status posed significant challenges for Franklin's credibility as a scientific author, regardless of the medium in which he communicated his work. But the fact that he circulated *Account* in print, and that he did not include the conventional and expected anti-authorial paratext as part of the work, certainly did not make it any easier for the ideas he articulated to be seen as serious experimental science by the Royal Society's *virtuosi* and the other genteel natural philosophers he seems to have hoped to impress with the pamphlet. Franklin had failed to account for the continuing importance of manuscript circulation in mid-eighteenth-century science, a fact that influenced the pamphlet's reception then and continues to do so now.

Electric Letters and a Paratextual Apology for Print

If *Account*'s form as a printed pamphlet, combined with Franklin's status as a colonial printer who had himself printed the work, hurt the credibility of Franklin's theories about heat energy, his broader scientific ambitions were not much dampened, and neither was the pamphlet a total failure. The novelty and enjoyable style of the writing, as well as the evident "ingeniousness" of its author, seem to have helped Franklin insert himself into the correspondence networks of Enlightenment science. The pamphlet made clear, as another of Colden's correspondents put it, that Franklin was "a man of Sense & of a good Stile."[28] Indeed, Joyce Chaplin argues that *Account*'s appealing style gave Franklin an opportunity to use his pamphlet as "a kind of calling card . . . a way to introduce himself" to natural philosophers who were his social superiors.[29] Moreover, even though *Account* did not result in a formal testing of Franklin's theories by the likes of Desaguliers, Franklin seems to have learned an important lesson from the tenor of the work's reception: print was not the best medium to communicate scientific ideas in the Republic of Letters, at least not initially.

Franklin continued his program of scientific experimentation and, having sold active control of his printing business for a considerable sum in the late 1740s, devoted much of his greatly increased free time to a thorough study of electricity. Unlike his work on convection, Franklin's experiments on electricity did earn him a formal review by, and shortly thereafter the enthusiastic accolades of, the British Royal Society. Revealingly, however, Franklin disseminated his work on electricity in a manner quite different from his circulation of *Account*: no pamphlet was issued from Franklin's press describing his electrical work—no printed text we might imagine to have been entitled *An Account of the New-Invented Electrified Kite*. Moreover, and also unlike *Account*, when Franklin's work on electricity did appear in print, he included a substantial anti-authorial paratext claiming that he was largely unaware his work was being printed. That is, when Franklin agreed to print his work on electricity, he used both of the strategies genteel scientific authors deployed to deal with the general ambivalence about scientific work appearing in print.

Franklin circulated his work on electricity in manuscript letters for some years before any printed edition appeared. He kept detailed notes of his experiments and included copies of those notes in letters to his philosophical correspondents. Among the most important of those correspondents was Peter Collinson, a Londoner and member of the Royal Society whom Franklin had come to know well. Collinson had agreed to serve as the Library Company's book-buying agent in London as early as the 1720s, and he had increasingly become a patron to the group, sending it the first scientific instrument Franklin used for experiments with electricity: a glass cylinder that, when rotated, generated a static charge. Franklin's earliest letter to Collinson on any electrical subject, written in 1747, was a warm thank you for the device and Collinson's detailed instructions about how to use it. Collinson, intrigued by Franklin's interest, sent additional instruments from London and encouraged Franklin to continue and expand his electrical experiments.[30]

Bolstered by Collinson's positive response, Franklin began sending copies of his letters about his electrical experiments to others. His general practice was to keep copies of the letters he first sent to Collinson, making additional copies that he would send to other interested individuals. Colden, for instance, often received copies, and these, with Franklin's express blessing, Colden sometimes copied and forwarded to his own scientific correspondents. After a few years, this robust copying and exchanging of Franklin's electrical manuscripts effectively "published" Franklin's work to the Anglophone scientific community. Eventually, Franklin produced a summary collection of all his experiments and theories on electricity, asking his old friend, the cartographer Lewis Evans (who had drawn the diagrams of Franklin's stove included in *Account*), to make clean copies of all of Franklin's letters to Collinson, including the hand-drawn diagrams, and to organize them into a single manuscript book. Franklin then revised that text, making corrections and emendations to the manuscript that Evans had produced. A copy of that book has survived to the present day, one that Franklin sent to James Bowdoin, who was himself interested in electricity and who had requested the copy while visiting Franklin in Philadelphia. As many of the original letters Franklin sent to Collinson and others have now been lost, this manuscript book sent to Bowdoin is considered the most authoritative and complete "edition" of Franklin's *Experiments and Observations on Electricity*, given its priority to all printed editions. As the editors of *The Papers of Benjamin Franklin* note to explain why they chose to reprint the Bowdoin manuscript over any printed edition of *Experiments*, "The Bowdoin manuscript, though a copy, was supervised and corrected by Franklin. Made in 1750, it antedates the first printed edition of *Experiments and Observations*. It is also in several instances fuller than any printed version."[31]

Through all of this intense copying and exchanging of manuscripts we can see Franklin self-consciously adapting to the expectations of the *virtuosi* of the Royal Society about how to properly communicate scientific knowledge in the Republic of Letters: that is, Franklin's engagement with the scribal culture of the natural philosophers who were often his social superiors allowed him to project authorial modesty and thus to more easily join what Johns describes as the "learned sociability" of Enlightenment science. The shared practices of experimentation and the reading, copying, and exchanging of manuscripts about those experiments defined a kind of virtuous "public sphere" within which scientific ideas were introduced and tested. Indeed, it was for the most part only work vetted in this manner that was warranted by that community *as* knowledge. Such practices effectively allowed scientific authors to project the authorial modesty needed to communicate they were the sort of people worth believing and, simultaneously, to demonstrate that the claims of fact found in their texts had been properly socialized through a network of other well-regarded philosophical gentlemen. Thus, Franklin's circulation of his electrical work in manuscript conferred the credibility needed to have his work seriously reviewed within the community of "learned sociability" that defined the Royal Society, and it was only after his work had been publicized and validated in this manner that it became relatively safe to have it printed.

For Franklin, the process of review by the Royal Society occurred in this way: not long after first reviewing Franklin's electrical letters, Collinson showed copies to several other members of the Royal Society, including William Watson, who was the group's principal "electrician." Having been vouched for by Collinson, Franklin's theories were examined and approved of by Watson, who seems mistakenly to have thought they confirmed his own work. Watson subsequently quoted one of Franklin's letters in a formal paper he read before the society, a paper that was later printed in the society's official organ, the *Philosophical Transactions*. With the formal introduction of Franklin's electrical work complete, Collinson read some of Franklin's other electrical letters before the society, which then conducted a formal debate of their merits. Franklin's experiments were then assigned to individual members for attempts at replication. At last, after his experiments had been successfully replicated, Franklin's work received the society's formal approval and imprimatur. At that point, in 1751, Collinson collected all of Franklin's electric letters together, and, with Franklin's express approval (and some additional revisions), had them printed as the pamphlet we know today, *Experiments and Observations on Electricity, Made at Philadelphia in America, by Mr. Benjamin Franklin*.[32]

In all of these steps we see Franklin conforming to the reading and writing practices preferred by the *virtuosi* of the Royal Society. As Johns puts it, "Shared practices of reading both constituted a community of experimental philosophers and warranted what that community produced as knowledge."[33] Franklin's decision to first disseminate his work on electricity in manuscripts sent to multiple well-connected correspondents—that is, to engage in "scribal publication" with others of the community of Anglophone natural philosophers—allowed him to transcend his colonial origins and his status as a printer-craftsman. Through manuscript Franklin generated a more credible authorial persona than he had done in the printed pamphlet *Account*; with his texts on electricity he crafted a scientific authorial persona that was both modest and appropriately sociable, and one that was more clearly free from the commercial compromises associated with the act of printing.

Franklin also made sure that when his electrical work eventually was printed, it conformed to the anti-authorial expectations for printed science written by gentlemen. Unlike *Account*, *Experiments* included a substantial paratext that highlighted the work's prior circulation in manuscript. The title page of *Experiments* makes explicit how Franklin's work on electricity had first been circulated in the form of personal correspondence. After "Experiments and Observations on Electricity" in the title, Franklin is credited as the primary experimenter, but his authorship of the printed text is moved into the background: the title continues, "And Communicated in Several Letters To Mr. P. Collinson, of London,

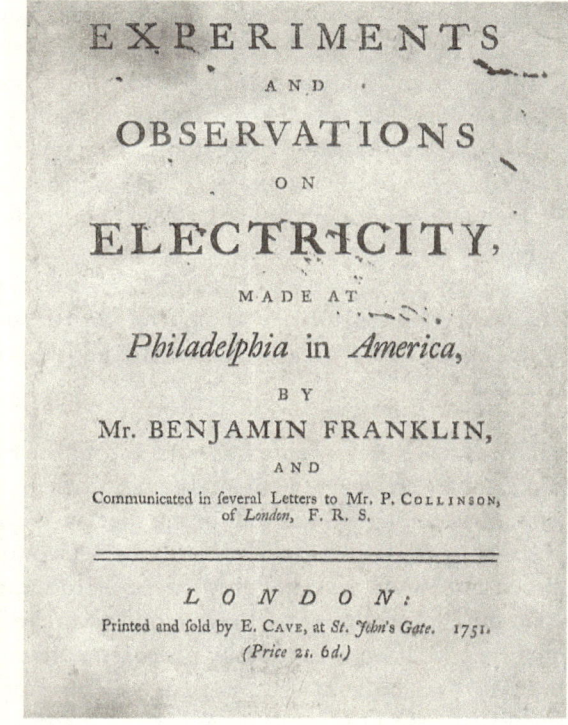

FIGURE 2. Title page of the first printed edition of Franklin's *Experiments and Observations on Electricity*. (Franklin 467 1751 1; General Collection, Beinecke Rare Book and Manuscript Library, Yale University)

F.R.S." Franklin's authorship of those letters, while reasonably assumed, is not mentioned directly, which distances Franklin from the printed pamphlet. Readers are thus put in a voyeuristic position, given the manner in which the paratext casts the pamphlet as a secondary extension of Franklin's manuscript letters addressed to Collinson. In addition, the title page highlights Collinson's expertise and prestige: the "F.R.S." suffix that follows his name—Fellow of the Royal Society—makes clear that the original recipient of Franklin's letters possessed substantial social and scientific credibility, and this, too, supports the text's legitimacy, despite its appearance in print (see fig. 2).

Reinforcing the priority of manuscript to print in *Experiments*, the pamphlet's preface describes in detail the process by which Franklin's work had earlier circulated in manuscript, and it likewise apologizes for the printed pamphlet's existence by denying Franklin had any intention to print the work:

> The following observations and experiments were not drawn up with a view to their being made publick, but were communicated at different times, and most of them in letters.... But some persons to whom they were read, and who had themselves been conversant in electrical disquisitions, were of the opinion ... that it would be doing a kind of injustice ... to confine them.... The Editor was therefore prevailed upon to commit such extracts of letters ... to the press, without waiting for the ingenious author's permission to do so.... He was only apprized of the step that had been thus taken, while the first sheets were in the press, and time enough for him to transmit some farther remarks, together with a few corrections and additions which are placed at the end.

The message is clear: readers should not think Franklin or his work compromised by appearing in print. Franklin, after all, was informed that his letters were being printed only as the sheets were drying. By that time, the preface suggests, it was too late for Franklin to stop the presses, so he was forced to comply, working only modestly to improve the text's accuracy. Also significant is how the preface calls Franklin "ingenious" without the qualifiers we have seen used by his correspondents at an earlier point in Franklin's scientific career. Franklin's manuscript circulation of his electrical letters and his subsequent use of an anti-authorial paratext in the printed *Experiments* thus appear to have succeeded in making Franklin into a serious and credible scientific author where *Account* had not, and the "in his way" qualifier was no longer seen as necessary or appropriate.

It should be noted that the "epistolary pamphlet" genre engaged by *Experiments* was recognized beyond the realm of scientific readers. Pamphlets that claimed to be printed versions of personal letters were also used for general news and political polemic. As Joad Raymond remarks about the broader genre, "The usefulness of the letter as a pamphlet genre was its ability to create virtual correspondence, an imaginary context that refracted a real one."[34] However, the manuscript correspondence upon which *Experiments* was based was not virtual but actual, and the work's paratextual insistence that Franklin's electrical experiments really had been circulated in letters (and, moreover, as a correspondence with the eminently reliable Peter Collinson, "F.R.S.") offered a more specific claim than a general invitation to readers to imagine a fictive exchange of letters. Instead, it made clear that Franklin's work had been properly socialized—that it had been circulated among established and credible scientific authors in accord with the norms of genteel natural philosophy and had been judged to contain information worth believing—before it appeared in print.

As anyone familiar with Franklin might guess, *Experiments'* image of an author surprised by print is not an accurate one. Franklin actually worked assiduously with Collinson and the printer to prepare his work for the press. But that is somewhat beside the point since, as we have seen, Franklin restricted the work to manuscript for some time before it was printed and, moreover, he deferred to a key member of the Royal Society, Collinson, about when it was proper to move the work into print. If Franklin instead had printed his electrical work immediately, as he did with *Account*, it is quite possible that it would have found a similarly muted reception. Indeed, the way *Experiments* apologizes for its very printedness, and the preface's related insistence that the work did in fact first circulate in manuscript correspondence, suggest that at least in the world of eighteenth-century natural philosophy the medium of print did not create an impersonal, virtuous, and newly rational public sphere; rather, it was suggestive of authors who were compromised by personal ambition and self-interest, and whose claims of fact were therefore not reliable. The rules of gentlemanly etiquette dictated that scientific authors should often use manuscript to publicize and socialize their work, and that they should at least claim to use print only to explicitly serve others. Even Benjamin Franklin, colonial America's foremost printer, had to conform.

Notes

1. Franklin, *Benjamin Franklin's Autobiography*, 10.
2. Tarantello, "Persona-lly Appealing." The literature on Franklin's creation of multiple and sometimes contradictory personae over the course of his life is substantial, but Tarantello provides an excellent recent summary of that literature.
3. Breitwieser, *Cotton Mather and Benjamin Franklin*.
4. Warner, *The Letters of the Republic*, 77.
5. Mulford, *Benjamin Franklin and the Ends of Empire*, 164–46. Mulford perceptively notes the care with which Franklin developed a correspondence network of well-placed gentlemen through which he could test and refine his political theories in manuscript form before making the decision to have them printed.
6. Love, *The Culture and Commerce of Texts*, 35 and passim.

7. Foner, *Tom Paine and Revolutionary America*, 38.
8. Wrightson, "[Those with] Great Abilities Have Not Always the Best Information.'"
9. As a teenage apprentice printer, Franklin participated in his brother James Franklin's excoriation in the *New-England Courant* of the Mathers' defense of smallpox inoculation, and Franklin's later *Poor Richard's Almanacks* often featured medical advice. Franklin had also printed, at his own expense, a new edition of *Every Man His Own Doctor: Or, the Poor Planter's Physician* in 1734: Finger, *Doctor Franklin's Medicine*, 2.
10. Franklin, *The Papers of Benjamin Franklin*, 2:419.
11. Lemay, *The Life of Benjamin Franklin*, 2:467; Franklin, *The Papers of Benjamin Franklin*, 2:419.
12. Lemay, *The Life of Benjamin Franklin*, 2:488. Lemay argues that Franklin likely met Desaguliers in London in 1725, introduced by their mutual acquaintance Isaac Greenwood, who was then serving as Desaguliers's experimental assistant: ibid., 1:263.
13. Franklin, *The Papers of Benjamin Franklin*, 2:439.
14. Ibid., 422.
15. Shapin and Schaffer, *Leviathan and the Air-Pump*, 60.
16. Franklin, *The Papers of Benjamin Franklin*, 2:423.
17. Johns, "The Ambivalence of Authorship in Early Modern Natural Philosophy."
18. Ibid., 78–79.
19. Ibid., 80.
20. Ibid.
21. Biagioli, "Scientific Revolution, Social Bricolage, and Etiquette," 38. Mario Biagioli argues that gentlemanly status was particularly important in Britain and its colonies, as compared with the rest of Europe, where monarchs were explicit patrons. Gentlemanly status was exemplified socially through rules of etiquette governing how claims of fact should be offered in writing, read, and debated. By engaging in and writing about "experimental philosophy, gentlemen fashioned matters of fact as they were fashioning themselves as gentlemen.... [Claims about] matters of fact did not 'insult' anybody because everybody was supposed to have cooperated (actually or virtually) in their production": ibid., 38.
22. Boyle, *New Experiments Physico-Mechanicall*, sig. A3.
23. Desaguliers, *Physico-Mechanical Lectures*, sig. A2.
24. Franklin, *An Account of the New Invented Pennsylvanian Fire-Places*.
25. Chaplin, *The First Scientific American*, 95.
26. Colden, *The Letters and Papers of Cadwallader Colden*, 3:91.
27. Lemay, *The Life of Benjamin Franklin*, 2:465.
28. Colden, *The Letters and Papers of Cadwallader Colden*, 3:83.

29. Chaplin, *The First Scientific American*, 92.
30. Ibid., 106.
31. Franklin, *The Papers of Benjamin Franklin*, 3:118.
32. Cohen, *Franklin and Newton*, 464.
33. Johns, "Reading and Experiment in the Early Royal Society," 248.
34. Raymond, *Pamphlets and Pamphleteering in Early Modern Britain*, 217–18.

Works Cited

Biagioli, Mario. "Scientific Revolution, Social Bricolage, and Etiquette." In *The Scientific Revolution in National Context*, edited by Roy Porter and Mikulas Teich, 11–54. Cambridge: Cambridge University Press, 1992.

Boyle, Robert. *New Experiments Physico-Mechanicall, Touching the Spring of the Air and Its Effects*. Oxford, 1660.

Breitwieser, Mitchell. *Cotton Mather and Benjamin Franklin: The Price of Representative Personality*. Cambridge: Cambridge University Press, 1984.

Chaplin, Joyce. *The First Scientific American: Benjamin Franklin and the Pursuit of Genius*. New York: Basic, 2006.

Cohen, I. Bernard. *Franklin and Newton: An Inquiry into Speculative Newtonian Experimental Science and Franklin's Work in Electricity as an Example Thereof*. Philadelphia: American Philosophical Society, 1956.

Colden, Cadwallader. *The Letters and Papers of Cadwallader Colden*, 9 vols. New York: New York Historical Society, 1922.

Desaguliers, John Theophilus. *Physico-Mechanical Lectures. Or, An Account of What Is Explain'd and Demonstrated in the Course of Mechanical and Experimental Philosophy*. London, 1717.

Finger, Stanley. *Doctor Franklin's Medicine*. Philadelphia: University of Pennsylvania Press, 2006.

Foner, Eric. *Tom Paine and Revolutionary America*. New York: Oxford University Press, 1976.

Franklin, Benjamin. *An Account of the New Invented Pennsylvanian Fire-Places*. Philadelphia, 1766.

———. *Benjamin Franklin's Autobiography*, edited by J. A. Leo Lemay and P. M. Zall. New York: W. W. Norton, 1986.

———. *The Papers of Benjamin Franklin, Volume 2: January 1, 1735, through December 31, 1744*, edited by Leonard W. Labaree et al. New Haven, CT: Yale University Press, 1960.

———. *The Papers of Benjamin Franklin, Volume 3: January 1, 1745, through June 30, 1750*, edited by Leonard W. Labaree et al. New Haven, CT: Yale University Press, 1961.

Johns, Adrian. "The Ambivalence of Authorship in Early Modern Natural Philosophy." In *Scientific Authorship: Credit and Intellectual Property in Science*, edited by Mario Biagioli and Peter Galison, 67–91. New York: Routledge, 2003.

———. "Reading and Experiment in the Early Royal Society." In *Reading, Society, and Politics in Early Modern England*, edited by Kevin Sharpe and Steven N. Zwicker, 244–72. Cambridge: Cambridge University Press, 2003.

Lemay, J. A. Leo. *The Life of Benjamin Franklin, Volume 1: Journalist 1706–1730*. Philadelphia: University of Pennsylvania Press, 2006.

———. *The Life of Benjamin Franklin, Volume 2: Printer and Publisher 1730–1747*. Philadelphia: University of Pennsylvania Press, 2006

Love, Harold. *The Culture and Commerce of Texts: Scribal Publication in Seventeenth-Century England*. Oxford: Clarendon, 1993.

Mulford, Carla J. *Benjamin Franklin and the Ends of Empire*. Oxford: Oxford University Press, 2015.

Raymond, Joad. *Pamphlets and Pamphleteering in Early Modern Britain*. Cambridge: Cambridge University Press, 2003.

Shapin, Steven, and Simon Schaffer. *Leviathan and the Air-Pump: Hobbes, Boyle, and the Experimental Life*. Princeton, NJ: Princeton University Press, 1985.

Tarantello, Patricia F. "Persona-lly Appealing: Benjamin Franklin's Poor Richard and Authorial Self-Representation." *Authorship* 5, no. 1 (2016): 1–13.

Warner, Michael. *The Letters of the Republic: Publication and the Public Sphere in Eighteenth-Century America*. Cambridge, MA: Harvard University Press, 1990.

Wrightson, Nick. "[Those with] Great Abilities Have Not Always the Best Information': How Franklin's Transatlantic Book-Trade and Scientific Networks Interacted, ca. 1730–1757." *Early American Studies* 8, no. 1 (Winter 2010): 94–119.

PART III
New Methods for Manuscript Studies

Amateur Manuscript Fiction in the Archives
An Introduction

EMILY C. FRIEDMAN

IN 1842, THE Right Honorable Lady Katherine Howard, spinster of Cheltenham, Gloucestershire, and third daughter of the Irish Countess of Wicklow, died, and her will was probated through the Prerogative Court of Canterbury. After some initial legacies, she bequeathed the life benefits of her stocks and funded property to "my entirely beloved and faithful friend Maria Frederica Minchin, widow now residing with me."[1] This was a substantial bequest, but certainly not the first gift from Howard to Minchin; forty-three years earlier, Howard had produced a 243-page novel that the title page advertised as "most humbly dedicated to Mrs. Richard Minchin by Lady Katherine Howard."[2] This novel exists in only one copy: a manuscript inscribed neatly in Roman hand and brown ink onto the blind-ruled wove-paper pages of a large calf-bound and gilt-embossed blank book, which is so substantial that the majority of its pages remain blank. Impressive, scrupulously neat, and imitating print from its title page onward, this novel was crafted with great care and yet was intended for only one pair of eyes.

In this essay I discuss this novel, *The Life of Frederick Harley*; the extraordinary friendship preserved on its title page; and the challenges that appear when finding and researching works like it—and there are, indeed, works like it. We are accustomed to understanding novels as being composed for a mass audience, especially by the late 1700s, after a century of growth and dominance for both mass print culture and the novel genre. But Howard was just one of many people in the eighteenth and nineteenth centuries who continued to understand what manuscript could do and print could not. These private writings, for the self or a very select circle, sometimes explicitly signaled their disconnection from the world of print and its pressures. By tracing what we can and cannot know about this work, I illuminate some of the challenges—and rewards—of creating a history of fiction that was conceptualized in manuscript during the age of print. The nature of our extant cataloguing and bibliographic standards provide a substantial barrier to discovering these items and to fully describing their features when they are found. By removing those barriers—bringing these texts together in a searchable online collection and creating a descriptive vocabulary based on their features—we may create a rich new corpus of literary works. Greater accessibility (e.g., through aggregation within public scholarship sites such as 18thConnect and Networked Infrastructure for Nineteenth-Century Electronic Scholarship, or NINES) can allow these works to appear alongside their print contemporaries. It can also allow them to be consulted and compared as a group, enabling a new and expanded view of manuscript circulation in the age of print. Finally, the process of digitizing and describing these objects using existing controlled vocabularies can reveal both the continued survival of genres and subgenres after they ceased to appear in new print fiction and the need for more accurate terminology to describe these works.

The examples in this essay derive from a project I am undertaking with a research team of undergraduate students at Auburn University to create a database of manuscript fiction with rich metadata, titled Manuscript Fiction in the Archive, 1750–1900 (manuscriptfiction.org). While still in its early stages, the project aims to form a vocabulary and taxonomy for discussing manuscript fiction in the age of print and, in the process, provide insights into the writing and reading lives of the period. Attending to the particular challenges manuscript works pose for digitization projects may also show the potential for new technologies to open up frontiers of research in archival studies.

THE LIFE OF FREDERICK HARLEY

Lady Katherine Howard's *The Life of Frederick Harley*—now in the collection of Chawton House Library—was one of three bound pieces of manuscript fiction that I first found on my desk in the spring of 2009. At the time, I did not have the bibliographic skill set to assess details about the format, binding, and other aspects of the volume, although I knew enough to say it was either a large octavo or quarto and that the paper was quite fine. Nor was I prepared for the puzzling contents of *Frederick Harley*. The narrative, to say the least, is not terribly thrilling. I had hopes, perhaps, of some sort of riff on Harley in Henry MacKenzie's *The Man of Feeling*, but this piece of fiction was neither tantalizingly fragmentary nor particularly rich with emotional detail. The life of Frederick Harley outlined on these pages is complete from birth to death while devoid of significant incident. But for the fact that it labels itself a novel on its title page, it could just as easily have been taken as straight biography.

It was the title page that first grabbed my attention and that I have been unpacking bit by bit ever since. The page meticulously mimics the conventions of late-century printed title pages, complete with a Dublin "imprint" and "publication date" of 1799 (see fig. 1). This was the first such manuscript title page I had ever seen. It presented a stark contrast to the other piece of manuscript fiction in Chawton's collection on my desk at the time: a smaller, much more informal manuscript by Charlotte Patte titled *The History of Ernestine* (see fig. 2), which may be an incomplete translation of Marie-Jeanne Riccoboni's *Histoire d'Ernestine* (1764). Patte's hand sprawls across the pages of this small octavo notebook, becoming less and less legible as the narrative continues, and seems to come to a halt due to the limitations of the tiny bound volume.[3] By comparison, when the manuscript novel *Frederick Harley* is placed next to a printed novel with similar title conventions, we can see how faithfully Howard has kept to the formal conventions of the late eighteenth-century and early nineteenth-century novel's paratextual material (see fig. 3). This is, of course, not the first such manuscript title page to imitate printed novels. We can look back, for example, to a 1740s translation of Anne-Marguerite du Noyer's 1716 *Letters Historical and Galant*, held by the University of Pennsylvania, to see how closely manuscript could imitate the conventions of print (see fig. 4).[4] Of course, this is just one of many such examples of the fluidity between manuscript and print that have existed since printed books began, with early printed books that aimed to resemble manuscript and manuscript copies that aimed to be similarly indistinguishable from their print corollaries.[5]

However, we lack a robust language to describe the very different audiences and aims that seem apparent when putting *Frederick Harley* beside these other two translations and, indeed, distinguishing between a

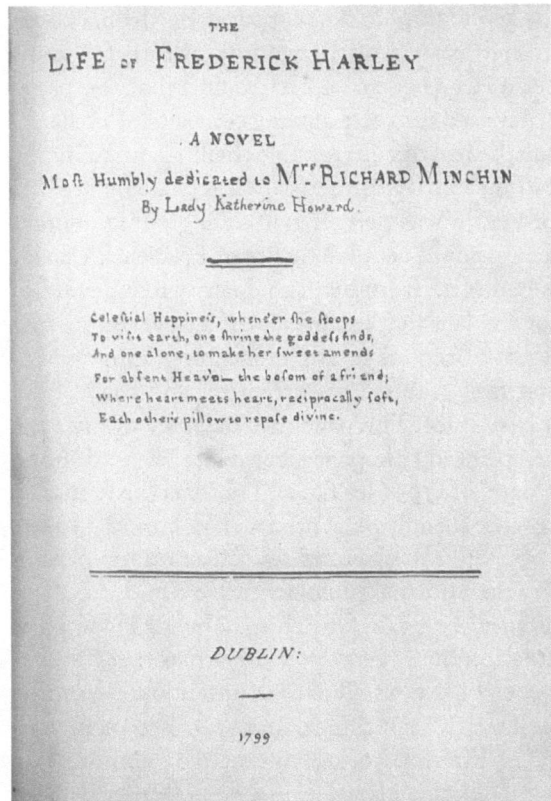

FIGURE 1. Title page to Lady Katherine Howard's *The Life of Frederick Harley*, with its dedication to her future legatee Mrs. Richard Minchin. (Manuscripts HOW, C3340; Chawton House Library)

translation that includes a multipage index (du Noyer) and one that lacks both legibility and completeness (Patte). In the absence of specificity, it is tempting to put Patte's translation and Howard's novel in the same category—that is, as juvenilia. But Howard was at least twenty-three, and more likely twenty-eight, at the time of the composition of *Frederick Harley*,[6] and the novel's dedicatee Maria Frederica Minchin was the same age and married, possibly for almost a decade, possibly with children of her own.[7] Moreover, there are other novelistic examples that further complicate a notion of manuscript fiction as primarily the realm of the young or apprentice writers:[8] Charles Isaac Mungo Dibdin and Warren Hastings both wrote fiction in their retirement that survives in their personal papers, and the anonymous author of *The Navy Officer* (ca. 1777–93) refers to a "young friend" as the intended recipient of the novel

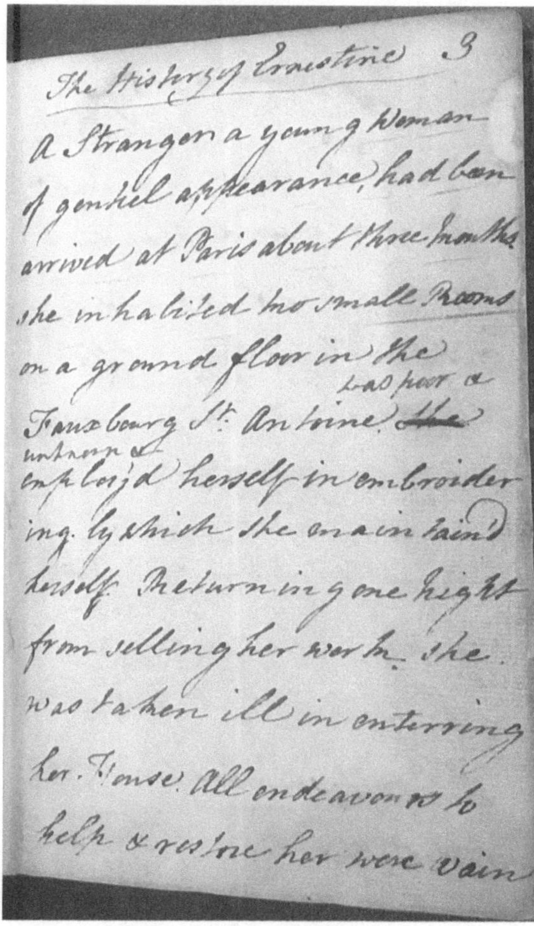
The History of Ernestine 3
A Stranger a young Woman
of genteel appearance, had been
arrived at Paris about three Months
she inhabited two small Rooms
on a ground floor in the
had poor a
Fauxbourg St. Antoine. she
unknown &
employ'd herself in embroider
ing. by which she maintain'd
herself. Returning one night
from selling her work, she
was taken ill in enterring
her House. All endeavours to
help & restore her were vain

FIGURE 2. First page of Charlotte Patte's *The History of Ernestine*. (Manuscripts PAT, C2594; Chawton House Library)

and its didactic warnings, implying that the author himself or herself was not necessarily young.[9] Lumping all manuscript fiction into a category of "juvenilia" does not make sense and may in fact hinder our comprehension of these works and their place within literary culture.

Manuscript Fiction: A Working Definition

What, then, do we make of these examples of manuscript fiction as a group? Had they been created at the end of the prior century—the seventeenth—we would be better equipped to place them in a context of

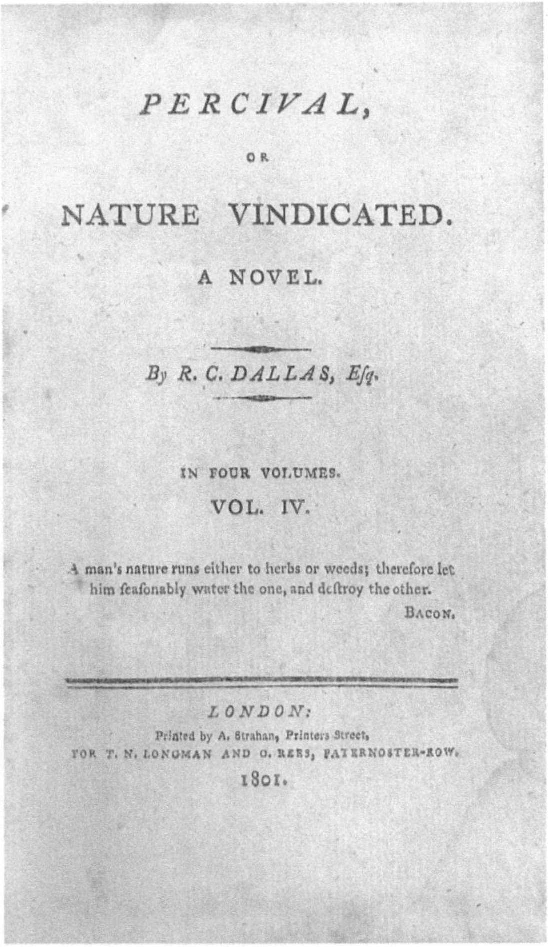

PERCIVAL,

OR

NATURE VINDICATED.

A NOVEL.

By R. C. DALLAS, Esq.

IN FOUR VOLUMES.

VOL. IV.

A man's nature runs either to herbs or weeds; therefore let him feasonably water the one, and deftroy the other.

BACON.

LONDON:

Printed by A. Strahan, Printers Street,

FOR T. N. LONGMAN AND O. REES, PATERNOSTER-ROW.

1801.

FIGURE 3. Title page to R. C. Dallas' *Percival; or, Nature Vindicated,* vol. 4 (London, 1801). (PR4525. D1243 P4 1801; Auburn University Libraries Department of Special Collections and Archives)

manuscript circulation practices with long roots. The early modern process of manuscript circulation and "publication" has been extensively discussed by scholars such as Margaret J. M. Ezell, Harold Love, and others following in their wake, but these accounts provide little in the way of a map of the terrain of manuscript publication and circulation of fiction after the rise of print culture in the early eighteenth century.[10] George Justice and Nathan Tinker's edited collection *Women's Writing and Circulation of Ideas: Manuscript Publication in English, 1550–1800,* worked to fill this gap, but even that promising title mentions late-eighteenth-century manuscript practice only in relationship to two famous—and published—writers, Lady Mary Wortley Montagu and Frances Burney, and does not tackle the wider range of manuscript writing that lies within its chronological bounds.

This is a limitation of prior scholarship but hardly an egregious oversight, given the nature of these documents in their respective archives. We cannot theorize or describe what we have not seen, and we cannot easily find that for which we do not have language. If we define manuscripts as "documents that do not attain printed form," as Marta L. Werner does, there is a built-in assumption that manuscripts are subsidiary

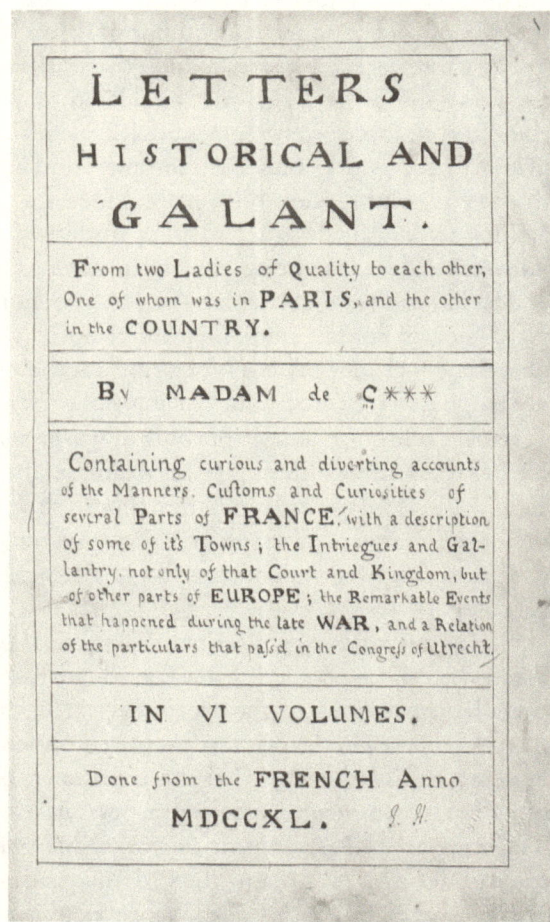

FIGURE 4. Title page of a manuscript translation of Anne-Marguerite du Noyer's *Letters Historical and Galant*. (UPenn Ms. Codex 227; Kislak Center for Special Collections, Rare Books, and Manuscripts, University of Pennsylvania)

to instantiation in print.[11] Such a definition overlooks manuscripts that do not have a connection to the world of print, either by publication or by association with an author engaged in print culture. While many works of manuscript fiction survive in the archival record (at the time of this writing I have identified more than 250), they tend to fall between definitional cracks. More often than not, manuscripts are insufficiently catalogued, especially when their authors are unknown or obscure. Since 2009, I have added examples from the National Library of Scotland, the British Library, the London Metropolitan Archive, the American Antiquarian Society, and elsewhere, finding unexpected needles in very large haystacks, often through painstaking examination of enormous boxes of personal papers. I now have thousands of pages of manuscript fiction, yet the task of collection feels as if it has only just begun.

My parameters are broad because the works are so rare compared with the verse and other forms that circulated more easily in manuscript or could be put into commonplace books, friendship albums, and the like. I primarily seek works of fiction, complete and incomplete, written during the age of print culture but not intended for print. Library catalogues are not necessarily designed to easily find items using these terms. As we know from decades of research on the novel's connection to true history and its ilk, what may seem on its face to be fictional may be factual, or vice versa—or, of course, some mixture of both. Moreover, whether a piece of writing was "not *intended* for print" can be profoundly challenging, if not impossible, to ascertain. During the current phase of the collection process, I rule out manuscripts only of works we know to have seen print during the author's lifetime—for example, the manuscript of Burney's *Camilla*. I also flag works by known published authors, such as the unpublished manuscript material of Jane Austen, as distinct in some way, though at this time I am unsure about whether they constitute a separate subcategory.

So far our work of collection, description, and transcription (undertaken with the assistance of undergraduate research assistants) has continually surprised us: we have seen survival of genres after they have fallen from popularity in the print marketplace, noticed hybridity of forms, and been startled by the ways that these writers choose to use the structures of fiction to comment on the world, personal or political, around them.[12] These are an odd assortment of works, ones we have not yet attempted to consider as a group and thus to analyze for similarities of physical shape or narrative technique. We do examine "important" manuscript material with great care and attention, as with manuscripts that achieve fame by association, such as the Brontë juvenilia, the Dickinson fascicles, and the working manuscripts of various published authors. There is also a substantial body of research on manuscripts that have value as social documents—friendship albums, commonplace books, and so on.[13] Given this foundational understanding of the larger world of manuscript circulation, I argue that the time is right to consider manuscript fiction as its own subset. My goal in collecting, taxonomizing, and contextualizing this material is to better understand what appear to be many different reasons for the existence of unpublished manuscript fiction after the establishment of print culture. I believe that we may elucidate both reading and writing practices and their change over time through these new data.

This enumeration and description takes the form of a digital database of manuscript fiction, 1750–1900. Its first goal is simply to create a catalogue of the locations of all known items, with the hope that archivists, librarians, and scholars can alert us to new items as they are discovered. But while we do need an enumerative bibliography of these works, we also need a richer model for describing them. These "modern manuscripts," as Donald H. Reiman has categorized manuscripts produced in this period,[14] fall between the descriptive categories of medieval and even Renaissance codicology and the bibliographic terms best suited to printed books. Best practices of codicology can get us a long way, but at a certain point many of these manuscripts are borrowing from the established norms of print culture and are inscribed in pre-bound blank books, which are themselves connected to the book trade. Thus, while we are not talking about "presswork" per se, we are often dealing with material that benefits from the application of methodology derived from Fredson Bowers's *Principles of Bibliographical Description* (1949) and Philip Gaskell's *A New Introduction to Bibliography* (1972).

I have created a rich metadata schema that allows for the entry of detailed physical description, provenance information, associated people (authors, recipients, and later owners), and features of the narrative itself.[15] To the best of our ability, we categorize each manuscript according to Reiman's categories of private, confidential, or public.[16] Elements of the database's information can be used by other data sets. For example, we will provide linked open metadata that will allow for these items to be discoverable by users of 18thConnect/NINES, major period-specific aggregators of commercial and nonprofit databases and sites. A more robust section of the schema can be combined with data from the Early Novels Database in order for our two teams of researchers to look for possible connections or parallels between the worlds of print and manuscript.[17] In addition, the schema includes "in-house" fields designed to track manuscript-specific features for future analysis that are not currently represented in MARC, Dublin Core, or RDF (the most common standards for description). These unique fields are designed to aid in visualizing change over time. Once the manuscripts are fully transcribed, both human and machine reading processes can potentially examine the corpus as a whole and reveal as-yet-unknown commonalities and diachronic change.

At the moment, my team at Auburn and I are entering extant catalogue data for the 250-plus items I have so far identified in collections primarily in Great Britain and the United States. For works I have visited and photographed, we are able to provide more information about format, binding, and other features not necessarily included in all catalogues. In addition, we are able to transcribe and encode those texts that are original manuscript fiction, a process that I anticipate will continue long after initial metadata entry has been completed.[18] The initial metadata tell us a significant part of the story, but ultimately full transcription and provenance research will be necessary to understand the stories these works tell: the stories within the pages, the stories of their provenance, and the larger stories of how they reflect or deviate from the world of print.

Finding Aids (and Hindrances)

One of the challenges of the project is that the sample set that is easily discoverable through traditional finding aids and more modern databases is very small. Consider *The Location Register of English Literary Manuscripts*, by any measure a massive and substantial reference work, now digitized for ease of use (having struggled with the oversize physical copies, I am certainly grateful for the digital version). When searching for unpublished manuscript holdings, the *Location Register*—in either medium—may as well not exist. To its credit, the *Location Register* faithfully catalogues "literary authors of all genres, from major poets to minor science fiction writers and romantic novelists," noting that "Enid Blyton, Marie Corelli and Ruby M. Ayres are included in the same way as Doris Lessing, Dorothy M. Richardson and Virginia Woolf." But there is no space for authors so minor that their work never entered the world of print, nor for that most famous and prolific of all authors, Anonymous.[19]

This is not a critique of the *Location Register* but, instead, an acknowledgment of a reality we all know about working with archival materials and with bibliographies and other compilations: that new knowledge is opened up to us by new and faster ways of sifting through information, and that how collections and databases are designed and organized rewards certain kinds of questions and uses more than others. A project that concentrates on the "unpublished" is often full of names who do not have substantial entries in the *Oxford Dictionary of National Biography* and whose work survives by happenstance. Moreover, it also includes those whose reputations do not derive from their fictional output, such as the philanthropist Maria Hackett, the politician Warren Hastings, and the theater manager Charles Isaac Mungo Dibdin. In these cases, finding aids, organizational methodology, and preservation priorities connected to the notion of *respects des fonds* will privilege the individual and thus the kind of work for which that person is best known. Evidence that gives us insight into Hastings's ideas about India, the exercise of colonial power, and the legal system are, rightly, of more interest to the average researcher than his thoughts on the novels of Samuel Richardson.

This project reminds me daily of how much we still rely on the capacious memory of librarians, archivists, and other colleagues; on the task of sifting through boxes marked "miscellaneous"; and on downright serendipity, especially when dealing with research tasks for which a given archive was not designed. Archival work, even in the digital age, is a complex and many-headed monster. Even digital resources designed to ease this process are not always successful. Gale's British Literary Manuscripts Online: c. 1660–1900 identifies the absence of provenance information and errors in attribution as a strength of its collection: the "bug" of poorly or unattributed manuscripts is flipped as an "opportunity for original scholarship to identify some of these items" that "is one of the contributions of the product."[20] Such "bugs" are compounded when we move from the study of print culture into the realm of manuscript, even with well-catalogued or duplicated examples.

Again, I note that we have inherited these challenges. Frank Burke traces the problem to the difference between what he terms the *archival* ("methodical, organized" and multigenerational) and the *personal* ("subjective, idiosyncratic, emotional, contemporary, and narrow") modes of collecting.[21] The latter category is frequently the home of manuscript material of the sort I discuss here. The differences are not always in form; sometimes they lie in why collections were produced, why they were kept, and thus how they are handled and how access is granted.[22] There are, as Burke notes, places of intersection: the personal papers of some people illuminate larger discrepancies. For example, where might we fit the surviving manuscript of Hester Thrale Piozzi's dialogic "Una and Duessa," a work of Spenserian fan fiction that was too overtly political for publication, although Piozzi had to be convinced not to publish it?[23] Does this belong alongside Piozzi's manuscript commonplace books or in some other category?

And as we know, whether an individual's personal papers survive depends on someone either benignly forgetting them in a safe place or actively committing them to some form of familial or institutional preservation. Thus, manuscript fiction is likely to appear in family papers, especially those connected to a great house. The most compelling manuscript novel I have yet read, Lady Charlotte Lindsay's *Mary Dawson*, is bound in one of many volumes of her aristocratic family's papers, between locks of hair and receipts for book purchases.[24] As this example shows, the formats of these pieces of fiction often vary widely. Some resemble print closely, including elaborate title pages, while others are barely decipherable. Some contain chapters and a clear plot, and some ramble in ways worthy of Tobias Smollett or Richardson (or are, indeed, parodies of those famous novelists). Some are found in archives bound and resembling printed books in sizes ranging from heavy tomes to tiny packets, while some survive only in fragments. At least one example, comprising Jessie Rivington's two Gothic novellas, was scribbled in the opposite end of a bookbinder's ledger from the prior year (1836), the ledger being the reason the book was acquired by the American Antiquarian Society in 2011. The volume is catalogued as a "Daybook"; only in the summary portion of the catalogue entry are the two novellas and their author mentioned.[25]

Frederick Harley, the first such manuscript fiction I ever encountered, is an excellent example of both the challenges of discovery and the possibilities of what these different approaches can yield. *Frederick Harley* first and foremost benefits from being housed in a reasonably well known, if small, collection at Chawton House Library, and clearly identified as both a manuscript and a work of fiction. Moreover, the case of *Frederick Har-*

ley's provenance, while challenging, is aided by the presence of multiple full names and bookplates.[26] Unlike most of the material I have collected so far, both the author's name and that of an intended recipient appear on the title page. But even with this information, constructing a complete chain of ownership from Lady Katherine and Mrs. Minchin through to Chawton will take time and may well be impossible. So far I have been able to trace the novel forward from Minchin to the turn of the twentieth century, but no further. There are exceptions to such provenance issues with manuscript fiction, but they are usually for works where the author is not only known but also notable in some way—for example, the lavishly bound presentation copy of Mary Delany's short fable *Mariana* given to Queen Charlotte sometime in the 1780s or '90s, also held at Chawton.

And while neither Lady Katherine Howard nor Maria Frederica Minchin is anywhere near as famous as Delany or Queen Charlotte, enough traces of their lives do remain to begin to tell a story about this novel. Howard appears in every Peerage, although in abbreviated form, given her status outside the line of succession. Both women were wealthy enough to have wills that document their existence in the historical record. When the 1841 census came through Sussex, Howard and Minchin were living together in the seaside resort of Worthing, as they would continue to do until Howard's death the next year. Minchin continued to live in Worthing for a time after Howard's death, long enough at least to write her will.[27] She died almost exactly six years later while living among her nieces and nephews in Reading.[28] The two women would be reunited after death in the graveyard of Trinity Church, Cheltenham, where they were buried side by side.[29] Aside from legal documents, the only thing that survives of their friendship of more than four decades is the novel, written by one for the other, probably when they were both twenty-eight years old.

In addition to the evidence from their wills, I have found their names in the correspondence of the Tighe family held at the National Library of Ireland, potentially connecting them in some way to Mary Tighe and the Ladies of Llangollen, who were also in this particular circle of correspondents.[30] Tighe, as is better known now, was the author of a manuscript novel of her own, *Selena*, which remained unpublished at the time of her death—and indeed, until 2012.[31] With consideration of Mary Tighe's other manuscript books now held at Chawton, there is at least the possibility of connecting the odd work of fiction *Frederick Harley* to a larger, better-known scribal community, including another group that circulated manuscript fiction in much the same format.

That said, there are frustrating gaps in the record, and full understanding of the *Frederick Harley* manuscript is hampered by the absence of the full chain of ownership. While several items in Minchin's will are singled out as having been Howard's, and there is a separate list of named bequests of special books mentioned repeatedly in the will, that list does not include *Frederick Harley*. As Minchin's will bequeaths all unnamed books to her niece Maria, one might assume that custody of the novel passed to her, but the 1848 signature on a flyleaf of the novel is that of Minchin's widowed niece, Harriet Mary Roder. Given that the date of the signature is the same as that of Maria Frederica Minchin's death, we can plausibly assume that Harriet claimed the novel as her own during the division of Minchin's assets that year. Harriet was a widow at the time of Minchin's death, and it is unclear whether she remarried, when she died, and to whom she left her estate.

The final clue to the afterlife of the novel is the elaborate bookplate from the late nineteenth-century from the library of Sir Charles Henry Stuart Rich, Bart. (see fig. 5). This seemed to be an unexpected leap of custody until Rich's name appeared in the same Chancery documents as that of William Henry Hervey Sandby, Minchin's nephew and executor of her will. Sandby served as plaintiff on the part of the seven-year-old Rich in a Chancery suit in 1867, and Rich was admitted as devises (named as a beneficiary) of Sandby's estate, in turn, after Sandby's death in 1885. Thus, it seems reasonable to assume that the novel passed from Harriet Roder to other members of Minchin's family and then into the estate of the Riches of Shirley House of Southampton. This is, frustratingly, where the trail currently runs cold: while the novel is now housed at an archive so close to Southampton that it is associated with the university there, it is unclear at what point the novel appeared on the open market and was purchased and subsequently donated to Chawton House Library.[32] So while the narrative within the pages of *Frederick Harley* is all too complete, the history of the object itself is frustratingly partial, though engagingly suggestive.

This, in short, is the delight and the challenge of this particular frontier of manuscript studies: the thrill of the hunt, the joy of discovery, and the wonder of a whole new set of questions to tackle. The works—the complete, the fragmentary, by authors famous, infamous, obscure,

Figure 5. Sir Charles Henry Stuart Rich's bookplate on marbled pastedown endpaper of Katherine Howard's manuscript novel *The Life of Frederick Harley*. (C3340; Chawton House Library)

or utterly unknown—have the potential to provide new insights into the practices of reading and writing beyond the world of the commercial print market. While I did not anticipate finding a hidden gem of literary brilliance among these works, I have nevertheless been profoundly moved and delighted by many of these texts: a hilarious children's book featuring an anthropomorphic dog, a harrowing fragment of a tale of transportation to New South Wales.

This is a report from early in the process: there is still much labor left to do, not only to find and contextualize these works, but also to learn to see patterns and trends within the new corpus. It is my hope that in bringing together these works that have been obscured for so long by the glare of the print record whose bibliographic details we know how to catalogue and understand, we will find they have a light all their own.

Notes

1. "Will of The Honorable, Lady Katherine Howard commonly called the Right Honorable Lady Katherine Howard, Spinster of Cheltenham, Gloucestershire," April 1, 1842, PROB 11/1961/43, National Archives, Kew, Richmond, U.K.
2. Katherine Howard, *The Life of Frederick Harley, a Novel*, 1799, C3340, Mss. HOW, Chawton House Library, Chawton, Alton, Hampshire, U.K.
3. Charlotte Patte, *The History of Ernestine*, after 1764, C2594, Mss. PAT, Chawton House Library.
4. *Letters Historical and Gallant from Two Ladies of Quality to Each Other*, 1740, Ms. Codex 227, Kislak Center for Special Collections, Rare Books, and Manuscripts, University of Pennsylvania, Philadelphia. Du Noyer's work is distinct from the 1716 English translation published by Mears and Browne: Madame du Noyer, *Letters from a Lady at Paris to a Lady at Avignon*.
5. Very early examples of this exchange are discussed in the Multigraph Collective's chapter on manuscript in *Interacting with Print*, 187–96.
6. None of the peerage accounts or other records I have found records Howard's baptism or even her place in the birth order. She was the third of four daughters out of eleven children total, but Cracroft's and Burke's peerages list male children followed by their sisters. She is listed as being between sixty and sixty-five in the 1841 census, and a Catherine Howard born to Ralph and Alice Howard was christened in Bath Abbey on October 11, 1771 (Howard's mother was Alice Forward Howard, Countess of Wicklow): "Catherine Howard, England Births and Christenings, 1538–1975," FamilySearch, https://familysearch.org/ark:/61903/1:1:JM2J-YSM.
7. Richard Minchins abound, as do Minchins who married women named Mary. However, so far only the marriage of Richard Minchin and Mary Gould in Chipping Campden, Gloucestershire, on December 7, 1791, fits any reasonable chronology or geographic logic: "Mary Gould, England Marriages, 1538–1973," FamilySearch, https://familysearch.org/ark:/61903/1:1:NVPZ-K58. The 1841 census records Minchin residing in Howard's household in Paragon Place, Broadwater, Sussex. Both Minchin and Howard are listed as sixty-five to sixty-nine, which would have made them between twenty-three and twenty-seven when *Frederick Harley* was composed. No firm data exist about Minchin's children, but five children were born in Wyck Rissington, Gloucestershire, to Richard and Mary Minchin in the

right time period: "Joseph Minchin, England Births and Christenings, 1538–1975," FamilySearch, https://familysearch.org/ark:/61903/1:1:NLJ2-NS7. That said, Maria Minchin left her estate to her nieces and nephews, so if she did have children they predeceased her or were profoundly estranged.
8. While manuscript studies in general embraces the study of letters, journals, commonplace books, and so on, of authors of all ages, genders, and walks of life, the existing research on manuscript fiction during the age of print primarily centers on the manuscripts of published authors.
9. *The Navy Officer, or True Blue Will Never Stain*, late eighteenth century, MS. 20446, National Library of Scotland, Edinburgh.
10. See Ezell, "Handwriting and the Book"; Ezell, "The Laughing Tortoise"; Ezell, *Social Authorship and the Advent of Print*; Love, *Scribal Publication in Seventeenth-Century England*.
11. Werner, "Reportless Places," 62.
12. Transcription and metadata entry have been undertaken by Auburn undergraduate students of great energy and talent, including Tristan Brown, Mary Butgereit, Brittany Conner, Savannah Downey, Kelsie Shipley, Hannah Skjellum, and Matthew Stinson.
13. As Melanie Bigold has recently noted, the print revolution of the eighteenth century has obscured how manuscript circulation continued to play a role particularly in the lives of female writers, as she shows through a consideration of correspondence as literary circulation: Bigold, *Women of Letters, Manuscript Circulation, and Print Afterlives in the Eighteenth Century*. I look forward to Michelle Levy's forthcoming book, *Literary Manuscript Culture in Romantic Britain*, which will help further contextualize these materials.
14. Reiman, *The Study of Modern Manuscripts*.
15. The schema's fields are designed to work with the granular MARC-based Early Novels Database data, as well as to distill down to the linked open data that is required of projects included in 18thConnect. These fields have been translated into Dublin Core and RDF thanks to the metadata specialist Dana Caudle of Auburn University Libraries, who has provided substantial assistance on this project with the support of the Digital Projects Department.
16. Reiman, *The Study of Modern Manuscripts*, 65.
17. Led by Rachel Sagner Buurma and Jon Shaw, the Early Novels Database includes records for more than 1,200 novels from collections at the University of Pennsylvania, Bryn Mawr College, the Library Company of Philadelphia, and the Free Library of Philadelphia. Their detailed MARC-based 2016 cataloguing guide, itself based on metadata fields developed by Michael Gamer and Lynne Farrington's Transatlantic Fiction Project, was provided to me during my visit to Penn in the summer of 2016 and formed part of the basis of our schema.

18. Translations and manuscript copies of printed works are included in the larger database for the ease of future research and to provide further context, but they currently are not a high priority for transcription compared with original fiction. According to my calculations based on timing student transcriptionists, we currently have 1,825 hours of work left on just the currently collected manuscripts. To put this in perspective, undergraduate research fellows at Auburn commit to seven hundred hours on such a project across their year of work, and my students who currently receive course credit for their contributions are required to commit to about ninety hours across the year, in addition to the hours they will spend learning about the project, the period, and the current debates in digital research and textual editing. The longer students work on the project, the more efficient they become, so this estimate of time is variable. It is worth noting that new items are also continually being added.
19. *Location Register of English Literary Manuscripts and Letters*, http://www.reading.ac.uk/library/about-us/projects/lib-location-register.aspx. See Batchelor, "Anon, Pseud, and 'By a Lady.'"
20. *British Literary Manuscripts Online, c. 1660–1900*, http://gdc.gale.com/products/british-literary-manuscripts-online-c.-1660–1900/discover/title-list.
21. Burke, *Research and the Manuscript Tradition*, 11.
22. Ibid., 13.
23. Hester Thrale Piozzi, "Una and Duessa; or, A Set of Dialogues upon the Most Popular Subjects," 1791, English MS 635, Thrale-Piozzi Manuscripts, John Rylands Library, University of Manchester, Manchester, U.K.
24. Charlotte Lindsay, "Mary Dawson: A Tale of the 18th Century," ca. 1836[?], Add MS 61985, Sheffield Park Papers, vol. 7, British Library, London, ff. 147–59ᵛ.
25. "Hoffman & White Daybook," 1836, Mss. Octavo Vols. H, American Antiquarian Society, Worcester, MA.
26. Chawton House Library has no provenance information for the novel, so all of the information that follows has been gleaned from physical elements of the book itself.
27. "Will of Maria Frederica Minchin, Widow of Worthing, Sussex," April 29, 1848, PROB 11/2073/281, National Archives.
28. In the probate records of her will, Minchin's nephew, William Henry Hervey Sandby, describes his aunt as formerly of "the county of Devon, afterwards of Worthing in the County of Sussex but late of Portland Place Reading." As Sandby is also listed as from Portland Place, Reading, Berkshire, it would seem that sometime between Howard's death in 1842 and drafting her own will in that same year, Minchin moved to be with her nieces and nephew.
29. "Will of Maria Frederica Minchin."

30. According to a collection of correspondence in the National Library of Ireland, "K. Howard of Cheltenham" was a correspondent of Sarah Howard (née Hamilton), Howard's niece by marriage and the mother of the fifth and sixth Earls of Wicklow. Sarah Howard was the daughter of Caroline Tighe Hamilton, who was a cousin of the poet Mary Tighe. Caroline's mother was Sarah Tighe, cousin of Sarah Ponsonby, one of the famous Ladies of Llangollen: "Tighe, Hamilton and Howard Papers, 1737–1919," *National Library of Ireland Catalogue*, http://catalogue.nli.ie/Collection/vtls000572704/HierarchyTree?recordID=vtls000573276.
31. Tighe, *Selena*.
32. Chawton House Library opened in 2003 thanks to Sandy Lerner, OBE, whose personal collection was a significant starting point for the holdings. *Frederick Harley* was in the collection as of early 2009.

Works Cited

Batchelor, Jennie. "Anon, Pseud, and 'By a Lady': The Spectre of Anonymity and the Future of Women's Literary History." In *Women's Writing, 1660–1830: Feminisms and Futures*, edited by Jennie Batchelor and Gillian Dow, 79–96. Basingstoke, U.K.: Palgrave Macmillan, 2016.

Bigold, Melanie. *Women of Letters, Manuscript Circulation and Print Afterlives in the Eighteenth Century: Elizabeth Rowe, Catharine Cockburn, and Elizabeth Carter*. Basingstoke, U.K.: Palgrave Macmillan, 2013.

Burke, Frank. *Research and the Manuscript Tradition*. Lanham, MD: Scarecrow, 1997.

Ezell, Margaret J. M. "Handwriting and the Book." In *The Cambridge Companion to the History of the Book*, edited by Leslie Howsam, 92–106. Cambridge: Cambridge University Press, 2015.

———. "The Laughing Tortoise: Speculations on Manuscript Sources and Women's Book History." *English Literary Renaissance* 38, no. 2 (May 2008): 331–55.

———. *Social Authorship and the Advent of Print*. Baltimore: Johns Hopkins University Press, 1999.

Love, Harold. *Scribal Publication in Seventeenth-Century England*. Oxford: Clarendon, 1993.

Madame du Noyer (Anne Marguerite Petit). *Letters from a Lady at Paris to a Lady at Avignon Containing a Particular Account of the City, the Politicks, Intrigues, Gallantry, and Secret History of Persons of the First Quality in France*, 2d ed., vol. 1. London, 1716.

Multigraph Collective. *Interacting with Print: Elements of Reading in the Era of Print Saturation*. Chicago: University of Chicago Press, 2018.

Reiman, Donald H. *The Study of Modern Manuscripts: Public, Confidential, and Private*. Baltimore, MD: Johns Hopkins University Press, 1993.

Tighe, Mary. *Selena*, edited by Harriet Kramer Linkin. Burlington, VT: Ashgate, 2012.

Werner, Marta L. "'Reportless Places': Facing the Modern Manuscript." *Textual Cultures* 6, no. 2 (2011): 60–83.

The Language of Notation and the Space of Manuscript Notebooks

COLLIN JENNINGS

Early modern notebooks often reveal the ingredients of their own composition. This is not meant figuratively. A receipt book from the 1680s includes recipes for blue and red ink as well as for coloring paper.¹ Likewise, a notebook of the natural philosopher Robert Hooke provides instructions for preparing erasable leaves for short "table books."² Notebooks were places for imagining how objects, ideas, and arguments could be combined, as well as how materials from different places could be reconfigured, rearranged, and remade. In John Dunton's idiosyncratic combination of digressive anecdotes and allegorical autobiography, *A Voyage round the World* (1691), the narrator, Evander, takes this idea to its logical extreme by suggesting that he has documented his own conception in a notebook. Evander inquires of the potentially skeptical reader: "Should I tell you, as the *virtuosi* do, that I was shaped at first like a Todpole, and that I remember very well, when my Tail *Rambled off*, and a pair of little Legs sprung out in the room on't: Nay, shou'd I protest I pulled out my *Note-book*, and slap-dash'd it down the very minute after it happen'd[?]"³ He speculates on the sources of his bodily material, writing, "There may have gone I know n't how many *perticles of a Lyon* into my Composition" and "my *great* Grandfather might be made out of a Whale or an Elephant."⁴ Dunton's narrator signals the almost farcical degree to which, in the late seventeenth century, notebooks served as sites for recording how things come together. Indeed, he similarly describes how a person gives life to his ideas: "Once *begot*, they must be *bred*—so out he turns 'em into the wide World to shift for themselves, after he has put a few *black and white Raggs"*—that is, ink and paper—"about 'em to cover their *Nakedness."*[5] Things, people, and ideas are born, "bred," and reborn in writing.

In this essay I explore the distinctive linguistic and spatial techniques by which early modern writers used manuscript notebooks to conceive of new combinations of things, most prominently in recipes that brought together substances found across an emergent system of global trade. However, I did not begin with this focus; rather, my interest in this topic originated with a question made possible by new methods in computational linguistics. I first asked: what kinds of passages—in terms of genres, topics, or media—feature the most unlikely combinations of words? To find such passages, I developed a new method of measuring what I call *lexical variation* to identify the words in a given set of texts that appear surrounded by the most unexpected sequences of other words. This is different from finding words that move across the widest range of contexts—such as the general verbs "take" or "have," which work in any number of semantic situations. The measure of lexical variation instead finds words that could be said to constitute arrangements of language that otherwise do not occur. When I refer to lexical variation, I mean the extent to which particular word combinations are likely (or not) to appear together according to the broader linguistic patterns found in a collection of texts.[6]

My computational method of observing lexical variation works by modeling in a word vector space all of the words that appear in the texts of the Early English Books Online Text-Creation Partnership (EEBO-TCP) corpus between 1640 and 1700.[7] Each word is represented as a three hundred-dimensional vector positioned in relation to the rest of the words according to how they co-occur in the corpus. In the word vector space, mathematical proximity corresponds to semantic similarity. One might imagine a lexical topography in which words occupy regions near frequently co-occurring words and far from rarely co-occurring words. In this way, the vector space is reminiscent of the memory palaces of classical rhetoric in which *topoi* are positioned in different areas of an architectural space envisioned in the mind. I measure the lexical variation of a given word by finding the average mathematical distance between the vectors of the ten words to the left and right of the word, respectively, across all of the appearances of that word. Words with high lexical variation scores are frequently surrounded by words that are positioned far from one another in the word vector space—that is, they appear alongside words that are otherwise unlikely to be near one another. This method allows me to further consider how subsets of the total corpus conform to or differ from the larger model. The subset could be delimited by any number of criteria, such as author, genre, format, or date. This comparative approach demonstrates a new way of reading relationally between particular texts and a model expressing how language tends to work.

This method, while trained on a corpus of printed texts, informs how I approach manuscript culture within the media ecology of seventeenth- and eighteenth-century Britain. Just as examining the linguistic features of particular texts or subsets relative to a broader model reveals patterns of diverse word combinations, reading manuscripts in relation to other contemporary media makes the distinctive linguistic and spatial flexibility of the medium observable. For this experiment, I isolated a five-year period from 1678 to 1682 in order to reduce the noise of diachronic language change. I chose this period because I initially thought the experiment might indicate that the disorder of the Exclusion Crisis and Popish Plot correlated with semantic variation in political poetry, but the results revealed something completely different. I examine them in detail later, but for now I note that the top words in terms of the lexical variation score include units of measure (*ounce, dram, bushel*), apothecary symbols (*ij* and *iij*), taxonomic terms (*major, minor*), and heraldry jargon (*arg., passant*), among others. By finding the passages in which these terms are most frequent, I discovered that they tend to function as structuring devices for bringing together physically and semantically diverse objects in a manner that corresponds to the genre of the notebook. Units of measure in particular make all objects and substances commensurate, drawing together otherwise unlike things. When I searched for the top lexical variation passages in databases of digitized and annotated manuscripts (including those of the Folger Shakespeare Library, Wellcome Library, and Cambridge University Library), I found that many of them appeared in multiple manuscript notebooks with various revisions. In addition to identifying the manuscript circulation of these passages, I observed that even in print they were often set apart in lists or tabular formats separate from the linear prose. Instead of typical grammatical connections between words, such passages feature symbolic units, technical jargon, and spatial arrangements that indicate how words are associated. These distinctive structures make possible a kind of semantic condensation in which dissimilar terms are brought into close contact.

Such structures produce the lexical variation I have described, but more specifically, they support the practices of "storing, sorting, summarizing, and selecting" that Ann Blair has called the "basic maneuvers" of note taking. I refer to the top lexical variation terms and other features of the passages I examine as constituting *notational form* for the way they use language and space to exhibit contrasting traits. Although first identified in print, these passages represent residual traces of distinctively manuscript practices. Note taking occurs in the moment—between language and experience, the public and the private—and the notational form I examine here stands out from its larger print context because in a sense it does not belong there. In the context of seventeenth- and eighteenth-century notebooks, the notational language and formats that are statistically aberrant in print make abstraction, collection, and combination easier to convey, suggesting an important yet underdiscussed affordance of manuscript. Early modern note takers used manuscript composition to collect and combine disparate terms that indexed emerging access to far-flung objects and substances. Roland Barthes theorized note-taking practices under the term *notatio,* claiming that such practices operate at the "problematic intersection between a river of language, of uninterrupted language . . . and a sacred gesture: to mark life (to isolate: sacrifice, scapegoat, etc.)."[8] What Dunton called note taking's "slap-dash" capacity creates a fundamental tension between recording ideas or events as they occur according to one's own idiosyncratic habits and contextualizing those occurrences within linguistic structures that make notes intelligible after the fact. Like Evander's speculative catalogue of the varied creatures that constitute his body's matter, the terms that organize recipes, taxonomies, and blazons reveal how early modern writers assembled the materials of an expanding world.

Of course, all print from this period began in manuscript, but part of what is distinctive about the passages I examine here is that they transferred manuscript forms and structures (various kinds of shorthand, notation, and nonlinear formats) to print.[9] Figure 1 shows a print version of a famous recipe, one for "The Countess of Kent's Powder," which was identified by the lexical variation measure as containing a high frequency of the top terms, while figure 2 is one of the numerous manuscripts in which the recipe appears. I return to this recipe at the end of the essay, but it is worth noting that printed versions of the countess's recipes explicitly make claims about their manuscript history—namely, that the recipes included were from the countess's own receipt book and thus that they gave the reader access to what had been previously limited to the

Pulvis Comitissæ Cantii, seu de Chelis Cancrorum.	The Countess of Kent's Powder: or, The Powder of Crabs-Claws.
℞. *Extremitatum nigrorum pedum majorum Cancrorum marinorum,* ʒiiij. *Oculorum Cancrorum fluviatilium, Margaritarum Orientalium, & Coralli Rubri præparatorum, an.* ʒj. *Succini Albi, Radicis Contrayervæ, Viperinæ, seu Contrayervæ Virginianæ, an.* ʒvj. *Lapidis Bezoar',* ʒiij. *Ossis è Corde Cervi,* ∂iiij. *Croci,* ∂ij.	℞. The black extremities of the feet of large Sea-Crabs, ʒiiij. River-Crabs-Eyes, Eastern-Pearls, and Red-Coral prepar'd, *an.* ʒj. White Amber, Root of Contrayerva, *Spanish*-Counterpoyson, *an.* ʒvj. Bezoar-Stone, ʒiij. Deer's Heart-bone, ∂iiij. Saffron, ∂ij.

All these being finely powder'd, let them be sprinkl'd with an ounce and a half of Spirit of Honey, and mix'd with Gelly of Vipers. Make up your Trochishes, dry them in the shade to be powder'd when use requires.

Take the Sea and the River-Crabs in the Month of *June*, while the Sun is in *Cancer*. Take and cut the Flesh from the extremities of the Claws, bruise the Claws and Crabs-Eyes in a Brass-mortar first, then grind them upon a Porphyrie, moist'ning them with some Cordial-water; and spread the Powder upon clean Paper, to be dry'd in the shade. Prepare the Pearl, Coral, and Amber-grise in like manner. Beat the Bezoar in a Brass-Mortar, and mix all the Powders. Then in a glaz'd-Earth'n-pot over a very gentle fire, boyl four large Vipers, well prepar'd, in a pint of Balm-water, till the Broth be reduc'd to the consistency of a Gelly. Strain it and press out the Vipers. Then put the Powders into a great Marble-Mortar; and when they have suckt up the Honey prescrib'd, add at several times the Gelly of Vipers, till the whole Mass be become thick and solid enough to make Trochishes, to be dry'd and us'd as before.

The Gelly of Vipers, is not only to unite and bind the Powders together, and reduce them to a proper Paste and fit solidity, but to impart to the Composition, the Cordial, and Poyson-resisting vertue of the Vipers, though the Ancients neglected the Gelly of Vipers, and refus'd it as Impertinent.

I might have plac'd this Composition in the Chapter of Trochishes, but I thought fit to imitate the English, from whence first it came, and who gave it the name of Powder.

This Powder is very famous, and in high request in *England*, against Epidemic Distempers, particularly against the Small-pox, and Measles. It is also highly commended for the Plague, as well to preserve, as cure. For it strength'ns the Heart, and all the Noble-parts, against the malignity of these Diseases, against Pestilential-Air, and preserves them from all sorts of Infection. Nor is it less esteem'd in *France*, by Persons that know the vertue of it, and who have often try'd it with good success. The Dose and manner of using it, is the same with that of the Spirit of Vipers.

FIGURE 1. Recipe for "The Countess of Kent's Powder" in Latin and English, in Moyse Charas, *The Royal Pharmacopœa* (London, 1678). (f RS79 .C46E*, 117; Williams Andrew Clark Memorial Library, University of California, Los Angeles)

countess's social circle. The recipe's recurrence in numerous subsequent notebooks also points to an often-overlooked fact of manuscript circulation, which is that it followed print publication as well as preceded it. Computational approaches to manuscript materials are limited and difficult. Aside from specific transcription projects, so far, manuscript archives are invisible to revolutionary new ways of programmatically studying histories of language and literature. But here I present a new way of bringing computational approaches to bear on historical manuscript practices by foregrounding their inextricable relation to print in the period.

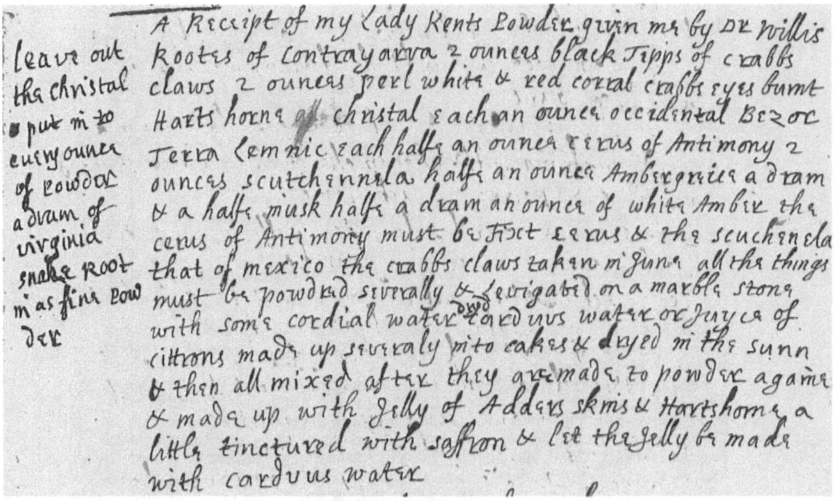
A Receipt of my Lady Kents Powder given me by Dr Willis
Rootes of Contrayarva 2 ounces black Tipps of crabbs
claws 2 ounces perl white & red corral crabbs eyes burnt
Harts horne christal each an ounce occidental Bezor
Terra Lemnic each halfe an ounce cerus of Antimony 2
ounces scutchinnela halfe an ounce Ambergriece a dram
& a halfe musk halfe a dram an ounce of white Amber the
cerus of Antimony must be first cerus & the scuchenela
that of mexico the crabbs claws taken in June all the things
must be powdred severally & levigated on a marble stone
with some cordial water Carduus water or Juyce of
cittrons made up severaly into cakes & dryed in the sunn
& then all mixed after they are made to powder againe
& made up with Jelly of Adders skins & Hartshorne a
little tinctured with saffron & let the Jelly be made
with carduus water

leave out the christal put in to every ounce of powder a dram of virginia snake Root in as fine pow der

FIGURE 2. The Countess of Kent's Powder recipe, in Johanna St. John's late seventeenth-century receipt book, with a marginal revision. (MS 4338, f. 138r; Wellcome Library)

Reading between print and manuscript media connects my method to recent scholarship by historians of note taking, including that of Blair and Richard Yeo. Their work has demonstrated how seventeenth- and eighteenth-century note-taking practices evolved in relation to the proliferation of print.[10] In his recent study *Notebooks, English Virtuosi, and Early Modern Science*, Yeo observes that the term "notebook" was not even coined until a hundred years after Johannes Gutenberg invented movable type.[11] Of course, the activity of note taking precedes the introduction of printing, but Yeo's contention is that many functions solidified as cultural practices well after print had spread across Europe in the sixteenth century. Yeo and Blair, among others, have explored early modern note taking as a tool for producing scientific knowledge, aiding memory, tracking economic transactions, and monitoring spiritual discipline. Moreover, scholars of early modern housewifery and recipe books have examined the formation of women's authority and subjectivity in personal notebooks in contrast to a print market dominated by men's voices.[12] This recent work has revealed how one technology developed and advanced in relation to a broader media environment instead of simply being surpassed by subsequent technologies. My computational method provides a new way into manuscripts through a profile of linguistic and graphical features that can be tracked across different media.

Measuring Lexical Variation

Before examining characteristics of notational form and then locating them in seventeenth- and eighteenth-century manuscripts, I will explain in greater detail how I have observed lexical variation in the context of early modern notebooks. Many studies of note taking have focused on how authors used their notebooks for recollection, whether of personal experiences or remarkable passages from other writers. Blair has posited that note taking served as an "art of transmission," a technology for communicating knowledge across generations.[13] Scholars of receipt books have argued that these collections functioned as repositories of familial and communal practices.[14] Given these observations, it might seem strange to examine this broad category of manuscripts as a source of variation and rarity. How does variation manifest in a format used to store "commonplaces"? The answer has to do with practices of producing knowledge that dealt with gathering, reducing, and arranging information. The Renaissance commonplace tradition is largely thought to have declined in popularity by the mid-seventeenth century, but during this period writers continued to develop new uses for and systems of note taking.[15] In academic contexts, the language theorist John Wilkins and the philosopher John Locke, for instance, proposed new methods of topical arrangement. Similarly, receipt books' authors and compilers explored different techniques of indexing and ordering. Indeed, in some notebooks both kinds of approaches can be observed in the same place, as in the case of the Masham family manuscript that began as a commonplace book of Latin passages (possibly collected by Locke while he lodged with the family) but was later converted into a collection of family recipes.[16] Early modern note takers recognized that new things and ideas required flexible systems into which to deposit them. To pose a question about lexical variation to manuscript culture, then, is to consider which linguistic and nonlinguistic features brought together new and disparate things in practices of composition.

Earlier I briefly described how I have measured lexical variation using new methods of semantic modeling. My specific form of modeling uses vector semantics—which entails embedding words in a multidimensional vector space—to represent the statistical likelihood that a given set of words will co-occur. Vector semantics starts from two premises: first, that words tend to occur in particular linguistic contexts; and second, that we can decipher the meaning of an unknown word based on the words that appear near it.[17] While many humanists interested in text analysis have just begun to consider the implications of these claims, computational linguists have been thinking about modeling language in this way since the 1940s and '50s. Zellig Harris, an early theorist of the "distributional structure" of language, explains, "The perennial man in the street believes that when he speaks he freely puts together whatever elements have the meanings he intends; but he does so only by choosing members of those classes that regularly occur together and in the order in which these classes occur."[18] His contemporary J. R. Firth put the idea even more plainly in his now-famous formulation, "You shall know a word by the company it keeps."[19] Since these foundational theories, linguists have produced methods for mathematically representing the tendencies of language. This computational framework makes it possible to ask: What are the conditions under which very different words are brought together in writing? And when words that are not typically used in the same context co-occur, what are they doing?

Word vector models provide mathematical representations of the distributional structure of language, which means that word vectors can be added and subtracted to find the words most similar in the model to the resulting composite vector. For instance, when the word vectors for *bounds* and *leaps* are combined using vector addition, and the vector for *limits* is subtracted, the most similar words to the resulting composite vector are *skips*, *leap*, and *fling*. But if *bounds* and *limits* are added, and *leaps* is subtracted, then the most similar words are *boundaries*, *confined*, and *precincts*. Any particular phrase or sentence will feature word combinations that to a greater or lesser degree correspond to linguistic patterns represented in the word vector model.[20] The lexical variation measure then is useful because it identifies pieces of text in which language is not being used as one would expect it to be in terms of the broader word vector model. If, as Harris claims, language operates according to classes and structures that writers are only partly aware of, the words found by the lexical variation measure defy the patterns that these structures anticipate.

To show what this looks like, table 1 presents a list of the top twenty words returned for the lexical variation measure for the 1678–82 subset of the EEBO-TCP corpus. The top fifty words can be broken down into the following categories: 35 percent Latin terms, 30 percent chemistry/natural philosophy, 17 percent apothecary symbols, 11 percent food/agriculture, and 7 percent other. As indicated earlier, the words that occur in

TABLE 1. Top twenty terms by lexical variation in EEBO-TCP corpus

Term	Score
strata	0.159
aq	0.158
basin	0.157
liquoris	0.157
deliquium	0.156
vena	0.156
curtis	0.155
sal	0.155
classis	0.155
sulphur	0.154
iij	0.154
cortex	0.153
latex	0.153
lignea	0.152
syrup	0.151
canon	0.150
acres	0.150
sem	0.150
specimen	0.148
lb	0.148

Note: Score refers to the average standard deviation of the vector positions of the words in the context windows (ten words to the right and left) surrounding each occurrence of a given term.

the most highly varied contexts tend to be notational terms operating in a range of technical and domestic discourses, including heraldry, medicine, agriculture, and natural history. On the one hand, the discourses come from learned contexts featuring a high prevalence of abstruse language; on the other, there are also terms (*acres* and *lb*, for instance) that are prevalent in household management and that connect the work of receipt books to that of chemistry and natural history books. This point of contact between public and private writing contexts is even more observable in the larger results.

In part because of the association with expert communities, the terms appear in genres that often combine English and Latin. I was initially tempted to remove Latin terms because they might appear more varied relative to a primarily English corpus, but the Latin words are often performing semantic functions similar to those of the English terms on the list. In addition, most of the Latin terms are coming from genres that contain Latin and English in the same context, such as botany and natural history. An unavoidable feature of late seventeenth-century English writing is that it creates a multilingual environment that operates across print and manuscript media.

To gain a better understanding of the sources of these terms, I visualized a sample of the vectors of the top 150 lexical variation words by reducing them from three hundred dimensions to two using a t-distributed stochastic neighbor embedding (t-SNE) visualization.[21] As in the larger three hundred-dimension model, the words are positioned near other words with which they tend to appear. This visualization functions as a map of the top words in terms of their semantic proximity to one another. The groupings of the words make it possible to observe the discursive coherence among the top terms. For instance, *bushel*, *bushels*, *wheat*, and *barly* are close to one another in the bottom left quadrant, while *fraction*, *numerator*, and *denominator* are clustered farther below them (see fig. 3). In the word vector model, *fraction* returns a similarity score of 0.81 with *numerator* and 0.82 with *denominator*, and *numerator* and *denominator* return a score of 0.94. The similarity score refers to the cosine distance between the angles of two vectors, with 1.00 being the maximum score. These scores denote a very high semantic similarity between the terms and thus indicate that the visualization accurately reflects the proximity between terms in the larger model. More generally, most of the words in the top half of the visualization are Latin or belong to natural-history texts in which Latin words are prevalent, and most of the English terms appear in the bottom half. Terms that belong to specialized discourses are similarly clustered, including heraldry (in the bottom center area) and ornithology (in the center right area).

The visualization makes it easier to observe the similarities among these words relative to their semantic functions and the different discourses in which they are likely to appear. That is to say, it demonstrates that the lexical variation measure has found not arbitrary terms but, rather, terms related to one another that perform comparable functions in specific discourses. I refer to these terms as *notational* because most of them operate within some type of technical sign system or more generally belong to annotating practices. The different systems indexed by these terms support processes of collecting unlike things—quantities, ideas, or observations—producing what Barthes, in his definition of *notatio*,

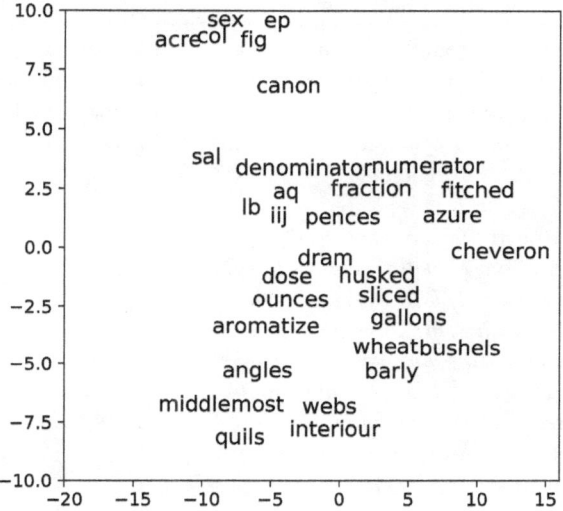

Figure 3. T-SNE visualization of a sampling from the top 150 terms in the 1678–82 subset of the EEBO-TCP corpus, according to the lexical variation measure.

calls "a layered text, a histology of cutups, a palimpsest."[22] The language of notation provides a linguistic framework of arrangement and combination (as in a list of ingredients for a medical recipe) without requiring the grammatical entailments of linear prose. The visualization helps to convey how notational language supports private and public dimensions of writing in terms of bringing together personal practices of observing, recording, and collecting in structures that would still be legible to outside readers. This is because the terms cluster closely in relation to their discursive affiliations, but they are also related by the fact that they support listing and cataloguing forms. They belong to knowledge-producing communities with specific practices of note taking, and it is these features that first indicate how manuscript-writing practices exerted pressure on print, an idea that I consider in detail in the next section.

I then took the different word clusters from the visualization and identified the texts in which they had the highest cumulative frequency. There appear to be four loose discourses in which these terms primarily occur. Table 2 breaks down the content of these discourses—Latin texts,

TABLE 2. Titles in the EEBO-TCP corpus featuring top lexical variation terms

Discourse	Exemplary titles	Top terms
Latin, botany, and natural history texts	Robert Morison, *Plantarum historiæ universalis Oxoniensis. Pars secunda seu herbarum distribution nova, per tabulas congnationis & affinitatis ex libro naturæ observata & detecta* (1680)	folio, sine, sit, major, minor, species, anno, sex, alias, classis, canon, plane, specimen, acre, lignea, strata
	Sir Robert Sibbald, *Scotland Illustrated, or, An Essay of Natural History in Which Are Exquisitely Displayed the Nature of the Country, the Dispositions and Manners of the Inhabitants . . . and the Manifold Productions of Nature in Its Three-fold Kingdom, (viz.) Vegetable, Animal and Mineral, Dispersed throughout the Northern Part of Great Britain* (1684)	
Ornithology	John Ray, *The Ornithology of Francis Willughby of Middleton in the County of Warwick Esq. Fellow of the Royal Society in Three Books: Wherein All the Birds Hitherto Known, Being Reduced into a Method Suitable to Their Natures, Are Accurately Described* (1678)	feathers, white, black, colour, middle, tips, dusky, exteriour, interiour, outmost
	John Josselyn, *New Englands Rarities Discovered in Birds, Beasts, Fishes, Serpents, and Plants of the Country* (1672)	
Heraldry	Sir George Mackenzie, *The Science of Herauldry, Treated as a Part of the Civil Law, and Law of Nations wherein Reasons Are Given for Its Principles, and Etymologies for Its Harder Terms* (1680)	argent, betwixt, azur, sable, bend, within, beareth, exeunt
	Robert Thoroton, *The Antiquities of Nottinghamshire Extracted out of Records, Original Evidences, Leiger Books, Other Manuscripts, and Authentick Authorities: Beautified with Maps, Prospects, and Portraictures* (1677)	

TABLE 2 (*continued*)

Discourse	Exemplary titles	Top terms
Chemistry and medical recipe books	Moyes Charras, *The Royal Pharmacopœa: Galenical and Chemical, according to the Practice of the Most Eminent and Learned Physicians of France* (1678)	half, ounce, two, drams, three, iij, bushels, ounces, fraction, denominator, gallons, aq, vitriolized, pulverized, lb, basin
	George Hartman, *The True Preserver and Restorer of Health Being a Choice Collection of Select and Experienced Remedies for All Distempers Incident to Men, Women, and Children: Selected from and Experienced by the Most Famous Physicians and Chyurgeons in Europe: Together with Excellent Directions for Cookery* (1682)	

ornithology, heraldry, and chemistry/medical recipes—in terms of the titles that contain numerous passages with high lexical variation.

The titles indicate writers attempting to share different bodies of knowledge using specific taxonomies and systems of notation, as illustrated in phrases such as the "science of herauldry" and an "essay of natural history." The taxonomies are often attributed to a particular person or group, which creates the need to reconcile an individual theory with the larger domain of shared knowledge. The top terms indexing the most varied contexts for each discourse include adjectives and numbers, but the most common types of terms, appearing across the clusters, are ones that seem to function as formal ligatures used in descriptions of different cases and examples positioned within the respective taxonomies and systems. In ornithology, all species of birds have an *exterior, feathers,* and *tips* with features that are *outmost* or in the *middle*. Likewise, in Latin natural histories, different species are arranged in hierarchical structures with *major* and *minor* divisions. Such structures are often presented in lists with branching diagrams. The chemistry and medical cluster features not only a large number of mathematical (*fraction, denominator*) and natural-philosophy terms (*vitriolated, pulverized*) but also a significant number of units of measure and symbols (*ounces, drams, gallons, iij, aq*). These terms provide the linguistic mortar for producing technical conventions—the descriptors, transitions, and abstract units that recur in lists and tables of various early modern knowledge domains. Set apart from the rest of the text, the contexts featuring high concentrations of these terms index, and rhetorically evoke, the note-taking practices that I examine in the next section.

Notation and Note Taking in Print and Manuscript Pages

The interaction between notational language and arrangement first identified in print indicates features to look for in manuscript works, which afforded even greater flexibility for writers to organize their materials. Working with the profile that I have described entails moving back and forth between manuscript and print sources that share lexical patterns, graphic formats, and even specific passages or recipes. Databases of digitized manuscripts featuring high-quality images and robust, searchable metadata produced by institutions including the Folger Shakespeare Library, the Wellcome Library, and Cambridge University Libraries have facilitated this approach. Using these databases, it is possible to observe how the statistically anomalous print passages found with the lexical variation measure depend on the semantic condensation afforded by notational structures and shorthand practices that are common in manuscript notebooks. In sampling the Folger's digitized manuscript collections of receipt and heraldry notebooks, I found that roughly 84 percent (or sixteen out of nineteen) of those from the 1670s through the 1700s contain features of notational form, ranging from lists and diagrams to loose paragraphs consisting of sets of steps. Of course, my analysis of notebooks addresses only a particular aspect of manuscript culture in seventeenth- and eighteenth-century Britain. Yet this focus demonstrates the unique semantic properties of manuscript composition. The discourses identified by the lexical variation measure concern the configuration of medicines, heraldic images, and even different plant and animal species in the case of natural history. In manuscript, the medium for composing language in writing, early modern authors also explored the composition of any number of substances and objects. It represented a distinctive space for considering how things were brought together.

Figure 4 presents English noblemen and their coats of arms in a tabular arrangement, a graphic format that tends to recur in passages featuring words with high lexical variation scores. The divisions between

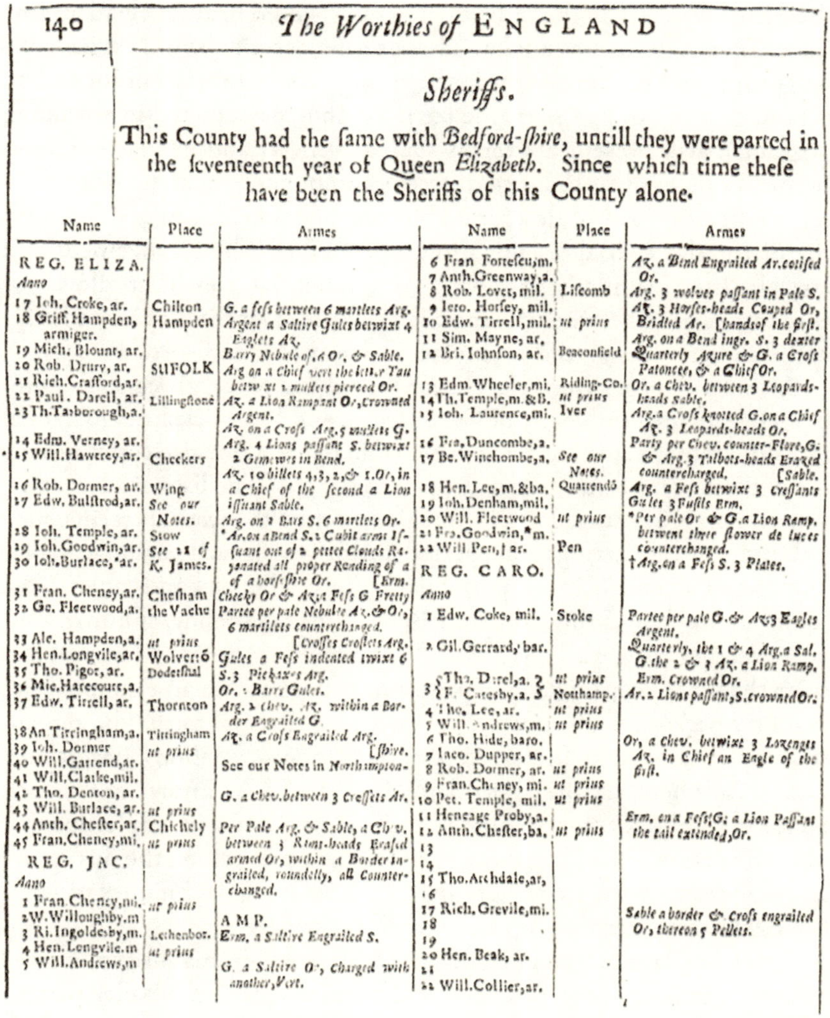

140 *The Worthies of* ENGLAND

Sheriffs.

This County had the ſame with *Bedford-ſhire*, untill they were parted in the ſeventeenth year of Queen *Elizabeth*. Since which time theſe have been the Sheriffs of this County alone.

Name	Place	Armes
REG. ELIZA. *Anno*		
17 Ioh. Croke, ar.	Chilton	*G. a feſs between 6 martlets Arg.*
18 Griff. Hampden, armiger.	Hampden	*Argent a Saltire Gules betwixt 4 Eaglets Az.*
19 Mich. Blount, ar.		*Barry Nebule of.6 Or, & Sable.*
20 Rob. Drury, ar.	SUFOLK	*Arg on a Chief vert the letter Tau betw xt 2 mullets pierced Or.*
21 Rich. Crafford, ar.		
22 Paul. Darell, ar.	Lillingſtone	*Az. a Lion Rampant Or, Crowned Argent.*
23 Th. Tasborough, a.		*Az. on a Croſs Arg. 5 mullets G.*
24 Edm. Verney, ar.		*Arg. 4 Lions paſſant S. betwixt 2 Gemewes in Bend.*
25 Will. Hawtrey, ar.	Checkers	
26 Rob. Dormer, ar.	Wing	*Az. 10 billets 4,3,2,& 1. Or, in a Chief of the ſecond a Lion iſſuant Sable.*
27 Edw. Bulſtrod, ar.	*See our Notes.*	*Arg. on 2 Bars S. 6 martlets Or.*
28 Ioh. Temple, ar.	Stow	**Ar. on a Bend S. 2 Cubit arms Iſſuant out of 2 pettet Clouds Rayonated all proper Rending of a of a horſ-ſhoe Or.*
29 Ioh. Goodwin, ar.	*See 22 of*	
30 Ioh. Burlace, *ar.	K. James.	*[Erm.*
31 Fran. Cheney, ar.	Cheſham	*Checky Or & Azure Feſs G Fretty*
32 Ge. Fleetwood, a.	the Vache	*Partee per pale Nebulee Az. & Or, 6 martilets counterchanged.*
33 Alc. Hampden, a.	*ut prius*	*[Croſſes Croſlets Arg.*
34 Hen. Longvile, ar.	Wolverton	*Gules a Feſs indented twixt 6*
35 Tho. Pigot, ar.	Dodeſhal	*S. 3 Pickaxes Arg.*
36 Mic. Harecourt, a.		*Or, 2 Barrs Gules.*
37 Edw. Tirrell, ar.	Thornton	*Arg. 2 chev. Az. within a Border Engrailed G.*
38 An Tittingham, a.	Tittingham	*Az. a Croſs Engrailed Arg.*
39 Ioh. Dormer	*ut prius*	*[ſhire.*
40 Will. Garrend, ar.		See our Notes in *Northampton-*
41 Will. Clarke, mil.		
42 Tho. Denton, ar.		*G. a Chev. between 3 Creſſets Ar.*
43 Will. Burlace, ar.	*ut prius*	
44 Anth. Cheſter, ar.	Chichely	*Per Pale Arg. & Sable, a Chev. between 3 Rams-heads Erazed armed Or, within a Border ingrailed, roundelly, all Counterchanged.*
45 Fran. Cheney, mi.	*ut prius*	
REG. JAC. *Anno*		
1 Fran. Cheney, mi.	*ut prius*	
2 W. Willoughby, m		A M P.
3 Ri. Ingoldesby, m.	Lethenbor.	*Erm. a Saltire Engrailed S.*
4 Hen. Longvile, m	*ut prius*	
5 Will. Andrews, m		*G. a Saltire Or, Charged with another, Vert.*

Name	Place	Armes
6 Fran Forteſcu, m.		*Az. a Bend Engrailed Ar. cotiſed Or.*
7 Anth. Greenway, a.		
8 Rob. Lovet, mil.	Liſcomb	*Arg. 3 wolves paſſant in Pale S.*
9 Iero. Horſey, mil.		*Az. 3 Horſes-heads Couped Or, Bridled Ar. [hands of the firſt.*
10 Edw. Tirrell, mil.	*ut prius*	
11 Sim. Mayne, ar.		*Arg. on a Bend ingr. S. 3 dexter*
12 Bri. Iohnſon, ar.	Beaconfield	*Quarterly Azure & G. a Croſs Patoncee, & a Chief Or.*
13 Edm. Wheeler, mi.	Riding-Co.	*Or. a Chev. between 3 Leopards-heads Sable.*
14 Th. Temple, m. & B.	*ut prius*	
15 Ioh. Laurence, mi.	Iver	*Arg. a Croſs knotted G. on a Chief Az. 3 Leopards-heads Or.*
16 Fra. Duncombe, a.		*Party per Chev. counter-Flore, G. & Arg. 3 Talbots-heads Erazed counterchanged. [Sable.*
17 Be. Winchombe, a.	*See our Notes.*	
18 Hen. Lee, m. & ba.	Quattendō	*Arg. a Feſs betwixt 3 creſſants*
19 Ioh. Denham, mil.		*Gules 3 Fuſils Erm.*
20 Will. Fleetwood	*ut prius*	**Per pale Or & G. a Lion Ramp. betwent three flower de luces counterchanged.*
21 Fra. Goodwin, *m.		
22 Will Pen, † ar.	Pen	*† Arg. on a Feſs S. 3 Plates.*
REG. CARO. *Anno*		
1 Edw. Coke, mil.	Stoke	*Partee per pale G. & Az. 3 Eagles Argent.*
2 Gil. Gerrard, bar.		*Quarterly, the 1 & 4 Arg. a Sal. G. the 2 & 3 Az. a Lion Ramp. Erm. Crowned Or.*
3 { Tho. Dirrel, a. / F. Cateſby, a. }	*ut prius* / Northamp.	*Ar. 2 Lions paſſant, S. crowned Or.*
4 Tho. Lee, ar.	*ut prius*	
5 Will. Andrews, m.	*ut prius*	
6 Tho. Hide, baro.		*Or, a Chev. betwixt 3 Lozenges Az. in Chief an Eagle of the firſt.*
7 Iaco. Dupper, ar.		
8 Rob. Dormer, ar.	*ut prius*	
9 Fran. Cheney, mi.	*ut prius*	
10 Pet. Temple, mil.	*ut prius*	
11 Heneage Proby, a.		*Erm. on a Feſs G. a Lion Paſſant the tail extended, Or.*
12 Anth. Cheſter, ba.	*ut prius*	
13		
14		
15 Tho. Archdale, ar,		
16		
17 Rich. Grevile, mi.		*Sable a border & Croſs engrailed Or, thereon 5 Pellets.*
18		
19		
20 Hen. Beak, ar.		
21		
22 Will. Collier, ar.		

FIGURE 4. A print example of heraldic descriptions, in Thomas Fuller, *The History of Worthies for England* (London, 1662). (PR3461.F8 H6 1684*, 140; Williams Andrew Clark Memorial Library, University of California, Los Angeles)

cells that organize various categories of heraldic information obviate any need for grammatical relationships between terms. The different entries for "Armes" exhibit features of the notational system of heraldry. Particular terms are repeated, indicating the similarities across coats even if the items depicted on the individual heralds would be unlikely to appear together in a different context. These terms describe standardized colors, forms, and patterns—for instance, *arg.* (the abbreviation for *argent*, meaning *silver*) and *passant* (the term for animals depicted in a walking position); also present are terms such as *betwixt* and *within* (common prepositions used to link the different components of the coats). This regimented method of describing blazons operates in conjunction with the distinctive spatial organization of the table. The arrangement and lexical pattern similarly support a comprehensive view that allows for easy comparison between the sheriffs from the seventeenth year of Elizabeth I's reign through the twenty-second year of Charles I's.

A series of pages from the Stevens family's eighteenth-century notebook organizes a catalogue of Oxfordshire and Warwickshire noblemen in a similar manner to the table depicted in figure 4 but also combines the list with images of the coats of arms (see fig. 5).[23] The lists of succeeding generations are arranged in a formulaic structure that repeats terms, such as Latin words referring to the period during which each person was alive and served as sheriff in his particular county. The lists and tables often found in notebooks thus illustrate Blair's "storing, sorting, summarizing, and selecting" at work.[24] Notational form operates across a range of formats that change from page to page. I have begun with an example from heraldry because it illustrates in linguistic and visual forms the semantic condensation that I referred to earlier. Indeed, Arthur Charles Fox-Davies calls heraldry the "shorthand of history."[25] As I move to focus on recipe examples for the remainder of the essay, I want to emphasize that even the printed heraldic table and other examples call on the distinctive affordances of manuscript note taking by featuring techniques of combining disparate terms in a small amount of space.

Attending to notational language and formats in manuscript as well as print entails tracing instances of difference within a broader pattern of similarity. Across disciplinary contexts, notation operates as a form of writing for translating subjective observations into shared systems of arrangement. Instances of revision or adaptation of notational formats or systems provide an opportunity for examining how authors adapted techniques of observation or experimentation to the demands of specific occasions. As a consequence, notational form offers a unique vantage point on the circumstances of a particular historical context. Several recipes for a horse-hoof ointment that appear in manuscript recipe books and printed hunting manuals illustrate a common approach to wounds

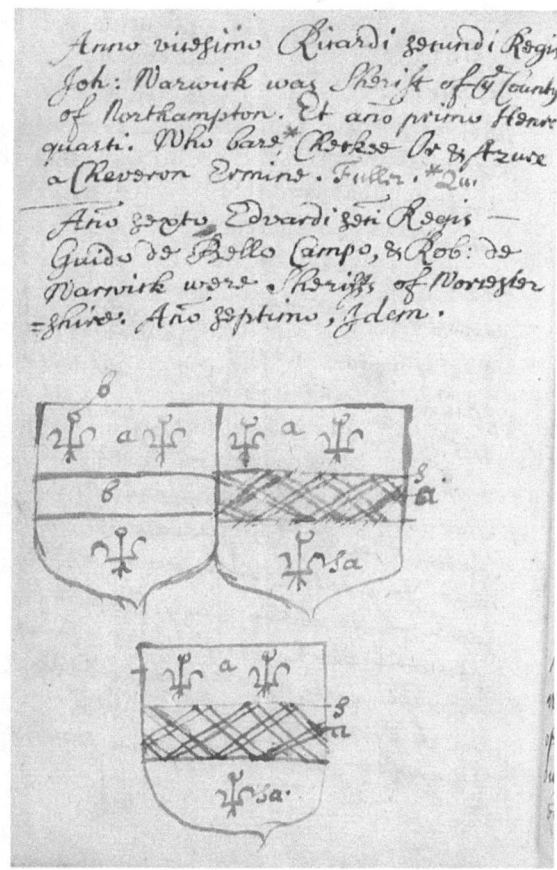

FIGURE 5. Manuscript version of heraldic descriptions, including drawings. ("Receipt book," ca. 1704–87, MS W.a.283, 144; used by permission of the Folger Shakespeare Library)

and swelling, but within this framework, successive versions reveal subtle changes that index larger cultural differences. An early instance appears in a manuscript receipt book from around 1600.[26] It features "hogges grease, baye salts, mayes butter and culvers donge," which refer to congealed animal fat, sea salt, springtime butter, and bird droppings, respectively.[27] A similar recipe was published in Nicholas Cox's popular 1686 hunting manual *The Gentleman's Recreation* and another one appears in the eighteenth-century Stevens family manuscript. (This list is by no means exhaustive; I even found a "horse grease" recipe from 1906 that features ingredients from the 1686 version.[28]) Each iteration of the recipe makes revisions, both to its contents and to its presentation. I first identified this recipe from the high lexical variation score of the Cox printed version, which lists all of the ingredients and their amounts in pints and ounces. Cox offers the recipe in a longer descriptive account of how a gentleman manages the care of his horses. The recipe is presented in paragraph form, following instructions regarding how one should hand-feed corn to the horse, and it illustrates how the shorthand notational form of notebooks could be transformed into a more accessible print format for a broader audience. By contrast, the eighteenth-century Stevens family manuscript includes the recipe as a list with units of measure conveyed in apothecary symbols among many other medical recipes for animal care (see fig. 6).[29] The manuscript presents the bare requirements for composing the ointment, suggesting the book's liminal position between private and public writing.

The quality and rarity of ingredients in the Cox recipe of 1686 and the very similar Stevens iteration position these versions in a higher socioeconomic realm than the one from the earlier seventeenth-century manuscript. In place of ingredients that likely would be found at any English farm, the Cox and Stevens versions add "Venice turpentine,"

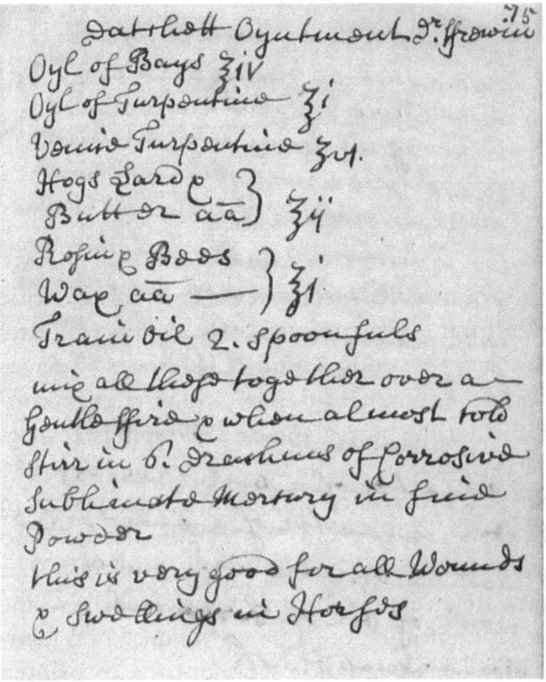

FIGURE 6. Recipe for horse-hoof ointment. ("Receipt book," ca. 1704–87, MS W.a.283, 75; used by permission of the Folger Shakespeare Library)

"train oil," and the "best Rosin," which were expensive items that would have had to be imported.[30] Train oil was produced by harvesting the fat from whale or cod, and in the late seventeenth century, the Dutch government largely controlled its production. K. G. Davies writes that in the 1680s, the Dutch government sent almost two thousand whaling ships to Greenland to catch ten thousand whales for the production of train oil.[31] Davies contends that the northernmost European settlement in the Americas (which was at the Churchill River near Hudson Bay) was so located as a result of members of the Hudson Bay Company observing thousands of white whales in the bay in 1686. In 1717, James Knight of the Hudson Bay Company established the Churchill River Post (which was subsequently renamed the Prince of Wales Fort) to gain a foothold for whaling. The demand for train oil in England launched thousands of ships. By including train oil in the ointment recipe, Cox signals the high status of the hypothetical gentleman who would be able acquire the ingredient. The Stevens manuscript similarly points to a family that fits this status level and contributed to the seventeenth-century demand for train oil. In this social context, the notational arrangement of the recipe serves to constitute a process by which train oil from the North Atlantic, turpentine from Venice, and lard from England could be combined. Notational form created the linguistic situation in which these disparate substances were brought into relation with one another. It served as a site of intersection between the public expansion of trade and the private space of household management, which were similarly united in the recurrent movement of the recipe between print and manuscript.

From a methodological perspective, what is striking here is that the presence of high lexical variation indexes the broader social and political context of the recipe. The bare notational form of the Stevens recipe indicates how manuscript functioned as a site for both written and material composition. One of the most famous medical recipes of the period was the previously cited Countess of Kent's Powder, supposedly the creation of Elizabeth Grey, Countess of Kent. The recipe was first printed in *A Choice Manual of Rare and Select Secrets* (1653), which purported to be a collection of the countess's favorite medical and culinary recipes, although her eponymous powder appears to have been the only original recipe in the collection.[32] *A Choice Manual* went through twenty-two editions, with the last one published in 1726. The powder recipe also appeared in *The Royal Pharmacopœa Galenical and Chimical* (1678). Part of the reason this later iteration scored highly in the measure of lexical variation is because, in that version, the recipe is set apart from the main text as a list, written in Latin and English in side-by-side columns, with each unit of the ingredients expressed in various apothecary symbols (see fig. 1). Originally published in French, the *Royal Pharmacopœa* validated the recipe by offering it to an international audience and presenting it in the scientific lingua franca of Latin. However, part of the recipe's appeal seems to have stemmed from the exotic items that it brought together, including "crabs' eyes" (small stones found in the stomach of crayfish), "white amber," and, most remarkably, "root of contrayerva," a "Spanish counterpoyson" that was imported from Peru.[33] Prominent figures, including Sir Thomas Osborne, Duke of Leeds; Johanna St. John, daughter of the Lord Chief Justice to Oliver Cromwell; and Bridget Hyde transcribed the countess's recipe in notebooks that tended to exchange its ingredients for even rarer items, such as viper skins and "unicorn horn," which was actually rhinoceros horn ground into a fine powder.[34] St. John's version even came with the endorsement of the noted chemist and member of the Royal Society Sir Thomas Willis.[35] It also featured a marginal note suggesting that users add a dram of "Virginia snake root," which was only found in North America (see fig. 2). In manuscript form, the recipe was only ever provisional; both the written and material dimensions of composition were subject to revision.

The recipe appears as a node in the network of early modern manuscript culture in that it links figures and ingredients from across emergent systems of global exchange. Items from the Americas and Africa listed in different versions of the recipe resemble the "puffs, powders, patches, Bibles, billet doux" catalogued in Alexander Pope's mock-epic *The Rape of the Lock*.[36] Like the countess's recipe, Pope's list displays a kind of private language in which grammatical relationships between words are exchanged for bare concatenation, and the affiliation between the objects is their mere presence on Belinda's toilet. Pope's mock-heroic catalogues are most often read in relation to the classical epic trope, but another rhetorical gesture is at work here. The lists participate in the shorthand of private access in which the poem revels. It is similar to the appeal of reading a printed version of a famous noblewoman's notebook, and it resembles the stylistic move toward shorthand in Samuel Richardson's epistolary novels, in which "writing to the moment" indicates closer proximity between the protagonist's interiority and the words on the printed page. It is manuscript notebooks that first create the distinctive discursive space wherein it might be said, "Tortoise here and Elephant unite."[37]

I have been examining two things with this experiment: first, how passages of text identified by a measure for lexical variation moved between print and manuscript; and second, how features of notational form made it well-suited for bringing together distant words, both in terms of their positions in the semantic model and in their geographical points of origin. The writers who copied and modified the Countess of Kent's recipe appear attracted to variety, especially as it registered the emergent capacity of the British economy to procure items from across the world. The notational system of units of measure and techniques of arrangement produced a constellation of things represented in language and space. The recipe bears out Barthes's view of *notatio* as "palimpsest," wherein multiple semantic domains correspond to social, cultural, and economic registers of meaning. The work of note taking indexes many more types of work that extend beyond the page and are implied by the histories of the objects and techniques implicated in lists and tables. This linguistic form represents one answer to the question posed by Bruno Latour: "How do we pack the world into words?"[38] Latour and theorists of new materialism have demonstrated how material produces language—that is, how networks of nonhuman agents, in part, produce the conditions of writing. Yet it is also true that, in notebooks enumerating the ingredients of inks, ointments, and powders, systems of language produce material.

Before theorizing the function of *notatio* in the notebook, Barthes first considered it in the nineteenth-century realist novel. In his essay on the "reality effect," he argues that concrete details service the "having-been-there of things" to create a referential illusion of "the real" in novels.[39] In this essay, I have been proposing that the language of notation in manuscript notebooks produces a different kind of reality effect in which lexical patterns signify historical realities, indicating a point of contact between private writing and public knowledge making. Developing this argument has entailed incorporating methods from the radically different perspective of computational linguistics. As relocating *notatio* from the novel to the notebook helped Barthes to recognize how the mode operates between writing and experience, approaching notational form from a foreign medial paradigm foregrounds the distinctive capacity of manuscript to produce rare semantic juxtapositions through a dynamic interplay of language and space. Manuscript, of course, differs from print in material and in the conditions of production, but a computational lens makes it possible to trace relationships between language and material that were typical of late seventeenth-century handwritten notebooks yet anomalous in contemporary print. Occupying a new medial standpoint thus helps to describe how manuscript and print mutually constituted a media environment that supported specific cultural and social structures, from the growth of the train oil trade to the broader relationship between colonial commodities and medical experimentation. Notational elements in manuscript notebooks did not merely reflect the contemporary world; rather, these linguistic and media technologies constituted how early modern writers engaged their world. The effect was to create reality in writing.

Notes

1. "Receipt Book," ca. 1679–94, MS V.b.363, Folger Shakespeare Library, Washington, DC, 32, 42.
2. Yeo, *Notebooks, English Virtuosi, and Early Modern Science*, 14.
3. Dunton, *A Voyage round the World*, 29–30.
4. Ibid., 27–28.
5. Ibid., 11.
6. Algee-Hewitt and his colleagues introduce a somewhat similar measure designed to observe redundancy in linguistic sequences. The key difference is that they measure the likelihood of one word following another, while I am measuring the likelihood of the ten words preceding and following a given word appearing together: see Algee-Hewitt et al., "Canon/Archive," 5–7.
7. The word space model was trained on 18,752 texts printed between 1640 and 1700 in the publicly released portion of EEBO-TCP Phase 1. I created the model using the Word2vec package in the Python programming language. The model was trained on context windows spanning ten words on either side of a given term, for words appearing at least forty times in the corpus. Word2vec uses a "shallow" neural network to generate a predictive word distribution model rather than a count-based model. This approach makes it more efficient and easier to train, and some computer scientists argue that predictive word space models perform better than count-based ones, but this is a highly contested argument. For arguments supporting count-based approaches to semantic modeling, see Levy and Goldberg, "Linguistic Regularities in Sparse and Explicit Word Representations"; Levy et al., "Improved Distributional Similarity with Lessons Learned from Word Embeddings." For the rationale behind predictive modeling, see Baroni et al., "Don't Count, Predict!" See also the paper that introduced the word2vec algorithm: Mikolov et al., "Efficient Estimation of Word Representations in Vector Space."
8. Barthes, *The Preparation of the Novel*, 18.

9. Rachael Scarborough King has introduced the "bridge genre" concept to describe forms (in King's case the letter) that transfer sets of "textual conventions" across different kinds of media. My lexical variation measure, in effect, identified such conventions that operate in different notational contexts across manuscript and print, showing how notational form operates as a "bridge genre." See King, *Writing to the World*, 2, 16–22.
10. See Blair, *Too Much to Know*, 63–116; Griffin, "Instruction and Information from Manuscript to Print," 667–76; Yeo, *Notebooks, English Virtuosi, and Early Modern Science*, 37–68.
11. Yeo, *Notebooks, English Virtuosi, and Early Modern Science*, 9.
12. See Leong, "Collecting Knowledge for the Family"; Nunn, "Home Bodies"; Theophano, *Eat My Words*.
13. Blair, "Note Taking as an Art of Transmission."
14. See Leong, "Collecting Knowledge for the Family," 81–103.
15. See Hobart and Zachary, *Information Ages*, 96–106; Yeo, *Notebooks, English Virtuosi, and Early Modern Science*, 17.
16. "Receipt Book," ca. 1700, MS E.a.4, Folger Shakespeare Library.
17. For recent digital humanities introductions to semantic modeling, see Allison et al., "Pamphlet 5"; Gavin, "Vector Semantics, William Empson, and the Study of Ambiguity"; Schmidt, "Vector Space Models for the Digital Humanities."
18. Harris, "Distributional Structure," 146.
19. Firth, *Papers in Linguistics*, 11.
20. There is still much work to do in using word space models to analyze phrases and sentences in computational linguistics. Word2vec has been used to identify words that tend to appear in phrases: see Mikolov et al., "Distributed Representations of Words and Phrases and their Compositionality." My measure uses the standard deviation between the vector positions of words occurring in the same context windows. The mean standard deviation value for each word in the subset 1678–82 corpus (averaged across all of the context windows of each word) is 0.11229. The mean for the top 150 terms that I present here is 0.139412, which is a little more than five standard deviations above the mean. While these terms stand out from the rest, it is, of course, true that there is only a relative difference between the lexical variation appearing in the context windows of the top terms and those of the rest of the words in the model. In the essay I focus on the contexts of the top terms, but the terms with the lowest values for the measure also indicate its efficacy. For instance, two of the bottom terms are *oge* and *ordeining*, which, like many of the top terms, are difficult to contextualize at first glance. In the subset, *Oge* primarily occurs in Irish genealogies in which formulaic phrases appear with great frequency, and the resulting context windows contain a lot of repeated words. Similarly, *ordeining* largely appears in formulaic phrases

in religious texts—most notably, *the power of ordeining others*. For a prime example, see Dodwell, *Separation of Churches from Episcopal Government*.
21. T-SNE is an algorithm for reducing the multiple dimensions of the word vectors to two dimensions that can be represented visually: van der Maaten and Hinton."Visualizing High-Dimensional Data Using t-SNE."
22. Barthes, *The Preparation of the Novel*, 18.
23. "Receipt Book," ca. 1704–87, MS W.a.283, Folger Shakespeare Library, 144–45.
24. Blair, "Note Taking as an Art of Transmission," 85.
25. Fox-Davies, *A Complete Guide to Heraldry*, v.
26. "Receipt Book," ca. 1600, MS V.a.140, Folger Shakespeare Library, f. 8^r.
27. Tobey, "No Foot, No Horse."
28. *Scientific American Supplement*, vol. 62, no. 1608, October 27, 1906, 25772.
29. "Receipt Book," ca. 1704–87, MS W.a.283, 75.
30. Cox, *The Gentleman's Recreation*, 46.
31. Davies, *The North Atlantic World in the Seventeenth Century*, 157.
32. Duffin, "Historical Survey of the Internal Use of Unprocessed Amber," 53.
33. Charas, *The Royal Pharmacopœa*, 117. The substance definitions are from *The "Cecil" Glossary of Materia, Medica, and Medical Terminology*.
34. Sir Thomas Osborne, "Sir Thomas Osborne Recipe Book," 1670–95, MS 3724, f. 78^r; Johanna St. John, "Johanna Saint John Recipe Book," 1680, MS 4338, f. 138^r; Bridget Hyde, "Bridget Hyde Recipe Book," 1676–90, MS 2990, f. 109^v, Wellcome Library, London.
35. Hyde, "Bridget Hyde Recipe Book," MS 2990, f. 109^v.
36. Pope, *The Rape of the Lock*, 9.
37. Ibid.
38. Latour, "Circulating Reference," 24.
39. For an extended analysis of how Barthes's understanding of notation changed from "The Reality Effect" essay to *The Preparation of the Novel* lectures, see Buurma and Heffernan, "Notation after 'The Reality Effect.'"

Works Cited

Algee-Hewitt, Mark, Sarah Allison, Marissa Gemma, Ryan Heuser, Franco Moretti, and Hannah Walser. "Pamphlet 11: Canon/Archive. Large-Scale Dynamics in the Literary Field." Stanford Literary Lab, January 2016, https://litlab.stanford.edu/LiteraryLabPamphlet11.pdf.

Allison, Sarah, Marissa Gemma, Ryan Heuser, Franco Moretti, Amir Tevel, and Irena Yamboliev. "Pamphlet 5: Style at the Scale of the Sentence." Stanford Literary Lab, June 2013. https://litlab.stanford.edu/LiteraryLabPamphlet5.pdf.

Baroni, Marc, Georgiana Dinu, and Germán Kruszewski. "Don't Count, Predict! A Systematic Comparison of Context-Counting vs. Context-Predicting Semantic Vectors." *Proceedings of the Association for Computational Linguistics* 1 (2014): 238–47.
Barthes, Roland. *The Preparation of the Novel: Lecture Courses and Seminars at the Collège de France*, 3d ed. New York: Columbia University Press, 2010.
———. "The Reality Effect." In *The Rustle of Language*, 141–48. Berkeley: University of California Press, 1989.
Blair, Ann. "Note Taking as an Art of Transmission." *Critical Inquiry* 31, no. 1 (Autumn 2004): 85–107.
———. *Too Much to Know: Scholarly Information before the Modern Age*. New Haven, CT: Yale University Press, 2011.
Buurma, Rachel Sagner, and Lauren Heffernan. "Notation after 'The Reality Effect': Remaking Reference with Roland Barthes and Sheila Heti." *Representations* 125, no. 1 (Winter 2014): 80–102.
The "Cecil" Glossary of Materia, Medica, and Medical Terminology. London: Royal Holloway, University of London, 2010.
Charas, Moyse. *The Royal Pharmacopœa*. London, 1678.
Cox, Nicholas. *The Gentleman's Recreation*. London, 1686.
Davies, K. G. *The North Atlantic World in the Seventeenth Century*. Minneapolis: University of Minnesota Press, 1974.
Dodwell, Henry. *Separation of Churches from Episcopal Government*. London, 1679.
Duffin, Christopher. "Historical Survey of the Internal Use of Unprocessed Amber." *Acta Medico-Historica Adriatica* 13, no. 1 (2015): 41–74.
Dunton, John. *A Voyage round the World, or, A Pocket-Library Divided into Several Volumes*, vol. 1. London, 1691.
Firth, J. R. *Papers in Linguistics, 1934–1951*. London: Oxford University Press, 1957.
Fox-Davies, Arthur Charles. *A Complete Guide to Heraldry*. New York: Bonanza, [1909] 1978.
Gavin, Michael. "Vector Semantics, William Empson, and the Study of Ambiguity." *Critical Inquiry* 44, no. 4 (Summer 2018): 641–73.
Griffin, Carrie. "Instruction and Information from Manuscript to Print: Some English Literature, 1400–1650." *Literature Compass* 10, no. 9 (2013): 667–76.
Harris, Zellig. "Distributional Structure." *Word* 10, nos. 2–3 (1954): 146–62.
Hobart, Michael E., and Zachary S. Schiffman. *Information Ages: Literacy, Numeracy, and the Computer Information*. Baltimore: Johns Hopkins University Press, 2000.
King, Rachael Scarborough. *Writing to the World: Letters and the Origins of Modern Print Genres*. Baltimore: Johns Hopkins University Press, 2018.

Latour, Bruno. "Circulating Reference: Sampling the Soil in the Amazon Forest." In *Pandora's Hope: Essays on the Reality of Science Studies*, 24–79. Cambridge, MA: Harvard University Press, 1999.

Leong, Elaine. "Collecting Knowledge for the Family: Recipes, Gender and Practical Knowledge in the Early Modern English Household." *Centaurus* 55, no. 2 (May 2013): 81–103.

Levy, Omer, and Yoav Goldberg. "Linguistic Regularities in Sparse and Explicit Word Representations." *Proceedings of the Eighteenth Conference on Computational Language Learning* (2014): 171–80.

Levy, Omer, Yoav Goldberg, and Ido Dagan. "Improved Distributional Similarity with Lessons Learned from Word Embeddings." *Transactions of the Association for Computational Linguistics* 3 (2015): 211–25.

Mikolov, Tomas, Kai Chen, Greg Corrado, and Jeffrey Dean. "Efficient Estimation of Word Representations in Vector Space." September 7, 2013. arXiv:1301.3781.

Mikolov, Tomas, Ilya Sutskever, Kai Chen, Greg Corrado, and Jeffrey Dean. "Distributed Representations of Words and Phrases and their Compositionality." October 16, 2013. arXiv:1310.4546.

Nunn, Hillary. "Home Bodies: Matters of Weight in Renaissance Women's Medical Manuals." In *The Body in Medical Culture*, edited by Elizabeth Klaver, 15–36. Albany: State University of New York Press, 2009.

Pope, Alexander. *The Rape of the Lock*. London, 1714.

Schmidt, Ben. "Vector Space Models for the Digital Humanities." October 25, 2015. http://bookworm.benschmidt.org/posts/2015-10-25-Word-Embeddings.html.

Theophano, Janet. *Eat My Words: Reading Women's Lives through the Cookbooks They Wrote*. New York: Palgrave Macmillan, 2002.

Tobey, Elizabeth. "No Foot, No Horse." *Shakespeare's World*. March 2, 2016. https://blog.shakespearesworld.org/2016/03/02/no-foot-no-horse.

Van der Maaten, L. J. P., and G. E. Hinton. "Visualizing High-Dimensional Data Using t-SNE." *Journal of Machine Learning Research* 9 (2008): 2579–605.

Yeo, Richard. *Notebooks, English Virtuosi, and Early Modern Science*. Chicago: University of Chicago Press, 2014.

The Circulation of John Keats's Letters on Land, on Sea, Online

BRIAN REJACK

Some of John Keats's most notable letters were sent across the Atlantic to his brother and sister-in-law George and Georgiana Keats after the couple emigrated from England in the summer of 1818 and eventually settled in Louisville, Kentucky. In the nearly two centuries since then, many more of Keats's letters have made it to the United States, where the majority of them now reside (including eighty-six autograph letters in the Harvard Keats Collection). In the last half-century, almost all of these have, so to speak, gone out of circulation, and if we narrow that range to the last quarter-century, only a handful could be said to have circulated extensively in some physical manner. But one aim of this essay is to resist the assumption that once manuscripts end up in an archive they cease to move. Archives are living institutions and the materials they house remain vital and mutable in several senses. Perhaps the greatest archival transformations now occurring result from the recognition that, as Jerome McGann puts it, "The whole of our cultural inheritance has to be recurated and reedited in digital forms and institutional structures."[1] As a beginning assumption, then, we can say that one way that manuscripts reenter circulation is through processes of digitization. With Keats's letters and other eighteenth- and nineteenth-century manuscript collections, significant recurating and reediting has already brought many materials into the digital realm (the William Blake Archive and the Emily Dickinson Archive being just two prominent examples). However, my focus in this essay concerns not those initial processes of making manuscripts accessible in digital form, but other kinds of activities scholars can undertake with those new forms to further our understanding of manuscripts' past movements and interactions.

Doing this kind of work requires that we first recognize that we are dealing not with the simple binaries of print and manuscript, digital and physical, or mobile and fixed. Archives and the objects they hold are not eternal universals existing apart from the world; they consist of and operate through contingent material networks that must be vigilantly maintained to keep cultural memory operable, and in the twenty-first century cultural memory is inextricably bound up with computational systems. At the same time, we ought not to think that Keats's letters in the nineteenth century were divorced from the media ecological systems of that era. Rather, they existed in relation with forms of nineteenth-century mediation like the postal system, printed books and magazines, and forms of visual reproduction. With the advantage of a few decades of digital curation behind us, we now benefit from easier access not only to materials such as the letters themselves but also to other digitized records, which, through further curation, can help resituate the manuscripts in a network of relations across temporal moments and through various media.

That work of what we might call secondary curation is one aim of the Keats Letters Project (KLP), an initiative for which I serve as one of the founding coeditors (keatslettersproject.com).[2] My colleagues and I began our work on the project by recognizing that digital materials related to the letters (primarily in the form of digitized images of the manuscripts and digital copies of earlier print editions of the letters) already existed in abundance. Our work, then, would not be the construction of an edition of the letters; instead, we sought to create a venue for re-presenting extant digital resources while also creating new content in the form of responses to individual letters: scholarly analyses from a wide variety of contributors, creative responses from poets and artists, pedagogical resources, and, in the spirit of the oft-punning prankster who was John Keats, a decidedly silly YouTube series called "This Week in Keats" hosted by two of the KLP's cofounders. In practical terms, the site features an introductory post about each of Keats's 252 surviving letters posted on the date of its two-hundredth anniversary (usually with links to a digitized print edition of the text, along with images of the manuscript when possible), as well as additional content of the sorts mentioned above. The KLP purposely does not offer a new digital edition, or even transcriptions, of the texts of Keats's letters. Instead the site orients readers to the wealth of resources related to the correspondence already available. By bringing together new scholarly content with existing digital resources, the site suggests a variety of possible forking paths for further exploration of the letters' pasts and futures.

One reason that we gravitated toward Keats's letters as the locus of the project is that his epistolary writing is so consistently marked by insightful reflections upon media, mediation, and the complex interrelations between different forms within broader systems. As scholars of the letters such as John Barnard, Heidi Thomson, Timothy Webb, and Susan Wolfson have observed, the generic, rhetorical, and material circumstances of epistolary communication in the early nineteenth century significantly informed how Keats crafted his letters.[3] My essay follows their work as well as other recent scholarship by Romanticists engaged in media studies.[4] With regard to Keats specifically, I embark from Yohei Igarashi's contention that "communicative mediation constitutes a significant, although still largely unremarked, concern of Keats's poetry and letters."[5] Given the tenuous state of the early nineteenth-century transatlantic postal system, it comes as no surprise that in his transatlantic correspondence we find Keats pondering fundamental questions about mediation and the deep uncertainty it involves. After receiving, in October 1818, brief news from George Keats that the new couple had arrived safely in Philadelphia, Keats would have no further communications from them for another seven months, during which time he sent three long journal letters across the ocean in the other direction. In each of these missives, Keats expressed discontent with the vagaries of transatlantic communication while still clinging to the hope that some signal was being transmitted. In December 1818 he wrote, "I think we ought to have heard of you before this—I am in daily expectation of Letters—Nil desperandum—."[6] By February, he seemed to be a bit closer to despair: "How is it we have not heard from you from the Settlement yet? The Letters must surely have miscarried—I am in expectation every day."[7] The problems of posting became the content of his letters.

An attention to the material history of Keats's letters requires us to develop a focus on the infrastructural, institutional, and discursive networks that supported the circulation of letters during the period. Like all texts, letters "bear within themselves the history of their own making," as McGann puts it, paraphrasing D. F. McKenzie.[8] But letters often demonstrate a higher degree of self-reflexivity and markedness than other texts, if for no other reason than that, as Bernhard Siegert points out, letters record not only their own making but also their own transmission: "What is recorded is the necessary trace of posting."[9] The process of posting only works, as Siegert claims, through withdrawal, interruption, and interception, through those moments when a letter exits circulation and receives or produces some marker of its movements. Those kinds of moments lend themselves well to further engagement via a digital environment, in which—in contrast to a textual edition—one can reproduce images of features like postage marks, tears in paper, and wax seals, while also using other contextual digital resources to understand those elements' meanings (then and now).

At the same time, we should keep in mind that Keats's thinking on epistolary mediation was not unique—in fact, his comments are emblematic of how correspondents viewed the post in the early nineteenth century. Particularly with overseas communication during this period, when the transatlantic postal system was a provisional hodgepodge of exaptations built onto other, already existing structures, letter writers were likely to have keen "awareness of the mechanism."[10] While provoking awed contemplation of the amazing distances that they could bridge, letters also spurred reflections on how the medium was imperiled by crossing those distances. As Susan Manning writes of transatlantic correspondence at the time, "The burden of distance is to render communication provisional, partial and contingent on the conditions of transmission."[11] Similarly, Mary Favret argues, "Correspondence is never a transparent medium; rather, it promises blockage, limits and distance."[12] While the epistolary medium would become more transparent and consistent thanks to the regularizing effects of the global postal system in the second half of the nineteenth century, during Keats's brief period of epistolary production (1815–20), at least, writers remained attentive to the medium's palpable fragility. Keats's frequent reminders of the limitations and failures of nineteenth-century media thus provide the KLP with ample opportunity to reflect on the challenges we face with twenty-first century media—which similarly can both enable and endanger connection. Given that rhetoric around digital technology tends toward the triumphalist and the utopian, modes of resisting that logic from within a digital project help root us in a historical, though not teleological, frame of networked connections among print, manuscript, digital, and other modes. Rather than attempting to seal off the letters in an illusory total reproduction of a past moment, the KLP models the work of scholarship as one that must always be an ushering of cultural memory into the future, always a process of transformation. This is especially true as we exist in a moment when, as so many scholars have by this point recognized, the materials that make up our cultural memory are radically transforming through digitization efforts and the associated fallout.[13] To have some say over how those transformations take place, scholars need to actively engage with and extend the collective "record of textual makings and remakings," which will continue to evolve with or without us.[14]

In reckoning with mediation in a digital era, therefore, we should not delude ourselves into thinking that computational media will answer all our questions or circumvent the precarity of cultural preservation. We ought to cultivate our awareness of how mediation works in the twenty-first century—which means analyzing its limitations as much as its affordances, its complex place within deep time as much as its incessant drive toward an ever-updated now. With that cultivation we can bring our critical knowledge to bear on continuing efforts to make scholarship matter in a contemporary media environment. In this essay, then, I first explore in further detail how the KLP attempts to capitalize on the digital medium while also using the bicentennial temporal frame of Keats's letters to insist on a historicized view of epistolary mediation. As an illustration of the need for and potential significance of such work, I then turn to an analysis of the history of one letter: Keats's November 12, 1819, letter to George and Georgiana Keats, which endured a precarious nineteenth-century journey across the ocean, only to face another ordeal almost two hundred years later, when the manuscript was stolen from the Historical Society of Pennsylvania.[15] My analysis of the letter's travails in 1819–20 shows how digital tools can aid in reimagining manuscripts' past histories, while the tale of its theft and eventual recovery points toward the importance of continuing to support the physical and archival mechanisms necessary to make meaning out of the cultural record in general, and of manuscripts in particular, even as those materials continue to migrate into digital instantiations.

Curating Digital Keats

The main impetus behind the Keats Letters Project is the timely, bicentennial reproduction and recirculation of Keats's letters. The KLP has many origin stories—some of which begin in a pub in Cardiff—but it is rooted in the founders' shared commitment to rethinking the purpose and the nature of scholarship within the broader media ecology of the twenty-first century. We do so by contextualizing the letters' pasts, drawing attention to the ways we encounter them now, and, finally, commissioning scholars and poets, teachers and students, and writers and thinkers of many stripes to correspond with these texts anew. As of this writing (August 2019), the site has featured content for 143 of Keats's letters. Much of the material thus far has been in the form of short, scholarly essays, but we have also featured poems, visual art, an audio interview, and several kinds of responses during the week of December 21–27, 2017, which marked the two-hundredth anniversary of the letter in which Keats coined the term "negative capability." While we always encourage contributors to consider producing responses to letters in alternative forms, even in the traditional modes that make up the majority of the site's posts our contributors have done innovative work.

As an example of some of the potential that this platform enables, let us take Matthew Sangster's response to Keats's November 1, 1816, letter to Joseph Severn.[16] The manuscript of this letter resides at Harvard's Houghton Library, along with dozens of other Keats manuscripts, all of which have been digitized and made freely available via the library's website.[17] This letter to Severn features little in the way of the content that scholars of Keats's letters typically examine. It runs to only about seventy-five words and mostly shows Keats apologizing to Severn for being unable to visit him the next day. But with attention to what we know about the letter's movements in London in 1816, in his post Sangster asks us to rethink how we usually approach Keats with respect to temporality. As Sangster notes, Keats's poems are noted for their luxurious indolence—their "slow Time." In many of his most famous letters, Keats likewise writes meditatively, using epistolary form to dwell on serious topics. But here we instead find the poet zipping off a letter with the hopes that it will arrive a few miles away in London later that day or early the next morning so as to alert Severn in time about Keats's prior engagement. To enhance how readers conceived of that space and the rapidity with which Keats physically and textually traversed it, Sangster directs us to his own digital project, Romantic London (romanticlondon.org). That project overlays images from Richard Horwood's *Plan of the Cities of London and Westminster* (1792–99) onto existing web mapping services such as Google Maps.[18] Users can thus find on the digital version of Horwood's plan the two locations noted by Keats's letter: the poet's lodging at 8 Dean Street, from which he sent his letter, and Severn's at 128 Goswell Street, to which it was sent. Switching between views of Horwood's map and different contemporary online maps, users can visualize not only the movements of the letter, but also the temporal layering on which the KLP is based. In other words, the site functions as a digital space in which to reenact and reimagine the dispersed events of the manuscript letter's creation, transmission, and reception.

Another post that brings together speed, space, and movement is Richard Marggraf Turley's "Keats Underway." It responds to Keats's April 15, 1817, letter to his brothers George and Tom Keats, sent from Southampton to London, out of which Keats had traveled by mail coach the previous afternoon. Turley's essay focuses on the layered significations of Keats "going places"—his first book having just been published, he was embarking on the next stage of his burgeoning poetic career, with his travel to Southampton being the first leg of his journey to the Isle of Wight, where he planned to seclude himself in order to begin work on his next book (*Endymion*).[19] The letter itself is also going places. Obviously, it travels back to London via the mail coach in which Keats had spent the previous fourteen hours; it also displays a breezy rapidity like that of the letter to Severn analyzed by Sangster. Turley notes that the letter, "like the mail coach itself, speeds easily on, its own velocity echoing the vehicle's thundering progress through Surrey and Hampshire." Much of the letter contains what Turley calls an "em-dashed itinerary of the Mail Coach Road," or a list of sights Keats took in during the night of travel and then enumerated, with his characteristic dashes, in an extended list. Using contemporary resources, including Daniel Paterson's *Roads* (the fifteenth edition, published in 1811), Thomas Rowlandson's 1792 print "Barber's Shop, Alresford" (a location Keats mentions in his list of sights), and a map of Winchester from an 1806 Ordnance Survey by Edmund Crocker, Turley fills in some of the details Keats leaves out in between em-dashed items. Turley's post includes images from all three sources along with links to them should readers feel inclined to, say, learn about the distance along the mail coach road between Alresford and Winchester (seven-and-three-quarter miles).

This kind of reimagining of Keats's journey, which he narrates in the content of the letter, is overlaid upon the journey that the letter would take back to London the next day. One of the postage marks indicates the letter's arrival in London at "10 o'Clock / Ap 16 / 1817 FNn [forenoon]," which means that it would have left Southampton sometime the previous afternoon in order to cover the 77 miles before the next morning.[20] This congruence between Keats's narrated journey and the remarkable efficiency of the letter's return trip ought also to be understood in relation to the letter's more complicated movements leading up to its eventual archival home at Princeton University. In our introductory post for the letter, the editors of the KLP provide digital images of the manuscript that we requested from Princeton, and we also comment upon the uncertainty of the letter's movements in the twentieth century. The letter is part of the Robert H. Taylor Collection, which includes six autograph letters by Keats. Thanks to a seemingly throwaway remark in the *Princeton University Library Chronicle*, we know that Taylor acquired this one in late 1976 or early 1977.[21] Before that time, the letter was alternately pasted into Benjamin Robert Haydon's diary (along with several other of Keats's letters), owned by Maurice Buxton Forman, and in the possession of (an) other unknown owner(s) after Forman removed the letter from Haydon's diary and sold it off (along with other Keats letters). The provenance of this letter is typical in that we can confidently know some details of its movements but can only speculate about many more of them. By emphasizing the uncertainty inherent to the manuscripts and their histories, the KLP illuminates what textual uncertainty might have meant for Keats during his time and in his media situation, as well as how our ongoing efforts to make sense of the letters exists in relation to the particularities of twenty-first-century media and its affordances.

Jerome McGann has recently called for a reinvigoration of philology as a means to maintain scholarship's role in curating cultural memory in light of the large-scale digital reproductions occurring today. As he writes, "to the philologian, all possible meanings are a function of their historical emergence as material artifacts," and the nature of the material artifacts constituting the cultural archive is increasingly shaped by processes of digital mediation largely outside scholars' control or even ken.[22] Instead of despairing at this prospect, the KLP proposes ways to respond to these new conditions. There are dozens of editions of the letters accessible via HathiTrust, Google Books, and the Internet Archive. The Harvard Keats Collection also makes freely available digital reproductions of the eighty-six autograph and twenty-four transcribed manuscripts housed there, out of Keats's 252 total extant letters. Our site's recirculation of the letters consists of collecting, filtering, and amplifying these digital archives (while, of course, also alerting readers to existing print editions). We thereby insist on each letter as a multiply mediated artifact—or, rather, as a nexus of many artifacts. That gathering of objects reproduces new materialities each time a letter enters a new context, such as when Sangster's reading of the letter to Severn offers us a way to imagine its movements between Dean Street and Goswell Street, or when Turley helps to re-create Keats's journey to Southampton with Keats's own words and contemporary multimedia materials.

All of this is not to say that the KLP and its founders play fast and loose with the plenitude of untrustworthy, poorly produced, or ambiguously marked digital materials flowing freely through cyberspace. Editions of the letters available in digital form and other related resources vary widely with respect to coverage, editorial accuracy, and fidelity of reproduction. But one area of focus for the KLP is precisely how these conditions affect our understanding of the correspondence, for it is not only in 2019 and 1819 that these letters exist but also across those two centuries. Reading letters written in 1819 while sitting comfortably in front of one's computer screen in 2019 happens only thanks to innumerable past material contingencies, such as the existence of the early nineteenth-century transatlantic postal system. That infrastructural reality enabled many of Keats's letters to make the journey across the ocean to his brother George Keats, and it also afforded John Jeffrey, the second husband of George's wife, Georgiana, the chance in 1845 to come across a notice in a Kentucky newspaper indicating that, in London, Richard Monckton Milnes was preparing a life of Keats. Jeffrey sent a letter back across the ocean to Milnes, offering to send transcripts of the Keats manuscripts in his possession, which he did later that year. Milnes then used those materials for his *Life, Letters, and Literary Remains of John Keats* (1848). Although it is unfortunately true that Jeffrey was a rather dismal transcriber, his work remains a crucial element in establishing the legacy of Keats's manuscript letters, particularly as Jeffrey's transcriptions are now the only sources we have for six letters, including for the letter in which Keats coined "negative capability," arguably his most famous and influential phrase. By 1845, when Milnes received transcripts from Jeffrey, the global postal system had come a long way from the 1810s, thanks to steamships traveling on regularly scheduled routes, the increasing development of inter-governmental cooperation, the beginnings of inland railroad travel, and, in England, the adoption of Rowland Hill's postal reforms in 1839–40. The two key temporal moments for our understanding of Keats's American letters—the composition and first movement of the texts around 1817 to 1820, and the second wave of travel in the 1840s leading up to Milnes's *Life*—demonstrate how crucial the development of international, transoceanic communication was to the makings of the Keatsian legacy. By attending to such histories and making them visible through the venue of our collaborative website, the KLP offers contributors and readers the opportunity to become the new philologians that McGann hopes will emerge. Even though we arrive "Too, too late for the fond believing lyre" of Keatsian immediacy, our project seeks to "build a fane" where our collective "branched thoughts" are "new grown with pleasant pain," propped up on the "wreath'd trellis" of working brains, networks, texts, and, of course, manuscripts.[23]

Tracking Keats at Sea

Thus far I have focused primarily on two aspects of the KLP: how it benefits from already existing digital resources in the process of adding to what we know about Keats's letters, and how it offers us opportunities to reflect upon contemporary media through the bicentennial lens orienting the project. But what does a digital endeavor like this reveal to us about manuscripts and other related media from 200 years ago? In what remains, I will analyze one of Keats's letters that has had a particularly varied history of movements and interactions in order to suggest that even though it is tempting to view computational media as an evolution from and progression beyond older forms, our contemporary situation can just as easily remind us of the continuing richness of what came before. In particular, I use this example to illustrate how digital media can help us insist upon a commitment to materiality despite the tendency in digital rhetoric toward immateriality and disembodiment.[24]

First, then, an anecdote about my attempts to seek out this particular letter in digital form. The letter is owned by the Historical Society of Pennsylvania (HSP), and since physical travel there was not possible for me, I requested a digital image of the manuscript. Doing so required first locating the details of the letter within the archive's cataloguing system. Scholars who work with archival manuscripts well know that locating items remotely can sometimes require careful digital detective work, as most archives have grafted their digital databases onto the branches of older, physical systems. The HSP's recent strategy for doing so was to digitize the nearly one million cards in the card catalogue that had slowly grown over the decades along with the archive itself. Eventually I came across the card for Keats's letter, and despite not holding the card in my hand, I nonetheless immediately took some pleasure in noting the two-dimensional presentation of texture indicating that the card had experienced some folding in its day, and at some point required a bit of tape to

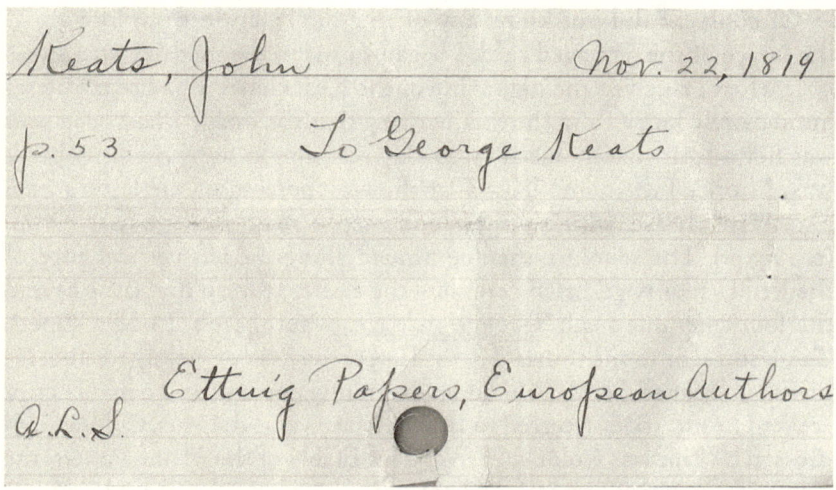

FIGURE 1. Index card catalogue entry for John Keats's November 12, 1819, letter to George Keats. (HSP manuscripts card catalogue record; Historical Society of Pennsylvania)

heal its battle scars, which remain present even if they seem not to matter in this digital instantiation (see fig. 1).

It was months later that I would learn about the origins of these creases and tears, which date to a harried period in the life of this letter and its associated archival record. This card, along with the Keats manuscript it indexed, was stolen from the library in late 2010 or early 2011 by Barry Landau and his accomplice Jason Savedoff, who worked together to surreptitiously remove approximately ten thousand documents from twenty-two different institutions during a months-long spree of cultural plunder. To prevent institutions such as the HSP from realizing that items had gone missing, Landau and Savedoff tore the corresponding cards out of the institutional catalogues. They also kept careful records of what they stole, which meant that when they were caught in July 2011, their trove of stolen documents was fairly well organized, and individual items were often still accompanied by catalogue records, such as the card pictured in figure 1, although in at least one case Savedoff ingested an HSP card to avoid detection by library staff. Luckily for those of us who care about cultural preservation, no highly valued archival artifacts were themselves eaten, and at this point all recovered items, including four documents that Landau managed to sell before being arrested, have been returned to their owners.[25]

Of course, I did not know any of this information from looking at the image of the damaged card. I began to suspect something was amiss only when I received the digital file of the Keats letter I had requested. I immediately knew from the handwriting that the image I had been sent was not a Keats letter, but after quickly scanning it to figure out what it was, I noticed the name "Keats" at the very bottom of the letter's final page. The phrase, with a double underscore, read "Get me that Keats" (see fig. 2). The sentence then continued along the left vertical edge of the letter's first page, briefly crossing the earlier text, so that the line and the following one read: "Get me that Keats autograph. I had a superb Tennyson sent to me tother day by Tupper, written expressly for this individual. [Signed,] BM."[26] I had inadvertently encountered a manuscript seeker like me. "BM" referred to Brantz Mayer, and the "cher Colonel" addressed by him was Colonel Frank Marx Etting of the Etting Papers, the collection in which my desired Keats letter was held. I assumed a simple clerical error was behind my receiving the wrong letter, but after corresponding with the staff at the HSP, the connection with the Landau case was brought to my attention. Among the thousands of stolen documents recovered from Landau's New York apartment by federal agents in July 2011 was Keats's November 1819 letter to his brother George Keats. The letter was miscatalogued when it returned to HSP from its kidnapping; thus, I received the images of Mayer's letter to Etting instead of Keats's to his brother.

This letter's misadventure reminds us of the enduring significance of the material systems and institutions that continue to care for and preserve the cultural record. Among these are nonprofit organizations such as the HSP, university libraries (Landau and Savedoff stole from Yale and Columbia, among others), and the federal government of the United States. The Library of Congress (an agency of the legislative branch) was another targeted institution, and when the thieves were caught, the investigative arm of the National Records and Archives Administration, with help from the Federal Bureau of Investigation, took charge of the complicated process of returning thousands of stolen materials to many different institutions. All of the documents were taken to the National Archives in College Park, Maryland, where they were inventoried, placed in acid-free folders, and stored until they could be returned to their owners. So for at least a brief period of time, a small part of Keats's legacy was under the aegis of the United States government—just one more example of Americans being true friends of Keats.[27]

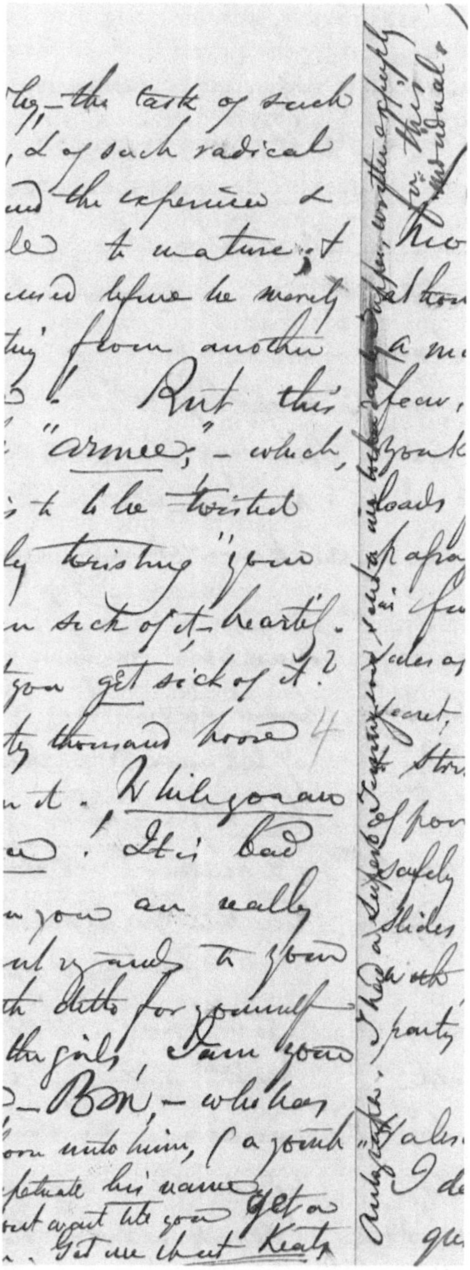

FIGURE 2. Letter from Brantz Mayer to Frank Marx Etting. (Frank Marx Etting Papers, March 18, 1869; Historical Society of Pennsylvania)

Keats's American story first began two hundred years ago, when his brother and sister-in-law left England for the wilds of Kentucky in the summer of 1818. As mentioned, Keats's transatlantic correspondence contains some of his most memorable musings, particularly on the nature of the epistolary medium itself. While in the content of the November 12 letter Keats does briefly lament the difficulties of communicating across the ocean (he writes that "the Posts [are] so uncertain"[28]), we garner a more vivid picture of those difficulties thanks to what the material letter tells us about its own movements. Traces of the voyage, including specific geographical coordinates, still exist and point toward the letter's complicated making and transmission (see fig. 3). In addition to the address written by Keats — "Mr George Keats / Louisville / Kentucky" — there are four endorsements in different hands on what was the outside of the folded sheet. The first was written and signed by John Capper, of the firm of Capper and Haslewood, through whom Keats sent several of his America-bound letters. Capper noted that the letter was sent on the ship "the William via New York," information that helps us reconstruct a history of the letter's movement in a way that is often lost to us with archival letters.[29] Two other marks on the letter offer specifics about where, when, and how it traveled. Remarkably, on February 16, 1820, someone named Dane W. Threlkeld noted the *William*'s coordinates — "Lat. 40.23 N / Long. 72 W.," which would place it "about fifty miles south of Montauk, Long Island," according to Hyder Edward Rollins, editor of *The Letters of John Keats*. The next mark ("Edgartown M^s Feb 23 Ship 27") locates the letter one week later, still on the *William*, now at Edgartown, Massachusetts, on Martha's Vineyard. As Rollins suggests, the ship likely encountered bad weather on its way to New York and turned back to Edgartown.[30]

Using these paratextual traces on the letter, and supplementing them with other existing textual records, we can place the letter in a broader network of travels and interactions. What results is a surprisingly full catalogue of moments, places, and events within which our humble Keats letter surfaces and enters a knowable cultural record. First there is the ship, the *William*, about which many records exist. For instance, notices in several New York newspapers announced the arrival of the *William* in New York on February 26, 1820. On the same day, the *Commercial Advertiser* wrote that the ship was "56 days from London" and that it "Spoke off the Isle of Wight, the needles bearing north, ship Rosseau, of Philadelphia, 126 days from Batavia, bound to Amsterdam." The newspaper also

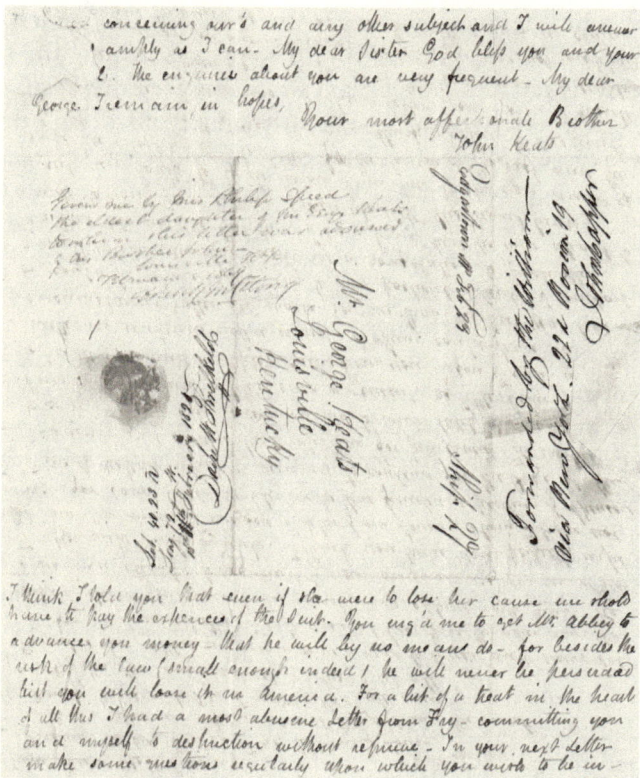

FIGURE 3. Letter from John Keats to George Keats with added notes in a variety of hands on what was the outside address panel. (Frank Marx Etting Papers, November 12, 1819; Historical Society of Pennsylvania)

contains a small piece of information concerning Dane W. Threlkeld: he appears to have been a servant traveling with a "Mrs Ellis and family."[31] Why he would have noted on Keats's letter the ship's latitude and longitude on February 16, 1820, remains a mystery, but it nonetheless functions as an illustrative moment when the letter's transit was interrupted, leaving the unmarked space of its aqueous passage and, for a moment, reentering the realm of signification. While we can speculatively reconstruct some of this letter's movements and makings, this must always occur with a high level of uncertainty.

This newspaper notice also serves as a reminder that when we situate Keats's letter in the global postal network, we situate it in the network of imperial commerce. The *Commercial Advertiser* notes the *William*'s encounter with the *Rousseau*, which was owned by the famed, wealthy Philadelphian Stephen Girard. Girard's ship was making the trip from Batavia, now Jakarta, to Amsterdam when it passed the *William* off the Isle of Wight, probably sometime in early January 1820, around the same time that George Keats was returning to England from America because he had not been able to secure money through his brother due to delays with the post. All of these details are partial, of course, and they require a sort of "greeting of the Spirit to make them wholly exist"—to make them affect our understanding of this letter or of Keats's correspondence more generally.[32] But particularly in a multimedia environment, we are well equipped to unearth and re-present materials such as these. Doing so does not and ought not create a seamless narrative. Instead, following the circulations of manuscripts—movements in the past, present, and future—can construct a discontinuous archive of materials that point toward the meanings of an object that will remain always to some degree closed to us.

Another archaeological finding related to this particular object helps us recapture some sense of how transatlantic circulation continued after letters reached the shore. Two days after the *William*'s arrival in port, on Monday, February 28, the *Mercantile Advertiser* ran the same notice from the *Commercial Advertiser* with the addendum: "The letters by the William were put into the Post Office at Old Town, and have not yet reached town."[33] "Old Town" refers to Brooklyn, which means that Keats's letter required more travel by water before reaching Manhattan ("town") and then proceeding to the rest of its journey. For a brief period, at least over the weekend of February 26–27, 1820, we know that Keats's letter spent some time at the hardware store/post office owned by Joel Bunce and Thomas Birdsall, the latter of whom was postmaster at the time. Their building was located at the corner of Fulton Street and Front Street, which Henry Reed Stiles discussed in his 1869 *History of the City of Brooklyn*.[34] Today that site is an empty lot located more or less directly under the Brooklyn Bridge. We know something about the building's appearance in 1820 thanks to the painter Francis Guy, who worked out of a studio at that location and enjoyed his view so much that he painted several different versions of the scene, at least five of which still exist. The version owned by the Brooklyn Museum, titled *Winter Scene in Brooklyn*, shows in clear detail the very building where Keats's letter waited before continuing westward to Kentucky (see fig. 4). The lower entrance of the large yellow building dominating the painting's right side

FIGURE 4. Francis Guy's *Winter Scene in Brooklyn* (ca. 1819–20). The building on the right was the hardware store and post office where Keats's November 12, 1819, letter was held. Oil on canvas, 58 ⅜ × 74 ⁹⁄₁₆ inches (148.2 x 189.4 cm). (97.13; Brooklyn Museum, transferred from the Brooklyn Institute of Arts and Sciences to the Brooklyn Museum)

has two signs posted over it, attesting to the dual-purpose nature of the location: the upper sign reading "Post Office" and the lower "Thoˢ W. Birdsallˢ / Hardware Store." Given that Guy may still have been working on this painting in February 1820, we can go so far as to imagine that Keats's letter sat within those walls while Guy completed his painting. In a sense, we can assert that the painting mediates more than this imagined winter scene—it also participates in mediating for us part of the past of Keats's letter.

As we can see, this single manuscript letter conveys much to us about its own making and movements. The ink on the paper tells us about the people involved in its journey, as well as when and where it became momentarily fixed in time and space, both on its initial voyage and when it began its slow march toward finding an archival home in Philadelphia.[35] The letter also harbors many secrets. Using materials such as digital databases, to which I have access thanks to my university affiliation, and also publicly available resources like HathiTrust and Google Maps, we can begin to tell some of those secrets. The speculative narratives that emerge are not stories of singular times and places, but of networks of relations spreading across decades and centuries, across continents and oceans, and across a wide array of media objects. But we should not assume that such narratives are only available from a twenty-first century media perspective. What the movements of Keats's November 1819 letter show is the extent to which its existence *then* was a networked one, even if *now* it exists within a network of different media. That network almost lost a central node when Landau and Savedoff betrayed the trust of so many public institutions of cultural memory. What this letter's theft and recovery shows is that as our digital tools, resources, and platforms change the way we work with manuscripts and other materials of the past, we must still insist on a commitment to the material supports that have gotten us to this point, and on which we will continue to rely in the future. Only by bringing material texts together with traditional archival structures and emerging digital methods can we arrive at the new knowledge about historical manuscripts that twenty-first-century resources make possible.

Notes

1. McGann, *A New Republic of Letters*, 1.
2. Many thanks to those involved in the project thus far, especially my founding coeditors: Anne McCarthy, Ian Newman, Kate Singer, Emily Stanback, and Michael Theune.
3. Barnard, "Keats's Letters"; Thomson, "Keats's Letters"; Webb, "Cutting Figures"; Wolfson, "Keats the Letter-Writer."
4. For an overview of some of this scholarship, see Burkett, *Romantic Mediations*.
5. Igarashi, "Keats's Ways," 173.
6. Keats, *The Letters of John Keats*, 2:15.
7. Ibid., 2:58.
8. McGann, *A New Republic of Letters*, 168.
9. Siegert, *Relays*, 11.
10. Kirschenbaum, *Mechanisms*, 1.
11. Manning, *Poetics of Character*, 165.
12. Favret, *Romantic Correspondence*, 56.
13. McGann's *A New Republic of Letters* represents one significant voice in this conversation. In the realm of Romanticism and nineteenth-century liter-

ature more broadly, Andrew Stauffer has also written extensively on the effects of mass digitization efforts: see esp. Stauffer, "My Old Sweethearts."

14. McGann, *A New Republic of Letters*, 123.
15. The letter has in the past been dated either November 22 or November 19, 1819. The former date is due to the endorsement written on it by John Capper—the merchant through whom Keats sent the letter—who wrote "Forwarded by the William via New York. 22ᵈ Novem '19 John Capper." That date, however, refers to when Capper forwarded the letter, not when it was written. Keats wrote "Friday Evening / Novʳ" at the beginning of the letter, which leaves November 5, 12, and 19 as the three Fridays prior to November 22. Hyder Edward Rollins, editor of Keats's letters, decides on November 12 because Keats refers to William Hazlitt's "last Lecture," during which he quoted from Keats's "Sleep and Poetry." That lecture took place on November 5: see Keats, *The Letters of John Keats*, 2:228–30.
16. Sangster, "John Keats and Urban Time."
17. John Keats Collection, Houghton Library, Harvard University, Cambridge, MA, https://hollisarchives.lib.harvard.edu/repositories/24/resources/1309.
18. Sangster, "Creating the Online Plan."
19. Turley, "Keats Underway."
20. "Letter 16: To George and Tom Keats, 15 April 1817," *Keats Letters Project*, April 15, 2017, http://keatslettersproject.com/letters/gtk15apr1817.
21. Wickenheiser, "Fifty Years of Collecting."
22. McGann, *A New Republic of Letters*, 19.
23. Keats, "Ode to Psyche," 37, 50, 52, 60.
24. *How We Became Posthuman* is an influential early example of work analyzing the tendency toward what N. Katherine Hayles calls an "ideology of disembodiment" and the way that "the body's dematerialization depends in complex and highly specific ways on the *embodied* circumstances that an ideology of dematerialization would obscure": Hayles, *How We Became Posthuman*, 193. More recent media scholars have continued to demonstrate the ways that seemingly "immaterial" computational processes and systems have their own material particularities, as with Matthew Kirschenbaum's focus on the hard disk drive in *Mechanisms*; Nicole Starosielski's focus on the network of undersea cables which make most internet traffic possible in *The Undersea Network*; or Jussi Parikka's focus on the geological requirements of computing in *A Geology of Media*.
25. Lee Arnold, senior director, Library and Collections, Historical Society of Pennsylvania, in discussion with the author, October 12, 2016. Special thanks to Lee Arnold for agreeing to be interviewed so I could learn more about this case. Details of the case mentioned here and elsewhere in this essay come from that interview, unless noted otherwise. The story did gain

some national attention when the thefts occurred, so several accounts exist in major newspapers, many of which can still be found online. I also thank Kaitlyn Pettengill, digital services archivist at the HSP, with whom I corresponded in the process of requesting images of the Keats manuscript and who first informed me of the Landau case.
26. Brantz Mayer to Colonel Frank Marx Etting, March 18, 1869, Etting Papers, Historical Society of Pennsylvania, Philadelphia. The Tennyson autograph mentioned by Mayer now resides at the Buffalo and Erie County Public Library and is printed in Lang and Shannon, *The Letters of Alfred Lord Tennyson*, 518.
27. For an account of the significance of Keats's reception in America, see Rowland, "Loving, Knowing, and Illustrating Keats."
28. Keats, *The Letters of John Keats*, 2:229.
29. John Keats to George Keats, November 12, 1819, Historical Society of Pennsylvania. I quote directly from the manuscript for this and the letter's other paratextual marks, since I differ slightly from Rollins's transcriptions in Keats, *The Letters of John Keats*, 2:228.
30. Ibid., 2:229
31. "Port of New-York," *Commercial Advertiser* (New York), vol. 23, no. 60, February 26, 1820.
32. Keats, *The Letters of John Keats*, 1:243.
33. "Port of New-York," *Mercantile Advertiser* (New York), no. 8995, February 28, 1820.
34. Stiles, *A History of the City of Brooklyn*, 58–59.
35. When Frank Marx Etting received the letter as a gift from Emma Keats Speed, the poet's niece, he wrote this inscription perpendicular to Threlkeld's coordinates: "Given me by Mrs Philip Speed / the eldest daughter of Mr George Keats / to whom this letter was addressed— / by his Brother John— / Louisville KY— / February 1869— / Frank M. Etting."

Works Cited

Barnard, John. "Keats's Letters: 'Remembrancing and Enchaining.'" In *The Cambridge Companion to Keats*, edited by Susan Wolfson, 120–34. Cambridge: Cambridge University Press, 2001.

Burkett, Andrew. *Romantic Mediations: Media Theory and British Romanticism*. Albany: State University of New York Press, 2016.

Favret, Mary. *Romantic Correspondence: Women, Politics and the Fiction of Letters*. Cambridge: Cambridge University Press, 1993.

Hayles, N. Katherine. *How We Became Posthuman: Virtual Bodies in Cybernetics, Literature, and Informatics*. Chicago: University of Chicago Press, 1999.

Igarashi, Yohei. "Keats's Ways: The Dark Passages of Mediation and Why He Gives Up *Hyperion*." *Studies in Romanticism* 53, no. 2 (Summer 2014): 171–93.

Keats, John. *The Letters of John Keats, 1814–1821*, 2 vols., edited by Hyder Edward Rollins. Cambridge, MA: Harvard University Press, 1958.

———. "Ode to Psyche." In *Keats's Poetry and Prose*, edited by Jeffrey N. Cox, 463–64. New York: W. W. Norton, 2009.

Kirschenbaum, Matthew. *Mechanisms: New Media and the Forensic Imagination*. Cambridge, MA: MIT Press, 2008.

Lang, Cecil Y., and Edgar F. Shannon Jr., eds. *The Letters of Alfred Lord Tennyson, Volume 2: 1851–70*. Cambridge, MA: Harvard University Press, 1987.

Manning, Susan. *Poetics of Character: Transatlantic Encounters, 1700–1900*. Cambridge: Cambridge University Press, 2013.

McGann, Jerome. *A New Republic of Letters: Memory and Scholarship in the Age of Digital Reproduction*. Cambridge, MA: Harvard University Press, 2014.

Parikka, Jussi. *A Geology of Media*. Minneapolis: University of Minnesota Press, 2015.

Rowland, Ann Wierda. "Loving, Knowing, and Illustrating Keats: The Louis Arthur Holman Collection of Keats Iconography." In *Transatlantic Literature and Author Love in the Nineteenth Century*, edited by Paul Westover and Ann Wierda Rowland, 267–92. Basingstoke, U.K.: Palgrave Macmillan, 2016.

Sangster, Matthew. "Creating the Online Plan." *Romantic London*. http://www.romanticlondon.org/the-online-plan.

———. "John Keats and Urban Time." *The Keats Letters Project*. Nov. 1, 2016. http://keatslettersproject.com/correspondence/john-keats-and-urban-time.

Siegert, Bernhard. *Relays: Literature as an Epoch of the Postal System*, translated by Kevin Repp. Stanford, CA: Stanford University Press, 1999.

Starosielski, Nicole. *The Undersea Network*. Durham, NC: Duke University Press, 2015.

Stauffer, Andrew. "My *Old Sweethearts*: On Digitization and the Future of the Print Record." In *Debates in the Digital Humanities 2016*, edited by Matthew K. Gold and Lauren F. Klein, 218–29. Minneapolis: University of Minnesota Press, 2016.

Stiles, Henry Reed. *A History of the City of Brooklyn: Including the Old Town and Village of Brooklyn, the Town of Bushwick, and the Village and City of Williamsburgh*. Brooklyn, NY, 1869.

Thomson, Heidi. "Keats's Letters: 'A Wilful and Dramatic Exercise of Our Minds towards Each Other.'" *Keats-Shelley Review* 25 (September 2011): 160–74.

Turley, Richard Marggraf. "Keats Underway." *Keats Letters Project*, April 15, 2017. http://keatslettersproject.com/correspondence/keats-underway.

Webb, Timothy. "'Cutting Figures': Rhetorical Strategies in Keats's Letters." In *Keats: Bicentenary Readings*, edited by Michael O'Neill, 144–69. Edinburgh: Edinburgh University Press, 1997.

Wickenheiser, Robert J. "Fifty Years of Collecting: The Collector and His Books." *Princeton University Library Chronicle* 38 (Winter–Spring 1977): 84–85.

Wolfson, Susan. "Keats the Letter-Writer: Epistolary Poetics." *Romanticism Past and Present* 6, no. 2 (1982): 43–61.

Cooking Hannah Woolley's Printed Recipes from a Manuscript Recipe Book
UPenn Ms. Codex 785

MARISSA NICOSIA

I BURNED THE lemon cakes.[1] This is a risk that comes with cooking from a seventeenth-century recipe. The vague instructions that are typical of early modern recipes could lead any accomplished, modern cook to struggle, let alone someone like me: a scholar of English literature and an adventurous home cook working on a project that combines these skills. But this challenge—cooking from early modern manuscripts and learning from that practice—is a central concern of the ongoing public food history project I am working on called *Cooking in the Archives: Updating Early Modern Recipes (1600–1800) in a Modern Kitchen*.[2] The project seeks to identify, research, and cook recipes from manuscript recipe books produced in the early modern era.[3] Since June 2014, I have been testing recipes and documenting my experiments on my website rarecooking.com. Recipe manuscripts and printed cookbooks line the shelves of research libraries and, especially in recent years, have become important resources for scholars interested in food studies and the history of science and medicine. These recipes belong in the kitchen as well as the library. After all, what are recipes if not instructions for cooking? If, as Pamela H. Smith shows in the ongoing Making and Knowing Project at Columbia University, following how-to instructions from our archives can produce historical knowledge, then cooking is a valuable methodological tool for the study of early modern culinary manuscripts and printed books.[4] I began from a place of wondering how I might prepare these historical recipes in a modern kitchen and what they might taste like. These were my questions when I sat in the Kislak Center for Special Collections, Rare Books, and Manuscripts at the University of Pennsylvania, opened Ms. Codex 785, and first saw the recipe for "Lemmon Cakes."[5] I wondered how they would taste.

As I researched and prepared the "Lemmon Cakes," I learned that the recipe was closely copied from Hannah Woolley's well-known cookery book, *The Queen-like Closet or Rich Cabinet* (1670).[6] Woolley's recipes were a touchstone for cooks in the late seventeenth and early eighteenth centuries, when this manuscript was most likely compiled. Moreover, the manuscript's compiler not only copied Woolley's recipe for "Lemmon Cakes" but also copied, in a single opening early in the manuscript, recipes for the decadent banqueting dish "Portugal Eggs"; for a useful preserve, "Marmalaid of Apricocks"; and for a handy recipe for wafers.[7] Modern cooks know instinctively that recipes are not always new; so did those in the eighteenth century. The compiler of Ms. Codex 785 selected a few of Woolley's recipes to complement other items that they had already collected in their recipe book.[8]

On the one hand, Ms. Codex 785 is a simple case of manuscript copying print rather than preceding print. As the Multigraph Collective recently wrote, even recipe books, "These highly domestic books, which exist without any ambition for print, are not somehow cordoned off from it: such miscellanies could contain both original material and extracts or complete texts copied from both handwritten and printed sources."[9] At the same time, limiting this case to manuscript following print obscures the other afterlife Woolley's recipes have had in, and beyond, Ms. Codex 785. Her recipes were copied into a manuscript that cooks used, and might still use, to prepare food. Woolley's recipes were printed, copied into manuscript, possibly cooked in the seventeenth and eighteenth centuries, and, more recently, prepared in my kitchen. In this essay, I consider Ms. Codex 785 as a case study for print afterlives in early modern manuscripts by tracing two aspects: considering the dynamic between Woolley's popular printed cookbook and the recipe manuscript, and cooking Woolley's recipes. Moreover, I discuss how cooking these recipes is a method for manuscript studies that sheds light on concepts of taste. After testing recipes for "Lemmon Cakes" and "Portugal Eggs," two of the recipes that can be found in both the manuscript and Woolley's book, I have as many questions as answers—questions that I asked only because I was cooking. In this essay I show that cooking from manuscripts both returns them to their original purpose and forces scholars to grapple with the results. Recipes are not simply texts but, rather, instructions for action, a fact that encountering them in a library reading room often obscures. I understand Woolley's dramatic dish of Portugal eggs far better after preparing it than I did when I first transcribed the recipe. Cooking recipes from early modern manuscripts has forced me to consider and reconsider practices, ingredients, methods, and tastes that I never would have understood through transcription, codicology, book history, and traditional bibliography.

This approach should not be entirely unfamiliar to scholars of the early modern era. We constantly encounter dramatic, poetic, and prose texts that were performed, read aloud, set to music, copied onto objects, and adapted among literary forms. Moreover, the field of performance studies has long asserted that premodern plays, songs, masques, and entertainments come to new life with each performance.[10] A recipe is not all that different from a play—it simply requires different materials.[11] Moreover, decades ago Hugh Amory proposed the methodological concept of "ethnobibliography," or a bibliography that shares contextual concerns with ethnohistory.[12] Amory coined the term when he encountered a medicine bundle excavated from a Pequot cemetery that contained, among other items, a page from a Bible.[13] Traditional bibliographical methods may have enabled Amory to determine from which edition of the Bible the page was extracted, but it told him neither what this Bible meant to the community that extracted the page nor why it was included in a burial. To consider these questions, Amory proposed an ethnobibliographical method that was attentive to context, use, cultural practices, and other aspects of ethnohistory. When our objects of study exceed established methodologies—as they did in Amory's case—then our methods must adapt. Cooking from culinary manuscripts is a kind of ethnobibliography that brings together traditional study of the material text and maker's knowledge.[14]

The discipline of history also has a long history of grappling with concepts of making and reenactment. In the introduction to their collection *Ways of Making and Knowing*, Pamela H. Smith, Amy R. W. Meyers, and Harold J. Cook note that, although the artisans employed by early modern states have been objects of study for historians of science and art, and while there has been "a growing interest in using material culture as a method to connect head and hand," the hand has been far less studied than one might expect.[15] Any division between abstract knowledge and "how to" know-how would not be readily accepted by early modern artisans, medical practitioners, and scientists.[16] Discussing the modern glassmaker Ian Hankey's reconstruction of Venetian glassmaking, Smith, Meyers, and Cook show "how very difficult—but how very important—it is for historians to consider carefully the material things with which actors once worked and from which they derived tacit skills and tacit knowledge that they subsequently attempted to articulate in the form of concepts."[17] Katherine Johnson's work on historical reenacting, historiography, and bodily knowledge engages with similar issues and more directly addresses the biases against re-enacting within history as a discipline.[18] Johnson points out that "while the ethnographic turn in history facilitated the study of numerous Indigenous communities, many of which have a rich repertoire of bodily, performance-based histories, this interest rarely extends to embodied practices closer to home" and, in turn, discounts reenactment as a form of knowledge in cases in which other archives, sources, and accounts are available. In the face of this resistance within the discipline, the recent turn to performance and making demonstrates a reevaluation and revaluing of embodied knowledge.[19]

Humanities disciplines are not the only place where scholars are rethinking the connection between knowledge and practice. In sociology, Loïc Wacquant has called for a methodological turn to "carnal sociology" or "enactive ethnography" to examine the link between culture and cognition through practice.[20] Wacquant claims that this method highlights "the primacy of embodied practical knowledge arising out of and continuously enmeshed in webs of action, upon which discursive mastery comes to be grafted."[21] Building on Wacquant's work, Karen A. Cerulo's research on scent and cognition suggests "that neither brain nor mind nor body can, independently, explain the deciphering of smell" and thus a holistic approach is necessary to investigate "olfactory meaning."[22] Embodied research practices such as enactive ethnography show that knowledge is the preserve not only of the mind, but also of the body.

As scholars of early modern recipe culture have insisted, receipts for culinary and medicinal preparations required a range of skills in botany, distillation, brewing, chemistry, and, especially, handwriting.[23] These are the very types of embodied knowledge that Wacquant calls "the reality and potency of *carnal know-how*, the bottom-up, visceral grasp of the social world."[24] These manual literacies were necessary for caring for the family and a means to participate in society at large. In her study of women's friendship networks, *Female Alliances: Gender, Identity, and Friendship in Early Modern Britain*, Amanda Herbert argues that these skills were essential for women navigating social networks wherein a gift of something like preserved quinces accompanied by a trusted receipt was a prized form of intellectual and social capital.[25] Most recently, Rebecca Laroche and Jennifer Munroe have considered recipes through an ecofeminist lens to show how they record social relations as well as relations between human and nonhuman actors such as animals, plants, and climate.[26] Recipe books were repositories for gendered knowledge that connected cooks to the world around them and enabled performances of preparation.

Making Manuscript Recipe Books

Manuscript recipe books are thus prompts for skilled activity. "Recipe book" is truly an umbrella term for a messy category of household manuscripts that were compiled and used in England between the sixteenth century and the nineteenth century.[27] To earn this name instead of another moniker in the slippery taxonomy of early modern manuscript culture, the majority of the contents must be "receipts" for medicine and food. Many of these books also include household accounts, birth and death dates of family members, poems, prayers, proverbs, and other miscellaneous content. Some are small and covered up to the margin on every page; some are left mostly blank after a datable period of use; some are individual scribal productions that later give way to an array of other users; some were used for more than a century; some change in orientation partway through; some contain detailed indices that the user has attempted to keep up to date over a period of use; some are large; some are in an oblong format; and some include notes on specific recipes—source attributions, ambiguous ticks, or an occasional statement about the effectiveness or failure of a dish or cure.

Early modern recipes are more suggestive than prescriptive in their structure, which implies that cooks would possess tacit skills and might also innovate or adapt recipes as needed. Recipes usually took the form of a narrative paragraph that combined ingredients, amounts, and instructions for preparation. As Ken Albala reminds us in *Cooking in Europe, 1250–1650*, "The modern recipe format is an invention of the twentieth century. It is advantageous because it offers a list of ingredients with precise measurements and explicit instruction, along with cooking times and temperatures."[28] Early modern recipes vary between incredible precision in weight and volume, on the one hand, and entirely customizable adjustment to the cook's taste, on the other. Moreover, cooking early modern recipes on a hearth with variable fire types and temperatures demanded a skilled cook who could manage heat effectively. Early modern recipe books assume a high level of skill from their users: the servant cooks and ladies of the house who were responsible for the nourishment and welfare of the family.[29]

In addition, very few books divide what we would now call medicine from what we would now call food. Narrative recipes compiled in recipe books covered topics from furniture varnish to sugar candy, face cream to macaroons, restorative tonics to home brewing. Elaine Leong writes, "Many families had a designated notebook in which to record, create and communicate these necessary bits of practical knowledge and hundreds of such books now survive in archives and libraries, each representing the varying needs, interests and aspirations of generations of men and women."[30] While recipe books have often been thought of as the exclusive purview of women—and, indeed, care of the body both gastronomical and medical was women's labor in the home—recent work by scholars such as Leong suggests that the contents of these books were fundamentally collaborative at the level of the family, with men and women contributing recipes to and using recipes from these books.[31]

We know what we know about England's food culture from herbals, household accounts and inventories, court records, dietaries, paintings and engravings, kitchen architecture, garden designs, and menus. But first and foremost, we obtain this information from printed and manuscript recipe books. Food in early modern England was a site of pleasure and danger, the locus of many ailments and the source of many cures. A failed harvest could mean starvation, so preserving food was a priority in early modern households. Fresh fruit such as apples, currants, and pears, and vegetables such as green beans, cucumbers, and mushrooms were preserved as jams, jellies, pickles, and pies. Fresh herbs were used to season dishes and were distilled with alcohol to make spirits of violets and rosewater and tinctures of rosemary. Meat dishes took a nose-to-tail approach and used the entire animal. But despite the prevalence of thrift, printed and manuscript recipe books also prized decadent concoctions, rare or expensive spices, and remarkable skills.[32] Products that came from farther afield were likely consumed only by the very wealthy. For instance, wheels of Parmesan cheese imported from Italy were given as gifts among royalty: Pope Julius II reportedly gave a hundred Parmesan cheeses to King Henry VIII.[33] The diarist and epicure Samuel Pepys buried a wheel of Parmesan cheese along with wine in his garden when the Fire of London threatened his property. Spices such as nutmeg, mace, cloves, cinnamon, and pepper arrived in England from the East Indies. Citrus such as oranges, lemons, and thick-skinned floral citrons in fresh or dried form came from southern Europe.[34] Sugarcane grown and processed by enslaved Africans in the West Indies arrived in England in hard cakes ready to be scraped into elaborate candies and cakes.[35]

This growing range of ingredients shaped English recipe culture in manuscript and in print. In *Recipes for Thought*, Wendy Wall shows that printed recipe books saw a unique popularity in England between 1573 and 1630, while continental publications more frequently took the form of dietaries.[36] These printed guides offered instructions for cooking and brewing, setting the table and managing servants, healing the sick, and preparing confectionary. Wall argues that over the course of the printed English recipe book's popularity, authors crafted ideas of the "good housewife," the professional cook, and, in later decades, English culinary identity.[37] However, manuscript recipe books disrupt Wall's timeline because they are difficult to place into any of these overarching trends. Each manuscript recipe book is unique in its contents, organization, size, and duration of use. I have consulted and cooked from many recipe manuscripts produced between the early 1600s and the 1820s and can attest to their infinite variety.

Although manuscript recipe books vary so greatly that it is difficult to establish standards or norms, Ms. Codex 785 is not an especially complicated case. An inscription inside the front cover—"November the 19 1726 paide the poores rates and tel Lady day next"—a few dates in the manuscript itself, and the style of handwriting and binding, date this manuscript to the late seventeenth and early eighteenth centuries. Most of Ms. Codex 785 is written in a neat italic hand, with a few additions by three later users on the final folios. The majority of the manuscript is either a scribal production or the handiwork of its original user. Either way, most of the manuscript was created at one time, and the efficacy notes marking best recipes for various dishes are copied in the same deliberate hand as the recipes themselves. The final pages of the manuscript feature an alphabetical index that catalogued the first 215 recipes in one hand and was subsequently updated to include the later additions. The inclusion of recipes from Woolley's late seventeenth-century printed books also helps locate this manuscript in time and in traditions.

"Lemmon Cakes" and "Portugal Eggs" are among the plethora of recipes that Hannah Woolley committed to paper in her career as, essentially, a seventeenth-century lifestyle guru. Woolley lived from 1622 to 1674 and throughout her married life and widowhood she made a living as an author of recipe books and a medical practitioner, as well as giving private instruction in these fields.[38] Woolley, along with authors Robert May and William Rabisha, set the standard for culinary writing in the last decades of the seventeenth century.[39] Although she is best known as a purveyor of culinary and medical knowledge, her works also provided guidance on etiquette, homemaking, and interior design.

The idea that knowledge is produced through practice—making and knowing, embodied skill—would not have been unfamiliar to Woolley. Indeed, she advertised her availability for lessons to supplement her printed instructional works. The poem "To all Ingenious Ladies and Gentlewomen" that prefaces the 1674 supplement to *The Queen-like Closet* argues for making as a kind of learning. Woolley insists that her readers will improve their skill if they "practice what I teach" and move beyond any errors or inconsistencies in the text itself.[40] The text can only provide suggestions for practices, but the body is necessary to enact them. Furthermore, she describes the writing and learning process as one of distillation and gathering, using a conventional but powerful image of a bee sucking nectar from flowers and producing honey. Like eager bees, her readers will transform the nectar of written instructions into the honey of skilled cookery:

> The Quintescence of what I have I send;
> Accept it really, as I intend,
> For to accomplish those who want the skill,
> Their Tables to adorn and Closets fill.[41]

Through reading and cooking, attention and practice, Woolley's readers will develop the skills she promises—skills that they simultaneously lack and desire. They will find pleasure and knowledge, method and portable skill, pantries full of delicacies and a personal repertoire of talents. Woolley always knew that a recipe was useful only if it was used. Printed and manuscript recipe books are replete with instructions for making and thus are well suited to enactive methods of study.

Making "Portugal Eggs"

Given Woolley's widespread popularity, it is not surprising that her recipes appear in a contemporary manuscript recipe book such as Ms. Codex 785. The four recipes from Woolley's *Queen-like Closet* appear early in the manuscript. The compiler first copied "Portugal Eggs," then "Lemmon Cakes," "Marmalaid of Apricocks," and "Wafers" (see figs. 1–2). We will never know whether the compiler was copying these recipes directly from Woolley's printed book or which of the five possible editions of Woolley they may have used.[42] The compiler may also have seen these recipes in another culinary manuscript or a letter, but the order of the last three recipes in the group matches the order in which they were originally printed in Woolley's cookbook.[43] "Portugal Eggs," however, appears a few pages before the other three recipes in *The Queen-like Closet*. The compiler of Ms. Codex 785 may specifically have sought out "Portugal Eggs." I was also intrigued by the recipe and decided to try to prepare it. It reads:

> To make portugal Eggs
>
> Take a very large Dish with a broad brim lay in
> it some naples Biscake in the form of a star, then
> put so much sack into the Dish as you think
> the biscakes will drink up, ~~on~~ then slick them
> full with little peices of preserv'd orange, and
> green Citron peele, and strow Store of French
> Comfits over them of Divers Colours, then butter
> some Eggs and lay them here and there upon
> the biscakes then fill up the hollow places in
> the dish with severall colour'd jellyes and
> round about the brim thereof lay Laurell
> Leaves guilt with Leaf Gold, lay them slanting
> and between the Leaves severall colour'd Jellies.[44]

As I embarked upon preparing Hannah Woolley's recipe for Portugal eggs, I could have used some further guidance from the author herself. I needed to make six subrecipes in total to assemble this dish, and four of these components needed to be made at least a day in advance to set, cool, or dry. Without some modern tricks, such as using powdered gelatin for the jelly, this would have been an even more labor-intensive endeavor.

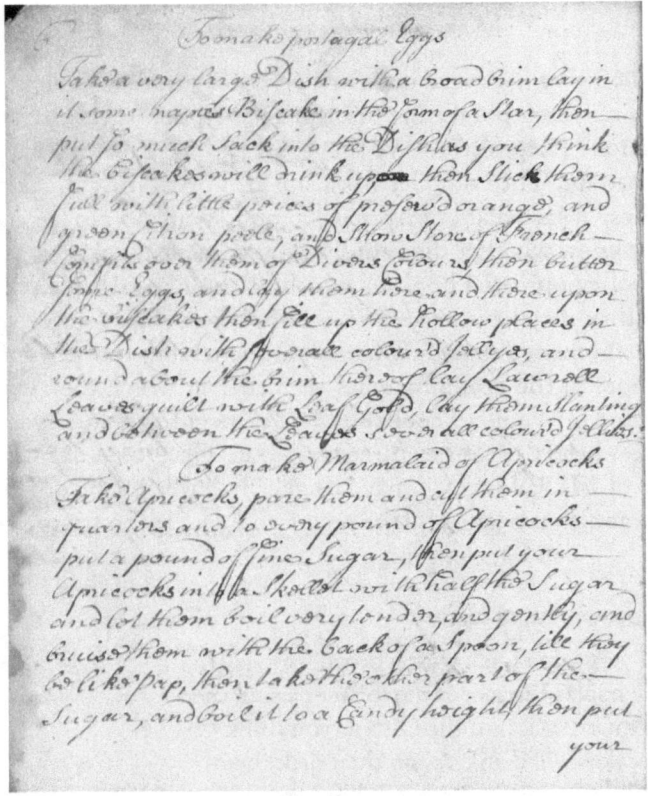

FIGURE 1. Recipe for "Portugal Eggs." ("Recipe book," 1705–1726, Ms. Codex 785, 6; Kislak Center for Special Collections, Rare Books, and Manuscripts, University of Pennsylvania)

My preparation of Portugal eggs was visually striking, yet was one of the more extreme flavor combinations I have encountered so far in this project, bringing together sweet, savory, and rich elements (see fig. 3). This dish is most at home at a banquet. As Albala notes, "banquet" derives from the word for the boards on which large meals were served.[45] The food historian Ivan Day has called these spreads "Tempting Tables."[46] According to Albala's account in *The Banquet: Dining in the Great Courts of Late Renaissance Europe*, English banquets usually consisted of cold dishes served after or between other courses.[47] Indeed, Portugal eggs were among the many dishes served at the coronation of James II.[48] Woolley's Portugal eggs are decidedly on trend for a Restoration-era banquet.

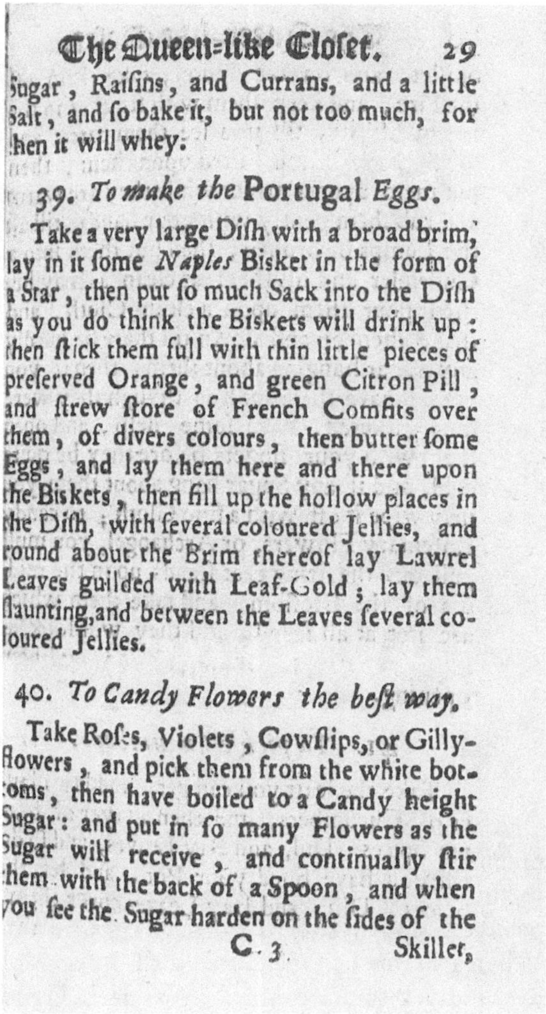

> **The Queen-like Closet.** 29
>
> Sugar, Raisins, and Currans, and a little Salt, and so bake it, but not too much, for then it will whey.
>
> **39. *To make the* Portugal Eggs.**
>
> Take a very large Dish with a broad brim, lay in it some *Naples* Bisket in the form of a Star, then put so much Sack into the Dish as you do think the Biskets will drink up: then stick them full with thin little pieces of preserved Orange, and green Citron Pill, and strew store of French Comfits over them, of divers colours, then butter some Eggs, and lay them here and there upon the Biskets, then fill up the hollow places in the Dish, with several coloured Jellies, and round about the Brim thereof lay Lawrel Leaves guilded with Leaf-Gold; lay them flaunting, and between the Leaves several coloured Jellies.
>
> **40. *To Candy Flowers the best way.***
>
> Take Roses, Violets, Cowslips, or Gillyflowers, and pick them from the white bottoms, then have boiled to a Candy height Sugar: and put in so many Flowers as the Sugar will receive, and continually stir them with the back of a Spoon, and when you see the Sugar harden on the sides of the Skillet,

FIGURE 2. The recipe for "Portugal Eggs" in Hannah Woolley, *The Queenlike Closet or Rich Cabinet* (London, 1670). (W3282, 31–32; used by permission of the Folger Shakespeare Library)

Her contemporary Robert May also published recipes for "Portugal" and "Spanish" eggs in *The Accomplisht Cook* (1660).[49] Although these eggs may also have been intended for the banquet table, neither recipe harnesses the pageantry of Woolley's dish, which includes colored jellies, glistening comfits, and gilded laurel leaves. A plate of eggs and sweets, Woolley's Portugal eggs could easily hold its own among the pies and sculptured sugar subtleties.

FIGURE 3. My preparation of Portugal eggs.

Although I have made this all sound very complicated (and it is), read on and let me guide you through one way a cook using Ms. Codex 785 might prepare Woolley's elaborate recipe. As both the manuscript and printed recipe make clear, Portugal eggs are much more than an egg dish. When I decided to make this dish, I began by delineating the component parts: biscuits, candied citrus peel, "French Comfits" (sugar-coated seeds), jelly, buttered (that is, scrambled) eggs, and gilded laurel leaves.[50] To prepare the various components, I used recipes from the manuscript as well as from Woolley's cookbook. I adapted the recipes from Ms. Codex 785 for "Jelly of Hartshorn," or a jelly made from deer antler and flavored with lemon and cinnamon, and "the best bisket Cakes," as they are similar to recipes for the Naples biscuits the recipe calls for.[51] I experimented with a recipe for fennel comfits in Woolley's cookbook. I used a tried-and-true modern recipe for candied citrus peel. Finally, I decorated my dish with colorful, store-bought, sugarcoated fennel seeds and fresh bay leaves. In the essay's appendix, I provide complete transcriptions of the historical recipes I used, as well as my updated recipes.

This dish is fit for a feast. The flavors and textures were truly exceptional, if unfamiliar. The boozy cookies paired nicely with the candied peel and fennel comfits but clashed with the rich eggs. It made me wonder about the perfect forkful of this dish: should its many elements be eaten in combination or isolation? Was I supposed to try some eggs and then some sugary cake? Or should I eat a bit of everything in one cacophonous bite? The pale yellow, lemon-and-cinnamon-flavored jelly did not complement any of the other flavors. Since the manuscript and print sources insist only on the various colors of jelly, not the various flavors, savory aspic or even an orange-flavored sweet jelly might be a better pairing for the eggs and seasoned cake.

This dish of eggs and sweets challenged, perplexed, and delighted me. Only by putting these items on the same plate did I finally grasp the variety, the mélange, intended in Woolley's receipt copied into Ms. Codex 785. And only by thinking about this as a banqueting dish did it begin to make any sense at all. Banquets are about *Concordia discors*, variety, and performance—as are Portugal eggs.[52] I needed to experience the taste, smell, and sight of these eggs, biscuits, jellies, sugar sweets, and decorative laurels to make sense of their place in early modern food culture.

What else can we learn about early modern culinary books and manuscripts by using them? Perhaps not exactly as they were intended— Hannah Woolley did not have a blender or a gas range—but in the spirit of their composition? I knew that banqueting dishes celebrated variety, and by making Portugal eggs I sampled that array of textures and flavors by the forkful. By cooking in the archives, I hope to both transform and re-create dishes to consider what we can learn by experiencing them anew. I hope to do what Woolley asked of her readers: put both my culinary and book-history skills into action in the pursuit of pleasure and knowledge.

We have much more to learn about early modern and eighteenth-century manuscripts in general, and about messy, practical, domestic manuscripts in particular. With the current interest in transcribing and encoding early modern manuscripts, I hope scholars will discover more connections between print and manuscript recipe books so we can pursue diverse studies of the lives, and afterlives, of recipes. Moreover, I urge scholars to consider what might be gained by pursuing practical literature, such as cookbooks, through making, as well as reading, transcribing, contextualizing, and the other quotidian aspects of literary and historical inquiry. It may be messy; it may involve burned sugar; it may require guesswork; it may ultimately be inconclusive. But it may also be enlightening and delicious.

Appendix

"To make portugal eggs" using Ms. Codex 785 and Hannah Woolley's *Queen-like Closet*:

1. Biscuits (Ms. Codex 785, 5)

To make the best bisket Cakes

Take four new laid Eggs, leave out two of the
whites, beat them very well, then put in two
Spoonfulls of Rosewater, and beat them very
well together, then put in a pound of double
refin'd sugar beaten and search'd and beat
them together one hour, then put to them
one pound of fine flour, and beat them
together a good while, then put them upon
plates rubb'd over with butter, and set
them into the Oven as fast as you can
but have a care you do not bake them
too much.

This recipe was relatively straightforward to update. It makes about 24 cookies.

> 4 eggs (2 whole, 2 whites only)
> 2 tsp. rosewater
> 1 lb. sugar (2 ⅔ cups)
> 1 lb. flour (3 ⅔ cups)
> Butter or baking spray to coat the baking sheets

Preheat your oven to 350°F. Grease two baking sheets with butter or your preferred baking spray.

Beat the eggs in a large bowl. I used a hand mixer for this, but a standing mixer would also work well. Add the rosewater to the eggs and continue beating. Add the sugar and beat on a high setting until the mixture starts to look fluffy (about 1 minute). Add the flour in three batches, allowing each to mix in fully.

Shape the dough into rough ovals. I did this by picking up about 2 tbsp. of the dough and rolling it roughly in my hand. Make sure that you leave about a half-inch between the cookies, as they expand a lot as they cook.

Bake fifteen minutes. The bottom of the biscuits should be nicely browned and the top still a little spongy.

Eat immediately with a cup of tea or allow to cool on a rack before storing.

2. French Comfits (Woolley, *Queen-like Closet*, 157–59)

Comfits are sugar-coated seeds. Although I adapted Woolley's recipe to coat fennel seeds in sugar, I also could have used this method to candy coriander or caraway seeds.

> CCLV. How to cover all kinds of seeds, or little pieces of Spices, or Orange or Limon Pill, with Sugar for Comfits,
> First of all you must have a deep bottomed Bason of Brass or Latin, with two ears of Iron to hang it with two Cords, over some hot coals. You must also have a broad Pan to put Ashes in, and hot Coals upon them.
> You must have a Brass Ladle to let run the Sugar upon the Seeds.
> You must have a Slice of Brass to scrape away the Sugar from the sides of the hanging Bason if need be.
> Having all these things in readiness, do as followeth;
> Take fine white Sugar beaten, and let your seeds and Spice be dry then dry them again in your hanging Bason:
> Take to every two pounds of Sugar one quarter of a pound of Spices or Seeds, or such like.
> If it be Aniseeds, two pounds of Sugar to half a pound of Aniseeds, will be enough.
> Melt your Sugar in this manner; put in three Pounds of sugar into the Bason, and one Pint of water, stir it well till it be wet, then melt it very well and boil it very softly until it will stream from the Ladle like Turpentine, and not drop, then let it seeth no more, but keep it upon warm Embers, that it may run from the Ladle upon the seeds.
> Move the seeds in the hanging Bason so fast as you can or may, and with one hand, cast on half a Ladle full at a time of the hot sugar, and

rub the seeds with your other hand a pretty while, for that will make them take the sugar the better; and dry them well after every Coat.

Do thus at every Coat, not only in moving the Bason, but also with stirring of the Comfits with the one hand, and drying the same, in evrey [sic] hour you may make three pounds of Comfits; as the Comfits do increase in bigness, so you may take more Sugar in your Ladle to cast on:

But for plain Comfits, let your sugar be of a light decoction last, and of a high decoction first, and not too hot.

For crisp and ragged Comfets [sic], make your decoction so high, as that it may run from the Ladle, and let it fall a foot high or more from the Ladle, and the hotter you cast on your sugar, the more ragged will your Comfits be; also the Comfits will not take so much of the sugar, as upon a light decoction, and they will keep their raggedness long; this high decoction must serve for eight or ten Coats, and put on at every time but one Ladle full.

A quarter of a pound of Coriander seeds, and three pounds of sugar, will serve for very grear [sic] Comfits.

See that you keep your Sugar in the Bason always in good temper, that it burn not in Lumps, and if at any time it be too high boiled, put in a spoonful or two of water, and keep it warily with your Ladle, and let your fire be always very clear, when your Comfits be made, set them in Dishes upon Papers in the Sun or before the Fire, or in the Oven after Bread is drawn, for the space of one hour or two, and that will make them look very white.

This is a long and complex recipe. Here's what I did.

¼ cup sugar
⅓ cup water
1 tbsp. fennel seeds

In a small saucepan, bring the water and sugar to a boil.
   A) Add the fennel seeds and simmer for one minute.
   B) Strain the mixture to remove the fennel seeds, reserving the sugar syrup. Spread the seeds out on a plate and allow to cool for two minutes.

Bring the syrup back to boil and repeat the straining and simmering steps (A and B) as many times as you like.

I did this three times before the seeds were too sticky to work with. The seeds were sweeter each time they came out of the hot syrup and cooled. Woolley suggests eight to ten coats of sugar. However, Woolley also instructs you to roll the hot seeds in the syrup with your bare hands.

In any case, reserve the syrup at the end. This fennel-infused simple syrup is excellent in cocktails and adds a refreshing flavor to sparkling water.

Allow the seeds to cool completely. Store them in a glass or plastic container for future use.

3. Candied Citrus Peel

The method for making comfits includes a method for candying citrus peel. Instead of simplifying the recipe, as I did in the case of the comfits, I turned to a tried-and-true modern recipe.[53] The outcomes of the modern and early modern processes are similar.

> 1 cup orange peel, in strips
> ½ cup white sugar
> ¼ cup water

Cook the peel. Place peel in a large pot with the water. Bring to a boil and simmer for fifteen minutes. Remove peel.

Add water to ensure that you have one-quarter cup, but do not discard the orange-flavored cooking water. Add sugar to the water and bring to a boil. Place peel in sugar mixture and simmer for fifteen minutes. Remove peel with a slotted spoon and allow to dry on a wire rack overnight. Store the finished candied peel in an airtight container until you are ready to use it.

4. Various Jellies (Ms. Codex 785, 4)

To make Jelly of Hartshorne

Take a pound of Hartshorne and four quarts of
Water, lett it boil until it will Jelly, then take
it off, then take it off [sic], and strain it through a
Jelly bag, then put it into shellet with a
little mace and Cinnamon, season it with
Sugar to your taste. the whites of three Eggs

and the Juice of Lemmons, boil all these
together almost a quarter of an hour, then
put into your bagg a Roll of Lemmon peele,
pour out your Jelly into your bagg and set
Glasses under it to drop in, and lay warm
Cloths upon the bag that it may not cool
too fast; Slit some Lemmon peele in long slices
and put them into the glasses.

Inspired by the rich seasonings in the "Hartshorn Jelly" recipe, I prepared a lightly sweetened jelly infused with lemon and cinnamon. This sub-recipe must be made in advance because jelly needs to set in the refrigerator for at least three hours.

> 1 packet Knox Gelatin
> 1 cup water
> ¼ cup sugar
> The peel of one lemon cut into strips
> 1 cinnamon stick

Sprinkle the gelatin over one-quarter cup of the water in a medium-size bowl. Set aside.

Place the other ingredients and the remaining three-quarter cups water in a small saucepan. Bring this mixture to a boil. Once the sugar dissolves, reduce the heat to a simmer and allow to cook for another three to five minutes, until the mixture smells strongly of lemon and cinnamon. Discard the lemon peel and cinnamon stick. You can do this by scooping them out of the mixture or straining the whole thing and reserving the liquid.

Add the hot, fragrant liquid to the gelatin mix and stir to dissolve. Transfer your jelly mix to a flat-bottomed dish for easy shaping. I used a square, glass storage container for this.

Refrigerate for at least three hours before using.

5. Buttered Eggs

Buttered eggs are just an early modern way to talk about scrambled eggs cooked with butter and cream. Do not scramble the eggs until you have prepared all the other subrecipes and are ready to assemble the entire dish. See the "Portugal Eggs" recipe below for when in the process this component should be prepared and added to the banqueting plate.

> 2 eggs
> 3 tbsp. butter
> 3 tbsp. heavy cream
> Twist freshly ground black pepper

Whisk together the eggs and cream.
Melt the butter in a frying pan.
Add the egg mixture and stir the eggs until they are fluffy and cooked through to your preferred texture.

Portugal Eggs

Once your jelly is set, your biscuits are baked, and your citrus peel and seeds are candied, you are ready to begin to assemble Portugal eggs. The quantities below amply filled a standard dinner dish. Increase them if you plan to use a larger banqueting platter. The subrecipes produce enough ingredients for a significantly larger platter (or more small dishes), so feel free to adjust this recipe to the scale of your banquet.

> 5 biscuits
> 3 oz. sack
> 1 tbsp. comfits
> 3 tbsp. candied citrus peel
> 1 batch of buttered eggs
> 4 tbsp. jelly (or more to taste)
> 2–3 sprigs fresh bay leaves to garnish, gilded if you prefer

Arrange the biscuits in a star shape on your dish. Pour about 3 ounces of sack, or substitute brandy or sherry, over the biscuits. When the biscuits cannot absorb any more liquid, stop pouring.
Prepare the buttered eggs.
Return your attention to the main plate. Place comfits and candied orange peel on top of the soaked biscuits. Stick your candied peel into the biscuits or scatter it on top.
Add dollops of the buttered eggs to the plate.
In the remaining space on the plate, add jelly by the spoonful.

Arrange the bay leaves around the edge of the plate. Step back and admire your handiwork. Serve.

Notes

I thank Rachael Scarborough King for the opportunity to share this work at the "After Print" symposium in 2015 and for her precise and thoughtful feedback on earlier drafts. I also thank the cofounder of the *Cooking in the Archives* project, Alyssa Connell; my inspiring and enthusiastic mentor, Peter Stallybrass, for supporting the project when it was a mere proposal; Claire Falck, Carissa Harris, Joseph Malcomson, Lydia Pyne, Laura A. Orrico, Alisha R. Walters, Thomas Ward, and the anonymous readers who all made suggestions that improved this essay immensely; and the librarians at the Kislak Center for Special Collections, Rare Books, and Manuscripts at the University of Pennsylvania and the Folger Shakespeare Library for sharing their expertise and providing access to crucial materials.

1. Nicosia, "To Make Lemmon Cakes."
2. Nicosia, *Cooking in the Archives*.
3. There are a range of other projects and blogs that take on related challenges: see *The Recipes Project*, June 21, 2018, https://recipes.hypotheses.org; Alex Ketchum, ed., *The Historical Cooking Project*, June 20, 2018, http://www.historicalcookingproject.com; Alma Igra, Jordan Katz, and Avner Aarak, *Leftovers: History of the World in 1000 Cookbooks*, July 26, 2016, http://www.leftovershistory.com; Sarah Lohman, *Four Pounds Flour*, February 20, 2018, http://www.fourpoundsflour.com; Karen Hammonds, *Revolutionary Pie: Historic American Cooking in a 21st-Century Kitchen*, July 17, 2017, https://revolutionarypie.com; Ken Albala, *Ken Albala's Food Rant*, April 20, 2018, http://kenalbala.blogspot.com. For medicinal recipes, see also "1,000-Year-Old Onion and Garlic Eye Remedy kills MRSA," *BBC News*, March 30, 2015.
4. The Making and Knowing Project: Intersections of Craft Making and Scientific Knowing, Center for Science and Society, Columbia University, https://www.makingandknowing.org. See also Ken Albala's article on cooking as a research method: Albala, "Cooking as Research Methodology."
5. "Recipe book," 1705–26, Ms. Codex 785, Kislak Center for Special Collections, Rare Books, and Manuscripts, University of Pennsylvania, Philadelphia (hereafter, Ms. Codex 785).
6. Hannah Woolley, *The Queen-like Closet or Rich Cabinet: Stored with All Manner of Rare Receipts for Preserving, Candying and Cookery* (London, 1670), W3282, Folger Shakespeare Library, Washington, DC. I consulted

the first edition of Woolley's cookbook on Early English Books Online (EEBO). The microfilm was created from a copy held at the British Library. I also used the full-text search available through Early English Books Online Text-Creation Partnership (EEBO-TCP) to seek out other recipes from Ms. Codex 785. The recipe "XXXIX. *To Make the* Portugal *Eggs*" appears on page 31, sig. C4ʳ, and the other recipes are clustered later in the same gathering: "XLVIII. *To make Marmalade of Apricocks*," 37–38, sig. C7ʳ⁻ᵛ; "XLIX. *To make Limon Cakes*," 38, sig. C7ᵛ; "L. *To make Wafers*," 38, sig. C7ᵛ. Woolley's book was quite popular, and the two volumes went through five editions over fifteen years: 1670, 1672, 1675, 1681, and 1684. I have consulted at least one copy of each edition in person or using EEBO to confirm that the order of the recipes remained the same across editions. The recipe for Portugal eggs that I include as figure 2 comes from the third edition of *The Queen-like Closet* held at the Folger Shakespeare Library (29, sig. C3ʳ).

7. Ms. Codex 785, 6–7.
8. I use the gender-neutral pronoun "they" to refer to the compiler of Ms. Codex 785. Alyssa Connell and I write about cooking "Lemmon Cakes" and our method in more detail in Connell and Nicosia, "Cooking in the Archives."
9. Multigraph Collective, *Interacting with Print*, 199.
10. Roach, *Cities of the Dead*; Worthen, *Print and the Poetics of Modern Drama*. Performance requires skill, as Evelyn Tribble's recent work on cognition and skill has shown, as do cooking, handwriting, iron forging, mathematics, and needlework: Tribble, *Cognition in the Globe*.
11. Recent publications on Shakespeare and food have made the connection between eating and performance: see Coles and Shahani, "Introduction to Forum"; Fitzpatrick, *Food in Shakespeare*; Goldstein and Tigner, *Culinary Shakespeare*.
12. Amory, "The Trout and the Milk."
13. Ibid., 1
14. Scholars of the history of material texts, especially conservation specialists, archivists, and librarians, have long understood the need to develop maquettes of books and to research technologies of paper making, parchment preparation, sewing, binding, typesetting and type forging, and calligraphy—the processes that enable texts to be imprinted or inscribed. See D'Ambrogio, *Dictionary of Letterlocking*; Heather Wolfe and Peter Stallybrass's work on filing that Wolfe discusses in "Filing." See also Timothy Barret and his colleagues' Paper through Time: Nondestructive Analysis of 14th- through 19th-Century Papers Project, University of Iowa, Iowa City, http://paper.lib.uiowa.edu.
15. Smith et al., "Introduction," 6.

16. Ibid., 9.
17. Ibid., 8–9.
18. Johnson, "Rethinking (Re)Doing." See also Agnew, "History's Affective Turn"; McCalman and Pickering, *Historical Reenactment*.
19. Johnson, "Rethinking (Re)Doing," 194, 196.
20. Wacquant, "For a Sociology of Flesh and Blood."
21. Ibid., 2.
22. Cerulo, "The Embodied Mind," 38.
23. Wendy Wall has called these "kitchen literacies": Wall, *Recipes for Thought*, 112–66.
24. Wacquant, "For a Sociology of Flesh and Blood," 3.
25. Herbert, *Female Alliances*, 52–59.
26. Laroche and Munroe, *Shakespeare and Ecofeminist Theory*.
27. I use the word "messy" here following Margaret Ezell's work on domestic books: Ezell, "Invisible Books."
28. Albala, *Cooking in Europe*, 27.
29. Pennell, *The Birth of the English Kitchen*.
30. Leong, "Collecting Knowledge for the Family," 83.
31. Elaine Leong, *Recipes and Everyday Knowledge*, 1–45.
32. Herbert, *Female Alliances*, 52–59.
33. Dalby, *Cheese*, 7.
34. Dalby, *Dangerous Tastes*.
35. Hall, "Culinary Spaces, Colonial Spaces." See also Mintz, *Sweetness and Power*.
36. Wall, *Recipes for Thought*, 7.
37. Ibid., 65–111.
38. Considine, "Wolley, Hannah."
39. Wall, *Recipes for Thought*, 36–40.
40. The supplement to Woolley's *The Queen-like Closet or Rich Cabinet* is considered part of the 1675 edition of the cookbook: supplement, "To all Ingenious Ladies and Gentlewomen," in Woolley, *The Queen-like Closet or Rich Cabinet*, W3284, sig. A2^r.
41. Ibid., sig. A2^v.
42. I have consulted the five editions of Woolley's recipe book that the compiler might have seen and see no distinctive trends in spelling that makes any edition a more likely copy-text than any other.
43. To date, I have not identified any other print sources for recipes in Ms. Codex 785. Although Woolley's books include many recipes for dishes also included in the manuscript, the compiler uses other sources for the majority of the entries.
44. "To make portugal eggs," Ms. Codex 785, 6.
45. Albala, *The Banquet*.

46. Day, "The Tempting Table."
47. Albala, *The Banquet*, 23 and passim.
48. *A Complete Account of the Ceremonies Observed in the Coronations of the Kings and Queens of England*, 75. There are very few mentions of "Portugal eggs" in the EEBO-TCP and Eighteenth-Century Collections Online corpuses. This may simply be a result of the construction of the corpus at the time of searching.
49. Robert May, *The Accomplisht Cook, or, The Art and Mystery of Cookery* (London, 1660), M1394, Folger Shakespeare Library, 422–23.
50. Since I want recipes that I post on *Cooking in the Archives* to be accessible to a wide range of readers, I do not purchase ingredients from eBay. I did not gild the laurel leaves because this element of the recipe is for presentation, not consumption. I did, however, decorate the dish with fresh bay leaves.
51. Alyssa Connell prepared a version of these biscuits when she made "Artificial Potatoes": Connell, "Artificial Potatoes."
52. Albala and Wall both write about the classic example of the bleeding deer pie: Wall, *Recipes for Thought*, 80.
53. I adapted this recipe from Jill, "Candied Citrus Peel," *AllRecipes*, http://allrecipes.com/recipe/18999/candied-citrus-peel.

Works Cited

Agnew, Vanessa. "History's Affective Turn: Historical Reenactment and Its Work in the Present." *Rethinking History* 11, no. 3 (2007): 299–312.

Albala, Ken. *The Banquet: Dining in the Great Courts of Late Renaissance Europe*. Urbana: University of Illinois Press, 2007.

———. "Cooking as Research Methodology: Experiments in Renaissance Cuisine." In *Renaissance Food from Rabelais to Shakespeare: Culinary Readings and Culinary Histories*, edited by Joan Fitzpatrick, 73–88. Aldershot, U.K.: Ashgate, 2010.

———. *Cooking in Europe, 1250–1650*. Westport, CT: Greenwood, 2006.

Amory, Hugh. "The Trout and the Milk: An Ethnobibliographical Essay." In *Bibliography and the Book Trades: Studies in the Print Culture of Early New England*, edited by David D. Hall, 11–33. Philadelphia: University of Pennsylvania Press, 2005.

Cerulo, Karen A. "The Embodied Mind: Building on Wacquant's Carnal Sociology." *Qualitative Sociology* 38 (2015): 33–38.

Coles, Kimberly Anne, and Gitanjali Shahani. "Introduction to Forum: Diet and Identity in Shakespeare's England." *Shakespeare Studies* 42 (2014): 21–31.

A Complete Account of the Ceremonies Observed in the Coronations of the Kings and Queens of England. London, 1727.

Connell, Alyssa. "Artificial Potatoes." *Cooking in the Archives: Updating Early Modern Recipes (1600–1800) in a Modern Kitchen.* February 18, 2015. http://rarecooking.com/2015/02/18/artificial-potatoes.

Connell, Alyssa, and Marissa Nicosia. "Cooking in the Archives: Bringing Early Modern Manuscript Recipes into a Twenty-First-Century Kitchen." *Archive Journal* 4 (July 2015). http://www.archivejournal.net/notes/cooking-in-the-archives-bringing-early-modern-manuscript-recipes-into-a-twenty-first-century-kitchen/.

Considine, John. "Wolley, Hannah (b. 1622?, d. in or after 1674)." In *Oxford Dictionary of National Biography*. Oxford: Oxford University Press, 2004. https://doi.org/10.1093/ref:odnb/29957.

D'Ambrogio, Jana, and Daniel Starza Smith. *Dictionary of Letterlocking.* November 1, 2016. http://www.janadambrogio.com/letterlock/#letterlocking-format-catgories.

Dalby, Andrew. *Cheese: A Global History.* New York: Reaktion, 2009.

———. *Dangerous Tastes: The Story of Spices.* Berkeley: University of California Press, 2000.

Day, Ivan. "The Tempting Table." *Historic Food.* 2006. http://www.historicfood.com/Tempting%20Table.htm.

Ezell, Margaret J. M. "Invisible Books." In *Producing the Eighteenth-Century Book: Writers and Publishers in England, 1650–1800,* edited by Laura Runge and Oat Rogers, 53–69. Newark: University of Delaware Press, 2009.

Fitzpatrick, Joan. *Food in Shakespeare: Early Modern Dietaries and the Plays.* Aldershot, U.K.: Ashgate, 2007.

Goldstein, David B., and Amy L. Tigner, eds. *Culinary Shakespeare: Staging Food and Drink in Early Modern England.* Pittsburgh: Duquesne University Press, 2016.

Hall, Kim F. "Culinary Spaces, Colonial Spaces: The Gendering of Sugar in the Seventeenth Century." In *Feminist Readings of Early Modern Culture: Emerging Subjects,* edited by Valerie Traub, Lindsay Kaplan, and Dympna Callaghan, 168–90. Cambridge: Cambridge University Press, 1996.

Herbert, Amanda E. *Female Alliances: Gender, Identity, and Friendship in Early Modern Britain.* New Haven, CT: Yale University Press, 2014.

Johnson, Katherine M. "Rethinking (Re)Doing: Historical Re-enactment and/as Historiography." *Rethinking History* 19, no. 2 (2015): 193–206.

Laroche, Rebecca, and Jennifer Munroe. *Shakespeare and Ecofeminist Theory.* London: Bloomsbury, 2017.

Leong, Elaine. "Collecting Knowledge for the Family: Recipes, Gender and Practical Knowledge in the Early Modern English Household." *Centaurus* 55, no. 2 (2013): 81–103.

———. *Recipes and Everyday Knowledge: Medicine, Science, and the Household in Early Modern England.* Chicago: University of Chicago Press, 2018.

McCalman, Iain, and Paul Pickering, eds. *Historical Reenactment. From Realism to the Affective Turn*. Basingstoke, U.K.: Palgrave Macmillan. 2010.

Mintz, Sidney W. *Sweetness and Power: The Place of Sugar in Modern History*. New York: Penguin, 1986.

Multigraph Collective. *Interacting with Print: Elements of Reading in the Era of Print Saturation*. Chicago: University of Chicago Press, 2018.

Nicosia, Marissa. *Cooking in the Archives: Updating Early Modern Recipes (1600–1800) in a Modern Kitchen*. June 15, 2018. http://www.rarecooking.com.

———. "To Make Lemmon Cakes." *Cooking in the Archives: Updating Early Modern Recipes (1600–1800) in a Modern Kitchen*. March 26, 2015. https://rarecooking.com/2015/03/26/to-make-lemmon-cakes.

Pennell, Sara. *The Birth of the English Kitchen, 1600–1850*. London: Bloomsbury, 2016.

Roach, Joseph. *Cities of the Dead: Circum-Atlantic Performance*. New York: Columbia University Press, 1996.

Smith, Pamela H., Amy R. W. Meyers, and Harold J. Cook. "Introduction: Making and Knowing." In *Ways of Making and Knowing: The Material Culture of Empirical Knowledge*, edited by Pamela H. Smith, Amy R. W. Meyers, and Harold J. Cook, 1–16. Ann Arbor: University of Michigan Press, 2014.

Tribble, Evelyn. *Cognition in the Globe: Attention and Memory in Shakespeare's Theatre*. New York: Palgrave, 2011.

Wacquant, Loïc. "For a Sociology of Flesh and Blood." *Qualitative Sociology* 38 (2015): 1–11.

Wall, Wendy. *Recipes for Thought: Knowledge and Taste in the Early Modern English Kitchen*. Philadelphia: University of Pennsylvania Press, 2015.

Wolfe, Heather. "Filing, Seventeenth-Century Style." *The Collation*. March 23, 2013. https://collation.folger.edu/2013/03/filing-seventeenth-century-style.

Worthen, W. B. *Print and the Poetics of Modern Drama*. Cambridge: Cambridge University Press, 2005.

Epilogue

MARGARET J. M. EZELL

U NLIKE A printed work's "afterword," which typically summarizes for the reader highlights of the text preceding it and delivers the final word on what came before, an "epilogue," with its associations with the dynamic space of the theater rather than the static printed page, typically involves a character in the performance stepping outside the world of the play and suggesting how the action will continue. In contrast, the "characters" of textual media—those chiseled into stone, written on a page, printed on paper, or even formed on a screen—typically are thought of as literally the final word. Human characters offering epilogues onstage often adjust their performances to suit the desires of the immediate audience, but we think of graphic characters on a page as being static, promising predictable linearity leading to a conclusion, not pointing to an open or changing future. All of these graphic characters, whether carved, scripted, or typed, at one point in time represented the height of technology used to transmit literary, scientific, and domestic texts from writer to reader: for graphic characters and their mediums, afterlife is typically seen as either a termination or a translation into another form, and it is suggested that improving technology drives replacement, from clay tablets, to scrolls, to paper, to the screen. "While print is not yet dead," one media critic observed in 2008, "it is undoubtedly sickening."[1]

As a group, the essays in this collection strongly contest this model of media change and textual graphic characters' lack of an afterlife. The essays in this volume demand an epilogue rather than an afterword, requiring a looking forward as well as back. The very multiplicity of the active, lively modes of textual transmission in the centuries covered by the volume leads one to ask: When does a literary medium become useless, obsolete, or simply unknown to writers and readers? Does it ever? It certainly does not happen when a new and presumably better technology comes into being and is made widely available to replace it. I have a clear memory of a meeting in my English Department in the mid-1980s in which we collectively declined the offer of free computers from Texas Instruments. We preferred instead to purchase IBM Selectric typewriters with the interchangeable font balls and correction tapes. Even after we did switch to computers with printers, most of us kept a typewriter of some sort in the office or department because computer technology had yet to encompass such necessary tasks as filling in forms and addressing envelopes (a confession: I still handwrite addresses on envelopes).

Indeed, had we accepted the generous offer and taken those early personal computers with their 5.25-inch disks, all that we wrote, rewrote, recorded, and saved on them would be largely lost today. As computer hardware evolved, those large-format disks would have become obsolete; even had the technology to read the disks been preserved, the disks would have had a limited life because chemical and magnetic decomposition and degradation would render them unreadable.[2] As media scholars have observed, in the words of Jonathan Sterne, "The computer industry has applied the logic of planned obsolescence to media hardware more thoroughly than any other media industry before it. Computers and digital media are no long 'new' with respect to other media. They are primarily new with respect to themselves."[3] A developing field within digital humanities is in fact now devoted to strategies to retrieve materials stored on early digital platforms created in the 1990s and to find ways to archive them and sustain older sites and links.[4]

From the perspective of a literary historian, this loss of digital texts, images, and data because of the evolution of the technology used to record and preserve them stands in contrast to the ways we find that some older media—oral, scribal, and print—complemented and competed with each other. As the essays in this volume clearly demonstrate, there was an extended transition period from handwritten copies to the new print opportunities in the post-1700 world, and, notably, there was a pattern of deliberate, strategic return to older media modes. Remodeling the earlier linear, progressive history of technology in which one superior mode replaces another, the essays in the collection invite us to consider what the strategies or motives might be for retaining or even returning to an earlier media form.

Popular debates playing out in the news media today draw attention to our changing habits surrounding creating and disseminating texts. In 2013, a series of articles appeared in multiple newspapers about the elimination of teaching cursive handwriting in American public schools. The Common Core adopted in 2010 left it up to individual states whether to require the teaching of handwriting. Steve Graham was quoted in a *Washington Post* article making the point that the argument for keeping cursive handwriting in the curriculum "centers more on tradition than practicality": "When you think about the world in the 1950s, everything was by hand. Paper and pencil.... Right now, it's a hybrid world."[5] "Cursive should be allowed to die," Morgan Polikoff declared in a panel debate in the *New York Times* in 2013, and Kate Gladstone agreed that "handwriting matters, but cursive doesn't." "Mandating cursive to preserve handwriting resembles mandating stovepipe hats and crinolines to preserve the art of tailoring," she argued.[6] On the other side, the occupational therapist Suzanne Baruch Asheron argued that the "Benefits of Cursive Go Beyond Writing," and Jimmy Bryant called cursive writing "A Cultural Tradition Worth Preserving," arguing that "e-mail messages are routinely deleted and not saved for posterity," but "letters written in cursive tend to be saved and cherished. And let's be honest, receiving a letter written in cursive is much more meaningful than one that is computer-generated."[7]

Certainly, older media technologies can have this nostalgic function for their users, and the appeal of being part of a tradition should not to be underestimated or trivialized. Roger Chartier has pointed out that the conventions of print itself are marked by "a durable nostalgia for a lost orality."[8] Discussions of contemporary media evaluating the impact of the digital environment on reading and writing habits—as opposed to its technology or hardware—suggest, however, some of the ways in which old practices can be preferred to new for practical rather than aesthetic purposes, even when the new becomes ubiquitous. In his recent study *The Revenge of Analog*, David Sax notes that in the twenty-first century "certain technologies and processes that had recently been rendered 'obsolete' suddenly began to show new life, even as the work around them was increasingly drive by digital technology."[9] Speaking of the return of vinyl records, film photography, and independent bookstores, and of the persistence of printed reading materials in the digital age, he suggests that "it was as though analog was becoming newly relevant, right as its very obsolescence was supposedly assured." This present-day analogy leads us to ask: did handwriting function in a similar fashion in a culture where print was becoming commonplace?

Recent scholars of new digital media typically have dwelled on the eradication of the old by the new, even as they draw on the vocabulary from Raymond Williams's early paradigm of dominant, residual, and emergent media.[10] Williams, unlike those who predict the death of libraries and paper books with the advent of the digital, highlighted how, as Jay David Bolter and Richard Grusin write, "media are continually commenting on, reproducing, and replacing each other, and this process is integral to media. Media need each other in order to function as media at all."[11] Scholars of the early modern period likewise reject a simple replacement pattern. As Peter Stallybrass has argued, the expansion of cheap print encouraged and preserved the art of handwriting; printing "indeed produce[d] a revolutionary transformation in communications, but not primarily through books. Its most radical effect was its incitement to writing by hand."[12] Discussing writing that is generated in response to "the stimulus of print," whether it is the completion of preprinted fifteenth-century Indulgence forms or the use of seventeenth- and eighteenth-century printed almanacs to structure personal diaries and daily notes, Stallybrass writes that the "assumption that printing means the printing of *books* has helped to reinforce the further false assumption that printing somehow displaces manuscript." He has argued instead that print ushered in a "revolution" in handwriting practices, creating an environment that encouraged and preserved the scribal medium.[13]

When I was writing *Social Authorship and the Advent of Print* in the 1990s, it was widely argued that the presence of print was a marker of important cultural change and therefore represented the shift toward a modern intellectual culture. From the time of Sir Francis Bacon, print has been associated with the term "revolution": the proliferation of cheap print during the English Civil War was tied to a growing idea of political participation that would later blossom into democracy. Print had been used as a signal for increasing literacy and for the expanding professionalization of literature. In such studies, print was highlighted as "new," associated with the "modern," and hailed as a democratizing force.[14] My argument about manuscript being a more accessible medium than print for authors in the seventeenth century has evolved to appreciate that print could be "democratic" for readers, in the narrow sense that, unlike with the circulation of manuscripts in literary coteries, anyone living in an urban area who had a penny could purchase a broadside or a pamphlet or, at no cost, see it posted on a wall or hear it read aloud. Cheap printed texts such as ballads and broadside proclamations, however, were in many senses still "social" in nature and required more than simple purchasing power to enjoy.[15] They were intended to be read aloud, performed, and copied and curated. The variety of literacies in operation well after 1700 in the English-language world meant that, alongside print, one still needed skills in both oral and handwritten cultural traditions.

Part of the complexity of defining a "culture" by its media forms is highlighted in recent debates over the nature of the very phrase "print culture." Jason McElligott and Eve Patten's recent collection *The Perils of Print Culture* points to the problem of defining when a period can be described as having a "print culture." The "reader is told on numerous occasions that a particular period, such as the 1590s, or the 1640s, or the 1680s, or the 1720s, saw the development of print culture in Ireland," they observe, making the point that "print circulated [in Ireland] for over 200 years before a discernable print culture, as such, existed."[16] "In other words," McElligott and Patten conclude, "'print' and 'print culture' are not interchangeable concepts or categories." It becomes increasingly problematic to define a period by a dominant technology when the label elides issues raised by physical location, gender, and genre.

This is most apparent in places where access to existing printing presses is geographically limited, as in Ireland or Iceland. Ireland had a flourishing literary culture during the medieval period, but after the English gained control over the country and regulated printing in Dublin, Gaelic fonts were so rare and expensive to create that anyone writing in Gaelic required the services of scribes to circulate their writings. Although relatively few books in Gaelic were printed in Ireland in the eighteenth century, more than four thousand Irish-language manuscripts have been preserved, and it is estimated that more than two hundred scribes were active in Cork during the period, existing side by side with the Dublin printing industry producing English texts.[17] Likewise, although Iceland had had an established press since 1530, it published exclusively religious texts, resulting in a flourishing scribal culture for the preservation and circulation of secular, vernacular writings that continued well into the nineteenth century.[18]

While one might feel that writers in such circumstances were disadvantaged in not having easy access to print, the continued practice of handwritten textual production suggests we should not overlook the possible positive benefits for the authors. Essays in this collection by Philip S. Palmer and Collin Jennings, employing very different methodological approaches, explore the allure for the pen-and-ink writer of blank white spaces as "places for imagining how objects, ideas, and arguments could be combined, as well as how materials from different places could be reconfigured, rearranged, and remade," as Jennings puts it. Likewise, as Michelle Levy's chapter points out, this preference for blank space is not necessarily a nostalgic or anachronistic turn but can be a creative and curatorial one. As the essays in this volume so clearly demonstrate, handwriting, print, and performance enjoyed a complicated, complex network of relationships in eighteenth-century England and America, leading to what in the introduction Rachael Scarborough King calls "the multimedia eighteenth century." Perhaps it could be said that England after 1700 was "the age of print," but, as we see in Leith Davis's account of accessing news during the Glorious Revolution and Kathryn R. King's exploration of mid-eighteenth-century periodical publications, it was so only in conjunction with the conscious employment of earlier traditions of oral and scribal practices that supported and sustained it.

Thinking about post-1700 writings in English in the context of the publishing conventions of other countries highlights how writers used multiple media to circulate their works effectively in a transatlantic world. Brian Rejack traces the various intercontinental fortunes of one of John Keats's letters from the nineteenth century through the twentieth century and its twenty-first-century recovery and preservation in the online Keats Letters Project. In the same way that manuscripts have tended to be associated with the "old-fashioned," they have also tended to be thought of as more limited in their geographical reach than printed texts—just as, too, the digital tends to highlight its own "universality" and dismiss the range and availability of mechanical printing methods. This is true in terms of numbers of copies made and the speed at which they can be done, but as Beth Fowkes Tobin's reconstruction of the circulation of John Abbot's drawings and field notes demonstrates, naturalists in England, as well as in America and France, were able and eager to collect and curate his writings. Likewise, while one might assume that new experimental scientists would naturally embrace the newest and fastest media technologies, Colin T. Ramsey shows how the perception of Benjamin Franklin as a "celebrity" early scientist was created by a strategic use of multiple modes of publication forms. He writes that "even ... colonial America's foremost printer" found it "necessary to communicate his scientific ideas in manuscript, at least initially, if he was to have his work seriously reviewed by the transatlantic community of natural philosophers."

In the same way that one might have assumed that scientific writing would have been embraced and subsumed by print in the post-1700 literate world, novels as a genre are rarely discussed as being part of a manuscript culture. While we might long for the rough drafts of Samuel Richardson's *Pamela* or Ann Radcliffe's *The Mysteries of Udolpho*, it is the texts' lives in print that have dominated discussion about their composition, content, and distribution and that have highlighted their mass audiences as an important feature of the genre itself. Emily C. Friedman's recovery of post-1700 full-length manuscript novels, not as isolated or anomalous artifacts but, indeed, as an emerging archive of more than 250 titles at this point in time, jolts us into remembering that "many people in the eighteenth and nineteenth centuries . . . continued to understand what manuscript could do and print could not" and that a text's length was not a primary concern when deciding how it should reach its intended audience.

Simultaneously with the attention being focused on the vitality and viability of manuscript texts and with hybrid media in the post-1700 period, there have been a series of recent studies focusing their attention on how specific groups comfortably employed multiple modes of literary production as a means to secure their identities and to reach out to larger audiences. Catholic monasteries and nunneries had been the repository of forbidden books and writings in the post-Reformation period; their devotional practices also encouraged the creation, preservation, and circulation of handwritten devotional texts: reading, copying, annotating, and writing were all part of a monastic spiritual life.[19] It is to this literary culture that we owe the survival and circulation of the medieval mystic Julian of Norwich's writings, which were repeatedly copied and carried into Antwerp and Paris prior to their publication in 1670.[20] In a similar fashion, as Andrew O. Winckles argues in this volume, in the eighteenth century the early Methodists confounded the distinction often made between "private" handwritten accounts and "public" printed texts. "Oral and manuscript media were inherent to conversion experiences for these women, not simply a result of conversion. It was through hearing and then writing their spiritual experiences that women became Methodists," he argues. Although Rachael Scarborough King argues that we have been reductive in positioning letters written in the post-1700 world as a "private" and "feminine" genre, suggesting instead that "letters composed by male and female correspondents do not split in terms of subject matter or tone," it is nevertheless important to note that manuscript texts could and did preserve space for women's voices in post-1700 England and America. Winckles's example of Sarah Crosby's bound blank book to record the events of her career as a minister created a public record during a time that Methodist print publications were increasingly less accommodating to women's voices. Levy likewise draws attention to the ways in which, over the course of the nineteenth century, the dismissal of manuscript materials as being "rough" or unfinished work fails to recognize the extent to which the bound blank book offered the possibility of a multimedia creation that eclipsed print. In her bound blank journal Dorothy Wordsworth found the space to create and archive her writings without the limitations of the conventions that controlled the appearance and content of printed books. "Without rule lines or margins," Levy observes, "pages can be turned into surfaces inviting the incorporation of other media, of print and engraving and drawing."

The study of pre-1700 English-language manuscript texts as a media form now has a well-established history. Its texts are becoming the focus of digital and distant reading possibilities. With the continuing improvements in OCR (optical character recognition) and transcription projects such as the Folger Shakespeare Library's Early Modern Manuscripts Online project, it will be possible in the future to do large-scale linguistic analysis of early modern handwritten materials. Post-1700 manuscripts and hybrid works, however, are just now emerging both as a new field of study and as fascinating individual objects that tease us to see them not as tiresome textual problems that do not fit within our current taxonomies for describing books or tidy narratives of technological progress, but as textual creations that challenge us to examine our assumptions about literary cultures, writers, and readers. Marissa Nicosia's essay, for example, urges readers to consider how the practice of reconstructing recipes from manuscript volumes in a modern kitchen, an exercise in critical making, can offer us insights not only into early modern tastes but also into the significance of collective writing (and cooking) projects.

Handwritten characters flourishing in the context of print culture highlight that there are still questions to be posed about the relationships among oral, handwritten, print, and digital texts and how they are created and disseminated. Exploring handwritten texts' creation, as well as the ways they moved through space and time and encountered different types of readers, the study of manuscripts is ready to take on the recent challenge posed by the Multigraph Collective to consider the question, "How does a particular configuration of media become associated with historically specific practices to produce new kinds of social configuration?"[21] Like the approach taken by the Multigraph Collective's multi-author academic book, the afterlife of handwritten characters in later periods disrupts "the habitual narratives of book history—indeed, its identity as 'book history'": handwritten texts help us to nuance and complicate the model of "mutually exclusive 'spheres' to understand the impact of print culture" by highlighting how media interact.[22] Perhaps most important to the future of the study of manuscripts in print cultures, post-1700 handwritten texts resist traditional book history narratives to insist that we think about gender, of both the writer and the reader, and, in particular, to examine with care the implications in labeling past practices as either anachronistic or nostalgic.

Notes

1. Gomez, *Print Is Dead*, 3.
2. Kirschenbaum, *Track Changes*, 220–21.
3. Sterne, "Out with the Trash," 22.
4. See Earhart, *Traces of the Old, Uses of the New*.
5. T. Rees Shapiro, "Cursive Handwriting Is Disappearing from Public Schools," *Washington Post*, April 4, 2013.
6. Morgan Polikoff, "Let Cursive Handwriting Die," *New York Times*, April 30, 2013; Kate Gladstone, "Handwriting Matters; Cursive Doesn't," *New York Times*, April 30, 2013.
7. Suzanne Baruch Asherson, "The Benefits of Cursive Go beyond Writing," *New York Times*, April 30, 2013; Jimmy Bryant, "A Cultural Tradition Worth Preserving," *New York Times*, April 30, 2013.
8. Chartier, *The Author's Hand and the Printer's Mind*, 22.
9. Sax, *The Revenge of Analog*, xiv.
10. Williams, *Marxism and Literature*, 162–63.
11. Bolter and Grusin, *Remediation*, 55.
12. Stallybrass, "Printing and the Manuscript Revolution," 111.
13. Ibid., 114–15.
14. See Ezell, *Social Authorship and the Advent of Print*, 8–10.
15. Ezell, "Seventeenth-Century English Reading Cultures and Multimodal Literacies," 357–73.
16. McElligott and Patten, "The Perils of Print Culture," 4.

17. Brown, *The Irish Enlightenment*, 133; Ni Úrdail, *The Scribe in Eighteenth- and Nineteenth-Century Ireland*, 199–225.
18. Driscoll, *The Unwashed Children of Eve;* Olafsson, "Vernacular Literacy Practices in Nineteenth-Century Icelandic Scribal Culture."
19. Lay, *Beyond the Cloister.*
20. Watson and Jenkins, "Introduction," 13.
21. Multigraph Collective, *Interacting with Print*, 14.
22. Ibid., 7–8.

Works Cited

Bolter, Jay David, and Richard Grusin, *Remediation: Understanding New Media.* Cambridge, MA: MIT Press, 1999.

Brown, Michael. *The Irish Enlightenment.* Cambridge, MA: Harvard University Press, 2016.

Chartier, Roger. *The Author's Hand and the Printer's Mind*, translated by Lydia G. Cochrane. Cambridge: Polity, 2014.

Driscoll, Matthew J. *The Unwashed Children of Eve: The Production, Dissemination and Reception of Popular Literature in Post-Reformation Iceland.* Enfield Lock, U.K.: Hisarlik, 1996.

Earhart, Amy E. *Traces of the Old, Uses of the New: The Emergence of Digital Literary Studies.* Ann Arbor: University of Michigan Press, 2015.

Ezell, Margaret J. M. "Seventeenth-Century Reading Cultures and Multimodal Literacies." *Eighteenth-Century Studies* 51, no. 3 (Spring 2018): 357–73.

———. *Social Authorship and the Advent of Print.* Baltimore: Johns Hopkins University Press, 1999.

Gomez, Jeff. *Print Is Dead: Books in Our Digital Age.* London: Palgrave Macmillan, 2008.

Kirschenbaum, Matthew G. *Track Changes: A Literary History of Word Processing.* Cambridge, MA: Harvard University Press, 2016.

Lay, Jena. *Beyond the Cloister: Catholic Englishwomen and Early Modern Literary Culture.* Philadelphia: University of Pennsylvania Press, 2016.

McElligott, Jason, and Eve Patten. "The Perils of Print Culture: An Introduction." In *The Perils of Print Culture: Book, Print and Publishing History in Theory and Practice*, edited by Jason McElligott and Eve Patten, 1–16. London: Palgrave Macmillan, 2014.

Multigraph Collective. *Interacting with Print: Elements of Reading in the Era of Print Saturation.* Chicago: University of Chicago Press, 2018.

Ni Úrdail, Meidhbhín. *The Scribe in Eighteenth- and Nineteenth-Century Ireland: Motivations and Milieu.* Münster, Germany: Nodus, 2000.

Olafsson, Davið. "Vernacular Literacy Practices in Nineteenth-Century Icelandic Scribal Culture." In *Att läsa och att skriva: Två vågor av vardagligt skriftbruk i Norden 1800–2000*, edited by Ann-Catrin Edlund, 65–86. Umeå, Sweden: Umeå Universitet og Kungl, 2012.

Sax, David. *The Revenge of Analog: Real Things and Why They Matter*. New York: Public Affairs, 2016.

Stallybrass, Peter. "Printing and the Manuscript Revolution." In *Explorations in Communication and History*, edited by Barbie Zelizer, 111–18. New York: Routledge, 2008.

Sterne, Jonathan. "Out with the Trash: On the Future of New Media." In *Residual Media*, edited by Charles R. Acland, 16–31. Minneapolis: University of Minnesota Press, 2007.

Watson, Nicholas, and Jacqueline Jenkins. "Introduction." In *The Writings of Julian of Norwich: A Vision Showed to a Devout Woman and A Revelation of Love*, edited by Nicholas Watson and Jacqueline Jenkins, 1–59. University Park: Penn State University Press, 2006.

Williams, Raymond. *Marxism and Literature*. Oxford: Oxford University Press, 1977.

CONTRIBUTORS

LEITH DAVIS is a Professor in the Department of English at Simon Fraser University. She is the author of *Acts of Union: Scotland and the Negotiation of the British Nation* (1998) and *Music, Postcolonialism and Gender: The Construction of Irish National Identity, 1725–1875* (2005), as well as coeditor of *Scotland and the Borders of Romanticism* (2004) and *Robert Burns and Transatlantic Culture* (2012). She has just completed the draft of a new book titled, *Mediating Cultural Memory in Britain and Ireland, 1688–1745*.

MARGARET J. M. EZELL is Distinguished Professor of English and the John and Sara Lindsey Chair of Liberal Arts at Texas A&M University. She is the author of many studies on manuscript culture and women's participation in seventeenth-century literary and intellectual life. Her books include *Writing Women's Literary History* (1993), *Social Authorship and the Advent of Print* (1999), and Volume 5 in the Oxford English Literary History series, *1645–1714: The Later Seventeenth Century* and its *Companion Volume*.

EMILY C. FRIEDMAN is an Associate Professor of English at Auburn University and the director of 18thConnect.org, a peer-reviewed digital aggregator. She is the author of *Reading Smell in Eighteenth-Century Literature* (2016) and of articles and essays on book history and women's writing. Her current project is the monograph and database *Manuscript Fiction in the Age of Print, 1750–1900*.

COLLIN JENNINGS is an Assistant Professor of English at Miami University of Ohio. His work has appeared in *Eighteenth Century: Theory and Interpretation*, *English Literary History*, and *Literacy and Linguistic Computing*. He is at work on a book manuscript titled *An Enlightenment History of the Link*.

KATHRYN R. KING is a Professor Emerita of Literature at the University of Montevallo and former director of faculty development. Her research focuses on the lives, texts, and professional careers of female writers in the long eighteenth century. Her books include *A Political Biography of Eliza Haywood* (2012) and *Jane Barker, Exile: A Literary Career 1675–1725* (2000). She is coeditor (with Alexander Pettit) of Haywood's *Female Spectator* (2001) and has published articles in *RES, ELH, JEMCS, Eighteenth Century: Theory and Interpretation, Studies in the Novel,* and many other journals. She has held ACLS, NEH, and other fellowships and is a former editor of the eighteenth-century section of *Literature Compass*.

RACHAEL SCARBOROUGH KING is an Associate Professor of English at the University of California, Santa Barbara, and the author of *Writing to the World: Letters and the Origins of Modern Print Genres* (2018). She is a Senior Fellow in the Society of Fellows in Critical Bibliography at Rare Book School.

MICHELLE LEVY is a Professor in the Department of English at Simon Fraser University. She is the coeditor of the *Broadview Reader in Book History* (with Tom Mole, 2014), the coauthor of the *Broadview Introduction to Book History* (with Tom Mole, 2017), and the author of *Family Authorship and Romantic Print Culture* (2008). She has published extensively on female writers of the Romantic period, and her book *Literary Manuscript Culture in Romantic Britain* is forthcoming from Edinburgh University Press. She also directs the Women's Print History Project, 1750–1836, a comprehensive bibliographical database of women's books.

MARISSA NICOSIA is an Assistant Professor of Renaissance Literature at Pennsylvania State University, Abington College. She has published articles in *Modern Philology*, *Milton Studies*, *Papers of the Bibliographical Society of America*, *Postmedieval*, and *Studies in Philology*. She also runs the food history website *Cooking in the Archives*. Her research has been supported by the Andrew W. Mellon Fellowship of Scholars in Critical Bibliography at Rare Book School.

PHILIP S. PALMER is the Robert H. Taylor Curator of Literary and Historical Manuscripts at the Morgan Library and Museum. His work centers on early modern material texts, annotated books, Renaissance travel writing, and Thomas Coryate. His publications include articles in *Renaissance Studies*, *Huntington Library Quarterly*, and *The Library*, as well as an edition of the library of Sir Thomas Roe for *Private Libraries in Renaissance England*.

COLIN T. RAMSEY is a Professor of English at Appalachian State University. He has written widely on early Americanist topics. His work recently appeared in the edited collection *The Cinematic Eighteenth Century* (2017) and in *Studies in Eighteenth-Century Culture*.

BRIAN REJACK is an Associate Professor of English at Illinois State University. He is the coeditor (with Michael Theune) of the essay collection *Keats's Negative Capability: New Origins and Afterlives* (2019). He is also one of the co-founders of the Keats Letters Project and is at work on a monograph on John Keats and media theory titled *John Keats and Romantic Imaginary Media: The Secrets of Wondrous Things.*

BETH FOWKES TOBIN is a Professor of English and Women's Studies at the University of Georgia. She specializes in eighteenth-century natural history and its cultures of collecting. Her books include *Superintending the Poor: Charitable Ladies and Paternal Landlords in British Fiction, 1770–1860* (1993), *Picturing Imperial Power: Colonial Subjects in Eighteenth-Century British Painting* (1999), *Colonizing Nature: The Tropics in British Arts and Letters, 1760–1820* (2005), and *The Duchess's Shells: Natural History Collecting in the Age of Cook's Voyages* (2014).

ANDREW O. WINCKLES is an Assistant Professor of CORE (Liberal Arts) at Adrian College. He is the coeditor (with Angela Rehbein) of *Women's Literary Networks and Romanticism: "A Tribe of Authoresses"* (2017) and the author of *Eighteenth-Century Women's Writing and the Evangelical Media Revolution: "Consider the Lord as Ever Present Reader"* (2019).

INDEX

Abbott, John, 12, 52, 54–68, 69n7, 70n18, 70n23, 70n32, 71n35, 71n37, 315; drawings of, 52, 54–68, 69n7, 70n18, 70n23, 70n32, 71n35, 71n37
Accomplisht Cook, The (Robert May), 295
"Account of Mrs. Planche, The," 42, 44
Account of the New Invented Pennsylvanian Fire-Places, An (Franklin), 196, 198–203, 205–6, 208, 210–11
Addison, Joseph, 2, 15, 18, 175; *Spectator*, 8, 15–17, 175–76, 189n1; *Tatler*, 8, 15–17, 189n1
affect theory, 13, 177–79, 185–89, 190n14
Allan, David, 20n28, 108
Albala, Ken, 289, 294, 304n3, 307n52
Albemarle, 3rd Earl of (George Keppel), 81–82, 83
Algee-Hewitt, Mark, 258n6
Allestree, Richard, 132–36, 142, 146n20; *The Causes of the Decay of Christian Piety*, 132–36, 142, 146n20; *The Whole Duty of Man*, 146n20
American Ornithology (Wilson), 65
American Philosophical Society, 64–65
Amory, Hugh, 287
Anne, Queen, 172n77
annotation, 123, 125–26, 130–31, 139, 142, 144, 145n9
antiquarian writing, 8
apothecary symbols, 239, 244, 256
archival research, 5, 6, 10–11, 14, 75, 81, 90, 100, 217, 224, 227–28, 230, 272, 280
Arlington, 1st Earl of (Henry Bennet), 169n27
Arminian Magazine. See *Methodist Magazine*
Arnold, Lee, 281n25
artisans, 197, 202, 204, 208, 287–88

Asheron, Suzanne Baruch, 312
Athenian Mercury (Dunton), 8, 176, 182, 189n1
Atherton, Ian, 149, 151, 168n19, 168n24, 169n29
Audubon, John Jacob, 12, 52, 55
Austen, Jane, 89, 224; *Northanger Abbey*, 89
Austin, Margaret, 36
authorship, professional and individual, 98, 108, 116–17, 175, 188
Autobiography of Benjamin Franklin, The (Franklin), 195
autograph collecting, 274

Bacon, Francis, 313
Baird, Spencer Fullerton, 71n35
Baker, Frank, 29
Banks, Joseph, 53–54, 61
Bannet, Eve Tavor, 7, 76, 77, 90n6, 154
banquets, 294–95, 297, 302
Barker, Jane, 179; *A Patch-Work Screen for the Ladies*, 179
Barker, Mary, 108
Barnard, John, 265
Barthes, Roland, 240, 246, 257
Bartram, William, 65
Becket, Thomas, 18n5
Bee (Budgell), 1
Bellanca, Mary Ellen, 102
Benson, Joseph, 27–28, 37–38
Biagioli, Mario, 212n21
bibliography, conventions of, 4, 10, 218–19, 225, 232, 287
Bigold, Melanie, 233n13
Biographical Sketches of the Lives and Public Ministry of Various Holy Women (Taft), 37, 48n3

Birdsall, Thomas, 278–79
Black, Jeremy, 77
Blair, Ann, 9, 240, 242–43, 252
Blair, Hugh, 76
Bland, Mark, 95, 113
blanks, 3, 9, 96, 313
blogging, 116
Boisduval, Jean Alphonse, 52, 65–68, 69n7, 70n30, 70n32; *Histoire Générale et iconographie des lépidoptères et des chenilles de l'Amérique septentrionale*, 52, 58, 65; *Histoire naturelle des insects; species général des lépidoptères*, 65
Bolter, Jay David, 313
book history, field of, 4, 287, 297, 305n14, 317–18
bookplates, 229, 230
Bosanquet Fletcher, Mary, 27, 31, 38, 39–42, 44, 48
Boswell, James, 7; journals of, 7; *Journal of a Tour to the Hebrides*, 7
botany, 54
Bowdoin, James, 206–7
Bowers, Fredson, 225
Boyle, Robert, 197–202; *New Experiments Phyisco-Mechanical, Touching the Spring of Air and Its Effects*, 197, 201
Bradshaigh, Lady, 190n31
Brant, Clare, 77, 81, 89, 176, 184
Breitwieser, Mitchell, 195
Brief Treatise of the Nature, Causes, Signes, Preservation from, and Cure of the Pestilence, A (Kemp), 139–41, 142
British Literary Manuscripts Online: c. 1660–1900, 227
Brooke, Frances, 13, 176–77, 179–82, 184–88, 191n41; *The History of Lady Julia Mandeville*, 179; *Old Maid*, 13, 175–78, 180–89, 191n33, 191n35, 191n41; *Virginia, A Tragedy*, 191n33
Brooke, John, 190n13
Brooklyn, 278
Bryant, Jimmy, 312
Budgell, Eustace, 18; *Bee*, 1
Bulstrode, Richard, 152–55, 158–66

Bultitude, Elizabeth, 49n23
Burke, Frank, 227–28
Burnet, Gilbert, 149, 167n6
Burney, Frances, 7, 223, 224; *Camilla*, 224; "journal letters" of, 7
Burrish, Onslow, 82
Bushell, Sally, 105, 108
Butterflies of the Eastern United States and Canada (Scudder), 66
Buurma, Rachel Sagner, 233n17

Calhoun, John, 66
Cameron, Sharon, 106, 109
Camilla (Burney), 224
Capel, Anne, 84–86, 88, 89
Capper, John, 276, 281n15
Catesby, Mark, 55
Causes of the Decay of Christian Piety, The (Allestree), 132–36, 142, 146n20
censorship, 150, 157, 164–65, 168n18, 168n20, 170n71
Cerulo, Karen A., 288
Chandler, Wayne, 124–25
Chaplin, Joyce, 205
Charles II, 152
Charlotte, Queen, 229
Chartier, Roger, 90n6, 312
Choice Manual of Rare and Select Secrets, A, 255
Civil War, English, 131
Clarkson, Catherine, 110–11
Clarkson, Thomas, 111
coffeehouses, 149, 151, 168n18, 175, 179–81
Cohen, Matt, 10
Colden, Cadwallader, 202–6
Coleridge, Samuel Taylor, 111
Collinson, Peter, 206–11
Comitini, Patricia, 99
commendatory verse, 123–26, 130–32, 135, 138–39, 141–43, 144, 145n5, 146n16
Common Core State Standards Initiative, 312
commonplace books, 7, 20n28, 31, 41–42, 44–47, 101, 103, 107, 108, 110, 179, 224–25, 228, 243

computational linguistics, 13, 238–39, 242–44, 246, 257, 258nn6–7, 259n20
Connell, Alyssa, 307n51
Connoisseur, 175, 179, 186, 191n35
Conway, Francis Seymour, Marquess of Hertford, 86–87
Conway, Henry Seymour, 12, 77, 79–80, 86–89
Cook, Harold J., 287–88
Cooke, John, 152, 154, 159, 161
cooking, 285–87, 290, 292–93, 296–97, 304n3, 305n10
Cooking in the Archives: Updating Early Modern Recipes (1600–1800) in a Modern Kitchen, 14, 285, 307n50
Cornell Wordsworth, The, 116–17
Coryate, Thomas, 126–30, 131–32; *Coryats Crudities*, 126–30, 131–32, 136, 142, 143, 145n13
Cox, Nicholas, 253–55; *The Gentleman's Recreation*, 253
critical making, 14, 285–88, 292, 297, 305n14, 317
Crosby, Sarah, 27–28, 29–32, 33, 37, 39–40, 41, 47, 50n42, 317; "Letter book" of, 27, 29–32, 33, 39, 41, 47, 317
Culley, Amy, 39
cultural materialism, 177–78, 188–89
Culverwel, Nathanael, 46
Curll, Edmund, 1
Curtis, Jared, 109

Davis, K. G., 255
Day, Ivan, 294
de Selincourt, Ernest, 95–96, 110
de Sylvius, Sir Gabriel, 153
Declaration of His Highnes William Henry by the Grace of God Prince of Orange, &c. of the Reasons Inducing Him, to Appear in Armes in the Kingdome of England, The, 149, 150, 167, 167nn5–6
Defoe, Daniel, 1, 189n1; *Review*, 1, 189n1
Delany, Mary, 229; *Mariana*, 229
Derrida, Jacques, 109

Desaguliers, John Theophilus, 198–202, 205, 212n12; *Fires Improved*, 198; *Physico-Mechanical Lectures: or An Account of What Is Explain'd and Demonstrated in the Course of Mechanical and Experimental Philosophy*, 198–99, 201
Designe, Susannah, 35, 36, 47
Dibdin, Charles Isaac Mungo, 220, 227
Dickens, Melchior Guy, 81, 82–83
Dickinson, Emily, 98, 106, 109, 225; fascicles, 225
Dierks, Konstantin, 6, 75
digital databases, 4–5, 14, 143–44, 218, 224–27, 231, 234n18, 250, 279–80; problems of digitization, 5, 125, 143
digital humanities, 4, 11, 14, 226, 238–39, 241–44, 257, 267, 311, 317; popular-scholarly projects, 14, 264, 266–72, 285, 307n50, 317; sustainability, 311
digital media, 3, 11–12, 14–15, 263, 266–67, 270, 272, 280, 311–12, 315; association with incorporeality, 272, 281n24; interaction with analog media, 312; temporality of, 267, 280
Donne, John, 126
Drury, Dru, 54, 60–62, 66–68, 69n7; *Illustrations of Exotic Insects*, 61, 69n16
Dublin Core, 226, 233n15
Dubois, Dorothea, 76; *Lady's Polite Secretary, or New Female Letter Writer*, 76
Duguid, Paul, 10
du Noyer, Anne-Marguerite, 219–20, 232n4; *Letters Historical and Galant*, 219, 232n4
Dunton, John, 8, 176, 182, 189n1, 237, 240; *Athenian Mercury*, 8, 176, 182, 189n1; *A Voyage round the World*, 237
duplicate copies, 144

Early English Books Online (EEBO), 4, 143–44
Early English Books Online Text-Creation Partnership (EEBO-TCP), 238, 244, 258n7
Early Modern Manuscripts Online, 317

Early Novels Database, 226, 233n15, 233n17
Edwards, George, 62
Eighteenth Century Collections Online (ECCO), 4, 143–44
18thConnect, 218, 225, 233n15
Emily Dickinson Archive, 263
endpapers, 125, 141–42, 143
Endymion (John Keats), 269
Englesing, Rolf, 195
English Botany (Smith), 54
English Flora (Smith), 54
English Manuscript Studies 1100–1700, 3, 175
Entomologia systematica (Fabricius), 54
entomology, 52, 54, 56, 61, 67–68; lepidoptery, 63, 65–66
epistolary manuals, 75, 76, 83, 88, 90, 90n6
errata lists, 4, 9
Essex, 3rd Earl of (William Capel), 83–84, 86, 89
ethnobibliography, 287
Etting, Frank Marx, 274, 282n35
Evans, Lewis, 206
Evans, Mary (née Downing), 139–41, 142
Exclusion Crisis, 239
Excursion, The (Wordsworth), 116
experiments, scientific, 196, 198–200, 205–8, 210; and artisans, 197; electricity, 196, 205–8, 210; thermodynamics, 196–200
Experiments and Observations on Electricity, Made at Philadelphia (Franklin), 13, 196, 206–11; manuscript book of, 206–7
Every Man His Own Letter-Writers: Or, the New and Complete Art of Letter-Writing, 76
Ezell, Margaret J. M., 5, 13, 33, 95, 99, 104, 166, 176, 178, 180, 187, 222, 306n27

Fabricius, Johann Christian, 53; *Entomologia systematica*, 54; *Species Insectorum*, 54
Fagel, Gaspar, 167n6

Fairer, David, 176
fan fiction, 228
Faringdon, Alexander, 149
Farrington, Lynn, 233n17
Favret, Mary, 74, 81, 266
Feder, Rachel, 100
Female Spectator (Haywood), 175, 180
feminist criticism, 74, 99
Fielding, Henry, 1; *Shamela*, 1
Fires Improved (Desaguliers), 198
Finch, Anne, 190n24
Fingal (Macpherson), 18n5
Firth, J. R., 244
Fleming, Daniel, 149
Fletcher, John, 40, 44
Foner, Eric, 197
food culture, early modern, 290–91, 297
Forman, Maurice Buxton, 270
Fothergill, John, 61
Four Pounds Flour, 304n3
Fox, George, 28
Fox-Davies, Arthur Charles, 252
Francillon, John, 62, 66–68, 69n7, 70n23
Franklin, Benjamin, 13, 15, 195–211, 315; *An Account of the New Invented Pennsylvanian Fire-Places*, 196, 198–203, 205–6, 208, 210–11; *The Autobiography of Benjamin Franklin*, 195; *Experiments and Observations on Electricity, Made at Philadelphia*, 13, 196, 206–11; *Pennsylvania Gazette*, 195, 198; *Poor Richard's Almanac*, 195, 212n9
Franklin, James, 212n9
Fraser, Peter, 168n20, 168n25, 169n41
Fuller, Thomas, 131–32, 142, 143; *Good Thoughts in Bad Times, Together with Good Thoughts in Worse Times*, 131–32, 142
Furnivall, Margaret, 35, 36

Gaelic, 314
Gamer, Michael, 233n17
Gaskell, Philip, 225
Gauger, Nicholas, 198; *Mechanique de fue*, 198

gender roles, 75, 177, 184–85, 187–88
Genette, Gérard, 124–25, 145n4
Gentleman's Journal (Motteaux), 176, 180
Gentleman's Magazine, 185, 187, 191n34
Gentleman's Recreation, The (Cox), 253
Georgia (state of), 12, 55–56, 60, 65
Gifford, Richard, 181, 190n13
Gill, Stephen, 105
Gilroy, Amanda, 6, 81, 90n2
Girard, Stephen, 278
Gitelman, Lisa, 96–97
Gladstone, Kate, 312
Goldsmith, Elizabeth, 74
Goodman, Dena, 74
Good Thoughts in Bad Times, Together with Good Thoughts in Worse Times (Fuller), 131–32, 142
Goodyear, Henry, 127, 129
Google Maps, 268, 280
Grace, Robert, 197–98
Grangerization, 53
"Grasmere—A Fragment" (D. Wordsworth), 105–6
Grasmere Journals (D. Wordsworth), 101, 103; editing of, 101, 103; notebooks of, 101, 117n20
Gray, Asa, 71n37
Greenwood, Isaac, 212n12
Griffith, Humphrey, 152–53
Grigson, Martha, 40
Gronovius, Johann, 202
Grusin, Richard, 313
Guenée, Achille, 65; *Historie naturelle des insects; species général des lépidoptères*, 65
Guillory, John, 11
Gutenberg, Johannes, 242
Guy, Francis, 278; *Winter Scene in Brooklyn*, 278

Haarlem Gazette, 165, 170n41
Habermas, Jürgen, 6, 17, 75, 80, 175, 178, 195
Hackett, Maria, 227
Halfpenny, Elizabeth, 35

handwriting, 31–32, 35, 36, 41, 89, 177, 179, 184, 288, 305n10, 312; cursive, 312
Hankey, Ian, 288
Harris, Moses, 61
Harris, Thaddeus William, 65
Harris, Zellig, 244
Hartley, Anthony, 133–36, 142, 146n18
Hastings, Warren, 220, 227
Haydon, Benjamin Robert, 270
Hayles, N. Katherine, 281n24
Haywood, Eliza, 180, 182; *Female Spectator*, 175, 180
Hazlitt, William, 281n15
heating, 196–200, 202–3, 205
Henry VIII, 289
heraldry, 239, 245–46, 248–52
Herbert, Amanda, 289
Hill, John, 185
Hill, Rowland, 271
Hindmarsh, Bruce, 35
Histoire d'Ernestine (Riccoboni), 219
Histoire Générale et iconographie des lépidoptères et des chenilles de l'Amérique septentrionale (Boisduval and LeConte), 52, 58, 65
Histoire naturelle des insects; species général des lépidoptères (Boisduval and Guenée), 65
Historical Cooking Project, 304n3
Historical Society of Pennsylvania, 14, 267, 272–74
History of Ernestine, The (Patte), 219
History of Lady Julia Mandeville, The (Brooke), 179
History of the City of Brooklyn (Stiles), 278
Holland, printing in, 148–49
Hooke, Robert, 237
Horwood, Richard, 268; *A Plan of the Cities of London and Westminster*, 268
Howard, Katherine, 217–18, 220, 229–30, 232nn6–7, 234n28, 235n30; *The Life of Frederick Harley*, 217–20, 228–30, 232n7, 235n32
Howard, Sarah, 234n30

Hudson Bay Company, 255
Hutchinson, George, 111
Hutchinson, Sara, 107–8, 111, 118n23, 118n38
Hyde, Bridget, 256

Igarashi, Yohei, 265
Illustrations of Exotic Insects (Drury), 61, 69n16
ingredients, 237, 240, 244, 247, 254–57, 290–91, 307n50; global circulation of, 255–58
ink, 31–32
"Irregular Stanzas: Holiday at Gwerndovennant" (D. Wordsworth), 109
Israel, Jonathan, 149

Jacobites, 85
Jakobson, Roman, 91n18
James II, 148–50, 152–53, 156, 158, 162–64, 166–67, 168n18, 294
Jay, Stephen, 131–32, 142
Jeffrey, John, 271
job printing, 9
Johns, Adrian, 5, 9, 200, 207–8
Johnson, Katherine, 288
Johnson, Samuel, 1, 7–8, 18n5, 76, 80, 180; *Rambler*, 76, 175, 180
Jones, Margaret P., 38
Jonson, Ben, 126, 129
Journal of a Tour to the Continent (D. Wordsworth), 114
Journal of a Tour to the Hebrides (Boswell), 7; manuscript circulation of, 7–8
Julian of Norwich, 316
Julius II (pope), 291
Junto, the, 197
Justice, George L., 2–3, 5–6, 33, 222
juvenilia, 220–21, 225; of the Brontës, 225

Kauffman, Linda S., 74
Keats, George, 263, 265, 267, 269, 271, 274–76, 278
Keats, Georgiana, 263, 267, 271, 276

Keats, John, 263–72, 274–79, 281n15, 315; *Endymion*, 269; letters of, 263–72, 274–79, 281n15, 315
Keats, Tom, 269
Keats Letters Project, 14, 264, 266–72, 315
Keith, Robert Murray, 81, 83
Kemp, William, 139–41, 142, 143; *A Brief Treatise of the Nature, Causes, Signes, Preservation from, and Cure of the Pestilence*, 139–41, 142
Ken Albala's Food Rant, 304n3
Kent, Countess of (Elizabeth Grey), 240, 255–57
Kernan, Alvin, 3
King, Kathryn R., 33
King, Rachael Scarborough, 159, 170n54, 176, 186, 259n9
Kingston, Eleanor, 138
Kirschenbaum, Matthew, 281n24
Knapp, Susannah, 40
Knight, William, 103, 118n24

Lady's Polite Secretary, or New Female Letter Writer (Dubois), 76
Ladies of Llangollen (Eleanor Butler and Sarah Ponsonby), 229, 235n30
Landau, Barry, 273–74, 280, 281n25
Lanser, Susan, 187–88
Laroche, Rebecca, 289
Latin, 245–46, 247–48, 256
Latour, Bruno, 257
Lawrence, Sarah, 40
LeConte, John Eatton, 52, 65–68, 68n1, 69n7, 70n30; *Histoire Générale et iconographie des lépidoptères et des chenilles de l'Amérique septentrionale*, 52, 58, 65
LeConte, John Lawrence, 67–68, 71n35
LeConte, Louis, 65
Leftovers: History of the World in 1000 Cookbooks, 304n3
Lemay, Leo, 198, 204, 212n12
Leong, Elaine, 290

Lerner, Sandy, 235n32
letters, 6–7, 12, 14, 15, 80, 90, 263–68, 316; association with privacy, 12, 75–77, 81, 82, 84, 90, 90n2; in cipher, 78, 82; communal production, 35–36; and correspondence circles, 76, 81–82, 84, 86, 88; diplomatic correspondence, 6, 12, 75, 77–80, 80–84, 87–88, 150–55, 158, 165, 168n25; enclosure of printed materials, 82, 88–89; "express," 160; as feminine genre, 6, 12, 35, 74–77, 80–81, 84, 88–90, 90n2, 316–17; and gossip, 77, 83, 84–85, 87–88, 90; letter books, 29–32, 78–80, 81, 88; letter-writing norms, 75–77, 79–81, 86, 88–90, 265; and literary circulation, 233n13; materiality of, 6, 16, 31–32, 35, 77–80, 88–89, 265–66, 269, 276, 279; merchants' letters, 6, 75, 78; mixed public-private status, 7, 18, 75, 77, 80–81, 82–86, 88–89, 155; movement/circulation of, 263–66, 268–72, 276–77; multimedia status, 7, 16, 18, 77, 176; and orality, 77, 86; in periodicals, 176–77, 180–83, 185, 187; personal letters, 6–7; phatic quality, 82, 84, 91n18, 265–66; political correspondence, 6–7; printed, 209–10; protocols of, 154; and reading aloud, 7, 77, 86; reflection on mediation, 265–66, 276; religious, 12, 27, 31, 35–36; of scientists, 52–53, 60, 202–4, 206–9, 211; and sentimentality, 75–76, 77, 80, 83–85, 87, 89, 157, 161; as source for newspapers, 6, 75, 82, 157–59, 169n41; temporality of, 268–69, 280; and transmission of news, 75, 77, 82–83, 84–85, 87–89, 149, 152, 154–55, 157, 159–61. *See also* newsletters
Letters Historical and Galant (du Noyer), 219
Levin, Susan, 96, 99
Levine, Caroline, 19n8
Levy, Michelle, 19n14, 233n13
Lewin, John William, 60

lexical variation, measure of, 238–40, 243–44, 246, 249–50, 253, 255–57, 258n6, 259n9, 259n20
Library Company of Philadelphia, 197, 206
Licensing Act, 8, 157, 164–65
Life, Letters, and Literary Remains of John Keats (Milnes), 271
Life of Frederick Harley, The (Howard), 217–20, 228–30, 232n7, 235n32
"Lilliburlero" (song), 149
Lindsay, Charlotte, 228; *Mary Dawson*, 228
"Lines Intended for My Niece's Album" (D. Wordsworth), 107, 109
Linnean Society, 54, 63
Linnaean taxonomy, 54, 61, 63, 67
Linnaeus, Carl, 54, 203–4
lists, 239, 247, 249–50, 252, 254, 256–57
Location Register of English Literary Manuscripts, 226
Locke, John, 243
London Courant, 165
London Daily Advertiser, 185
London Magazine, 185
London (Oxford) Gazette, 152, 157–58, 168n21, 170n41
Loughran, Trish, 9
Love, Harold, 5, 7, 13, 32, 154, 157, 178, 196, 222
Lyceum of Natural History, 65

Mack, Phyllis, 34, 35
MacKenzie, Henry, 219; *The Man of Feeling*, 219
Macpherson, James, 1; *Fingal*, 18n5; Ossian poems, 1, 18n5
magazines, 175, 185
Magnússon, Sigurður Gylfi, 19n14
Making and Knowing Project, 285
Mallett, Sarah (Sarah Mallett Boyce), 37, 40, 47
Manchester Natural History Society, 62
Man of Feeling, The (MacKenzie), 219

INDEX

Manning, Susan, 266
manuscript, medium of, 2, 6, 9, 13, 18, 53, 149–50, 177–78, 188, 196, 208, 211, 218, 223–25, 239–40, 242, 250, 257, 313, 316–17; accessibility of, 2, 19n14, 187, 313–14; affordances of, 2, 19n8, 151, 218, 239–40, 250, 252, 257; albums, 178, 185, 188, 224–25; archiving/cataloguing (present day), 12, 14, 29–32, 54, 101, 103, 125, 142–43, 146n28, 218, 223–28, 263–64, 270, 272–74, 279–80; association with amateurism, 2, 5, 12, 102, 178, 217–18; association with body, 177, 179, 184, 186, 188; association with domesticity, 286, 297; association with privacy, 2, 7, 12, 29, 33, 47, 95–96, 98, 101, 102, 218, 316; association with women, 2, 3, 5, 12, 32–33, 77, 233n13, 242, 317; audience for, 219; bequeathal of papers/books, 41, 67–68, 178, 217, 229–30; choice of, 5, 10, 13, 18, 33, 99, 315; circulation, 5, 11, 28, 32–34, 39, 44, 47, 60, 64–65, 66, 68, 81, 99, 180, 196, 200–202, 205–7, 209–11, 222, 230, 233n13, 241, 263–64, 315; collaborative production, 7, 12–13, 36, 98, 108, 111, 114, 117; collecting, 41, 47, 52–55, 66–68, 71n33; commendatory verse, 13, 123–27, 131–33, 136, 139, 141–43, 144; copying, 36, 41, 44, 46–47, 98, 100, 101, 108, 110–11, 116; creation of coteries/networks, 5, 12–13, 18, 19n14, 53, 98, 99, 102, 108, 111, 151–52, 162, 176–77, 180–82, 196, 207, 211n5, 218, 229–30, 313; digitization of, 125, 143–44, 218, 224, 226, 233n12, 234n18, 239, 250, 263–67, 270–73, 278, 280, 280n13, 297, 317; drafts, 13, 98, 102, 103–4, 108, 110–11, 116, 225, 316–17; drawings/illustrations, 52–56, 58, 62–66, 98, 111, 116, 179; fair copies, 98, 102, 103, 105, 110–11, 114, 115–16, 206; family papers, 227–28, 289; fiction, 7, 14, 15, 178, 181, 184, 218–21, 224–26, 228–30, 233n8, 234n18; flexibility of, 239, 250; fragments, 42, 44, 228; genres of, 3, 6–7, 12–14, 75, 100, 110, 123–24, 128–29, 132, 142–43, 150, 166, 168n19, 218, 224–25, 233n8, 289; as gifts, 63–64, 66, 68, 70n32, 113; imitation of print, 9, 115, 144, 217, 219, 225, 228, 286; journals and diaries, 7–8, 12, 31, 41, 95–96, 101, 103, 110, 317; ledgers, 228; memoirs, 27; mixed public-private status, 254–57; "modern manuscripts," 7, 96, 98, 102, 225; news, 149–50, 153; "originals" trope, 1–2, 15, 18n5; ownership inscriptions, 123, 144, 144n1; paratexts, 13, 124–28, 130, 132, 136–38, 141–42; poetry, 13, 19n15, 123–44, 176, 178, 181, 188, 190n24, 224; print editions of, 13, 29–30, 100, 102–3, 207, 264; publication, 3, 5, 7–8, 10, 11, 13, 19n15, 29, 32–33, 39, 47, 196, 201, 208, 219, 222; range of meaning, 2, 3–7, 9, 47, 76, 90, 95, 196, 218; and reading aloud, 28, 36, 41–42, 44–45; scientific texts, 3, 5, 7, 8, 12, 13, 52–55, 60, 66, 196, 205–8, 210–11; sermons, 32, 33, 45–47; temporality of, 95, 96–98, 100, 104, 116, 160–61, 170n41, 170n55; title pages, 9, 111, 217, 219, 229; translations, 219–20, 232n4. *See also* commonplace books; letters; newsletters; notebooks; recipe books; recipes
manuscript culture, 4, 6–7, 9–10, 19n14, 33, 34, 35, 52, 60, 76, 81, 90, 96, 100–101, 103, 166, 175–76, 187–88, 239, 243, 250, 256, 316; association with anonymity, 224, 227; association with failure to print, 3, 33, 99–100, 223–24; in eighteenth century, 3, 4, 6, 7; and gender, 317–18; in Iceland, 19n14, 314; in Ireland, 314; periodization of, 2–4, 12, 19n12, 19n15, 222–23, 317–18; in science, 52, 60, 68, 196, 207, 316; "script affect," 178–79, 188; and sociability, 12–13, 95–96, 100, 103, 105, 110, 126, 225; and "stigma of print," 3, 5, 19n13, 33
Manuscript Fiction in the Archive, 1750–1900, 218, 225–26, 233n12, 234n18

INDEX

manuscript-print interaction, 2, 3–6, 8–10, 11–12, 13–14, 96, 100, 126, 157, 166, 176, 187–89, 219, 224, 232n5, 240–41, 247, 257–58, 311, 313, 316; back-formation of manuscript, 242; imitation of print in manuscripts, 9, 115, 144, 217, 219, 225, 228, 286; incorporation of manuscripts in periodicals, 8, 15–18, 27, 176, 179, 181; interaction between newsletters and printed news, 151, 152–53, 157–59, 161, 165, 168n20, 169–70n41; letters in periodicals, 8, 13, 15–16, 18, 176–77, 180–83, 185, 187; manuscript as source for print, 1–2, 3, 4, 6, 8–9, 14, 18, 75, 82, 157–59, 169n41, 240; mixed manuscript-print forms, 3–5, 8–9, 128, 130–32, 313. *See also* blanks; marginalia; multimedia interaction

manuscript studies, 3, 14, 15, 176, 230, 233n8, 286, 317–18

Manuscript Studies, 3

MARC (machine-readable cataloguing), 226, 233n15, 233n17

marginalia, 4, 5, 9, 13, 53, 125–26, 128, 132, 144

Mariana (Delany), 229

Marotti, Arthur, 19n15, 154

Mary II, 148

Mary Dawson (Lindsay), 228

Mathews, Mary, 44, 46

May, Robert, 292, 295; *The Accomplisht Cook*, 295

May, Steven, 19n13

Mayer, Brantz, 274

McDowell, Paula, 9, 19n7

McElligott, Jason, 314

McGann, Jerome, 263, 265, 270, 272, 280n13

McKenzie, D. F., 2, 10, 265

McKitterick, David, 10, 53

Mechanique de fue (Gauger), 198

media ecology/environment, 149–51, 164, 166, 167n13, 177–78, 188, 239, 242, 258, 264, 267

media shift, 3, 4, 10–11, 18, 266, 310–13; developmental model of, 10, 15, 18, 29, 33, 53, 175–76, 189, 242, 266, 272, 310–11, 313, 317; nostalgia for old media, 312, 315, 318; revolutionary model of, 4–5, 9, 11, 233n13, 313

media studies, 2, 4, 10–11, 265, 281n24, 310, 313

medical texts, 139–41, 197, 212n9, 245, 249–50, 255, 289–90, 292

Mee, Jon, 105

Memoirs of William Wordsworth, 102

memory palace, 238

Merian, Maria Sibylla, 63

metadata, 142–43, 218, 225–26, 233n15, 233n17, 250

Methodism, 12, 27–29, 33–35, 47, 316–17; conversion narratives, 35–36, 38, 41; female preaching, 27, 31–32, 33, 36–37, 39, 41, 45–47, 49n23, 50n42; itinerant preaching, 27, 35, 41, 47; journals and diaries, 33, 36; letters, 27, 31–33, 35–36, 38, 39, 41, 44; manuscript publication practices, 12, 28–29, 31–36, 39, 41, 44–45, 47, 316; orality, 12, 34–36, 41–42, 44–45; restrictions on women in print, 28, 33, 37–39, 44, 47, 317; role of print, 12, 28–29; sermons, 32, 41–42, 45–47; single-sex classes and "bands," 28, 34–36, 37, 41; women's roles within, 12, 27–28, 31, 33–35, 36–37, 39–40, 47, 317

Methodist Book Room, 29

Methodist Conference, 27, 36, 47

Methodist Magazine (Arminian Magazine), 27–28, 37–39, 41, 42, 44; publication of women's texts, 27–28, 37–39, 44

Meyers, Amy R. W., 287–88

Middleton, Earl of (Charles Middleton), 155

Midwife, or The Old Woman's Magazine (Smart), 185

Milnes, Richard Monckton, 271; *Life, Letters, and Literary Remains of John Keats*, 271

Minchin, Maria Frederica, 217, 220, 229–30, 232n7, 238n28
monastic manuscript production, 316
Montagu, Mary Wortley, 223
Mori, Jennifer, 82
Morton, Thomas, 138
Motteux, Peter Anthony, 176, 180; *Gentleman's Journal*, 176, 180
Moxon, Joseph, 136–39, 141, 142, 143; *A Tutor to Astronomie and Geographie*, 136–39, 141, 142, 143
Muddiman, Henry, 151–52, 168n21, 168n24, 169n41
Mullan, John, 179, 183
Multigraph Collective, 2, 9, 318
multimedia interaction, 2, 10–12, 35, 44, 149–50, 159, 189, 264, 266, 270, 280, 314–15, 317; in eighteenth century, 2, 12; eighteenth-century self-reflection on, 2, 4, 11, 18; in present, 3, 11–12
Munroe, Jennifer, 289
Murphy, Arthur, 190n13
Mysteries of Udolpho, The (Radcliffe), 316

natural history, 12, 52–54, 60, 63, 67–68, 196–202, 204–8, 210–11, 244–46, 249–50, 315; anti-print norms, 200–201, 205–6, 208; correspondence networks, 196–98, 202–9, 211, 211n5; culture of collecting, 52–55, 58, 60–63, 66–67; culture of sociability, 53–55, 59–60, 61, 64, 68, 207–8, 210–11; drawings, 52–53, 55–56, 58–59, 61, 62–63, 68; gentlemanly norms, 200–202, 204–7, 211, 212n21; in "the field," 55–56, 63; networks of natural historians, 60, 64–65, 66, 68; and printed illustrations, 58, 68; urban centers of, 55–56, 60, 65
Natural History of the Rarer Lepidopterous Insects of Georgia, 52, 58, 63
Navy Officer, The, 220
"negative capability," 268, 271
Networked Infrastructure for Nineteenth-Century Electronic Scholarship (NINES), 218, 225

New and Complete British Letter-Writer, The; or, Young Secretary's Instructor in Polite Modern Letter-Writing, 76
New Experiments Phyisco-Mechanical, Touching the Spring of Air and Its Effects (Boyle), 197, 201
newsletters (manuscript), 13, 150–66, 168nn18–19, 169n29; chronological organization, 160, 167; circulation, 151, 153; commercial, 150, 168n20; distinctions from printed news, 157–58; enclosure of printed texts, 151, 158; genre conventions of, 150–51, 153–54, 164; interaction with printed news, 151, 152–53, 157–59, 161, 165, 168n20, 169–70n41; official, 150–55, 157, 159, 161–67; mixed public-private status, 150, 155, 157, 166; multimedia status, 153, 157–59, 161, 166; newsgathering methods, 152–53, 155, 158, 159–61; news on the Revolution of 1688, 158; periodicity, 160–61, 167; personalization, 153–56, 161, 165–66; physical form of, 150, 155, 162; use of epistolary conventions, 154
Newton, Isaac, 201
Northanger Abbey (Austen), 89
Norton Anthology of English Literature, The, 101
notational form, 240, 243, 246–47, 249–52, 254–55, 257–58; as bridge between manuscript and print, 254–55, 259n9
notebooks/blank books, 8, 12–13, 14, 8, 12, 32, 53, 60, 95–99, 100, 101–3, 109, 111, 113, 116, 217, 219, 225, 237–43, 250, 252, 254, 256–58, 315, 317; association with domesticity, 95, 102, 103, 104, 113; audience for, 95, 98–99, 103, 105, 107, 111; incorporation of print, 97, 104, 108, 114–15; materiality of, 96–99, 100, 102, 103–4, 109–10, 113, 116; and orality, 108; sharing of, 98, 100–102, 105, 108, 110–11; travel, 101, 110; used to archive other materials, 12, 96–98, 103–4, 108–11, 116

note taking, 239, 242–43, 245, 247, 250, 252, 257. *See also* scientific notes
novels, 14, 15, 90, 184, 217–19, 224, 227, 257, 316; epistolary, 7, 75, 88, 184, 256; manuscript, 7, 14, 15, 218–21, 224–26, 228–30, 233n8, 316; material forms of, 219–20, 228; rise of, 4, 90, 217–18
Nussbaum, Felicity, 38

Ockley, Ann, 183
Ólafsson, Davíð, 19n14
Old Maid (Brooke), 13, 175–78, 180–89, 191n33, 191n35, 191n41
optical character recognition (OCR), 317
orality, 2, 11, 19n7, 35, 44, 149–50, 159, 166, 314–15; interaction with manuscript and print, 166, 314–15 (*see also* multimedia interaction); and news transmission, 149, 159, 161; songs, 149–50; temporality of, 160
ornithology, 54, 65, 246, 248–49
Orrery, 5th Earl of (John Boyle; 5th Earl of Cork), 181, 183, 190n13, 190n17, 191n34
Osborne, Thomas, Duke of Leeds, 256
Ossian: debate, 1; poems of, 1, 18n5. *See also* Macpherson, James
Oxford Dictionary of National Biography, 227

Pamela (Richardson), 316
pamphlets, 186, 196, 198, 200, 202, 204–5, 208–10, 314; epistolary, 210
paratexts, 13, 124–27, 130, 132, 136–42, 144, 145n4, 196, 201–2, 205–6, 208–10, 219, 276
Parikka, Jussi, 281n24
Parmesan cheese, 291
Patch-Work Screen for the Ladies, A (Barker), 179
Paterson, Daniel, 269; *Roads*, 269
Patte, Charlotte, 219–20; *The History of Ernestine*, 219
Patten, Eve, 314
pencil, 105, 107, 109

Pennsylvania Gazette (Franklin), 195, 198
Pepys, Samuel, 291
performance, 287–89, 305nn10–11
periodicals, 4, 8, 13, 15, 27, 160, 175–77, 179, 181, 185, 187–88, 189n1, 315; association with print medium, 15–17; club trope, 177, 183; eidolons, 176–77, 182, 186–88; and gender, 177, 180–83, 184–85; incorporation of manuscripts, 8, 15–18, 27, 176, 179, 181; and interactivity, 180, 185–86; periodical essay, genre of, 175, 180, 183–84, 186–88, 189n1; reader communities, 181–83, 186–87; reader correspondence, 8, 13, 15–16, 18, 176–77, 180–83, 185, 187; and sociability, 176–77, 180, 185
periodical studies, field of, 4, 177, 188
personae, authorial, 182–84, 186–87, 195–96, 208, 211n2
Perry, Ruth, 74
philology, 270, 272
Philosophical Transactions of the Royal Society, 7, 208
Physico-Mechanical Lectures: or An Account of What Is Explain'd and Demonstrated in the Course of Mechanical and Experimental Philosophy (Desaguliers), 198–99, 201
Piper, Andrew, 9
Piozzi, Hester Thrale, 228; "Una and Duessa," 228
Plan of the Cities of London and Westminster, A (Horwood), 268
Poley, Edmund, 152–66, 169n27, 172n77
Polikoff, Morgan, 312
Ponsonby, Sarah, 235n30. *See* Ladies of Llangolen
Ponton, Thomas, 136–39, 143, 146n24
Poor Richard's Almanac (Franklin), 195, 212n9
Pope, Alexander, 1, 2, 15, 176, 256; *The Rape of the Lock*, 256
Popish Plot, 168n20, 239
Portland, Duchess of (Margaret Cavendish Bentinck), 54, 61, 70n18

postal systems, 6, 8, 10, 264–66, 269, 271, 276–78; postal reform of 1839–40, 271; transatlantic, 263, 265–66, 271, 277–78
Portugal eggs, 286–87, 291–98, 302, 304n6, 307n48
Powell, Manushag, 187
Preceptor, 89
print, medium of, 4, 11, 18, 97, 148–50, 167n13, 185–86, 195–96, 218, 313; associations with fixity and authority, 9, 53, 103, 105, 115; association with incorporeality, 179, 187–88, 195, 211; association with masculinity, 77, 242; association with professional authorship, 2, 313; association with publicity, 2, 7, 77, 316; broadsides, 314; as container/archive of manuscript, 123, 144; creation of communities, 188; critiques of (eighteenth century), 4, 13, 18, 200–202, 205–6, 208–11; "death" of (present day), 310, 313; as dominant medium, 2, 4, 6, 16, 53, 188–89, 314; as eighteenth-century new medium, 177; illustrations, 12, 53, 58, 63, 68, 114–16; instability of, 53; newsbooks, 151; newspapers, 151, 152, 157–60, 165, 186; origins in manuscript, 3, 8, 9, 15, 18, 240; paratexts, 124–28, 130, 132, 137, 140, 144; piracy, 200–201; political role of, 148–50, 157; propaganda, 148–49; quantitative increase in eighteenth century, 8–10, 14; scientific publication, 196, 200–202, 205–6, 208–11; temporality of, 97, 160. *See also* novels; pamphlets
print culture, 2–3, 6, 11, 15, 18, 19n7, 33, 35, 75, 167n13, 175–76, 188, 217, 222, 224–25, 314, 317–18; association with mass audience, 217, 224; association with modernity, 9, 195, 313; and democratization, 313; in eighteenth-century, 2–3, 5; in Iceland, 314; in Ireland, 314; in science, 52–54, 200, 202, 207, 315–16
printing, 195–97, 200, 202, 204–5, 208, 242
print-manuscript hierarchy, 4, 6, 10, 15–18, 33, 52–53, 102, 175–76, 178, 189, 209, 223–24
print marketplace, 3, 5, 6, 9–10, 14, 64, 224, 231, 242
"Print 2.0," 8
private sphere, 7, 33, 150, 188; association with manuscript, 7, 12, 33
provenance, 142, 226–27, 229–30, 234n26, 270
public sphere, 7, 17, 36, 150, 175, 178, 188–89, 195, 207, 211; association with print, 7, 13, 17–18
Pulteney, Richard, 63

Queen-like Closet or Rich Cabinet, The (Woolley), 286, 292–93, 298–99, 304n6, 306n40, 306n42
queer studies, 13, 177–78, 182–83, 186–89

Rabisha, William, 292
Radcliffe, Ann, 316; *The Mysteries of Udolpho*, 316
Rambler (Johnson), 76, 175, 180
Rape of the Lock, The (Pope), 256
Raven, James, 5, 149
Raymond, Joad, 148, 210
RDF (resource description framework), 226, 233n15
rebinding, loss of text, 125, 142
recipe books, 240, 242–43, 245, 252–53, 285–87, 289–93, 296–97
recipes, 8, 14, 139, 142, 237–38, 240, 247, 249, 252–57, 285–93, 295–302, 306n43; and ecological criticism, 289; formats of, 289; and women, 289–91
Recipes Project, 304n3
Recollections of a Tour Made in Scotland (D. Wordsworth), 102, 110–14; manuscripts of, 110–13
reenactment, 287–88
Reiman, Donald H., 7, 96, 150, 167n17, 225
remediation, 11, 13, 150, 287
Republic of Letters, 196, 205, 207
residual processes, 177–79, 188–89, 240, 313

Restoration, 4, 14, 131, 150, 151, 294
Review (Defoe), 1, 189n1
revision, textual, 105–6, 108–9, 113, 239; preservation of multiple versions, 105–9, 115–16
Revolution of 1688, 13, 148–51, 153, 157–58, 161, 164, 166–67, 315; role of print in, 148–49
Revolutionary Pie: Historic American Cooking in a 21st-Century Kitchen, 304n3
Riccoboni, Marie-Jeanne, 219; *Histoire d'Ernestine*, 219
Rich, Charles Henry Stuart, 230
Richardson, Samuel, 184, 227, 228, 256, 316; *Pamela*, 316
Ritchie, Elizabeth, 40
Rivington, Jessie, 228
Roads (Paterson), 269
Robinson, Henry Crabb, 114
Roder, Harriet Mary, 230
Rogers, Hester Ann, 41
Rollins, Hyder Edward, 276, 281n15
Romantic period, 4, 12, 19n14, 75, 101, 103, 116–17, 265
Romantic London (digital project), 268
Rousseau (ship), 278
Rowe, Elizabeth Singer, 33
Rowlandson, Thomas, 269
Royal Letter Writer or Every Lady's Own Secretary, The, 76
Royal Pharmacopœa Galencial and Chimical, The (Charas), 255–56
Royal Society, 7, 14, 53, 196, 198–99, 204–11, 256
Ryan, Sarah, 40, 41
Rydal journals (D. Wordsworth), 101

Sabor, Peter, 191n31
Saice, Elizabeth, 35
Saint Louis Conference on Manuscript Studies, 3
Sandby, William Henry Hervey, 230, 234n28
Sangster, Matthew, 268–70

Savedoff, Jason, 273, 280
Sax, David, 312
Schaffer, Simon, 199
Schellenberg, Betty, 5
Schwoerer, Lois, 148
scientific drawings, 52, 54–60, 61, 63, 65–68; of birds, 52, 62, 71n35; of butterflies and moths, 52, 61, 63, 65–66, 70n18; for classification purposes, 56, 58–60, 66, 68; collection of, 52–54, 58, 61, 63, 65–66, 66–68; engravings of, 12, 52, 58; of insects, 52, 54–56, 58–59, 61, 62, 63, 68; publication of, 52, 55, 58, 63, 65–66, 68; of spiders, 56, 62
scientific notes, 3, 8, 12, 52–56, 60–62, 66–67
scientific specimen collection, 12, 53–55, 59–62, 65–68, 70n20
Scudder, Samuel H., 66, 68, 70n32; *Butterflies of the Eastern United States and Canada*, 66
secretaries of state, offices of, 150–53, 155, 157–58, 164–66, 168nn20–21; circulars (newsletters), 151; Northern Department, 151–53, 155; Southern Department, 151–53, 155, 168n21
Selena (Tighe), 229
sensibility, 178–79, 183, 185–86, 188–89
sentimental literature, 179
Severn, Joseph, 268
Shamela (Fielding), 1
Shapin, Steven, 199
Shapiro, Barbara, 149
Shaw, Jon, 233n17
Shelley, Percy, 103
Shelton, Samuel, 138
Sherman, William, 9
Shevlin, Eleanor, 32
Siegert, Bernhard, 265–66
Singleton, Mary (eidolon of the *Old Maid*), 176–87
Siskin, Clifford, 167n13
Smart, Christopher, 182, 185; *Midwife, or The Old Woman's Magazine*, 185
Smeathman, Henry, 60, 61

Smith, Helen, 124, 145n4
Smith, James Edward, 54, 63, 66–68, 69n7; *English Botany*, 54; *English Flora*, 54
Smith, Pamela H., 285, 287–88
Smollett, Tobias, 228
social media, 11, 185
Sommerville, John, 160
Southey, Edith, 108
Species Insectorum (Fabricius), 54
Spectator (Addison and Steele), 8, 15–17, 175–76, 189n1
Speed, Emma Keats, 282n35
Stallybrass, Peter, 9, 313
Starosielski, Nicole, 281n24
Stauffer, Andrew, 280n13
Steele, Richard, 8, 15, 18, 175; British Library collection of letters to, 8, 15–17; *Spectator*, 8, 15–17, 175–76, 189n1; *Tatler*, 8, 15–17, 189n1
Sterne, Jonathan, 311
Stiles, Henry Reed, 278; *History of the City of Brooklyn*, 278
St. John, Johanna, 256
Strahan, William, 204
structures of feeling, 178, 188
Stuart, James Edward, 167n5
Sunderland, 2nd Earl of (Robert Spencer), 155
Sutherland, James, 151
Swainson, William, 69n7
Swift, Jonathan, 18

t-distributed stochastic neighbor embedding (t-SNE) visualization, 246–47, 260n21
Taft, Mary Barritt, 37, 40
Taft, Zecheriah, 37, 48n3; *Biographical Sketches of the Lives and Public Ministry of Various Holy Women*, 37, 48n3
Tatler (Addison and Steele), 8, 15–17, 189n1
Taylor, Robert H., 270
Temora (Macpherson), 18n5
Tempest, Rowland, 153

temporality: of digital media, 267, 280; of letters, 268–69, 280; of manuscript, 95, 96–98, 100, 104, 116, 160–61, 170n41, 170n55; of orality, 160; of print, 97, 160
textbooks, 136–39
theft of documents, 267, 273–74, 280, 281n25
Thomas, Naomi, 35
Thomson, Heidi, 265
Thornton, Bonnell, 182
Tighe, Mary, 229, 235n30; *Selena*, 229
Tinker, Nathan, 5, 222
"To Dora Wordsworth" (D. Wordsworth), 107–8
Tolar Burton, Vicki, 28, 38
Toola, William, 138, 146n24
Tooth, Mary, 39, 40–42, 44–48
Townshend, Albinia, 84–86, 87, 88
train oil, 255, 258
Transatlantic Fiction Project, 233n17
Tribble, Evelyn, 305n10
Tripp, Ann, 27–28, 40
Turley, Richard Marggraf, 269, 271
Tunstall, Marmaduke, 61
Tutor to Astronomie and Geographie, A (Moxon), 136–39, 141, 142, 143

"Una and Duessa" (Piozzi), 228
Universal Intelligence, 164
Universal Magazine, 185
UPenn Ms. Codex 785, 286, 291, 293, 296–98, 301, 306n43

van Citters, Arnout, 158–59
vector semantics, 13, 238–39, 243–44, 246, 257, 258n7, 259n20
Verhoeven, W. M., 6, 81, 90n2
Villettes, Arthur, 83
Virginia, A Tragedy (Brooke), 191n33
Voyage round the World, A (Dunton), 237

Wacquant, Loïc, 288
Wahrman, Dror, 8
Walker, R. B., 164
Wall, Wendy, 291, 306n23, 307n52

Wallis, John, 164
Warner, Michael, 17–18, 35, 195–96
Warner, William, 167n13
Warre, Richard, 153, 165
watercolors, 52, 56, 58, 64
watermarks, 32, 35
Watson, William, 207–8
Webb, Timothy, 265
Werner, Marta L., 98, 102, 223
Wesley, Charles, 35–36, 39, 44, 47
Wesley, John, 27–29, 31, 33–36, 37–38, 39, 40, 41, 44, 47, 50n42
Whitaker, Laurence, 129
Whitefield, George, 36
Whole Duty of Man, The (Allestree), 146n20
Whyman, Susan, 81
Wilkes, John, 87, 88
Wilkins, John, 243
William (ship), 276–78, 281n15
William III (William of Orange), 148–49, 152–53, 156, 157, 160–67, 172n77
William Blake Archive, 263
Williams, Charles Hanbury, 12, 77–84, 88–89
Williams, Frances Hanbury (Frances Capel, Countess of Essex), 79–80, 84–86, 87, 88
Williams, Franklin B., Jr., 124, 145n4, 146n16
Williams, Raymond, 177–79, 188–89, 313
Williamson, Joseph, 151–53, 168n24
Willis, Thomas, 256
Wilson, Alexander, 52, 55, 64–65; *American Ornithology*, 65
Wilson, Edward, 149

Wilson, Louise, 124, 145n5
Winter Scene in Brooklyn (Guy), 278
Wolfson, Susan, 265
Woof, Pamela, 96, 101
Woolley, Hannah, 286–87, 291–99, 301, 304n6, 306n40, 306nn42–43; *The Queen-like Closet or Rich Cabinet*, 286, 292–93, 298–99, 304n6, 306n40, 306n42
Wordsworth, Dora, 111
Wordsworth, Dorothy, 12, 95–117, 317; "Grasmere—A Fragment," 105–6; *Grasmere Journals*, 101, 103; "Irregular Stanzas: Holiday at Gwerndovennant," 109; *Journal of a Tour to the Continent*, 114; "Lines Intended for My Niece's Album," 107, 109; notebooks of, 95–96, 98–117; print publication of writings, 102; *Recollections of a Tour Made in Scotland*, 102, 110–14; Rydal journals, 101
Wordsworth, John, 113
Wordsworth, Mary, 102, 111, 118n23, 118n38
Wordsworth, William, 15, 98–99, 101–2, 104, 105, 108–10, 116–17; *The Excursion*, 116; *Memoirs of William Wordsworth*, 102; use of Dorothy Wordsworth's writing, 118n23
World, 175
writing manuals, 4
Wyche, Peter, 153–58, 160–62, 165–66
Wynne, Owen, 152, 155

Yale, Elizabeth, 53, 67, 71n33
Yard, Robert, 152–53
Yeo, Richard, 242

www.ingramcontent.com/pod-product-compliance
Lightning Source LLC
Chambersburg PA
CBHW021341300426
44114CB00012B/1033